The Loyal Opposition

The Loyal Opposition

Americans in North Vietnam, 1965–1972

JAMES W. CLINTON

UNIVERSITY PRESS OF COLORADO

© 1995 by the University Press of Colorado

Published by the University Press of Colorado
P.O. Box 849
Niwot, Colorado 80544
303-530-5337

The University Press of Colorado is a cooperative publishing enterprise supported, in part, by Adams State College, Colorado State University, Fort Lewis College, Mesa State College, Metropolitan State College of Denver, University of Colorado, University of Northern Colorado, University of Southern Colorado, and Western State College of Colorado.

The paper used in this publication meets the minimum requirements of the American National Standard for Information Sciences — Permanence of Paper for Printed Library Materials. ANSI Z39.48-1984

Library of Congress Cataloging-in-Publication Data

Clinton, James W., 1929–
    The loyal opposition: Americans in North Vietnam, 1965–1972 /
James W. Clinton
        p.   cm.
    Includes index.
    ISBN 0-87081-412-5
    1. Vietnamese Conflict, 1961–1975 — Protest movements — United
States.   2. Americans — Vietnam (Democratic Republic).   I. Title.
DS559.62.U6C55 1995
959.704'3373 — dc20   95-49998
                                                   CIP

10   9   8   7   6   5   4   3   2   1

Contents

Foreword ix

Preface xv

Acronyms xxxi

Chap 1   Mary Clarke 1

Chap 2   Michael Myerson 7

Chap 3   Harold Supriano 10

Chap 4   Herbert Aptheker 12

Chap 5   Dave Dellinger 25

Chap 6   Hugh Manes 62

Chap 7   J. B. Neilands 69

Chap 8   Julius Lester 77

Chap 9   Betty Boardman 88

Chap 10 Bill Heick 103

Chap 11 John Pairman Brown 111

Chap 12 Anne Weills 118

Chap 13 Madeline Duckles 136

Chap 14 Ethel Taylor 148

Chap 15 Cora Weiss 165

Chap 16 Noam Chomsky 183

Chap 17 Peter Weiss 201

Chap 18 Irma Zigas 206

Chap 19 George McT. Kahin 220

Chap 20 George Wald 236

Chap 21 Ramsey Clark 251

Chap 22 Paul Mayer 265

Chap 23 Susan Miller-Coulter 268

Chap 24 Telford Taylor 273

Appendix: U.S. Citizens Who Traveled to North Vietnam, 287
    1965–1972

Index 297

Forgive us our trespasses
as we forgive those who trespass against us.

Foreword

[The Vietnam War went on longer than any other American war. It was longer than the combined length of all world wars that had occurred up to that point in the twentieth century.] It was, in many respects, also a distinctive war, with many unusual features. One óf the most controversial aspects of the Vietnam experience was the stream of American antiwar activists who visited "the enemy," North Vietnam. During the early part of the war, these visitors were often castigated in the public press as virtual "traitors" or, at best, naive instruments of communist propaganda. Their visits were deeply resented by the U.S. government and were seen as expressing a lack of unity about the war effort. U.S. officials and media pundits alleged in a variety of settings, especially in the late 1960s, that such antiwar activity prolonged the conflict by encouraging miscalculations in Hanoi about the firmness of U.S. intentions to adhere to official war aims.

As U.S. war objectives shifted after the Tet Offensive in 1968, attitudes toward the war and its opponents became more confused. During this period, when both sides sought a negotiated solution, visits to Hanoi were never openly encouraged by the U.S. government, but at the same time, the secret channels were being relied upon by officialdom to explore the basis for an end to the war. My own experience was illustrative. Prior to going to Hanoi for the first time in June 1968, I was invited to meet informally with high officials in the Pentagon, briefed somewhat on the U.S. negotiating position, and told that if I were to desist from public criticisms of the government's Vietnam policies, I could meet with the secretaries of defense and state and carry a message to North Vietnamese leaders. It never occurred to me at the time to accept such a proposal for I felt then, and now, that it was improper to tie any role as a messenger with an abridgement of my rights to act on conscience as a citizen. Yet this experience is indicative of some less publicized aspects of this kind of private initiative and its quasi-official embrace, even at a time when the government was threatening citizens who wished to visit North Vietnam with criminal prosecutions under the Logan Act, an old, unused statute punishing private diplomacy.

In fact, my visit to Hanoi was an eye-opening experience in many respects. North Vietnam and its people became real. The other side in the Vietnam War had a human face; its leaders were surprisingly well educated, with strong cultural interests and, perhaps most unexpectedly, often possessing a sharp wit. I was moved by the beauty of the countryside and the villages, appalled by the damage from frequent bombing, and impressed by the ingenuity of the Vietnamese in seeming to have a response to the damage being inflicted, whatever its form. I think what impressed me most was that the Vietnamese bore no hatred toward the United States, as such, while at the same time, they were utterly unwilling to give up their struggle, no matter how high its costs.

Ho Chi Minh was an outstanding leader of his people, who imparted upon the whole of North Vietnam the distinction between the imperialist government in Washington and the American people and Vietnam's own anticolonial history. On one level, of course, this was a standard communist propaganda line, but in Vietnam, it meant more and seemed genuine. Possibly, this was because Ho as a young man, living in Paris during the peace talks in 1919, had been inspired by President Woodrow Wilson's advocacy of self-determination at the end of World War I. Ho Chi Minh considered the war against the United States to be one of national independence, retaining all the while an appreciation of America's own earlier anticolonial heritage, despite his turn after 1919 toward Marxism-Leninism for ideological guidance.

Throughout the Vietnam War, despite the terrible devastation of the country and the merciless pounding that Vietnam received, Vietnamese school children were required to memorize the U.S. Declaration of Independence, both for its message and as an expression of "the real America."

At the end of my visit to North Vietnam in 1968, I met with several American POWs being held in Hanoi. They seemed to be well treated and healthy. They were quite forthcoming in conversation, although I assume that our meeting was monitored and that the POWs were "prepared" for the meeting. Afterward, I felt uncomfortable about leaving them behind, realizing that I would return to the relative normalcy of America while they would remain imprisoned indefinitely. Such a sense of divided conscience was one inevitable dimension of these visits to Hanoi for almost all of us who chose this course.

No issue concerning the peace movement provoked more misunderstanding than this contact of visitors to North Vietnam with the American POWs. Several of the most prominent visitors, most notably Jane Fonda and Tom Hayden, went out on a limb by declaring that accusations of POW torture were false. Such a conclusion could genuinely emerge from such meetings as I had, which included reassurances by the POWs (possibly coerced but seemingly spontaneous and sincere) that were reinforced by further persuasive insistence of good treatment by our Vietnamese hosts. My own suspicions at the time were that prisoner abuse undoubtedly occurred, especially in the immediate aftermath of capture and possibly more systematically in the earlier phases of the war, before the well-being of the American POWs became such a major diplomatic concern of the U.S. government. My impressions along these lines in 1968 were reinforced four years later when I accompanied William Sloane Coffin, David Dellinger, and Cora Weiss to Hanoi once again, this time to escort three American POWs back to the United States after their early release by North Vietnamese authorities as a gesture of support for the U.S. peace movement, undoubtedly motivated by public relations goals.

Professor Clinton has performed an enormously useful scholarly service by rescuing this neglected dimension of the Vietnamese experience. It is particularly appropriate for him to have undertaken this task, given his own military service and his early attitudes of intense anger about these visits by his fellow Americans. I cannot think of a better expression of some kind of reconciliation between Americans of equivalent conscience who responded to the confusing challenge of the Vietnam War in contradictory ways. The interviews brought together here, I think, suggest two important lines of interpretation.

First of all, the interviews manifest a consistent purity of intention: the participants all saw the war as a tragedy for both sides and wanted, above all, to bring the fighting to an end. The individuals whose voices are heard in this book, although speaking with the benefit of hindsight, were, by and large, ordinary citizens who were aware that they were embarked upon a politically and physically hazardous journey; they went to Hanoi because of a sense of duty, as they understood it, not unlike soldiers embarked on a different mission, full of fear and foreboding. These are not, and were never, disloyal Americans but rather citizens who saw the war in different terms, not as a part of the necessary struggle against communism as much as a misguided effort by their government to deny Vietnam national unity and self-determination. These antiwar citizens also generally believed the war was waged in violation of both the U.S. Constitution and international law.

The second impression that is powerfully expressed by these interviews is the diversity of backgrounds and orientations of these American visitors to Hanoi. The spectrum runs from those who interpret their visits almost exclusively in humanitarian and often pacifist terms with no political content to those who grasp the experience in loaded ideological terms of a partisan character.

In the end, as with those who fought in the war, the visitors to Vietnam deserve neither wholesale respect nor censure. Some exhibited, in my view, poor judgment by allowing themselves to be used as propaganda instruments, undoubtedly influenced at the time by their strong sense of how terrible the war was for the Vietnamese people and a low-technology society being devastated by high-technology instruments of war. Others were moved by the hospitality of the North Vietnamese and their absence of animosity, and they made assertions of solidarity that perhaps they didn't fully mean when removed from the immediacies of the war zone. Others were more prudent, but I think almost everyone who went to Hanoi was changed as a result and saw the war differently henceforth, generally deepening the antiwar convictions that had led them to receive an invitation in the first place.

Did these visits make any real impact upon North Vietnam or the U.S. government's perceptions of the war — strengthening the will to persevere in Hanoi, weakening it in Washington? We shall never really know. These visits were a small piece in a large, complex puzzle. Perhaps archival research by historians will give us a more solid response some day about how such visits were perceived by leaders in both Hanoi and Washington. In the meantime, I think, it is best to assume a minimal impact; possibly, the morale of the peace movement in the United States was raised and the North Vietnamese interest in gaining sympathy for their cause among the American people was enhanced. At most, then, the visits were a minor factor yet by no means irrelevant.

Whatever one's sense of the Vietnam War, the testimony of the individuals collected in this book is of great value. For each testimony is a rendering of feelings, ideas, and recollections that are deeply felt even after many years. With the calming impact of the passage of time, these testimonies can also be read as a kind of Cold War history from the perspective of dissenters, thereby exhibiting one set of critical views about how U.S. power was being used. From the perspective of 1995, with the Soviet Union no longer in existence and the remaining Communist countries (including Vietnam) having embraced market economics and welcoming foreign investment, the Vietnam War, which once summoned such ideological fervor, now indeed seems remote, almost unreal.

Walking through Ho Chi Minh City (Saigon) less than a year ago, I would have assumed that the war had been won by the South! Corporate billboards were everywhere, no police were in sight, and the surging crowds had the same feeling of vitality as in any other large city in South Asia. Such are the ironies of history. But these ironies don't detract from the very real drama that led men and women in the United States to take diametrically opposed, yet equally sincere, views as to what was at stake in Vietnam and what, as citizens, they should do about it. This book, more than any other I know, brings us into direct contact with that part of the drama waged by civilian opponents of the war.

RICHARD FALK

ALBERT G. MILBANK PROFESSOR OF INTERNATIONAL LAW AND FINANCE

CENTER OF INTERNATIONAL STUDIES, PRINCETON UNIVERSITY

Preface

This manuscript consists of excerpts from twenty-four interviews of individuals who shared one common experience: all traveled to North Vietnam between 1965 and 1972 during the course of the Vietnam War. They expressed opposition to the war openly and in a variety of ways, and they believed they were absolutely right to oppose the war, which they felt was responsible for an enormous and unnecessary loss of life on both sides. Most of those interviewed were highly critical of the U.S. government's political leaders who allowed the war to continue. Those interviewed included professors, ministers, members of the Communist Party, attorneys, members of Women Strike for Peace, activists, and pacifists — strong-minded individuals with definite opinions. They were not ambivalent or halfhearted in the way they expressed themselves in these interviews. The United States could use politicians with such character.

ORIGINS OF THIS PROJECT

My most compelling motivation for this project was an image that I was unable to erase from my mind — a photograph of actress Jane Fonda sitting atop a North Vietnamese tank, smiling. It was the summer of 1972. I was a career U.S. Air Force officer, a "lifer," on assignment as an ROTC instructor at the University of Missouri, Rolla. It was bad enough that an internationally known American movie actress was fraternizing with the enemy in time of war, but for her to appear to support our battlefield enemy on his home ground was, to me, beyond belief and intolerable. Americans who traveled to Hanoi and consorted with our enemy, I then believed, had to be traitors.

I had returned to the States in November 1971, after serving a twelve-month tour of duty in Vietnam as navigator in a Special Operations UC–123 aircraft unit based in Nha Trang, South Vietnam. Vietnam duty was a career ticket punch item and necessary for promotion and career-track duty assignments. I had not the slightest misgiving about our nation's armed struggle against the North Vietnamese: the usual Communist menace that all democracies reflexively opposed.

I had enlisted in the air force twenty years earlier, in 1950, to help defeat the North Korean Communists who had attacked South Korea without provocation. As it turned out, I flew as a navigator in transport aircraft for the length of the war, both at home and in the Pacific.

Jane Fonda was a lightning rod for those, like myself, who supported the Vietnam War. She represented all that was wrong with America. Despite her professional success in Hollywood, she had, I felt, contemptuously turned on the country that had acclaimed her and made her wealthy. Her strident criticism of her native country, which was attempting to bring democracy to South Vietnam, was a slap in the face to all patriotic Americans. Ms. Fonda apparently did not understand that if not for U.S. economic power and military might, it would be only a matter of time before the rest of the world became Russian-speaking citizens of the Global Union of Socialist Republics.

As an air force blue-suiter, I experienced no difficulty in finding coworkers who shared my distasteful perceptions of the woman labeled "Hanoi Hannah." Her unequivocal, defiant opposition to the war was unsettling. How could the U.S. government tolerate such flagrantly unpatriotic behavior? Moreover, if U.S. citizens refused to support the government in its fight against communism, what was to become of this nation? In 1975, I left Rolla, Missouri, for an assignment with the Joint Chiefs of Staff in the Pentagon, still harboring hatred in my heart for Jane Fonda — to my mind, America's number one Communist-lover.

Prior to entering the air force in 1951, I had graduated from Columbia University in New York City with a bachelor's degree in business administration. Later, while on active duty with the air force, I received a master's degree in business administration from the University of Washington in 1961 and a doctorate in business administration from St. Louis University in 1973. The air force and I agreed on two things: advanced education was a worthwhile end in itself, and Jane Fonda was no friend of the military services.

I retired from the air force as a lieutenant colonel in 1977 to teach management at the University of Wisconsin, Whitewater. Jim Mescall, a fellow instructor from Chicago, often razzed me about Jane Fonda and knew that he need only mention her name to get my blood boiling. I left Whitewater in 1980 to teach management at the University of Northern Colorado in Greeley.

I still couldn't shake my strong distaste for Jane Fonda, and it irked me that in 1983, ten years after American POWs had returned to the

States, she returned to her money-making ways in Hollywood. Such commercial behavior seemed hypocritical since these United States, whose free enterprise system made her wealth possible, had been the object of her loathing during the war. Six years ago, after repeatedly telling others how disgusted I was with both Jane Fonda and Tom Hayden for traveling to Hanoi during the Vietnam War and speaking out on Radio Hanoi against this country's role in that conflict, I decided to find out exactly what Fonda and Hayden said and did during the war and expose their near-treasonable behavior.

I requested information from the Federal Bureau of Investigation and the Central Intelligence Agency through the Freedom of Information Act concerning Fonda's antiwar efforts and her Radio Hanoi broadcasts during the summer of 1972. FBI and CIA reports of her activities and verbatim transcripts of Fonda's Hanoi speeches confirmed my belief that if U.S. citizens were made aware of this information, she would become an outcast in this society. I also accumulated additional information about other U.S. citizens who had traveled to North Vietnam during the war.

In the process of identifying possible publishers for this material, I contacted John Hubbell, director of the Kent State University Press. He suggested that, instead of relying upon secondary sources, I should personally contact and interview those Americans who had traveled to Hanoi during the war. I followed his advice and wrote to about one hundred individuals whose addresses I found in telephone directories, directories of university and college instructors, directories of attorneys, newspaper and journal articles, books, and so forth. In my letter of inquiry to these individuals, I asked to visit with them and discuss their reasons for traveling to North Vietnam, as well as what they did while they were there and how today, with benefit of hindsight, they viewed their actions.

At this point, part of our country's history came to my attention in a way that caused me to moderate my previously uncompromising support of the war. In the summer of 1989, my wife, Shirley, and I drove to Washington, D.C., to review Central Intelligence Agency files in the CIA's Roslyn, Virginia, office pertaining to Americans heard over Radio Hanoi during the Vietnam War. While in Washington, Shirley and I visited a special exhibit at one of the Smithsonian Museums concerning the internment of Japanese American citizens during World War II, "And Justice for All." It was an emotional experience to see the photographs of innocent children, parents, and grandparents, most of them U.S. citizens, who were forcibly evicted from their homes. As a result, many, if not most, of these displaced American citizens lost essentially all that they owned to greedy, intolerant neighbors. Families were transported under tight military security to subsistence-level camps, encircled with barbed wire, and located in isolated areas of the western United States. Armed soldiers and guard towers prevented those confined from escaping.

The imprisonment of over one hundred thousand Japanese Americans was wrong: our government had made a tragic mistake that was in part racially motivated. My belief that our government was incapable of doing wrong had suffered a serious setback. I wanted to learn more about this black mark in our history and find out how it could have happened in the good old United States. Two books in our local library covered the story of the internment of Japanese Americans in great detail. One of the books — John Tateishi's *And Justice for All: An Oral History of the Japanese American Detention Camps* (New York: Random House, 1984) — had inspired the Smithsonian exhibit. The major finding of the second book — Michi Weglyn's *Years of Infamy: The Untold Story of America's Concentration Camps* (New York: Morrow, 1976) — was that government officials in California and Washington, D.C., were aware that Japanese Americans living on the West Coast, who also happened to be U.S. citizens, presented no security risk in this country's war against Japan. But President Franklin Roosevelt decided that to do nothing would be politically unpopular. Both federal and state officials, including California Attorney General (and former U.S. Supreme Court Justice) Earl Warren, ignored investigative reports that concluded that Japanese Americans should not be interned in "relocation camps" and deliberately uprooted over one hundred thousand Japanese Americans because it served either their personal political objectives or their racial biases.

The folly of the internment of U.S. citizens who happened to have ancestors in Japan or who had become naturalized American citizens since coming to this country from Japan made me less sure that the government had acted properly toward Vietnam. If the government could treat its own citizens as badly as it did the Japanese Americans, it wasn't difficult to picture government officials cut from the same cloth once again behaving just as odiously toward another nonwhite population, with lethal consequences. I was now more eager than ever to interview those who had traveled to Hanoi, to determine for myself whether their trips were justified and how they viewed the nature of the war.

The "Choice" of Interviewees

Most of those to whom I wrote did not answer. They included: the Reverend Daniel J. Berrigan; writer Elaine Brown; Rennie Davis; actress Jane Fonda; author Seymour Hersh; editor Andrew Kopkind; historian Staughton Lynd; journalist Robert Scheer; author Susan Sontag; and college professors Grace Paley, Sidney Peck, and Howard Zinn. About two dozen individuals indicated that either professional or personal commitments made an interview impossible. Among this group were Tom Hayden and Joan Baez. Others, such as the Reverend Michael Allen, the Reverend William Sloane Coffin, Mary Anne Hamilton, and poet Denise Levertov, could not conveniently be fitted into the interview schedule. Anthony Lewis, columnist for the *New York Times,* was unavailable because of recent surgery. In some cases, I was unable either to discover a current address or find someone who knew an individual's whereabouts. Others, such as industrialist Cyrus Eaton, pacifist James Forest, foreign correspondent Joseph Kraft, pacifist A. J. Muste, and reporters Charles Collingwood, John Hart, and David Schoenbrun, were deceased. The two dozen individuals whom I interviewed simply comprised those who consented to be interviewed and who also made themselves available at a time and a place that was feasible for me to meet with them.

The Interviews

Each interview was unique and tended to focus upon those incidents, events, and views that were of importance to the person interviewed. In addition, I attempted to develop discussion in those areas that seemed appropriate, based on my prior knowledge of the individual's activities during the war. Those interviewed, have reviewed the material for accuracy and completeness.

I have restructured the interviews so that the questions I asked have been deleted. The comments of those interviewed have been reorganized in some cases so that related material is grouped together even though the comment may have been made at another point during the interview. In most cases, the comments of the interviewee needed no prefatory clarification and stand alone. In other cases, however, I have inserted a parenthetical phrase to substitute for the question that I asked, so that the reader can understand the context in which the response was elicited. The interviewees' comments were also subjected to minor editing to eliminate redundancies, awkward phrases, and grammatical inconsistencies and to clarify comments that some readers may have found ambiguous. Essentially, however, the words and meanings of those interviewed remain intact.

ORGANIZATION OF THE BOOK

To neatly categorize those interviewed into distinctive groups, unique and without overlap, proved to be an impossible task. Practically every individual had multiple associations and network affiliations: there were university professors, attorneys, and ministers; members of radical groups, Students for a Democratic Society, Women Strike for Peace, and the investigating teams of the Stockholm War Crimes Tribunal; counselors against the draft; New National Mobilization Committee organizers; Quakers; prisoner-of-war escorts; members of the Committee of Liaison; authors; pacifists; antiwar protesters; those who met with Ho Chi Minh; those who made multiple trips to Hanoi during the war; those who broadcast over Radio Hanoi; those who returned to Vietnam after the war, etc. Any classification scheme is, on its face, arbitrary and as likely to make as much sense as another.

The difficulty in categorizing these individuals is characteristic of them as persons as well. They do not fit into clearly differentiated categories, and, based on the interviews, they seem proud of their differences. I have no doubt that they would be uncomfortable with any attempt to categorize them, according to background, experience, or political views, within one niche rather than another. No attempt was made, therefore, to present the interviews in what I considered to be their order of significance, although the length of the Dave Dellinger interview does illustrate how important and unique I thought his experiences were. Consequently, the interviews are presented simply in chronological order, based upon the interviewee's date of arrival in North Vietnam during the war.

THE INTERVIEWEES THEMSELVES

One aspect of each interview that was singular and characteristic of all those interviewed was the extraordinary degree of articulateness, regardless of occupation or level of achievement. I also was repeatedly amazed at how open, frank, and accommodating these individuals were. Their willingness to meet with me was both surprising and striking. At the same time, I am sure they were curious as to who I was and what my purpose was. Ramsey Clark consented to the interview because, as he told me prior to the interview, I appeared to be obsessed with interviewing him and the others. Ethel Taylor asked me at the end of the interview, "Who are you?" Some might ask why she waited to ask that question, but I was glad that she did wait. Even though my motives were not clear to her and others (and even to myself), those whom I interviewed went out of their way to make themselves accessible. I never questioned why they agreed to meet with me, but I surmise that they believed, as I do now, that misconceptions persist about how and why the United States got into the war and that perhaps this combined effort — offering a perspective contrary to that of U.S. wartime political and military leadership — might help clear up some of the confusion pertaining to the war and continue the healing process, which is still ongoing.

What did most of those interviewed have in common with one another?

- The willingness to devote an overwhelming part of their daily lives, between 1965 and 1972, to expressing their opposition — by speech, by writing, and by action — to the Vietnam War
- The willingness to take an initially unpopular stand against the war and accept the criticism, ridicule, and scathing enmity of those who found their views intolerable
- A belief that the war, at a minimum, served no useful purpose and that it never should have taken place
- A belief that the war was the direct result of the unwillingness of the U.S. political leadership — beginning with President Truman and continuing with Eisenhower, Kennedy, Johnson, and ultimately Nixon — to tolerate a democratic voting process expected to demonstrate that the majority of the Vietnamese people preferred a government led by the Communist leader Ho Chi Minh
- A conviction that the Vietnam War was a struggle for independence by an indigenous population, similar in character to America's own Revolutionary War that freed the nation from a British army of occupation

- Outrage over the hundreds of thousands of Vietnamese, many of them innocent civilians, who were maimed, disabled, disfigured, tortured, and murdered as a result of the war
- A condemnation of the violence inflicted upon the Vietnamese people, their homes, their villages and cities, their land, their culture, and their wish to be one nation
- The belief that the Vietnamese would fight on, regardless of losses, until they wore down the U.S. military perception that absolute victory (the light at the end of the tunnel) was feasible and worth the unlimited loss of life of U.S. servicemen
- A deep concern that U.S. servicemen were dying needlessly for a cause that was ill conceived, racist, and based upon the belief that no price was too great to halt the spread of communism
- A belief that the military tactics and weapons (B-52 carpet bombing and "daisy-cutter" antipersonnel bombs) employed by U.S. armed forces were inhumane and should have been outlawed
- A conviction that the war was an environmental disaster of immense proportions and that nothing could justify such ecological terrorism
- A certainty that their continued efforts, through all means available to them, to bring home to the U.S. public the brutality of the war would eventually turn citizens against the harm (1) that was suffered by Vietnam and its people, (2) that was inherent in a domestic military draft selection process that was biased against the poor, (3) that was produced by heightened domestic cultural conflict, and (4) that resulted from the diversion of billions of federal dollars from unmet domestic needs to destructive purposes abroad. These individuals believed that once citizens internalized the price of the war, they would vent their outrage upon their elected representatives who, anxious to remain in office, would apply relentless pressure on presidents Johnson and Nixon to close down the war.

IMPACT OF THE TRIPS ON PUBLIC OPINION

Initially, I don't believe that the trips made by these individuals to North Vietnam had any perceptible impact on public opinion at home. Publicity associated with these trips probably reinforced preconceived public opinions, such as those that I once held, that their behavior was un-American, traitorous, and a disservice to the United States, particularly to servicemen fighting in Vietnam and the surviving relatives at home of those wounded, injured, or killed because of the war.

The trips to Hanoi that involved the return of U.S. servicemen held captive by the North Vietnamese probably were public relations coups for the North Vietnamese since the repatriation of these servicemen focused the attention of both the media and the public upon the personal nature of the war and how it reached out and ensnared young Americans: neighbors, relatives, family members, and even sons and daughters. The highly publicized trips to Hanoi by those of celebrity status, such as Ramsey Clark and Jane Fonda, were tempestuous and censured by many Americans. At the same time, however, they strengthened the resolve of those antiwar activists who saw Fonda and Clark as courageous and willing to defy an unresponsive government. The Americans who traveled to North Vietnam also were role models for those beginning to question the morality of the war, the motives of our government, and the human and economic costs incurred by both sides in the conflict. Their impact became increasingly effective as the war went on and, combined with public demonstrations at home, significantly affected this nation's political leadership.

IMPACT OF THE TRIPS UPON U.S. POLITICAL LEADERSHIP

The first visits by Americans to North Vietnam were made by a group of women headed by Mary Clarke. The initial reaction of the government was to attempt to seize her passport and determine if her visit constituted a treasonable action, punishable by fine or imprisonment. The government continued to harass these visitors in an attempt to punish any effort to stray from the official position that although this was an undeclared war, it was an ideological struggle between communism and democracy and that a patriotic citizen's only option was to choose democracy. This hard-nosed reaction by the government, as practiced by the State Department and continued throughout the war, probably had the immediate purpose of deterring others from considering this same action. Of more importance was the need to hold these individuals up to public scorn so that other Americans, in their revulsion, would support the U.S. war aims.

The trips themselves may not have unsettled government officials. But certainly, the ripple effect did, as these acts of defiance inspired those who opposed the war on principle, those young men of draft age reluctant to risk their lives in a war of questionable merit, and those who simply sought an end to the bloodshed on both sides, grimly and relentlessly portrayed on the evening network news broadcasts.

Highly visible opinion leaders such as Ramsey Clark and Jane Fonda offered role models that in effect said: "Look, I've risked my life, my personal resources, and my professional career to oppose my government because I think I am right and my government is wrong. You can do the same, and you don't have to go to Vietnam. You can achieve the same result here at home. Just speak out and publicly demonstrate your opposition to the war." It was this indirect, cumulative impact upon the rest of the population, translated into mass public demonstrations against the war (most keenly felt by local government officials, members of Congress, the federal bureaucracy, and Presidents Johnson and Nixon) that eventually pressured Congress and Nixon to withdraw from Vietnam.

The varieties of protest and defiance took many forms: speeches, parades, marches, revolutionary theater, coffeehouse dialogues, picketing, sit-downs, sit-ins, teach-ins, chainings to iron fences, unlawful occupation of public buildings, defacement of public property with simulated or animal blood, lawsuits filed against the government, congressional lobbying, letters to editors, journal articles, books, songs, meetings with government officials and noncombatants of North Vietnam and the National Liberation Front, distribution of leaflets, visits to schools, creation of both domestic and international antiwar organizations and expanded coalitions, counseling young men how to avoid the draft, assisting young men in relocating out of the country to avoid the draft, networking, media interviews, public debates, underground publications, and prayer vigils. The most extreme elements resorted to violence against people and property, and they, in my opinion, probably undermined the efforts of the vast majority of those opposed to the war, who achieved their aims through nonviolent means.

IMPACT OF THE TRIPS UPON THE INTERVIEWEES

The trips to North Vietnam were, for some, momentous. Their lives changed forever, reinforcing their pacifist beliefs in a way that no other activity could have done. The contrast between the devastation of North Vietnam and the untouched landscape of the United States was stark and produced feelings of outrage, sparking a renewed commitment to their antiwar cause.

Some of those interviewed expressed the conviction that the trip to Hanoi was the defining event in their lives and that the scope of the death, destruction, and privation they observed firsthand validated their actions and their beliefs. The trips strengthened their commitment toward ending the war, a crusade of personal conviction that they put into practice upon their return to the United States.

Exasperated and radicalized by a government that refused to yield to their appeals for peaceful negotiation, disturbed and disillusioned by their failure to influence their elected officials, and outraged that the war went on, they recognized that the U.S. military presence in Vietnam would persist as long as the American people believed the cause was just. They saw their task, in which they eventually were successful, as one of convincing others not that the war could not be won but that it should not continue.

Many of those interviewed continue to distrust government, believing that, too often, the U.S. public is manipulated to serve narrow economic, political, and personal agendas. Nevertheless, all are content to live in the United States, believing this system is superior to other forms of government. They also feel that perhaps a better-informed public will produce a more equitable and caring governance.

My Motivation

For myself, I wanted to learn why this particular group of individuals had been so adamant and outspoken in their opposition to the war. I also wanted to find out, if possible, whether they had been right all along about the U.S. role in the war. The interviews have served as a catharsis for my previously unresolved doubts, and I now count myself as one of their supporters rather than a critic. The interviews were conducted in the fall of 1990, while I was on six-month sabbatical for the express purpose of developing this project.

Tackling this project was consistent, I think, with my nature. I find it difficult to ignore injustice, and I don't like to see helpless people pushed around. I am very proud of the fact, for example, that the Jewish mothers of Tompkinsville, Staten Island, New York, awarded me the Peace Prize when I graduated in 1942 from P.S. 16. I felt good about a snowy New Year's Eve some forty years ago when I prevented a young soldier about my age from being kicked insensible by his "buddies," though I paid the price of blackened eyes, the loss of several teeth, and a badly bruised body. In a way, I tend to share one of the values that I think is characteristic of those whom I interviewed, namely, the compulsion to do what one is driven to do, for whatever reason, regardless of the consequences.

Just as Ramsey Clark was accused of being a dupe of the North Vietnamese, supporters of the war may believe that I similarly have been duped by those whom I interviewed. No matter what the political orientation of the interviewees, most of whom probably would not be accommodated within the mainstream of U.S. political ideologies (and perhaps this means that there is something defective in mainstream politics), I believe they were right to oppose the war and that it was a war that should not have been fought. As I said to Irma Zigas in San Francisco, over fifty thousand Americans died for nothing.

A RECAPITULATION

I began this project utterly convinced that any and all U.S. citizens who traveled to North Vietnam during the Vietnam War were traitors who evaded a justifiable prison sentence only because of loopholes in the law. During the course of my interviews with some of these same Americans, however, I began to believe that perhaps there were special circumstances that motivated them to travel to North Vietnam. Their visits, although not in the best interests of the United States (or so I thought) probably were more the result of poor judgment than a lack of patriotism.

I now believe that these individuals had the absolute right, which they never doubted at any time, to travel overseas and determine for themselves, insofar as possible, the validity of claims made by both sides with respect to the nature of the war. My old nemesis Jane Fonda did what she thought was right, even though her words and actions were very unpopular among my circle of friends. I respect her perseverance and total commitment to her beliefs and her willingness to endure the harassment she received from private citizens and her government, both during and after the war, which has continued to this day. Although I still have reservations about the content of some of her broadcasts over Radio

Hanoi and her critical remarks about American POWs, she was right to oppose the war. Fonda was and is a very courageous person. So, too, are those individuals who are the focus of this collection of interviews.

This experience has been one of the highlights of my life. I was not prepared to learn, or even accept, what I now believe to be the truth about the war and its origins. In retrospect, I am disturbed about how unresponsive the U.S. government was to citizens who objected to the war and the senseless destruction and loss of life that the government justified by the need to save the Vietnamese from themselves.

It is outrageous that a person such as Robert McNamara —who, as secretary of defense from 1961 to 1968, was in a position to exert significant influence on the course of the war — should have totally abdicated his moral responsibility to speak out against a war that he believed was unwinnable (as noted in his book *In Retrospect: The Tragedy and Lessons of Vietnam* [New York: Times Books, 1995]). As a former career officer who believes in civilian supremacy in policy making in the field of national defense, I find it unconscionable that McNamara would allow thousands of American servicemen to go to their deaths, knowing full well that theirs was a lost cause. It is reprehensible that those who entered the military service prepared to give their lives did not receive support from the civilian leader they were obliged to follow.

It seems that McNamara is only belatedly attempting to find peace with his conscience as a result of his failure to act when he must have known that the only right thing to do was to speak out against the war. The members of the "loyal opposition" showed more courage than McNamara, which may be surprising to many but not at all so to those who protested the war here at home and, at risk to themselves, in North Vietnam. Not long ago, I was asked if I thought the antiwar protesters were vindicated by McNamara's recent statements. I replied that I thought the protesters knew that the war was wrong and had thought so all along — it was not necessary for someone in McNamara's position, at this late date, to agree with them for them to experience vindication.

A Personal Assessment

I don't know if the trips to Hanoi made by those interviewed were necessary. I don't think they were justified on the basis of exchanging mail and gifts between American POWs and their families. I am sure that world opinion would have forced the North Vietnamese leadership, which was very alert to public sentiment, to accede to these exchanges. However, I am sure that those Americans who traveled to Hanoi to express their opposition to the war experienced a sense of renewal and were galvanized to continue their opposition to the war at home. And by their example and leadership, they motivated increasingly large numbers of other Americans to join them in their expressions of opposition. To the extent that their opposition helped to end the killing, they deserve our respect and thanks. This group of opinion leaders, who came from all walks of life and varieties of professions, did, I believe, significantly impact public opinion.

Some readers may be offended by the title of this manuscript because they continue to question the loyalty of those whom I interviewed. However, the United States can claim to be a free, democratic nation only if opinions that may be out of favor among the political leadership can be freely expressed without fear of retribution. Just as the political factions out of power in governments are described as the "loyal opposition," it seemed fitting to describe this group in the same way because they, out of conviction, opposed a war they believed to be wrong at the very least and criminal in the extreme, and they fought for what they believed to be right.

Given current discussions about resolving the issue of American POWs with the Republic of Vietnam and debate over what the nature of the U.S. relationship should be with Vietnam, the interviews that follow provide significant insights related to both of these areas.

ADDITIONAL INFORMATION

The Appendix lists the names of 172 individuals who are believed to have traveled to North Vietnam during the war. Where available, the individual's affiliation (which is seldom complete) and the year of his or her trip(s) are shown. The list was derived primarily from newspaper articles, books, Central Intelligence Agency files, and congressional hearing records. Those who were interviewed added about a dozen more names.

The list is not complete. Government documents and books on Vietnam indicate that perhaps as many as three hundred American citizens may have traveled to North Vietnam during this period. Furthermore, several individuals on the list may not have gone but were erroneously reported by others to have made the trip, or they may have traveled to North Vietnam after 1972, when active U.S. military involvement had ceased. The list, nevertheless, as far as I have been able to determine, is correct.

Map of Vietnam and neighboring countries, 1972. Cities shown were visited by one or more of the individuals interviewed in this book.

Acronyms

ABC	American Broadcasting Companies
ACLU	American Civil Liberties Union
AFSC	American Friends Service Committee
AQAG	A Quaker Action Group
ASEAN	Association of Southeast Asian Nations
AWOL	absent without leave
CBC	Canadian Broadcasting Corporation
CBS	Columbia Broadcasting System
CIA	Central Intelligence Agency
CNN	Cable News Network
COINTEL	the FBI's counterintelligence program
COLIAFAM	Committee of Liaison With Families of Servicemen
CORE	Congress of Racial Equality
DMZ	demilitarized zone
DRV	Democratic Republic of Vietnam
EC	European Community
EPF	Episcopal Peace Fellowship
FBI	Federal Bureau of Investigation
FBIS	Federal Broadcast Information Service
GI	government issue; soldier
GIM	a type of Russian automobile
HBO	Home Box Office
HUAC	House Un-American Activities Committee
ICC	International Control Commission
IMF	International Monetary Fund
JFK	John Fitzgerald Kennedy
LBJ	Lyndon Baines Johnson

MIA	missing in action
MIG	a Russian-made fighter aircraft
MIT	Massachusetts Institute of Technology
NAACP	National Association for the Advancement of Colored People
NBC	National Broadcasting Company
NCUP	Newark Community Union Project
NGO	nongovernmental organization
NLF	National Liberation Front
NSA	National Security Agency
PCPJ	People's Coalition for Peace and Justice
PG&E	Pacific Gas and Electric
POW	prisoner of war
PR	public relations
PRG	Provisional Revolutionary Government
PUSH	People United to Save Humanity
R&R	rest and relaxation
SAM	surface-to-air missile
SANE/FREEZE	formed through a merger of the Committee for a Sane Nuclear Policy and the Nuclear Waepons Freeze Campaign; now called Peace Action
SAS	Scandinavian Airlines System
SDS	Students for a Democratic Society
SNCC	Student Nonviolent Coordination Committee
UC	University of California
UCLA	University of California, Los Angeles
UCSB	University of California, Santa Barbara
UN	United Nations
UNDP	United Nations Development Program
UNICEF	United Nations Children's Fund
VFW	Veterans of Foreign Wars
WILPF	Women's International League for Peace and Freedom
WSP	Women Strike for Peace

The Loyal Opposition

1

Mary Clarke

Mary Clarke was the first citizen from the United States to travel to Hanoi during the war. She, along with other members of Women Strike for Peace, helped arrange an international women's peace conference in Djakarta, Indonesia, in 1965. Clarke returned to Hanoi in 1967 and met with American POWs. While visiting a Vietnamese family, she was a very close spectator to a U.S. air bombing and questioned her ability to remain a pacifist while under air attack. She also discussed her experiences as a member of the peace movement and counselor to young men of draft age. My interview with Mary Clarke took place on November 16, 1990, at her home in Los Angeles, California.

MARY CLARKE: I am a member of Women Strike for Peace. I went to Hanoi in May of 1965. Traveling with me was another Women Strike for Peace member, Lorraine Gordon. We were told by the Vietnamese that we were the first Americans to come in. Staughton Lynd [and I later], at an international conference on Vietnam held in Geneva, debated who went first [to Hanoi]. Lorraine and I had been invited by the Soviet Women's Committee to attend a celebration of the "The Defeat of Fascism" in Moscow in May 1965. Among the guests were resistance heroes from mostly European countries. The Soviet Women's Committee designated Women Strike for Peace as "peace heroines" and invited Lorraine and me to represent our group.

Before we left the States, we had been asked by Women Strike for Peace to make contact with the Vietnamese in Moscow in order to make arrangements for a conference between our women and their women from the North and South of Vietnam. We went [first] to the North Vietnam embassy and explained what we had in mind and then to the [National] Liberation Front [NLF], which was just setting up offices. We met with the head of that delegation. Apparently, one of the men we met notified the women in Hanoi, who invited us to come to Hanoi immediately after the end of the Moscow conference.

We flew from Moscow to Peking, where we stayed overnight. Then we flew to Nanning, a border town in China, where we spent two nights. We left Nanning in a small twelve-seater plane for Hanoi but had to return to Nanning. We were told it was because of bad weather, but the reason was because American planes were sighted. The bombing was going on then in the North.

[Traveling with us to Hanoi were:] Frances Herring, from Berkeley, California, a professor at Berkeley; a student from Ann Arbor; a woman lawyer from San Francisco; Margaret Russell from Washington, D.C.; Phyllis Schmidt from Long Beach; Shirley Lens from Chicago; and three others whose names I cannot remember.

In Hanoi, we met with Vietnamese women to discuss the possibility of holding a joint meeting. We then were invited by Premier Pham Van Dong to talk about our proposal. He was very enthusiastic and supported the proposal. We also suggested that the meeting be held at a site convenient for the Vietnamese women. He contacted President [Achmed] Sukarno of Indonesia, who agreed to play host to our meeting, which was planned for July of 1965. It was agreed that there would be five women from the North, five women from the South, and ten women from Women Strike for Peace.

[We were in Hanoi] three or four days. A very short visit because it was important to get back to the States to make plans for the Djakarta meeting. During that visit, we met a young girl whose father had been killed in front of her eyes (she was from the South) and who was at that point having mental problems. We also met a little boy who had been napalmed. He also was from the South. He was grotesque-looking. It was heartbreaking. They showed us what was happening as a result of the bombing. We visited hospitals, where we saw children who were victims of the cluster bombs.

Dagmar Wilson, Ruth Krause, [and I] were invited to come [in 1967], I guess as a testimonial to what U.S. firepower was doing there. We went to bear witness. They knew that we were very solidly against the war. By that time, there was quite a bit of travel [to Hanoi]. Ruth, Dagmar, and I went to Paris first, where we picked up our travel credentials. We then flew to Cambodia. We stayed several days in Phnom Penh and were confirmed for the once-a-week flight to Hanoi via Vientiane, on an old French plane with an aging French crew from the days of French Indochina. It was there for the most part for the diplomatic corps stationed in Vietnam. While in Phnom Penh, we spent some time with Wilfred Burchett, the Australian journalist.

We arrived at Hanoi during the day. On the flight with us was the Canadian representative, who was also representing American interests. The head of the International Control Commission, a man from India, was on board, too, as were several other diplomats. They were attending some sort of formal affair in Hanoi, we were told by the Canadian, who also told us, "You are very safe on this flight because we are all here, and they don't dare touch us." Which was true. We landed at the airport outside of Hanoi, which was completely devastated. We were ferried on rafts with the other travelers, together with machines and cargo, across huge craters filled with water to the airport building. The airport building was in shambles.

We were met at the airport by representatives of the women's organization. We were taken to a hotel in Hanoi. David Schoenbrun, the noted American journalist, was also staying there. We saw him in the bomb shelters quite often. There were bombing raids almost every night. [We stayed] one week. We went out to the countryside to visit schools that were literally underground. The children all wore thick woven hats, in case of bombings. They all carried kerosene lamps and studied by lamplight.

We went to hospitals. Outfitted with helmets and mosquito netting, we traveled south toward the central part of Vietnam in a camouflaged jeep. In two places, we had to wait several hours at a time, waiting our turn to ford rivers where the bridges had been blown up. We crossed on pontoons made of bamboo.

We stayed overnight at one place that was rocky, and we had to climb to reach our lodging. The next day, we drove to a village and saw the devastation. Dikes had been blown up. A church, still standing by some miracle, was bombed weekly, if not more often. The people showed us leaflets dropped by U.S. planes, signed by quite a number of U.S. senators, which laid out the terms for an end to the war, as if it was the Vietnamese who were the aggressors.

We visited a peasant family in their simple abode, with a dirt floor. With us was a war orphan, a small child whose parents were killed in one of the U.S. bombings. As we sat and talked, we heard U.S. planes approach. We all went under the table. I held the orphan in my arms. I'll tell you, I thought I was a pacifist, nonviolent. The sight of a gun does something to me. But if I had a gun then, I would have shot at that plane, no matter who was in it. We could see it, and we saw the bomb pass by. It hit the church again.

We saw the man in charge of the whole POW situation. Very gruff. A colonel, I think. He was not pleasant, and I can imagine that life for the POWs under this man would have been difficult. We went to the Hanoi Hilton, the POW camp on the outskirts of Hanoi. We met one POW who was from Arizona, whose family thought he was lost in action. He had been picked up and incarcerated only a couple of weeks before. We saw a young guy [Seaman Douglas Hegdahl] who was really a character. All he wanted to know was what was happening in the baseball arena, what the Dodgers were doing, and so forth. He had been on a ship, swept overboard, and fished out of the sea by the Vietnamese. We met [U.S. Navy Lt. Everett] Alvarez, who is now or was head of the Veterans Administration. We got to know his sister when we contacted her upon our return, just as we immediately called the family of the POW from Arizona as soon as we arrived home, to say that "he's alive. He's a POW, but he's alive, and sends his love."

[We brought back mail.] Not very much. There was a discipline among the Americans in the camps, one that I later read about in the newspapers, a sort of not fraternizing with the enemy concept. The Arizona man was just delighted to see us and tell us how to reach his family. The young man from the ship [Hegdahl] was not friendly but not unfriendly. They showed us where they lived. And that's where we met Alvarez and a couple of others. I think they thought that we were against them because we were against the war, and here they were, POWs. I could understand that. When we talked with them, we didn't try to shame them or any such thing because we felt that they had been caught up in something that wasn't of their own making.

Speaking of memories, at one time the North was going to execute an American GI in retaliation for the televised killing of a young NLF man by the Saigon chief of police. Women Strike for Peace intervened. We sent a long telegram [to the North Vietnamese] saying, "This is wrong. You are doing just what the U.S. is doing, and we feel that you will get no sympathy. In fact, people will turn against you." They let us know that because of our intervention, they did not execute the American GI.

[In 1967] we returned by way of Vientiane, then back to Cambodia, where we were met by Prince Norodom Sihanouk's aide. We then traveled from Cambodia to Hong Kong, where news correspondent Bernard Kalb interviewed us, then [to] Hawaii and Los Angeles. Many friends were there to meet us, along with a sizable representation of the media. The press were interested mainly in the POWs and wanted to know if we had seen any. We refused to give the name of the Arizona man because we felt his family should hear it first. The press wasn't friendly. There was some hostility. We met with that all the time.

[I was] called a traitor. The press [sometimes] twisted our words or took them out of context, taking a sentence here and not relating it to the whole paragraph or statement. The press also did not accurately report what we said at the Moscow conference in 1965. They reported us as saying that we called for the United States to disarm unilaterally. . . . We called for international disarmament under United Nations safeguards. That was a case of selective misrepresentation.

I belonged to [the] Committee for a Sane Nuclear Policy, and I was one of the founders [of Women Strike for Peace] in southern California. When we *struck* on November 1, 1961, it was really just a one-day strike. Here in Los Angeles, we had printed up a paper which said, "Now, when this is over, here are different peace organizations, their addresses, and phone numbers. Get involved." The women said, "No, we want to continue with this nonorganization." They were tired of organizations with hierarchies, clearing things with national headquarters, not being able to take action when a crisis developed. We don't elect officers, no factotums, no constitution. We have a national spokeswoman or coordinator.

So what we had expected to be a one-day action was a national phenomenon and a national movement. Fifty thousand women across the country in sixty cities turned out to protest nuclear testing by the U.S. and the Soviet Union. In Los Angeles, forty-five hundred women took part. They came by bus and car from San Bernardino, Santa Barbara, and San Diego. It was incredible. . . .

All of my time was devoted to working for an end to the war. Day and night, I did nothing else. We were all volunteers. We had no hired help. It was a full-time job with no pay. I didn't have time to consider if I was doing enough. I do have one regret, and that is that I didn't work harder to help obtain the proper treatment for the physically and mentally maimed men of the Vietnam War. They, too, were victims of government policy and indifference.

We counseled the altruistic and the pragmatic young men. There were some who were kicked out of their homes by parents who felt they should serve in the war. We found homes for them and provided counseling and legal assistance. We advised them of their rights. Some had medical problems. Some were the sole support of their families. Some qualified as conscientious objectors, and we helped place them in hospitals and community services. A lawyer's panel provided legal advice and help. Some we helped go to Canada, where we had contact with a women's organization that was sympathetic. We probably counseled ten to twenty a week. Also, we were a referral center, so if a call came from out of state, we sent them to the nearest draft-counseling service.

To break the law meant the possibility of going to jail, so we didn't encourage that. What we did was to help them *avoid* the draft. Some went to jail. Some received deferments, not many. Some were certified as conscientious objectors. Where the draft boards had large quotas to fill, we advised draftees to move to another area where they had a smaller quota and set up legal residence with members of their family or friends. The lawyers who worked with us were crucial to our work. . . .

We helped support other counseling services, such as the one in London, headed by a woman law student. Many young men were attending universities in Europe, so she was able to counsel them. We helped with a conscientious objector shelter in Canada and with several other counseling services. We sent modest sums of money. . . .

[The average member of Women Strike for Peace was] middle class, white, intelligent, flexible, and resourceful. The majority were married and mothers. They were drawn to Women Strike for Peace because our major concern was nuclear testing, the fallout, and the strontium in the milk their children drank. We have been called by some the beginning of the new feminist movement.

Many of us had been involved with other peace organizations run by men. We were allowed to do the typing and filing and other nitty-gritty work, but few were in leadership positions. As women, we were accustomed to working in carpools, acting in family crises, altering plans when a child was ill, and generally adapting to new situations. And we felt stifled by the slow pace of decision making and [by] our status in a male-dominated group. We had no problems about making decisions and shifting gears. The men moved at a snail's pace. Many men were supportive of us even though they took no part in decision making.

2

Michael Myerson

Michael Myerson was a former international secretary for the W.E.B. Du Bois Clubs. He and Harold Supriano traveled to Hanoi in 1965 after attending a peace conference in Helsinki, Finland, which Myerson co-chaired. He mistakenly believed that he was among the first group of Americans to visit Hanoi during the war. He spent ten years protesting against the Vietnam War and believes the majority of the U.S. population is politically naive. Myerson teaches labor studies at Empire State College in New York City. Because of conflicting commitments, my interview with him was conducted by telephone on October 9, 1990.

MICHAEL MYERSON: I was one of the founders of the United States Peace Council. For ten years, I served as its executive director. I resigned in February of this year but continue to serve on the board. In 1962 I wrote a pamphlet about the war in Vietnam. About 80,000 to 100,000 copies of the pamphlet, which was used in teach-ins, were sold. I participated in the demonstrations in San Francisco against Mme Nhu [Tran Le Xuan], wife of the South Vietnamese president, and attempted to prevent her from entering her hotel. I was active in student politics. I was a member of the Vietnam Day Committee [VDC] and the free speech movement. I was on the Fifth Avenue [Vietnam Peace] Parade Committee, the National "Mobe," and the National Coalition for Peace and Justice, the latter two organizations essentially being the same, representing only a change in names. Along with a black publisher named Carleton, I was co-chairman of the American Peace Conference held in Helsinki, Finland, earlier in 1965, attended by about fifty Americans [ninety-six, according to "U.S. The Main Target," *New York Times*, July 11, p. 9].

Attending the conference were delegates from the National Liberation Front of South Vietnam and North Vietnam. They had translated the pamphlet I had written about the war and were using the pamphlet for propaganda with their troops in South Vietnam. Members of the North Vietnam delegation invited me to come to Hanoi and bring other Americans with me. I invited Richard Ward, Christopher Koch, and Harold Supriano, [who were at the Helsinki conference, to join me]. We weren't sure when we would leave, and Harold and I traveled around Europe, including Greece and Italy, before we received word that the timing of our visit to North Vietnam was approved.

When I went to North Vietnam in August 1965, I was a member of the first group of Americans to visit North Vietnam during the war [Myerson and his group actually were preceded by Mary Clarke et al.]. At the time I made the trip, I was working as a shipping clerk in San Francisco. I was international secretary of the W.E.B. Du Bois Clubs, a socialist youth organization. I belonged to various antiwar coalitions in San Francisco and Oakland. The other members of the group were: Richard Ward, who was living in Paris and a writer for *The Guardian*; Christopher Koch, a journalist, who has since worked for the Public Broadcasting System on its radio program *All Things Considered*; and Harold Supriano, now a member of Service Employees International with offices in Oakland, California.

Koch and Ward, as journalists, intended to report what they saw in North Vietnam. There was no specific purpose to the trip other than just curiosity, the excitement, and to show our solidarity with the Vietnamese. We were able to see things that no American before had seen. We later decided that we should try to reach as wide an audience as possible through writing and speaking throughout the country about our trip. I traveled for six months cross-country protesting the war before I moved back to New York City. Later, in 1966, I joined the Communist Party and have been a member ever since [Myerson resigned from the party later in 1990].

We met in Paris and flew to Warsaw, then Moscow, Beijing, and a city in southern China, where we waited for the bombing to stop before entering North Vietnam. We were guests of the United States–Vietnam Friendship Committee, which was cohosted by the Vietnamese Youth Group. We spent two weeks in North Vietnam. We visited villages and spent four or five nights outside of Hanoi. We met with Pham Van Dong for several hours and saw Ho Chi Minh from a distance during the twentieth anniversary celebration of the Democratic Republic of Vietnam. It was during this state celebration that I had a cold, and Ho Chi Minh sent me a note about my health. I also received a medal, "Favorite Nephew of Ho Chi Minh."

While in Hanoi, we were interviewed, and those interviews may have been broadcast over Radio Hanoi, but I am not aware that they were. As the first visitors to Hanoi, we were like a trial run and test case to see if they would be putting us in jeopardy with the United States government and if the visit would have positive results or be counterproductive. They were feeling their way gradually about visits to Hanoi by Americans. We met one of the captured American fliers, a POW from Del Rio, Texas.

While we were in Hanoi, they reportedly shot down the five-hundreth American plane. When we returned to the United States, the Immigration Service took away our passports and Attorney General Nicholas Katzenbach threatened to prosecute us. Among the items we returned with were rings made from an American plane that had been shot down. . . .

The Vietnamese will be living with Agent Orange for years to come. No one invaded the United States or bombed the United States. . . . The American people do not understand the nature of the war in Vietnam. They are among the most politically ignorant in the world. They have been brainwashed. Americans don't know that much about their own lives, let alone those of other countries. Decisions are made in our government and by the Congress without debate. . . .

Patriotism is a very much misused and abused term. Patriotism, as I would define it, is looking out for the best interests of one's country. I believe the Vietnamese were very patriotic in defending their country. The peace movement was the single most patriotic force in this country in terms of defending the best interests of our nation. . . . What was most effective was the constant melding of mass demonstrations so that in the end, the majority was committed against the war. Americans today reflect a national mood of self-interest bordering on selfishness. We don't want Americans killed but don't worry about others being killed.

My visit to Vietnam was the single most important event of my life. It certainly made me more serious as a political person and less of a dilettante about American political affairs. I expressed my opposition to the war because I wanted our government to know what my views were and because I think I am entitled to have a say in what our government does. The Vietnam War consumed my full-time energies for ten years. I don't regret what I did and wish that I had done more. I would have liked to have gone to South Vietnam as well.

3

Harold Supriano

Harold Supriano, actively opposed to the war, traveled to Hanoi in 1965 with a youth group that included Michael Myerson. He was fired by several employers at the urging of the Federal Bureau of Investigation [FBI] because of his trip to Hanoi. A union organizer for twenty years, Supriano was interviewed the morning of November 14, 1990, by telephone because we could not arrange a satisfactory time for a face-to-face interview.

HAROLD SUPRIANO: I was disappointed and frustrated with our government's involvement in the war, which I considered to be racist. I am black, and I had come out of the civil rights movement. I worked with SNCC [Student Nonviolent Coordinating Committee] and CORE [Congress of Racial Equality] in San Francisco. I was a member of the W.E.B. Du Bois Clubs, a socialist youth organization made up of people from all walks of life. I was generally active in the peace movement and participated in the major demonstrations against the war on the West Coast.

I was a member of a group that I believe was the very first to travel to North Vietnam during the war. At that time, I was thirty-two years old. It was in August of 1965. I had attended a World Peace Congress in Helsinki, where I and others met a Vietnamese delegation. They invited us to a briefing and then extended an invitation to us to visit North Vietnam. We agreed to contact a trade delegation in Paris concerning the trip, and approval was granted. There were four of us, and we needed visas. We waited several days for the visas before leaving for Hanoi.

We flew from Paris to Moscow on an Aeroflot plane and continued on to Beijing, where we spent the night. We flew from Beijing to Hanoi in a very small diplomatic courier plane of about eighteen to twenty-one seats. We were in North Vietnam about ten days. We talked to various groups, including a peace committee. We met with premier Pham Van

Dong and interviewed an American POW, Robert Dotry of Eagle Pass, Texas. He had ejected from a plane and injured both arms. He had been operated on in a Hanoi hospital, and both of his arms were in casts. We also saw Ho Chi Minh at a gathering but did not speak to him.

On our return trip, we took the same route (Hanoi-Beijing-Moscow-Paris) until we arrived [in] Paris. We then split up and met again in New York City. We had lengthy discussions in New York about whether we should go public about our trip and what we saw while we were there. At first, we decided to keep it quiet because there was the fear we might be prosecuted for breaking the law in visiting North Vietnam. After talking with an attorney, we decided to hold a press conference and discuss our trip. The conference was well attended.

The other three members of our group — Richard Ward, Chris Koch, and Michael Myerson — and myself had frequent meetings and discussions before, during, and after our trip to Hanoi. We developed a good relationship. After the press conference, I returned to the Bay Area and went with Mike Myerson on a speaking engagement tour in the Bay Area and the West Coast. We returned with film that we had taken on our tour of North Vietnam and showed the film in the Bay Area as part of the speaking engagements.

After the trip, I lost my passport and lost several jobs because of the trip. I was hounded by the FBI because of my trip to Hanoi. Agents from the FBI would come to my place of work and notify my employer that I had gone to Hanoi, and as a result, I was terminated, at least twice. I had been working as a social worker on probationary status. My supervisor said that my work was excellent, but after the FBI agent talked to the director, I was terminated.

I helped form the Association of Social Workers after being separated in order to improve employee protection against arbitrary dismissal. Eventually, however, I was reinstated as a city of San Francisco employee through efforts of the union. I was placed in the Public Health Department. I eventually was hired by the union; they became tired of representing me in my disputes with management. I have now been with the union for just over twenty years.

4

Herbert Aptheker

Prof. Herbert Aptheker, born in 1915, is a prominent Communist and Marxist scholar. He has spent most of his adult life — and continues to this day — chronicling the life and writings of W.E.B. Du Bois, a black scholar who campaigned for racial equality earlier in this century. Aptheker's extensive and definitive writings on Du Bois are cataloged in *Who's Who in America, 1992–1993,* 47th ed. (New Providence, NJ: Reed Publishing, 1992). In our interview, he told of his admiration for Du Bois and described some of Du Bois's experiences.

Aptheker served in the U.S. Army field artillery in Europe during World War II, from 1942 to 1946, and achieved the rank of major. Almost twenty years later, in 1965, Professor Aptheker traveled to Hanoi with Tom Hayden and Staughton Lynd; he recalled that he had to persuade Hayden not to remain in North Vietnam. Aptheker believed that despite this trio's sensational reception on their return to the United States, no criminal charges were filed against him because the Johnson administration also would have had to prosecute Lynd, the son of two well-known and respected university researchers. According to Aptheker, the Johnson administration was unwilling to hazard the unfavorable publicity that such a criminal prosecution would produce.

Professor Aptheker made no apologies for being a Communist and explained how it was possible to reconcile being both a Communist and a patriotic American. He was interviewed in his book-lined office in San Jose, California, on November 14, 1990.

HERBERT APTHEKER: I teach at the [University of California] Law School in Berkeley. [I teach only] one topic, racism and the law. I also teach at the Hastings College of Law, which is part of the University of California. That's in San Francisco. I teach a seminar called "Seminar on Civil Rights," but I will not continue because it is a twelve-hour day for me. At my age, a twelve-hour day is too much. So I am going to give up the seminar at Hastings this term and just do Berkeley. It's very important for me to keep on teaching because I get that contact with young people.

[In 1965, when I decided to go to Hanoi], I was already part of the Left here and was director of the American Institute for Marxist Studies. I had been editor for about ten years of *Political Affairs,* a leftist monthly magazine, and I was very active in the Left movement, the black movement, the civil rights movement, and the peace movement. I deliberately undertook to break the ban against radical speakers at universities, and I did that probably in seventy-five to eighty universities: North Carolina, Buffalo, Berkeley, Ohio State, and so on. In most cases, we eventually succeeded. I broke the ban in Berkeley in 1963, and a year later, in 1964, came the free speech movement.

And then I sued to get rid of the passport provision of the McCarran Act, which made it a crime for a Communist or a so-called Communist, a fellow traveler, to apply for a passport — ten years in prison [if you] applied, and the clerk who handled your application was subject to a year in prison. That's a long story. But we sued, lost at first, and faced ten years, but we won in the Supreme Court in 1964. It's a rather famous case in constitutional law; it's called *Aptheker versus Rusk.* [Dean] Rusk was the secretary of state. And the Court ruled six to three that Rusk was wrong and that I was right. And so now anybody can get a passport. In 1964, [however,] there were all sorts of restrictions.

I was simultaneously part of the World Peace Council, which had some strength at that time. I was on the Presidium, and it was in connection with that office that I attended a world peace congress in Helsinki. It seems to me it was in '64, and while [I was] there, members of the delegation from North Vietnam sought me out and asked if I could arrange a delegation of citizens from the United States. They said they could handle maybe three because they had limited resources. They said come and see what the war was, what it was doing, and tour their country, examine their country, and talk to people, with the idea that this delegation would come home and try to persuade the American people that that war should be stopped.

Well, I certainly wanted the war to stop, and so I promised these friends that I would undertake it. When I came home, I got in touch with Staughton Lynd, whom I knew, and he was younger. He was a professor at Yale, a very fine historian, and the son of very distinguished parents: Robert Lynd was head of the American Sociological Society, and his wife,

Helen Lynd, was a professor of sociology. Staughton was very active in various struggles, as I was, although his politics were different. Sort of a Quaker background, pacifist. Very honorable. I admired him. Very courageous. I asked, "Staughton, will you join me?" We differed in views, but we wanted peace. He said, "Yes."

We wanted one more person, and the person we first agreed on was Robert Moses, a black man, a very courageous man, who was leading the civil rights struggle in the South, in Mississippi. He came to see me in New York, and he, as I understood it, agreed. He said he would. We arranged to meet in Paris, but then I got word that he couldn't do it. I never did find out why. And I wanted a third person. So the next person was Tom Hayden because Tom was the head of the SDS [Students for a Democratic Society], and he was young. He was only twenty-six. Staughton was thirty-six, I was fifty. So the age group was good. I *had* wanted a black person, for obvious reasons, but I couldn't get it. Staughton knew Tom better than I did.

There was great difficulty at first. They couldn't get together and said they couldn't do it. I told them I was going myself because I had promised I would be there. Of course, it was illegal to go. It was a criminal offense to go to North Vietnam at that time. Five years in jail. I don't remember the name of the law.

I don't know whether it's legal now to go to North Korea. It wasn't for a long time, and then they forbade going to Cuba. You still can't go to Cuba freely. Anyway, there was this law. I made this clear to Staughton and Tom, and, of course, they knew it, so this was not a light thing. They finally said, "Yes." And we got together and, of course, left with passports. By this time I had a passport, but we couldn't say where we were going because that was illegal. We would not have gotten permission. We went to Paris, and from there we made arrangements. We went from Paris to Prague, and from Prague to Moscow, from Moscow to Peking, and from Peking to Hanoi. We got to Hanoi in the latter part of '65. I think it was December. We were met by some officials. My book (*Mission to Hanoi* [New York: International Publishers, 1966]) is fairly detailed, and Tom and Staughton wrote their own book (*The Other Side* [New York: New American Library, 1966]). Their views are somewhat different from mine but perfectly honest and worth reading, and they both wrote prefaces to my book.

That's the story. We went and saw the war, saw some of the devastation; they were already bombing in the North. We were there during the

Christmas bombing of Hanoi. I was called by some of the American press. The Paris office of the *Herald-Tribune* called me in Hanoi for an interview, and I spoke to them.

We toured the country. We saw people and had a very moving interview in Nam Dinh. My host asked what or who would I like to see. That city was a center of Catholicism. I said, if possible, I would like to see the eldest priest in the city. I would like to talk to him. He said that could be arranged. I asked to see an elderly priest because I was sure that he would not be a Communist. That's the first thing. And I wanted one who was old because I thought he would have the colonial experience, which only ended in the 1950s. There was a revolution and so on, something like that. I figured he would have that relationship.

I had a memorable interview with this aged Vietnamese who spoke fluent French and who was quite elderly. He was a priest at the cathedral, which, by the way, was damaged by our planes. There were things there that I will never forget. He was a rather innocent man, very religious obviously, and he asked, when he learned that I was from the United States, in a very innocent sort of way, "Can you tell me why the Americans are bombing this city?" I didn't know what to say to him, and I said, "Father, there's a war on." He said, "But why are they bombing this city?" They had a very large concentration of Catholic people. I really couldn't answer him. I didn't know what to say to him. To go into the whole history of the war would have been a little absurd, and he was rather politically naive.

Then I said to him, "Father, how do you find functioning under the Communists?" He said, "Oh, it's all right." That surprised me a little. I said, "Really, what do you mean?" He said, "Well, we have church services. In fact, it's better than under the French." I was startled. I said, "Really, why is it better than under the French?" He replied, "Under the French, we used to have two masses — a mass for the French and a mass for us" — he meant Vietnamese. He said that was wrong. I said, "But Father, we have that in the United States, too." He said, "You do? What do you mean?" I said, "Well, we have a white Christ and a black Christ. We have black churches and white churches." I said, "The most segregated day is Sunday, when people go to worship God." He was very startled. . . . He said, "Well, we don't have that now. We have one mass for people to come, if they want to, to worship. It's better" [laughter]. Which I thought was quite amazing with all the other contrary propaganda.

The interview was interrupted because of an American bomber. A plane came, and my hosts were intent that I survive. I wanted to stay, but they would not permit me. No bombs were dropped. I guess it was surveillance or something. It was a strange experience for me because I was in the Second World War for over four years. So it was a little unnerving to see an American plane as an enemy, someone who might drop a bomb on me but didn't. But they insisted that we stop, and they took me away. I forget what happened, but we went away somewhere because they didn't know whether there was another bomber or not. And they felt responsible for us.

I remember before we went on, they asked what we wanted. I was sort of the head of the delegation because they considered me old — fifty years is old in Asia — and the others were relatively young. They always asked me what we should do and so forth. So I said, "Well, after a few days, we would like to go out and see the country and talk to people. If there's damage, we would like to see it." So they arranged it. That's when we went to Nam Dinh. I don't know how far south it is, but it is south of Hanoi. "Okay," they said. They would arrange it. They got two cars. So I went to bed that night, and I don't remember when, nine or ten o'clock, there was a knock on the door, and I went to the door and opened it. There was a Vietnamese chap, a small fellow. They are all small people. I hoped he spoke English or some French. His English was perfect. "Yes?" He said, "I am a physician, and I've been told" — I think he used the word *told* — "to examine you." I thought that maybe he had made a mistake, that he had come to the wrong room. I told him that I wasn't ill, that there wasn't anything wrong with me. In any case, he knew my name. He said, "You are going on a tour tomorrow morning."

We were to leave at around four in the morning. This was during a blackout. . . . He said, "I've been instructed to examine you and see whether you may go." I saw that he was going to stay there until he did it. I said, "All right," and he came in. He didn't ask me to undress. I just lay down on the bed. He examined me in a way that an American doctor would, with various instruments, and then he used Asian medicine. He did things to me that no doctor here would do (nerves, tapping; I don't remember exactly). He said I was all right, which didn't surprise me. I was in good health.

"Then," he said to me, "we'll be going at four in the morning." I said, "What do you mean, we?" He said, "Well, I will accompany you." . . . I said, "My heavens, your country is at war. You must be needed here at the hospital." He said, "Well, I am instructed to go with you, take care of you, and see that your health is all right on this trip." I expostulated. I thought it was ridiculous, but it was again clear that that's what was going to happen. I said "All right. You're certainly welcome." And he was with me on the whole trip.

[What I saw in Vietnam did] not really [surprise me]. I had been through a war. Although the damage was fairly extensive, it was not anything like what we [Allied forces in Europe during World War II] had done in my experience.

[The three of us] got along very well. I think Tom was a little afraid of me, a little worried about me. I think it might have been age, I'm not sure. He was a very delightful young man, very shrewd, very sharp. But I had a feeling he was a little concerned about where I stood, my motives. Was I being honest? Was I misleading him in some way? That was the impression. He was an innocent kid. I don't know how much traveling he had done but, for instance, he didn't bring a toothbrush. And for a while he was borrowing our toothbrush until we became so annoyed we went out and got him a toothbrush.

Tom came in very light clothing. It was December, and we traveled through Siberia. I can't tell you how cold it was. Forty below zero, some damn thing. And the poor kid was shivering. We finally got him the heaviest sweater we could buy. I think we got it in Peking [laughter]. He took just a handbag, and that was it. The peasants loved Hayden. I think it was because of his freshness and his youth, his openness. He was very charming. But I think it was because he was a kid, and it was Christmas, and he was running around with a tape recorder, taping them, although he didn't know a word of Vietnamese, and I don't know how he did that. I'd be interested to know. But he loved it. And I got word from Staughton, not from him, that Tom was saying that he was going to stay there. He didn't want to go home.

He was going to stay there. I was astonished at this, and I don't remember whether I spoke to him or through Staughton. I'm not positive. Anyway, I made it clear that this was nonsense, that this was not a pleasure journey, and that the reason we had come was to see whatever we wanted to see and make up our minds and go home and tell the American people and, presumably, to contribute towards ending this goddamned thing where everybody was killing everybody. It was just ridiculous. Well, Staughton persuaded him, so that we didn't have any further trouble about that [laughter]. That's the nearest thing to trouble.

Staughton got a little cockeyed. There was a moment when he had too many glasses of schnapps, and we had to put him to bed. Staughton, in particular, was a marvelous person. Tom was, too, I thought, at that time anyway. Hayden more recently has apologized for making the trip. I believe it's because he doesn't want to lose votes [Hayden was a member of the California Assembly].

The Vietnamese thought very highly of us, especially because it was Christmas. They thought we were making such a sacrifice. And leaving our families. This was a time, New Year's, when their families got together. We didn't see Ho Chi Minh. We saw Pham Van Dong, but Ho Chi Minh was visiting peasants. You see, he's everybody's uncle. They all considered him part of the family. I don't think he had his own family. I'm not sure about that. Anyway, he was visiting, and we couldn't see him. He was very modest. I was told he told people to go see Pham Van Dong. And I saw Pham Van Dong.

One afternoon, I was walking with Pham Van Dong in the garden of what used to be the Imperial Palace. Pham Van Dong is tall and dark. His ancestry is from Borneo. He pointed to a barred basement window. He said he had served time in that cell. He then looked at me and said I would be going to prison. He knew that by coming to Hanoi, I had violated the law. I said I wasn't sure. He repeated that I would be going to prison. He asked if I would like to stay in Hanoi. I said, "No," and told him that I wanted to go back to the States and talk against the killing. He said, "Yes, you must do that." I thought that was a very human thing of him to do, to offer to help me.

We asked to see and we interviewed [an American POW] at length. He was brought to us. It was rather formal. I admired him very much. I thought he was tremendously self-possessed, with great courage. He seemed in perfect health and shape and everything else. We had a long talk with him. They were present. We weren't alone. He asked all sorts of things, and so did we. He told us about his family and gave us letters, which Staughton took. We asked him about others and conveyed our concern to the Vietnamese, which may have had some impact. I don't know.

[When we returned], we were in headlines here. We were in *Time* magazine, *Newsweek,* and I think on the cover of something. It was in all the newspapers. It was a sensation, and it was illegal. So when we came back, all the television stations were there at Kennedy [Airport], I think it was. We knew we would be met. Each of us had a statement. Tom and Staughton read their statements, but when it came to be my turn, they pulled the plug. So I was not on national television. [It was] because I was a Communist. And we got word from some defense organization, I forget which one. They offered to defend us if we were prosecuted — but not me [laughter]. They told Tom and Staughton that "if you have legal problems, we will help you." And of course, they both told me that and indicated that this was ridiculous.

Now, we had violated the law. And I have seen my FBI files on this. J. Edgar Hoover was very anxious to send me to prison for five years. That was the penalty. There was a rather extensive correspondence. There was no doubt that I violated the law. In fact, I broadcast on the Vietnamese radio [Radio Hanoi] to our troops and told them that they ought to think twice about killing people. I don't remember [why I made the broadcast], but I was there, so this added to my criminality. Tom and Staughton did not want to [make a broadcast]. Maybe they were wise. I don't know. But I felt that if I could do anything at all to stop it, I ought to do it. So I did. I didn't say anything subversive to them. I just told them that I thought there were better things for them to do at the age of twenty or twenty-five than come over here and kill people.

So he, J. Edgar Hoover, had what he needed, but he was advised not to prosecute. Why? Because he couldn't sever the prosecution of Aptheker from Hayden and from Staughton. Now, to prosecute Aptheker is one thing, but to prosecute the head of the SDS and a professor at Yale who was the son of Robert and Helen Lynd was something else. There was no way in the world that the Department of Justice could indict me and not indict them. And they didn't want to go through the problem of putting them in prison or trying to. They thought it would be too costly a victory. That's in the correspondence. I've seen it myself.

We toured the country. Tom and Staughton were able to go to Canada also. I couldn't. The Canadians wouldn't let me in. But we very systematically toured the country, especially campuses. I was on TV almost every day of the week. And I did nothing else, except make myself available. I went all over the country. I spoke to millions of people. I toured by myself, traveling everywhere except Mississippi, Texas, Vermont, and Alaska. I delivered scores of speeches, usually but not always at universities. My schedule was very intensive between 1966 and 1968, and I continued making speeches up until about 1972. I would ask for the payment of my expenses. I don't remember whether there was a speaker's fee, too. There may have been. If it was, it was modest. I don't know about Tom and Staughton. I imagine they did what I did. The people who invited me, this college or that college, would say, "Come to Columbus, Ohio." I would say, "I'd be very happy to, but will you please provide airfare and put me up?" And they did. So that's what we did. The fact that I was a Communist may also have bothered Tom Hayden. I don't think it bothered Staughton. I didn't ever get a feeling from him, and I believe they became as fond of me as I was of them by the time it was over. I am still a member of the Communist Party.

[To say that the Communist Party was committed to the overthrow of the United States is] nonsense. It's a kind of McCarthyite myth. It has no connection with reality. When the party leadership was indicted, it was indicted for *conspiring* to teach [laughter], not for having done anything, because there was no evidence that we had ever done anything of this nature. I never had a gun.

Lawyers will tell you how relatively easy it is to convict on a conspiracy, especially a conspiracy to teach or advocate, not to do. To get a conviction, you just need two stool pigeons who say that they know that you did teach that. That's all you need, and that's all they had. They had paid witnesses. Infiltrators, monsters like Herbert Philbrick and other vermin paid by the government, who testified that they were present when they heard so and so say such and such a thing. One of them testified that he had taken a class from me in which I taught people how to kill people with a pencil.

I haven't [been back to Vietnam since 1965]. [Concerning what Americans misunderstand most about the Vietnam War], I hesitate to make these kinds of [laughter] sweeping kinds of statements. My whole training is in scholarship. You have a difficult time thinking on your own motives. I think, first of all, there has been a tremendous growth of understanding about that war. When we went there, we were thought of as pariahs in opposition to the war. I don't know of anyone who favors the war now. Is there anyone who says it was a great thing to do? I suppose there are some. Surely, they are a minority. Well, that wasn't true when we went [laughter]. So that's some progress.

I do think that the majority, I was going to say the vast majority, but I think the majority of the American people view that war as at least unfortunate. And that we, let's say, made a mistake (I think it was a crime) but that it was a mistake, and we shouldn't have done it.

I think Nixon in some interview said that we should have finished the job, and that if we had, by now they would be a prosperous country. He said something like that, I think. But I don't know who pays attention to him. I suppose they do. They interview him. He is about as awful a person as we have ever had, except maybe Buchanan, in the presidency.

I saw that movie *Born on the Fourth of July,* which I found an amazing movie in its persistence. I kept looking for some way out. But there's nothing there. Right to the end, it screams. It never stops screaming. It's very moving. And the scene where the man in the wheelchair, a veteran, has that confrontation with his poor mother, the religious woman. He screams about Christ, and he takes a crucifix from her.

Born on the Fourth of July was a terrible experience for me, but I wanted to see it. And I wanted to see if what my friend had said was really true. I couldn't believe it, that there was no escape in the movie, that this was horror, and we were wrong, and we shouldn't have done it, and what we did was awful, indescribable. That's the picture. And it presents that very dramatically. Tom Cruise was marvelous.

I thought that this war was a terrible crime, conducted by those who ruled the United States, and contrary to the interests of the *people* of the United States. It was defaming us in the world; it was killing our young men; it was killing millions of people in Asia; it was taking money from what we could have used in terms of a million social purposes here, spending it on bombs, and throwing it over there. For no good reason.

We spent billions and killed millions, literally millions of people. We hurled more bombs on Vietnam than we had hurled on Germany. And it's half the size. And we used what amounts to poison gas, Agent Orange. We sprayed the whole country with it. They never have recovered from it. We destroyed all their forests. We killed all their water buffalo. We deliberately sought out their water buffalo, machine-gunned them, and killed them. They can't live without water buffalo. So if ever there was a horrible example of colonialist adventure, this was about as bad as you can find in history, and that's saying a great deal. It was also racist. President Johnson said the Vietnamese were nothing but brown dwarfs armed with knives.

I think we ought to live up to the Treaty of Paris, in which we agreed to pay reparations and to recognize a united Vietnam. Now the unity of Vietnam has been achieved, but we never have paid the reparations. But under the peace treaty, we agreed that we would pay, I think it was three billion dollars. We've given this reason or that reason for this nonsense. I was very impressed by the fact that several groups of veterans here have gone back there and done wonderful things, built hospitals or camps for children. I think that's marvelous, and I am sure that they have been welcomed with love over there. So maybe we are on the verge of mending. I think things are getting somewhat better.

I was in World War II, and I rushed to get in it. I was a little older than most people, and I got in it as soon as I could. I went in on Lincoln's birthday. I thought that was appropriate, February 12, 1942. And we got in in December [1941]. I did it as fast as I could. I hesitated because my mother was a widow and had a terrible time. My father had died, and I knew that this would be an awful blow to her. But I knew that she would understand. And it was a terrible blow. She did die soon after. So I certainly didn't help her live long. But I had to go, and I went.

Of course, I had my country in mind [when I traveled to Vietnam]. I love this country. I could become quite sentimental about it. This was where I was born and grew up. That's why I'm on the Left. I think it's best for the country. I don't make any money on it. I think we need such a voice. I think we need such a view. *We,* the Left, produced Social Security; *we* produced trade unions; *we* were the ones who fought against racism; *we* were the ones who denounced lynching.

[Is a Communist Party a necessary political alternative?] Of course, that is a very big question, isn't it? It's an enormous question. I have written very extensively on that. There's a whole literature on it. I edited the party organ, *Political Affairs,* for ten years. It's in any library. First, of course, the commitment [of the party] was anticapitalist, anti-imperialist, anticolonialist, and antiracist. The Vietnam War was the perfect example, in our opinion, of a colonialist, racist, imperialist adventure, in which we replaced the French.

I went to the South as a young man and risked my life as the secretary of the Abolish Peonage Committee. It was in Georgia, and I lived surreptitiously. You'd think I was in Berlin under Hitler, fighting against peonage. Peonage was debt slavery. It involved over three million people, according to documents in Georgia. And it was completely illegal. But it didn't end until World War II. But why did I go down there? At twenty years of age? I didn't have to go down there. I went down there because peonage was wrong. How could you have this in the United States of America? Liberty and justice for all, and these people were slaves because they're black. Women, too. We helped free some and raised a holy storm. And it was in the newspapers. We didn't end peonage. Peonage was ended by the invention of the mechanical cotton picker by the Rust brothers near the end of the war (it changed everything) and by the war itself.

I've actually written or edited eighty books. This book I am now writing will be eighty-one, which is not bad. I have been rather busy with other work, also. [In addition] to the *American Negro Slave Revolts* [New York: International Publishers, 1963], I published my first little book in 1938, called *The Negro in the Civil War* [New York: International Publishers]. There's great excitement now with Civil War history. My book came out fifty-two years ago [laughter]. So they finally caught up with that. . . . When I began my writing in history, the state of historiography was rabidly racist. That was wrong. And I helped change it. . . .

It's a very long story, but Dr. [William E.B.] Du Bois asked me to edit his works and his letters in 1946. I said that I would, of course, do it. In 1986 it was finished. We have thirty-seven volumes of the collected, published writing of Du Bois, which I think is definitive.

And now the world is beginning to discover Du Bois. They buried him, of course, because he was too radical, and he finally went to Africa, where he died. He was the father of the Pan-African movement. He was the chief founder of the NAACP [the National Association for the Advancement of Colored People]. Nelson Mandela [of the Republic of South Africa] mentioned him twice in his speeches. All Africans know Du Bois.

The Du Bois Clubs. That was a left organization. My daughter was one of the founders of the Du Bois Clubs. It lasted a short time. It gave a place for progressive and radical-minded youngsters to associate themselves, and they did.

Du Bois was arrested in Washington, D.C. He was eighty-three years old when they arrested him, handcuffed him, and photographed him. He was charged with being an unregistered foreign agent because he headed the Peace Information Center. The Peace Information Center gathered information in the United States and dispersed it through publications and lectures. It led a petition campaign to ban the A-bomb and collected two million signatures in the U.S. despite terror — and two billion signatures were obtained worldwide. This was 1950 to 1951. Du Bois was actually tried. Of course, he was acquitted. [Jawaharlal] Nehru [a former prime minister of India] knew Du Bois. He sent a cable to President Eisenhower and wanted to know if everybody in Washington went crazy, to indict Dr. Du Bois.

I loved him. I knew him and loved him. He is a decisive figure in twentieth-century history. Decisive. Of course, in African American history but in U.S. history and world history as well. He was one of the founders of the modern peace movement. He was *the* founder of the Pan-African movement. He was *the* founder of the modern black liberation movement. He created it. I don't mean single-handedly. He was the leader of it. He was the editor of *Crisis*, the organ of the NAACP, for twenty-four years, 1910 to 1934. He's the father of the so-called Harlem Renaissance, people like Countee Cullen, who was his son-in-law. Langston Hughes published his first poetry in Du Bois's magazine. They all considered him their father, as did the African leaders: [Kwami] Nkrumah, first president of Ghana; [Nnamdi] Azikiwe of Nigeria; and [Jomo] Kenyatta, former president of Kenya, and so on.

[Du Bois was] born in Great Barrington, Massachusetts. He was free, as his folks were free. His great-great-great-grandfather, Tom Du Bois, fought in the Revolution. So he goes way back, you see. And this had a very decisive influence on his character. His assumption was that he was an American, whatever his complexion. Yes, this is one of the great figures of world history.

5

Dave Dellinger

Dave Dellinger discussed his lifetime of pacifist experiences. He described his management style in bringing together the various factions opposed to the Vietnam War and how they prepared for the mammoth demonstrations in New York and Washington, D.C. As head of the National Mobilization [the "Mobe"] and other antiwar coalitions, Dave probably was the most visible antiwar activist and appeared to have been its intellectual inspiration and strategist. He was the personification of the antiwar movement to many of his peers. His personal and organizational skills contributed significantly to the persistence of the movement and the relentless growth of the antiwar coalition.

Although less than enthusiastic about the objectives of some of the coalition organizations, Dave welcomed their presence because each addition to the coalition accelerated broader public acceptance of the belief that the war was wrong and had to end. Dave and Cora Weiss were co-chairs of the Committee of Liaison, which sent three Americans a month to North Vietnam over a three-year period. While in Hanoi, on the first of three trips, Dave had a private interview with Ho Chi Minh. He also served on the Stockholm War Crimes Tribunal.

A lifelong pacifist, Dellinger also spoke of his time in prison during World War II, when he refused to serve in the armed services. He described his involvement in the demonstrations at the 1968 Chicago Democratic National Convention and his subsqent conspiracy trial as one of the Chicago Seven. He currently delivers his pacifist message in lectures throughout the country. Dellinger's autobiography, *From Yale to Jail: The Life Story of a Moral Dissenter* (New York: Pantheon Books), was published in 1993. He is also the author of *Vietnam Revisited: From Covert Action to Invasion to Reconstruction* (Boston: South End Press, 1986); *Revolutionary Nonviolence: Essays* (Indianapolis, IN: Bobbs-Merrill, 1970); "Appeal to American and World Opinion," which appeared in *Prevent the*

Crime of Silence: Reports From the Sessions of the International War Crimes Tribunal (London: Allen Lane, 1971); and the introduction to Wilfred Burchett's *Vietnam Will Win! Why the People of South Vietnam Have Already Defeated U.S. Imperialism — and How They Have Done It* (New York: Monthly Review Press, 1970).

Our interview was conducted in the campus television studio of Colorado State University, Fort Collins, Colorado, on January 23, 1991. After the interview, I drove Dave through a snowstorm to Boulder, Colorado, where he was scheduled to lecture at the Naropa Institute.

DAVE DELLINGER: My father was chairman of the Republican committees of the town of Wakefield [a suburb of Boston] and Essex County in Massachusetts. Politically, we differed. But my father was a very warm, loving person who always listened to other people, didn't try to take them by storm, and always tried to bring people together. I lived in a white, Anglo-Saxon neighborhood in a section called the Park. With one or two exceptions, the [residents] were all Protestants. People constantly ran down the Catholics. My father always defended the Catholics and always tried to be friends with them. So politically, we had our differences, but I think that I did learn something from him. He was less intellectual than I am, but intellect is not the answer. The heart is the answer, and understanding people is part of it. Then I probably came under the influence of other people who helped me learn that.

I graduated from Yale with a degree in economics. But I wasn't entirely satisfied with the curriculum. It seemed sterile, too much emphasis on statistics and not enough on the human element in economics. I received a fellowship to study at Oxford in 1936 and 1937 and decided to take up philosophy when I found out that my economics adviser there also seemed to be preoccupied with a statistical approach that lacked humanist concerns. Consequently, I decided not to pursue a degree and studied those subjects that I enjoyed and were compatible with my humanistic philosophy.

While at Oxford, I visited Germany and stayed with Jewish families and eventually had contact with the anti-Nazi underground. I came back to this country and worked with others to get the U.S. to lower its immigration barriers and accept Jewish refugees, but it didn't. Whole boatloads were sunk after being turned away in American ports.

I went to jail in 1940 for refusing to register for the draft. I was at the Union Theological Seminary and was exempt if I registered, but I thought that was bribery of the religious and established a false idea that some people are religious and some people don't like to kill but other people have to do the real work of society. I never went back to the seminary and did not graduate. I was not necessarily going to be a minister. I am not sure. But I wanted to find out more about the text and church history. I was inspired by some aspects of the Christian Gospels and the Hebrew prophets but offended by other things in the Bible.

In 1940 I didn't want to take the easy way out. I refused to register rather than take that bribe. I was an active antiwar person. I was in prison for a year and a day, but I was out before Pearl Harbor was attacked. I was in Danbury, [Connecticut,] which had the reputation of being a milder prison. While I was there, I went on strike along with others, and as always, the prison tends to think of somebody as the ringleader, which completely underestimated my cohorts. I'm not saying they thought that completely. But the warden summoned the head of the Prison Bureau, James V. Bennett. I was told by a friendly officer that Bennett came to Danbury to talk to me. I was called in and met with him. He said: "Dellinger, you've got to straighten up. You're getting in trouble all the time, and it's going to ruin you. You've got a great future, and so on." I said:

> Well, Mr. Bennett, the first time I was put in the hole when I got in trouble was because I walked into my first Saturday night movie with a black friend, and they ushered him into the black section and me into the white section, and I went and sat with him. The next thing I knew, I was being dragged out and taken to solitary confinement. That's fascism. The country is finally saying that it's against fascism after supporting Hitler in the early days.

The next time I got in trouble was because I was summoned to the office by number without mentioning my name. So I didn't go. I said that if you used my name and my number, I'll come. Bennett leaned forward. It was like he was a little above me. I don't know if it's like the way they always do, like in the courtroom, the judge is up high in the grand jury chamber and you're out here. Anyway, I had this feeling that he leaned down on me and said, "Dellinger, the American prison system is the most authoritarian prison system in the world. Unless you straighten up now, the full weight of it is coming down on you."

Shortly after that, I was in solitary confinement, along with some others, for something we had done. I had been told by guards that I wasn't going to get out alive. I went through a night of agony in which I figured out that with Bennett hovering over me, I could see or at least I thought that I was in for a hard life, if I lived. I went through it all, and I decided that I wasn't going to change. During that night, I felt that I died. I faced my own death and came through on the other side and said (pardon the language), "F— it, I'm going to be myself, and if I don't make it, I won't."

When I first arrived at Danbury prison in 1940, I was idolized by a group of furriers from New York City who had been imprisoned for reasons not connected with the draft. But they admired my stand against the draft because they were members of the Communist Party, and it was the period of the Hitler-Stalin pact, and the Communists were opposed to having the U.S. go to war against Hitler. To show their solidarity with me, they gave me coffee and snacks when I visited them in the prison's tailor shop, where they worked. They treated me very well. Then one day, I walked into the shop, and they called me a fascist, berated me, and told me to get out. They didn't want anything to do with me. I couldn't understand such hostility in view of the warm relationship we had up to this point. I mentioned this to someone else right after it happened. He said: "Don't you know? Russia was invaded by Germany." The situation had changed insofar as they were concerned.

I am not sure where I stand with regard to my feelings about Communist Party members in the United States, even though many of the grassroots Communists formed the party for idealistic reasons because they supported civil rights and economic justice. I know I don't trust the party leadership. I believe they tend to distort the truth or manipulate people to suit their own ends. I know also that they had some of their opponents physically attacked and injured.

Later, I served a two-year prison term in Lewisburg Penitentiary in Pennsylvania. One day, a fellow prisoner, a young man, came into my cell in a very agitated state. He told me that the night before, two other prisoners had entered his cell and attempted to force him to have sex with them. Somehow, he had been able to talk them out of it. They relented but told him they would be back the following night and would not be talked out of it a second time. His fears were well founded. The inmates who worked in the prison machine shop manufactured keys that fit the cell doors, allowing them entry into the cells of the other prisoners. They also shaped metal into crude knives called shivs that they used to intimidate potential victims. Young men would be confronted in what they thought was the safety of their cells by other prisoners with shivs in their hands, challenging them to "f— or fight."

I wanted to help this young man but also wanted to avoid violence if possible. I finally decided I would do whatever it took to protect this young man. My left hand was permanently injured from a football injury and would be useless to me in a fight if I did not protect it. I had one of the other prisoners steal some adhesive tape, which I wrapped around my hand so that I could use it, if necessary. I stood outside the young man's cell and waited for the two inmates to arrive for the attack. They came that night as promised, accompanied by two other prisoners. One was called Steele. He had cold-blooded, steely eyes, and seemed capable of extreme violence. His eyes would look right through you. The other man was called Sarge, because he had been transferred to Lewisburg from a military prison.

I talked to them in jailhouse talk, asking them why they had been sent to Lewisburg and when they expected to get out. I kept on talking to them, stalling for time, but they just would not go away. One of the men said, "I know why you're here. You're Bill's boy" [Bill was the young man]. I said that was not the case, that Bill and I did not go in for that sort of stuff. Finally, I knew I had to do or say something. I told them that before they stabbed that young man with a shiv, they would first have to stab me. They grumbled and debated what to do and then left. Steele waited until the others had gone and told me I was one of the bravest m— f—ers he had ever seen. And so I was successful in avoiding violence. What surprised me was that I wasn't really afraid during the confrontation, but afterwards, when I went back to my cell, I physically shook.

Some prison officials threatened my life and asked people to beat the shit out of me. Sometimes, they killed you, like William Remington, the undersecretary of commerce, who was charged by [Sen. Joseph] McCarthy with being a Communist. He was sentenced to Lewisburg in Pennsylvania where I had been and where my life had been threatened. He was sentenced there shortly after I had been there. It was during the McCarthy period, and he was killed while at Lewisburg. The authorities said that he was killed in an altercation that came about because somebody had stolen some of Remington's goods and he had objected.

For twenty-three years, I was a working printer in what we call an "intentioned community," located in western New Jersey. A half-dozen families got together and bought property that allowed us to live in our separate homes but also enabled us to share some community resources. We shared ownership of the property but lived as separate families, and after a while, we all worked in the community's printing business and communal finances.

At the same time, I was editor of a magazine called *Liberation*, which was printed and published there. We had a board that met once a week. I would go into New York from western New Jersey and meet with some people who were moderately well known: Paul Goodman and A. J. Muste, who was sometimes called the father of American pacifism, although there were other fathers. Like everybody, he was a son as well as a father.

During this time, I pursued my pacifism and spoke out against the war in Vietnam and what I believed to be injustices. I was well known for this and had received death threats. Consequently, I tended to be cautious opening my mail. One day, I received a bottle of Johnnie Walker Scotch in a parcel wrapped in brown paper. I became suspicious because the return address on the package was "V.C., Fifth Avenue Parade Committee." I was a member of the committee but could think of no one at the office who would put such a return address on a parcel. After all, V.C. stood for Vietcong. I removed the outside wrapper and went no further. My son asked me what I was waiting for. Why didn't I open the bottle and pour us both a drink? He said I was just savoring the prospect of drinking the scotch. I separated a small part of the bottom of the package and looked inside. I saw some wires and black powder. I told my son to follow me, and I took the bottle in the package in my extended arms outside and laid it down in the snow far away from my home.

I called the bomb squad and told them what I had done, and they came the next day. I had placed the package in an isolated location, and it represented no danger at that time. A postal inspector also came out and said that this was the third attempt to bomb my home. He said two packages containing bombs addressed to me had previously blown up in the local post office, and one employee had been permanently disabled in a bomb blast. The bomb squad supervisor said he was determined to find those responsible, but I never heard from him again.

I believe the CIA was involved, some sort of agent provocateur. I believe the CIA told the bomb squad not to pursue the investigation. I have no other explanation. As soon as news of the bomb got out, a member of the local Veterans of Foreign Wars (VFW) group told me he had been approached at a national conference by someone who said, "Why do you allow that Dellinger to live in your community?" He had never told me that before. He said that neither he nor any of the members of the local VFW would ever do a thing like that. The bombs came after the community's printing presses were destroyed, and a message was left that said, "Next time it will be you." The printing business served as the economic link for the families, and after it was destroyed, the community lost its cohesion and dissolved. We never found out who wrecked the printing press. . . .

I often have been asked, for some years now, to talk basically about the sixties and what lessons we learned. But I always make it the sixties, seventies, and eighties because [although] I think certain things happened in the sixties, not to say that it all went wrong, but towards the end in particular, . . . the seventies and part of the eighties were important corrective periods. So I sort of link them together.

At the beginning of the sixties, I think a lot of people were naive about the war and thought, "Well, if you get the right sort of information through to President Kennedy or President Johnson, then he will understand that it really isn't working, that there are various negative aspects about it."

Towards the end of the sixties, people became impatient and angry and came into the movement. In the original movement, there was a lot of emphasis on what was called the New Left, which meant not to commit the mistakes of the sectarian Left, the Old Left, which consisted of the Trotskyites and the Communists and groups of that kind which, amongst other things, were bitter enemies.

Towards the end, people marched and rallied and sometimes got beaten up or spent time in jail, and the war was still going on, and two hundred GIs were coming home every week in body bags, and the Vietnamese were getting massacred from the bombing raids, and people got impatient and angry. That was a tendency that crept into the movement, a new kind of Old Left crept in, vanguard parties that had the single correct answer, and you had to do or think exactly as they did. There was a lot of pressure. And there was the infiltration by the COINTEL program, the FBI's counterintelligence program. I can't tell you how many times they tried to persuade me to bomb something or to pick up a gun. I was a pacifist all my life, and they knew it, but they tried to get me to turn to violence.

So I think a harshness came into the movement. I wince, almost feel sick, every time I hear about a GI coming home and being spat on. At the meeting I spoke at last night, there was a GI there who said that had happened to him. It was terrible if that ever happened, whenever it happened, and obviously, it did happen to some. But that becomes the thing that people, anti-antiwar people — who don't like the antiwar movement — focus on, that the media focus on. I feel it's been exaggerated, but I don't know. Obviously, it happened and shouldn't have happened at all. During the seventies and eighties, people relaxed a bit. There was a kind of self-examination, and people thought things through. The women's movement was extraordinarily important. Even though, like everything, all movements go astray, including ones I'm involved in. The spiritual search movement, for example, often ended up with somebody at the feet of a guru who was going to tell her or him exactly what to think and exactly what to do. On the other hand, out of that did come, I think, a new awareness and a new deepening.

Committees organized to oppose the Vietnam War went through several phases. The first committee was called the Spring Mobilization Committee. Next, it was called the National Mobilization Committee to End the War in Vietnam, and then the New National Mobilization Committee, and so forth. Originally, I was the sole chairman of the National Mobilization Committee. When I made my first trip across the country, I was aware of how pretentious it was for us to think of ourselves as organizing all of these things all over the country — because everywhere I went, just like when I was at Boulder, [Colorado,] the night before last, I am inspired by the people I meet — and I considered coming home and saying we shouldn't call ourselves the National Mobilization Committee because it's pretentious. I discussed it in a number of the cities where I went. I went to people sitting on our steering committee, and we agreed that if you didn't think everything was directed and controlled in New York by this, quote, National Committee, unquote, and if you understood that the strength and the lifeblood came from the grass roots, the grass roots inevitably would take their own initiatives in a lot of things.

Our job was to organize periodic national demonstrations, usually in Washington and San Francisco or Chicago, that kind of thing. It was all right. Initially, I was the sole chairman. There was no woman chairman. There was no black chairman. And step by step, I can't tell you how long it took, but eventually, I ended up being the co-chair. We had a woman chairman, and we had a black chairman. I don't know if there were more than three. And that was what I wanted.

They begged me to chair, even before I was chairman, the meetings of the antiwar coalition. Now they call it facilitator. I said if I was going to be chairman, we were not going to follow Robert's Rules of Order. We were not going to use trickery, even if it was not evil trickery, rules trickery, to win an argument. Because if we went out of there divided, we were not going to be effective. There were times when we took a vote to see what the sentiment was. It would be sixty to thirty, and I would say: "Thirty opposed. That's too many. I would like to ask somebody who voted for the thirty position to explain why, and I would like to ask the people who voted for the sixty position to listen to him and see if there's some way that it could be worked out."

Sometimes, we actually postponed a decision, and I and two or three others would negotiate, and then we would meet again a week later if possible. The other trick was — and it probably was trickery on my part . . . I don't know if you would call it trickery . . . in a way, I think it was right — when we would get to a certain point in a meeting and we hadn't resolved anything, I would say — and after a while, I used to feel like a recording saying the same thing — although there weren't that many recordings in those days: "It's three o'clock. People are going to be leaving soon for their airplanes to go back to California or Colorado, wherever it was, and we're hung up. We haven't decided anything, and meanwhile, GIs are coming home in body bags, Vietnamese children are being burned with napalm. We've got to resolve this." Then I would perhaps offer a resolution or ask somebody else to offer one. "How about this?" And right up until the split over civil disobedience in 1970, this was the way it always happened, even though sometimes a decision was postponed for a while.

The first organizations were natural emergences. First was probably the Fall Mobilization Committee. Then people realized that they worked together, and it worked well, and they should hold another one, so it was called the Spring Mobilization Committee. After that, it became the National [Mobilization Committee]. I don't recall why it changed from the National to the New "Mobe." But the one time a serious political split developed was when it became the Coalition for Peace and Justice. There was another group; I can't think of the name right now. In 1967, the numbers at the mass mobilizations had been growing, the war was getting worse and worse, and there had been various acts of civil disobedience locally at various campuses and in various cities, such as blocking a recruiting station. Many of the Mobilization people, including myself, had been involved in some of these. We felt the time had come to include civil disobedience in a mass mobilization.

I sometimes consider the October 21, 1967, rally in Washington at the Lincoln Memorial to be a model demonstration where we were at our best. Numbers are always disputed. We thought [however,] there were 150,000 to 200,000 people at the [Lincoln] Memorial. We began with a mass rally.

I was one of the emcees and speakers. I applauded and was thrilled, and said so, by the number of people who showed up and how important this was. When I told of actions to follow, instead of urging people to take part, I urged them not to unless they wanted to. We were going to march across the bridge to Virginia and the Pentagon. I explained that we had been having trouble with the police about the route. The police wanted to turn us, after we crossed the bridge, in a way we thought led into a kind of a trap, and we would never get to the Pentagon. So I said, "You should know that if you decide to go on this march, and if we don't get the route, we may have to sit down on the bridge." Many thousands did come, and we did sit down, and we did get the route.

At the Pentagon (and I explained this also at the Lincoln Memorial), we were going to hold another brief rally, not that we needed more speeches or more rallies but to serve as a break-off point, so that those who did not want to take the next action —which was to try to blockade the Pentagon, to shut it down, was our slogan — could rally, say good-bye to one another, and leave. We got to the Pentagon parking lot and had a rostrum set up, where we had a permit to meet. That's a whole other story — the negotiations that had gone on and the threats that if we didn't drop the disobedience the buses carrying the demonstrators into Washington would be stopped at the district line and not allowed to come in and that kind of thing.

We finally had worked that through and obtained a permit to rally at the parking lot at the Pentagon. Norman Mailer and a few others, mostly young people, couldn't wait for the rally, didn't observe our plan, and rushed ahead and beat on the door of the Pentagon. It was funny. But I was very upset at the time. Leaders of various contingents were each to go to a separate door of the Pentagon and surround the building. I was on one with Dr. Ben Spock and Msgr. Charles O. Rice, a Catholic monsignor from Pittsburgh. We had bullhorns. I forget how many. We had maybe thirty to fifty people in our contingent. Maybe it was up to a hundred. I'm not sure. We were to go out and find the entrance and blockade it. The troops did come out the door when we got close to it. We addressed them. It was the first time federal troops had been called out for a demonstration.

The night before, we had been up until four or five in the morning. People came in from around the country, and we were discussing plans and reactions. There were some people, a few but very noisy, who said, "The troops are over there killing people. They're the enemy. They're robots. They're fascists." Terrible things. And then every once in a while, a new one would come. Some of them I didn't know, not that I knew everybody. Some I thought might be government people, trying to provoke that kind of thing. We finally reached an overwhelming consensus, which I had announced from the Lincoln Memorial, that our slogans were going to be, "You are our brothers. Join us. You are victims, too. Join us." We wanted to do everything possible to reach out to the troops. Spock and Msgr. Rice and I and eventually two or three others addressed the troops in this way. I was thinking about my particular contingent — where we were.

At a certain point, a group of sheriffs and policemen attacked us, many people were beaten, and we were carried off to jail. As I was being carried off on a stretcher, groggy, somebody was running along beside me. It was Dr. Spock. He said, "Dave, they won't arrest me, they won't arrest me." He was such a popular doctor and baby doctor at the time that they didn't want to have his name in the paper. Of course, after that, I think a month later, he was in another action at the Whitehall Recruiting Station [in New York City] and was arrested. Gradually, as far as the media was concerned, he went downhill. But that time, he was the only one who wasn't either slugged or arrested or both. I call that a model action in the sense that there wasn't the self-righteousness: "I'm going to get beaten up, and if you really cared, you would too." You'd be out there — with no consideration about whether they had children at home to get back to or philosophically or politically didn't agree with that kind of tactic.

But I would be incomplete if I didn't say that afterwards, a lot of people, people who had been working for two or three years against the war, became discouraged. It was as if we hadn't gotten anywhere. Even *Ramparts*, which, on the whole, had been a pretty good magazine, put out in California, published an article or an editorial that expressed the viewpoint of the magazine — that it had been a failure. It totaled all the money it said had been spent getting people to Washington and spent paying fines or bail. That amused me at the time because I think most of us refused to pay fines.

We didn't stay very long but however long until they let us out without paying. And *Ramparts* said, "They didn't shut down the Pentagon, and they wasted all that money. They could have shut down the Pentagon better by burning twenty-five cars outside the Pentagon at each road entrance." It was a complete denial of the nature of human political movements that are worthwhile: the spirit in which you do the thing and the reaching out to the people who are being turned into your enemies artificially but in truth are not. And this was the message that went around the country and the message sent to the government. But a high military officer who had been in the Pentagon told me several months later, when I went out to speak in California, that he had been in the Pentagon during the demonstration, and everybody realized they could not continue the war the way that it was because the opposition was growing so big and reaching all different sections of the population. It still took years before it came to an end.

Daniel Ellsberg testified at one of my court trials, when I did civil disobedience with others against aid to the Contras, that he was in [Secretary of Defense] Robert McNamara's office that day, planning the invasion of North Vietnam. He said he and McNamara stood at their window and looked down, saw us, and saw what was happening to us. Like a lot of people in the military or connected with the military, Daniel had come to feel by then that the war was being presented dishonestly, and secondly, it was doing more harm than good. But like a lot of people, he was in the service. It was routine. It's your job. He testified in court, and I've heard him say this other times, that as he looked out, he thought, "Those people are putting their bodies where their mouths are. They're living up to their conscience. What would happen if I started living by my conscience?" Three to three and one-half years later, he released the *Pentagon Papers*, which was a very important, conscientious act.

Around a thousand people, including myself, were arrested. We refused to pay a fine. Within twenty-four hours, they released us, even if we hadn't paid the fine. I've never kept track of how many times I was arrested or jailed. I'm just thinking about different instances. Just as a wild guess — just to be sure — I'll say six to twelve, seven to fifteen, I don't know. It's probably closer to eight or nine.

In one of my talks out of town on the Gulf question, I met somebody who said, "You know, we were in jail together in '65 from a demonstration." We started talking, and I thought, yes, I was in and out in a day or two. He started talking about it, and I remembered that we were in a week or ten days, something of that kind.

After the demonstration at the Lincoln Memorial, there was this split. When we talked about civil disobedience as part of a national mobilization, there was opposition within the mobilization. In fact, one of those originally opposed was Dr. Spock. We had a nonexclusion policy. It didn't matter what your politics were if you wanted to unite on a nonviolent demonstration against the war. The Socialist Workers Party, a Trotskyite group, was one of maybe seventy organizations that belonged to the "Mobe," and they had played what I thought was usually a pretty constructive role. They were opposed to adding civil disobedience. But when we talked it all through in what I think was a pretty good spirit and worked out in a way that made the October 1967 demonstration the model, namely, that actions would be separated and nobody would be under pressure to do anything they didn't want to do, they went along with it. And Dr. Spock went along with it.

The Socialist Workers Party did not believe in civil disobedience. They felt all demonstrations should be within the law. That was a tactic on their part; it wasn't conviction. It was a tactic, not a long-range view. Secondly, as the youth movement grew, it reached out and took in all kinds of new people, amongst them people like Abbie Hoffman and Jerry Rubin who eventually called themselves Yippies and engaged in guerrilla theater. The day before the Pentagon demonstration, Rubin and Hoffman supposedly levitated the Pentagon. But they announced this ahead of time, "We are going to exorcise the evil spirits in the Pentagon."

A lot of people, including the Trotskyites, thought this was making light of a very serious thing and would antagonize congressmen and middle-of-the-roaders in various towns and cities. Then after a final demonstration, following the invasion of Cambodia and the shooting by the National Guard of demonstrators at Kent State, we held a rather hastily called demonstration in Washington where the whole idea of civil disobedience became controversial. I never mention Kent State without saying that around the same period, black antiwar demonstrators at Orangeburg, South Carolina, were shot. The country barely heard about it. To the media, it was the white students at Kent; that was the important thing.

Some people demanded that we engage in civil disobedience, and some people, including the Socialist Workers Party, didn't want any civil disobedience to take place. It was a mess in its own right. We never reached a real accommodation. You may as well know the truth. I was speaking at that rally, and this had to be May 1970. I was told by a co-chair of the marshals, a pacifist — who I think had a misunderstanding of the nature of pacifism — that he was afraid if there was civil disobedience, some people would be killed as they had at Kent State, and he thought it was wrong of us to allow people to be killed. Of course, my point of view is that somewhere in our ranks, we have to have people who take every risk that soldiers take, who are willing to be beaten or killed. Otherwise, how are we going to generate the moral power which soldiers have?

Anyway, this pacifist had a different view than I did, but he was co-chair of the marshals. He and the other co-chair, a very fine man, Fred Halsted, a leader of the Socialist Workers Party, told me when I went to the microphone that if I called for civil disobedience, they were going to shut off the mike. Well, I wasn't going to call for it anyway because I felt that it was so divisive at that point and so uncertain. I don't want to over-simplify, but that's the way I remember it, and I think that's probably true.

The next rally was larger. It was a protest against the Cambodian invasion and for bringing the troops home now, which was our slogan. We chose to be nearer the Washington Monument, out the back door of the White House, by the Ellipse. I said there probably was some disagreement about it, but it wasn't enough to rally, and I urged people to go home and take stronger action. Afterwards, Abbie and Jerry berated me for not calling for civil disobedience right then and there. The "Mobe" split after that because there had been splits as we argued this question out. If one of the co-chairman can't say what he wants and they threaten to shut the microphone off, I think that was a very wrong act. So the Trotskyites basically organized the other group, and I cannot remember what they called it. They organized it, and the non-Trotskyites organized the PCPJ, People's Coalition for Peace and Justice. So the one was totally legal, law-abiding, and respectable, as they conceived respectable. Of course, there were a lot of people, the Trotskyites, who didn't think it was. They had a lot of good organizers and a lot of signers and supporters.

The PCPJ organized something called May Day in Washington, which was an attempt to shut down the city this time, and that was civil disobedience. This was in '71. I don't wish to appear immodest, but I think one of my roles throughout that whole period was to try to be a mediator or reconciler. When I was named chairman of the National "Mobe," I was told it was because I was the only one who had the trust of the various, conflicting groups and that my emphasis was not on driving ahead with the total answer but on getting people to work together. Of course, there were many other people like me, but that was one of the things I dedicated myself to, trying to increase human understanding between competing groups, both within the movement and between the movement and those outside. We worked on some form of reconciliation. Sometime before May Day, before the civil disobedience action, there was a rally supported and organized by both groups, which had speakers from both groups. That was the largest, and again there was a big dispute over the numbers. Somewhere close to a million, I think.

I'll say one thing on numbers. It was at one of our demonstrations in Central Park of New York City. The platform at which the demonstration took place was a permanent platform for various events, musical and things. We let the press come up one at a time to the platform and call in their story on the one telephone at the back of the platform. I ushered the *Daily News* reporter to the phone at a time when I wasn't speaking. The exact numbers don't matter, but the principle does. I may have the numbers right. But the story doesn't depend upon that. I heard him call in and say there were four hundred thousand people here. The rally took a long time, and I was involved in a lot of things, so I didn't get away early. I walked out and down the street and picked up a copy of the *Daily News*. The headline said, "Two Hundred Thousand Rally in Central Park." They had cut the number exactly in half from what their reporter had told them.

To this day, that's a subject of dispute. Whether the press cuts it down or whether the organizers exaggerate. We went so far as to get three or four statisticians — supposedly impartial — to try to estimate the crowd for us. I don't remember how it turned out, but that particular demonstration, I think it was April 28, 1971, to my knowledge was the largest of them all, and we thought there were in the vicinity of a million people.

Another extraordinarily large demonstration took place earlier, in November 1969. That was during our Chicago Eight or Seven trial. I was associated with it, however, and I have to tell a sad truth. Namely, that I was lied to by some people connected with the Weathermen. They wanted to have a rally at the Justice Department after the major rally, and they wanted me to endorse it. I wouldn't endorse it because I was afraid it was going to be violent. Then one or two Weathermen and one or two others and I met, and I said why I wouldn't endorse it. They said how important it was because of the prominence of the trial at that point, plus I had more of an in with the more respectable movement. They promised me there would be no violence, no charging, or anything.

I not only endorsed it, but when I spoke at the rally, I said I was going to the Justice Department when this was over and that it would be a nonviolent action, and I asked people to go with me. It wasn't nonviolent. I don't know exactly what happened, but in a couple of cases, I did find out because they apologized to me years later. I don't remember the exact form the violence took, but there was a kind of angry hate, hostile shouting and acting. I felt betrayed.

From the *Pentagon Papers* and from the general I knew who had been in the Pentagon, I learned that the government decided the movement was getting out of hand and that unless something was done, they would not be able to maintain order or continue the war. But first, they had the so-called Boston Five trial, which included Dr. Spock and William Sloane Coffin, who was chaplain at Yale at the time — the more respectable leaders of the movement — to frighten such people off and to send the message that nobody was immune. After the Chicago convention, Attorney General Ramsey Clark and the Justice Department and others in Washington decided not to indict us. As a matter of fact, the government's own investigatory commission concluded it had been a police riot. They did not completely vindicate the demonstrators, but mostly they did. They blamed the police. They said it was a preplanned police riot.

But under the Nixon administration and Attorney General John Mitchell, we were indicted. What they decided, I think, was not who had been violent or nonviolent in Chicago. They wanted to get the more prominent people in each section of the movement. I represented the adult mobilization–type thing and was nonviolent. Tom Hayden and Rennie Davis were first-generation student leaders with SDS, and Bobby Seale was a Black Panther, who they were out to get. Bobby Seale came in for one night, a last-minute replacement for Eldridge Cleaver, who was on parole or something and couldn't get his probation officer's permission to go to Chicago. Seale came in and made a speech in Lincoln Park, which was not part of the Mobilization activities. Although we were friendly to it, I wasn't even there. I didn't even hear it. Seale stayed overnight, met with the Black Panthers, and then went back. He had nothing to do with organizing or carrying out the regular demonstrations. But the Nixon administration was out to get the Black Panthers. I had never met Bobby Seale. I knew other Black Panthers but not him. John Froines and Lee Weiner, there's a question about them. I had met John Froines when he was teaching at Yale. I had gone to speak there. Basically, I didn't know them. I think they just took the heads of certain sections of the movement and tried to make an example of them.

When the Boston trial took place, their lawyers advised them not to engage in antiwar activities during the course of the trial. One of them didn't comply, but the others followed their lawyers' advice. They tried to get free on what might be called a technicality. It was a legal battle. It's not surprising. That's quite common in such things. But we decided we wanted to take the opposite tack, which was to put the government on trial.

Whatever negative anybody says today about Jerry Rubin or whatever disagreements I had with Tom Hayden and his present philosophy and actions — and then, too, we were never monolithic and always had some disagreements — whenever people attack them, I always say, "Remember, Jerry Rubin was willing to go to jail for ten years in 1969 rather than be freed on a technicality." We tried instead to state our philosophy, to bring in witnesses who we knew would be unpopular, even with the jury. But we felt it was a broad, diverse movement and that the movement was on trial and the movement should be able to speak.

I agreed to bring in a woman named Linda Morse, who had been a pacifist but who decided after the Chicago police riots that pacifism didn't work. She was training with a squad in California for armed rebellion, which Tom Hayden was part of. I let her sit on the witness stand and let the prosecutor say, "What are you doing now? Do you know what an M-16 rifle is?" She was practicing with one. That's ludicrous, but we allowed that to happen. I felt that if Tom and some of the others believed in that and that was their philosophy, it was permissible to discuss those subjects in open court. The problem was that the judge allowed things like that to go on but didn't allow me to tell about how somebody who was an FBI agent and also worked for the Chicago police force, Irving Bork, had proposed a plan to me to bomb the amphitheater in which the Democratic National Convention was going to take place. We could never get that on the record, even when Bork testified. The question was ruled out of order.

As I recall, Cora Weiss wanted to testify at the trial, but the judge refused to accept her testimony. Ramsey Clark also wasn't allowed to testify on our behalf. He was going to testify that we had been trying to carry out nonviolent demonstrations, which was a denial of the charge of having conspired to create a riot. That was one of the charges. The other was crossing state lines to have a riot.

Of course, there was scattered violence around the city at one point or another, when police clubbed demonstrators, and sometimes, demonstrators fought back, but mostly they didn't. I was at the microphone, as emcee of the rally in Grant Park, for which we had a permit. At some point, we always suspected a government agent, somebody lowered the American flag and put up a bloody shirt. I think I met the guy years later. He was one of the demonstrators. But typically, we thought it was the police because they did so many things like that. He thought a bloody shirt was a more appropriate symbol of what was happening at the time. We didn't plan it, and it wasn't approved. Maybe some approved. I don't know.

At that point, the police charged. I was at the microphone, and some lunch boxes were thrown. That was the only thing I saw. I kept saying, "Sit down, sit down. We have nonviolent marshals to take care of this. That's just what they want. They want a riot. They want violence. It's a trap." I could never get that introduced into the trial. They had other quotations from me.

In San Diego, I told a TV man who turned out to be a government agent that I was going to go to Chicago, where there might be problems. They tried to interpret that, along with the fact that I invited people to go with me, that I meant we were going to create violence.

The trial went on almost five months. But one thing almost makes me cry. In his charge to the jury, the prosecutor, Tom Foran, said, "These are evil men. They pretend to be this and that. But they are evil, sophisticated men." Something like that. He said, "They talk about their relationship (or maybe friendship, I'm not sure) with Martin Luther King and Bobby Kennedy. But who could believe that (I wish I had the exact words) Martin Luther King would have anything to do with these men?"

My oldest daughter, Natasha, stood up and said, "I can, because it's true." And then they grabbed her and took her out. I'm not sure whether that was the time or another time because she got thrown out twice during the course of the trial. One of those times, when she got to the hallway and the door opened, I could see from our side of the courtroom one of the marshals slug her on the side of the face. I am going to cry if I am not careful now. I said, "Stop hitting my daughter. Stop that." The jury was on the opposite side of the room, so they couldn't see, and Foran, the prosecutor, turned to the jury. He said, "Nobody's hitting his daughter. See, that's the way they are. They make up things to get your sympathy."

A lot of my contact with Martin Luther King was indirect. In the beginning was the Montgomery bus boycott of December 1955. I did not meet King during that time, but I had been active in civil rights in Newark, New Jersey, and in New York. I was working closely with Bayard

Rustin, and he, myself, and three others were putting out a magazine, *Liberation*, and Bayard was black. He went down to Montgomery. A. J. Muste, Bayard Rustin, and later, Paul Goodman and Roy Finch, chair of the War Resisters League, and I were on the board of *Liberation*. At every meeting, we would talk about the Montgomery bus boycott, and either Bayard would be down there and talk with us by phone or he would be at the meeting and preparing to go down to Alabama. We talked with Martin sometimes on the phone, right from the meeting.

I was in Nicaragua in 1984 as part of a witness for peace team, which goes unarmed to the border where an attack is expected. Miles Horton, the leader of Highlander Folk School, which played a big influence on Martin, was a member of the team. Miles was a close friend of Martin's. He was in the South. He said: "King and I used to talk about Dellinger and Muste up there, telling us how to conduct the Montgomery bus boycott. King laughed about it but said, 'They're pretty smart; they're older than I am, and they've given me some good advice, but in the end, I do what I think I ought to.'" Which, of course, is exactly my philosophy. Everybody should do that. I hope that we weren't that pretentious.

During that period — it was later — I wrote an article for Martin Luther King. First, I asked him some questions, and then I wrote the article. But I became humiliated when a neighbor, who was praising the article, said, "I didn't know that King believed this." I wasn't sure that King believed that and had sent him the article before it was published, and it came back to me approved. I am going to be very honest. I knew that Bayard Rustin was capable and sometimes assigned by Martin to go over things, so I didn't know for sure that Martin had ever seen the article. But apparently, Martin liked the article well enough that he actually asked me to go to the Bahamas to write his first book.

But I didn't. I didn't go. First of all, because we had small children. Secondly, because I didn't feel right about having written the article. I just don't believe in it. I felt wrong that I had written an article and it was under Martin Luther King's name, even if he had seen it and approved it. I didn't want to go to the Bahamas. But I know that other people did write his books for him, drawing on his speeches, and so forth.

There were two other special moments from the Chicago trial. I'll be brief. There was a big split between Abbie Hoffman and Jerry Rubin, on the one hand, and Tom Hayden and John Froines, who at that point — just anything that Tom said, Froines followed. Lee Weiner was with Abbie and Jerry. Tom was a straight politico, more or less, and took a hard line on things. He didn't think we should speak up in court because he thought it would antagonize the jury or that we'd give the wrong picture.

One time I came into court and sat next to Jerry Rubin. First, he whispered in my ear and then wrote out that he was going to ask to be separated from the trial. The reason, Jerry said, was because Tom, who was sort of the coordinator of the defense — things went through him — was using all the straight politicos and not calling in any Yippies or youth of that kind. Rennie and I had always tried to unite the two factions and keep them together. Jerry showed me the statement he had written. He was going to stand up before the session was over and announce his withdrawal. I persuaded him to wait until lunch. We would all have lunch together and talk it over. We did, and finally he didn't withdraw.

We insisted to Hayden that some of the others be called, and Tom claimed, perhaps with some justification, that he wasn't consciously excluding certain people. He was calling people he could reach, who he knew best, on the phone first. He didn't do it deliberately. He had trouble meeting the Yippies. You never knew where they were anyway.

The other moment was when my bail was denied. There was a film shown on HBO called, I think, *The Great Chicago Conspiracy Trial*. From the dramatic movie point of view, it wasn't done right. At the Grant Park rally, Tom Hayden and I had a disagreement. When I called for nonviolence at the park, Tom accused me of being a pacifist at the wrong time. But I called for it at the end. I said, "There were different views, and let Tom express his. Some, after the rally, should just go home. Tom has one proposal. I have another." Mine was for a nonviolent march to the amphitheater, as far as we could get. I got Allen Ginsberg, Jean Genet, Robert Lowell, and others to be at the starting point to help lead it along with our regulars. At a certain point, we were stopped by what we call the "Daley Dozers," jeeps with barbed wire on them and guns. We tried to negotiate and say it was law-abiding and nonviolent. We couldn't.

When it began to get dark, we saw men in street clothes walking through the underbrush, in groups of three or four, joining each contingent of the march, as far as we could see. Of course, they were plainclothesmen, and they were going to attack us as soon as it got dark. We conferred, and we said, "All right, we've stayed here long enough. We're going to end the march now and gather at the Hilton Hotel. Make your way peacefully and individually over to the Hilton Hotel."

But I felt I had led our people into a trap, and so I stayed there until the last ones got out because I was worried about what would happen, the beating up. So I was late getting to the Hilton, and I went at the very end with twenty or thirty people. We didn't even all walk together. We just left.

There came on the witness stand one of the police inspectors, whom I always had thought of as an honest cop. I had negotiated with him, off and on, for months. When I had gone to Chicago, we met with the administration, and we met with the Police Department, trying to get permits and assuring them the demonstration would be nonviolent. I thought he was an honest cop. The prosecutor asked him, "What happened after the march stopped and broke up?" He said, "Mr. Dellinger was the first to leave with a group, carrying the NLF flag and chanting something or other." I'm not sure about the chanting part. I looked at him, and I didn't even stand up. I said: "Oh, bullshit. Why don't you tell the truth? Tell what you stand for, and what I stand for and if I deserve to be in jail for that, OK, but don't make up lies about me."

Down came the gavel. The judge dismissed the jury, said he had never heard such obscenity in court before, and revoked my bail. In the movie, it's not clear that my bail was revoked because the judge used what appeared to be an obscure technical phrase, which I don't even remember. As a result, I spent the last three or four weeks in Cook County Jail.

Seale was in jail because he already was in jail when he was indicted. He was in jail on a murder charge, which later was tried in New Haven, Connecticut. The jury was 10 to 2, I believe, but overwhelmingly for acquittal. But it was a hung jury, and they never retried it.

When Bobby Seale was bound and gagged at the trial, Rennie Davis and I believed, and so did Abbie and Jerry at the beginning, that we should refuse to go into the courtroom, as an act of solidarity and protest. Tom argued that that's exactly what they wanted. Tom said, "They want to get us into jail. We're playing right into their hands. I may vomit when I see him bound and gagged, but we have to be smart and accept whatever pain is involved."

I didn't agree. The marshal kept banging on the door. The judge was ready for open court. We finally decided to go in the courtroom, discuss it again at night, and then decide. That night, we met with Bobby Seale, and he took Tom's position. That ended it. I went along to preserve the fragile unity of the group, but maybe I shouldn't have. That's one of many questions from those days that I'm not sure of.

From the movie and other things, people get the impression that we were wild in the courtroom. That example of what I said earlier and what happened was more typical of how we acted. We said things, but we weren't disruptive until that event. But after my bail was revoked, Abbie and Jerry said we should have supported Bobby Seale then and we're going to support Dave now.

The next morning, when I was brought in from Cook County Jail, I arrived at the defense table first. Early amongst the defendants came Abbie and Jerry in judges' robes and sat down, one on either side of me. Then they were disruptive.

Abbie harangued the judge. He called him Julie. He said he was a disgrace to the name. He said "You're a *shtikum*," I don't know if that's the right word, "for the goyim." Abbie and the judge were both Jewish and had the same last name. Very often, people identify that as typical of how we acted, but this was after about four months of the trial, in which we typically had done no more than the kind of thing that got my bail revoked.

I wasn't surprised at the verdict. We were found not guilty of one thing and guilty of another: five of us. Froines and Lee Weiner were not. We were all accused of having firebombed or trying to firebomb the city and specifically a garage, I think. I assumed at the beginning that Weiner and Froines had probably done it, and that's why they were brought in as defendants, and that's the way they were going to get the rest of us, the ones they really wanted to get. Neither Lee nor John, wonderful people that they are, were prominent. They weren't known the way the others were. It turned out that there was no evidence against them or anybody else. But John was a chemist, and they thought he was the one who was preparing Molotov cocktails. That's what they tried to pin on him, but there was no evidence; it wasn't true, nothing about it. But then we, most people, concluded at the end that Weiner and Froines had been brought in as the safety valve, so that if the jury was split, they could be exonerated, and we could be convicted. That may be stretching a point.

We accepted the jury before the prosecutor expected us to because there were a couple people on it we thought were favorable and who the prosecution would challenge on the next round. A short time after the trial began, the judge announced that a threatening letter had been sent to one of the jurors. He called the juror in. She was one of the people we thought was very good, a young, intelligent, apparently sympathetic person. The judge read her the letter. It had never reached her. The letter was a threat on her life and was signed, "The Black Panthers." I was sitting next to Bobby Seale. Bobby Seale said, "We would never do that. We always sign anything 'The Black Panther Party.' They weren't even smart enough to do that."

After reading the letter to her, the judge said, "Do you feel you can give a fair trial after receiving this letter?" — which she wouldn't have received if he hadn't read it to her. She quivered. She said, "No." She was taken off the jury, and the first alternate was put on. The first alternate turned out to be the fiancée of one of Mayor [Richard] Daley's staff. It's not clear whether he was or was not a member of Daley's staff. Two of the jurors told me he was, but a Chicago reporter claims the connection was more indirect — through this job, working for Cook County. All during the trial, she sat with those who were favorable to us. She kept waving to us, smiling at us, and encouraging us. When they began to deliberate, she was the one who arranged the final compromise. I don't know if she pretended to be for us or not. I forget now. I heard this later, when I went to Chicago to speak. Two of the jurors, who to the end thought we were not guilty and thought we should receive a not guilty verdict came where I was speaking and told me about it. She finally convinced the jurors that the judge would keep them there indefinitely, that they wouldn't allow a hung jury, and the best they could get for us was not guilty on one count and two of the people not guilty on any count. That's the way it ended. I wasn't surprised. I don't think I was surprised at anything.

When Staughton Lynd went to Hanoi in 1965 with Herbert Aptheker, I was his first choice as the third member of the group. However, I wanted to be at home for some reason and declined the invitation. Staughton, as a result, chose Tom Hayden.

I was invited to Vietnam more than once. My first visit was in 1966 and was an indirect result of my being invited to Japan to a Beheiren, a Japanese anti–Vietnam War conference. I decided either before I arrived or shortly thereafter that I should take advantage of being that far over there and try to get into Vietnam, particularly since nobody, no American, had been to North Vietnam for months. I called A. J. Muste and his secretary, Dick Gilpin, and asked them to have telegrams sent to the Vietnamese backing me. Tom Hayden and Staughton Lynd had been over there about eight months earlier, before the heavy bombing had started. I had both of them, at least Staughton and probably Tom, to vouch for me. One of the people who sent a telegram vouching for me was Bertrand Russell. . . .

I might as well say it, I have always been suspicious of Communist governments from early on. I had read a book just before I went over to Vietnam about the mass slaughter during the agricultural reform of about 1928 in Vietnam when they collectivized the farms, and I had seen pictures of a POW being driven through the streets and people harassing him, shouting and threatening him. So I brought up these issues, and the day before I saw Ho Chi Minh and two days before I was going to leave, after I had gone south and out into the countryside, places which were under attack, I met with what they called the heads of major organizations, the women's organization, the youth organization, workers' or labor, agricultural, and so forth. I challenged them on all of these things, including the slaughter during the agricultural reform, and I specifically said, which I had read, that Ho Chi Minh had admitted it.

They explained their version, which I'm inclined to think from other sources is probably more accurate, that there had been some violence, and in some cases, peasants had killed a hated landlord, but it had not been nearly as extensive as I had read in this book, a book by Bernard Fall. They said Ho had not admitted it. Ho had condemned what violence there had been and called for a different approach, but he had not in any way done what I had gotten out of Bernard Fall's book. The next morning, I had an appointment with Pham Van Dong, the prime minister, whom I met a lot of times on my different visits. I don't know if this was the first time I met him or not.

My friend, Do Xuan Oanh, who wrote the Vietnamese national anthem, a poet and a musician, was my interpreter and had been my interpreter on most of my trips into the countryside and so forth. He was my interpreter that day. I was sitting and talking to Pham Van Dong when all of a sudden, Ho Chi Minh walks in. He stood there and smiled. We talked. He said to me in English, "I've listened to a tape of your discussion yesterday. It was very good."

Later, he told me about living in Brooklyn, New York, when he had been a seaman as a youth. He spent at least six months, maybe a year or so, in Brooklyn where, quote, "I served as a houseboy for a family in Brooklyn. They were very nice." Then he talked about taking the subway to Harlem and learning things there. At one point near the end, he said, "When you go back, say that I worked for very nice people in Brooklyn, and they paid me forty dollars a month, and now I am president of Vietnam, and I get paid forty-five dollars a month."

Ho talked about his attitude and the Vietnamese attitude toward the POWs and the GIs. I can remember it almost word for word. He said, "I feel very sorry for them. They come over here thinking they are saving the world from some horrible thing called communism." A little bit of what almost seemed to be a laugh came out. "And they get over here, and they find out that even the anticommunist Vietnamese don't want them here." This confirmed my own experience in Saigon. I'm not saying that about everybody.

Ho said, "We feel sorry for them. We want to treat them very well and hope that they go away from here better citizens or with better understanding than when they came here." It was just a very positive attitude. And I came to believe that was what Ho Chi Minh was really like. That's why he was so well loved. It also was the official line, which people who might not have been quite as sensitive and understanding as I think Ho was echoed. Everywhere I went, people said, "We have no quarrel with the American people. The American people are peace-loving people. Our quarrel is with the administration."

A man who later became a Vietnamese negotiator said, I thought naively, "America has always been on the side of the oppressed people. They always stood up for them. How did it happen," he asked, with a sincere and serious question, "that this time, they've turned around and suddenly become aggressors and try to put down a legitimate government?" I believe he thought this was true, and I replied, "Mr. Vy," Nguyen Vinh Vy was his name, "you have an exaggerated picture of the American view of history. There have always been two sides of America, and one is the idealistic side which a lot of people believe in at a time like this."

But I talked about the other side: slavery, the Mexican war, one thing or another. The other thing that I found out was that the Vietnamese didn't love Russia. The minister of education in Vietnam, Ta Quang Buu, had actually signed the Geneva Accords after the French war. Bu proudly told me that when they formed their government and began working on education, they had no models to follow except Soviet models and that regrettably that was the model they had followed for several years. But now at last, they had developed enough literacy and enough understanding and had experimented enough so that they now had a strictly indigenous Vietnamese code and administrative rules with which to go about educating the population and how thrilled they all were.

Over and over again, I heard negative things about both Russia and China. China and the Soviet Union didn't get along together. There was a split in the so-called international conspiracy. These were two nationalist sides that didn't like one [an]other. China was about to cut off Soviet aid [to North Vietnam]. From time to time, they shut the border so that Soviet aid had to be delivered [to North Vietnam] by ship instead of by rail. . . .

When I went to Hanoi, the United States was claiming, just as it's claiming in the [Persian] Gulf today, that this was surgical, precision bombing. It's only hitting steel and concrete. We're not hitting any civilians. The Chinese had published a story that Hanoi was in ruins from the bombing attacks. I had no idea, and no American had been there for a long time. As I think about it now, one would think that somehow through Western diplomats, the truth would have been known, but it wasn't. Nobody knew. I wanted to find out what was going on. When I got to Hanoi, contrary to the Chinese, it had been barely touched and could have been accidentally bombed. But on one or two occasions, bombs had fallen, and I saw some damage. The city as a whole was not touched.

Then I went ten kilometers outside of Hanoi and stood in the village of Phu Xa. It had been leveled. I remember talking to a woman there. I think it would have been imprinted in my mind forever. She talked about hatred for the American aggressors who had killed her children. It wasn't the official line. I guess it didn't violate it either because she didn't say the American people. I had a hard job getting the Vietnamese to let me go south very far into the countryside. But everywhere I went, I saw hospitals with big red crosses on the caved-in roofs that had been bombed. I saw whole streets of working-class homes demolished, in rubble. Everywhere I went, I talked to tearful parents whose children had been killed or to tearful children whose parents had been killed.

We traveled by night. I rode in a jeep that had no lights and was camouflaged with tree branches. It had a hood over the lights, so that there were just certain occasions when it could just barely illuminate, but most of the time it was off. One night, we were between towns, and the American planes came. It was probably two o'clock in the morning. In Hanoi and in the towns, there were air-raid shelters of one kind or another, but here we were in the countryside, and there was none. We got out and lay in the ditch, just a drainage ditch by the side of the road, and all of a sudden it became bright as noonday. The plane dropped flares, and then we heard the bombing. It shook the ground. It was in the nearest town. I thought we heard machine-gun fire. Everywhere I had been, I was told about how the planes would bomb and then strafe civilians or whomever. We survived it. The bombs were pretty close.

I saw so much in North Vietnam. I wasn't afraid, I think it was fair to say. For a long time, during the civil rights movement, I was in the South and almost got killed or was threatened to be killed. One night in '63, I was in the Americus County Jail, the only person there. Or when I was in Albany, Georgia, and some guy followed me. I was trying to negotiate to get some people out of jail. I went to the city hall, to the courthouse, and to see different people. Everywhere I went, there was a man walking behind me, about two paces back, with an open knife. I didn't know when he was going to stab me, but I really wasn't afraid. Psychologically, I had already died. When I lay in that ditch in Vietnam and probably shook a little, I flashed back to that. So many people were getting killed. Why should I claim some privileged exemption? It's easier to say it than always to live up to it. I'm sure I haven't always lived up to it.

In Haiphong, I walked through several miles of absolutely devastated civilian territory. Every town I went where there was a hospital, the hospital was bombed. They bombed the leprosarium. It's hard to believe they would. I couldn't believe it at first when I was told. They used cluster bombs, antipersonnel bombs, which are useless against steel or concrete or even wood but only penetrated human beings. When the Vietnamese doctors were able to operate and remove them from those who survived the bombing, the U.S. used some new, improved cluster bombs where the fragments couldn't be traced as easily in the body and couldn't be removed — some kind of plastic. And they used new, improved napalm to burn people more efficiently, so that it would actually not burn on the surface but eat into the body. I think the constraints were not humanitarian.

After my visit to North Vietnam in September or October of 1966, I protested to the Vietnamese about reports of mistreatment of POWs, and they assured me that it wasn't true. They had taken me in to see a prisoner, which I was very hesitant to do. I had been in prison, and I knew how the authorities stacked the cards, and when they brought people in, they didn't show them the true circumstances. I have some of this written down. The best I can remember now is that I just tried to express solidarity with him and get the name of his parents, so that I could communicate with them and tell them that he looked well. I never came out and said they were being treated well. I said right away to the prisoner that I had been in prison and I knew how they conducted tours of the prison. I believe, moreover, there were cases of mistreatment of American POWs during the Vietnam War. How many, I don't know.

I organized trips of other people to go to Vietnam through the "Mobe" and the War Resisters League and just informally. I also organized a women's trip, which included Diane Nash Bevel, a black woman active in the civil rights movement in the South; Patricia Griffith; it doesn't matter, various people. I organized a clergyperson trip and so forth.

Cora Weiss and I formed the Committee of Liaison after we heard complaints in this country that the mail wasn't getting through to the American POWs (I may have included that they couldn't receive medicine) and that they weren't hearing from their loved ones. We told the Vietnamese that if it was true, it was a disgrace. They said it wasn't true. Together, we worked out this plan. Barbara Webster became a full-time staff person. There might have been others. Cora and I were the co-chairmen. There were other people who supported it: Rennie Davis, possibly Bill Coffin.

I returned to Vietnam in 1967 with Nick Egleson, who was president of SDS. [Dellinger and Egleson visited American POWs Lt. Richard Stratton and Navy seaman Douglas Hegdahl at one of the North Vietnamese prisons.] While I was there, the Vietnamese asked me to arrange for a meeting at which they would have a certain number of NLF people and a certain number of North Vietnamese people, and I was asked to put together a team of U.S. antiwar people of a similar number, about thirty persons. I came back and called in, amongst others, Tom Hayden for consultations on that. I wanted to be fair and not load the conference with my type of people and supporters. Tom was very active, quite brilliant, and had contact with some people that obviously I didn't. He selected some of the people. We probably conferred about it. So that was the Bratislava conference. After the Bratislava conference, he brought back some POWs from Cambodia.

At different times, I was asked to take part in a POW release, and I always had somebody else go. Once I received a teletype message asking me to come over to release some POWs. But when this invitation came along, I consulted with people and decided to ask Fr. Daniel Berrigan and Howard Zinn.

Sometime between 1967 and 1972, I was in Vietnam when an American whose name I have forgotten was over there doing some preliminary work in connection with the Bertrand Russell War Crimes Trial. He was a young fellow working with Ralph Schoenman. I think he was from Philadelphia, but I am not sure. I returned to Vietnam once again in 1972 to bring back some POWs [Maj. Edward Elias, Lt. Norris Charles, and Lt. Markham Gartley]. Our group included Cora Weiss; Peter Arnett, who is now in Baghdad; Bill Coffin; and Richard Falk. Cora and I asked Congressman

Ron Dellums to go. At first, he was quite excited, but then his advisers told him he had an election coming up. I think he made the wrong decision, but people in political office are under a lot of pressures. One of the POWs we brought back was a black GI from his district. It would have been perfect for him to have done it.

I was asked to be on the Bertrand Russell War Crimes Tribunal by Ralph Schoenman. Staughton Lynd, my good friend, was also asked to serve on the tribunal but turned it down because he thought it would be more of a propaganda thing. But I thought, amongst other things, that the American side was constantly publicized all over the world, certainly to the American people and the Western world, and that it needed to be balanced by hearing the Vietnamese side. Participants included distinguished international people, like Bertrand Russell, Jean-Paul Sartre, and others. I thought it provided an international vantage point for people to become aware of the lies of the U.S. government that they were bombing only steel and concrete. I had seen and heard enough atrocities, had been told by GIs about them, although, of course, it was later that My Lai was made public. I was determined that it not be a one-sided tribunal. I remember that all of the tribunal members met with Bertrand Russell a few months before our first meeting in Stockholm, but I missed the meeting because I was in Vietnam.

I think the tribunal helped some. It was followed by the National Council of Churches, which published a book about war crimes in Vietnam. The tribunal was, of course, both neglected and caricatured by the press and by the government. One of the things that I insisted upon before I agreed to go was that we would invite the American government to come and state its side. They refused to go, and they mocked it. But that was one of the conditions under which I would be part of it.

My last visit to Vietnam was in 1985, ten years after the war ended. That also was attacked. I went to see old friends and celebrate the ending of the war and the reunification of Vietnam. I did not go to celebrate the military aspects of it. Besides myself and George Wald, the only other American was John McAuliff, who works for what I think is called the Indochina Reconciliation Project, out of a SANE/FREEZE office in Philadelphia. He organizes trips of Americans to Vietnam, including an educators' trip for people who teach courses on Vietnam. There have been so many veterans' trips, I don't know whether he has been organizing them or not.

John McAuliff had been chairman of something called the Committee of Returned Volunteers, people in the Peace Corps, various organizations that had done voluntary work abroad, not necessarily in Vietnam. He was within the Mobilization, which at one time could have had up to a hundred fifty organizations belonging to it. John was a representative of the Committee of Returned Volunteers.

In my book *Vietnam Revisited,* I talk about how in 1945, after World War II was over in August and the Vietnamese with Ho Chi Minh declared their independence, the Allied governments — Britain technically was in control but with the approval of the United States — released captured Japanese prisoners, armed them, and used them to put down the Vietnamese. I don't think Americans understand how long the war went on. I don't think they understand the secret war that went on.

I spoke on a panel in Colorado with a writer from out of state, Jerome Washington, who served in the Special Forces in Vietnam, at a time when Americans had no idea that there were any American combat troops there. He told about [what happened] when people were killed. He was a medic and put them in body bags. The body bags were flown to Germany or some other place. When they came back, the people in them were reported killed in an automobile accident or some other thing in some other country. That kind of thing is not widely known. An American pilot, for example, who flew explosives and dropped them to the French during the French Indochina War, eventually was killed. There are a lot of people not on the Vietnam War Memorial because they were killed, as far as the government and the public were concerned, when we didn't have anybody over there.

We can't necessarily rewrite our opinions of what happened historically. I think it helps to write books and articles about it, but I am more interested in people becoming more warm, human, sensitive, and loving. Imagine. The Bible even says it, "Love your enemies. Do good to them that persecute you." Love the people who have a different interpretation of Vietnam than you do, whether they are persecuting you or not.

I think the American government has carried on a war against Vietnam after the military war was over and after reunification took place. The economic embargo is an example and the use of U.S. influence in the World Bank and other places to deny Vietnam capital.

Our government supported Cambodia's Pol Pot, who is more of a Hitler than Saddam Hussein, for all the tyrant that Saddam Hussein is. Pol Pot is probably the only person after Hitler who comes anywhere near to equaling his evil, genocidal behavior. I think it rankles a certain type of people that we, quote, "lost the war." There is the illusion that they fought it (Bush said the other day) with their hands tied behind their backs. I don't think that's true. The bombing was just atrocious.

I often quote a secret State Department document of 1948, which I learned of first through Noam Chomsky, in which it says — I can almost quote it word for word:

> The United States controls 50 percent of the world's resources and has 6.3 percent of the world's population. We cannot help being the objects of envy and resentment by other parts of the world. But we need not fool ourselves that our foreign policy should be concerned with altruism or benefaction. Our policy (to paraphrase) must be to preserve this disparity.

I think that behind the idealism for which a lot of people fought the war, behind that idealism, was a cold-blooded greed for profits and power on the part of some members of the power elite. I don't mean to say that those people kick their children or don't have another side to them, but one way or another, they have accepted the system and part of its philosophy, and they're willing to lie and start wars in order to increase America's power and profits.

The power elite was responsible for American involvement in the Vietnam War. Absolutely. Eisenhower refused a lot of pressure to join the French when the French were being defeated at Dien Bien Phu, but he spoke about the tin and the tungsten and the invaluable resources in Indochina which we could not lose control of or access to. The philosophy to justify the power elite is widely circulated and adopted in the country. C. Wright Mills's book *The Power Elite* [London: Oxford University Press, 1956] was very important to the SDS generation. I am not making the power elite out as total devils, but people have contradictory impulses and attitudes within themselves. Our society teaches us that the object in life is to rise above your fellows, instead of working together to rise together. In a sense, there are a lot of junior members of the power elite who have accepted that philosophy. But our government preaches, and our society preaches, a high idealism, and there are two contradictory sides to society and within most people.

In a war like that in Vietnam and also in the Gulf, but less so in the Gulf, there's a strange coincidence in some people of the need to protect

American profits and superiority. Their idea is that America is superior because we're a free world democracy and these other places are dictatorships and evil. Another quote I often use is that of John Foster Dulles, Eisenhower's secretary of state and an important, key member of the power elite. He said that in order to justify an extravagant military or spend billions of dollars on the military, we have to create a nation-hero, nation-villain complex. And that's what we do, and people accept it. The other countries very often have enough bad things in them that it is easy to play them up. We play up their bad qualities, like the Communist countries or Saddam Hussein, and play down our bad qualities and play up the fact that we're all doing it for idealism. In fact, somebody has said, "If Saudi Arabia and Kuwait produced carrots instead of oil, our troops would not be over there."

It's not only the oil though, it's to maintain our position of superiority in the world, and that is a key area. [President George] Bush helped destroy Project Independence, which was supposed to free us from oil. If they were spending the billions of dollars on conservation and safer, renewable energy sources that they are spending there, we wouldn't need the oil. But America wants to be a superpower. It needs an excuse. It lost out economically to Germany and Japan because they were demilitarized after World War II and put their research and their money investments into civilian production. We put ours into armaments.

I don't think the Soviet Union was ever united enough or strong enough to take over Japan or the United States. But now, what the United States would like to do since it has lost out economically — the only way it can be the reigning superpower — is to be the world's policeman, the world's military superpower, and protect the resources that Japan, Germany, and other countries want. Therefore, we can throw our weight around. They have to give us a certain amount of obeisance.

After the Cold War, when the threat was ended, the money should have been put into the economy, to turn the country around, to solve the problems of homelessness, the poor, the infrastructure, unemployment, cheap wages, day care, health care for everyone, and all the other things. . . .

I have always been a journalist and a writer. I've written a few books and, for at least the last twenty years or so, I have been a part-time teacher. Twice, I taught briefly at Yale. I spent more time teaching in an adult degree program, first at Goddard College and then at Vermont College in Montpelier, Vermont.

At Goddard, as part of an independent studies program, I would go in for two weeks of heavy residency, and the students would come in from all over the country for two weeks. At Vermont College, I worked with Vietnam veterans, not always on the question of the Vietnam War or similar questions, but usually they would do their senior paper on something to do with the war. It was a fascinating experience.

I began with a lifer, that is, a black sergeant who didn't fly but worked in the air force as a sergeant. He had been a supporter of the war but, step by step, came to feel it had been a mistake. In his senior paper, he talked a lot about the disproportionate number of black people who were casualties in the war. He was making his final presentation, which was open to the entire student body. He was a very popular, wonderful man. As the faculty person he had worked with, I introduced him when he gave his senior paper, which was some years ago, maybe 1981 or 1982.

I think my wife invited the constable of Peacham, Vermont, my home, to come over and hear this presentation by Eddie Wright, the black man. My wife and I knew the constable was a veteran, but we didn't know much about him. We were friends, but he never talked about it. There was a lot of discussion. Just at the very end, this constable, who was very silent, stood up and said, "Everything this man says is right because I was there myself. I never talk about it to anybody except Dave." And then he sat down. But despite what he said, we had never discussed the war.

I no longer teach. Lecturing has been my main source of income. I travel a lot, but I don't go on tour, as people do, partly because I want to be home more and do local things related to my family, which includes both my youngest daughter and my youngest son who, along with their families, have moved to Vermont and live within striking distance. My youngest daughter has a five-year-old named after me and a twin boy and a twin girl, twenty-two months old. They live next door to us. I like to be with them. I go to a lot of places. I go to California. I just got back from Texas, not too long ago, and here I am in Colorado. But I don't go on tour. I go out for one or two talks, and then I go home.

At the anti–Gulf War rallies that I speak at, very often one of the other speakers is a wife or a mother of somebody who is in the Gulf. At our statewide rally in Vermont last Saturday at the capital, as it happened, the first speaker was a Vietnam veteran; the second speaker was a woman who had a son over there. She said, "I'm proud of my son, and I love him but I think this war is wrong." This woman's daughter, a little girl, also spoke. And then somebody else.

Our slogan in Vermont, which is typical of what I hear everywhere is, "Support the troops. Oppose the political leaders who sent them there." That also was my position during the Vietnam War and one most people had, but unfortunately, there were others who did not support the troops but apparently spat on them.

Last night at a meeting here in Colorado, a meeting against the Gulf War, a veteran stood up. He said first of all he was spat on when he came back, which is horrible and totally wrong. He also said he believed POWs were still being held in Vietnam, and that I doubt very much. . . .

I'm more interested in a common solidarity and sensitivity than I am in coming to a universal, intellectual position on what happened or didn't happen. I think it's important for people from different sides to talk to each other to find ways of uniting. The soldier, the veteran, who last night said he had been spat upon, also said to me, "More power to you. You're on the right track here." But what it was also emphasizing was what I said, and this was supported in many ways by other people from the audience later. I said, "Don't let your anger at George Bush for launching this Gulf War be turned against the people who have accepted the propaganda and believe what we think are lies. Don't turn against them. In particular, support the troops."

We may think that the soldiers have been lied to or that they're mistaken in what they are doing, but, I say this in so many of my talks, for most soldiers, military service was perhaps the one point in their life, the high point of their lives. It may be complicated by other factors, but when they really laid it all on the line, they risked everything for what they thought was the greater good of people beyond themselves, the community, or the country. I talk about the need to understand that when people in the American Legion or the Veterans of Foreign Wars just seem so off the wall, to use the phrase, we must remember they are harking back to the moment when they did something which, in our society in general, is not possible. Emphasis in our society is not on serving the greater good, except in war and a few other things, but mainly on rising above your fellows.

One thing I stay out of now that I did during the Vietnam era is that I do not go to national coalition meetings and plan things. I get consulted a lot. I think in many ways, I'm of more use speaking in, for example, Fort Collins last night and Boulder the night before and Greensboro, Vermont, another night and Texas City, Texas, another night. Even during the Vietnam War, I emphasized local action and grass roots. I just got caught up almost against my will in becoming the national chair of that kind of group. Partly, because I was a good mediator. I don't want to give you the idea that I'm on the road all the time. I do not go on long tours. I go out for a couple nights, and then I am home again. . . .

[With respect to my age], if you read the papers in Vermont, you would think I'm seventy-six. I'm joking, because I'm actually seventy-five. One paper a few weeks ago showed a picture of Dave Dellinger, "76 years old," without a coat, speaking in the freezing air. I feel great.

A. J. Muste [a lifelong pacifict] was a great individual. He was human, like I am. He made mistakes, like I do. But especially the last ten years of his life, he was a great inspiration for me. I'm sure that either I or someone else mentioned his name, either in Fort Collins or at Boulder, and people didn't recognize his name.

One thing that occasionally I slip into my discussions, if it seems relevant, is that I delivered the last three of my children at home. It was at my wife's initiative. Actually, the woman delivers the child, but I was the one that did what is usually called deliver.

In the case of my son, the cord was actually around his neck, and I had to carefully disentangle it and bring him out, cut the cords, and take the afterbirth. Was the first one in the forties? Is that possible? Yes; 1948. It was the most revolutionary thing that I did, and it did a lot for me in terms of understanding of life. It reminds me of what Rabindranath Tagore, an associate of Gandhi, who worked with him in his nonviolent campaigns, said. He said, "Every child comes with a message that God is not yet discouraged with humanity."

Whether one uses the word *God* or not, to me, every child comes with a message that Mother Nature is not discouraged with humanity, and no matter how hard or discouraging life seems at some point, we better not get discouraged either. We better hope our true human nature, which I think is to love one another, will come out.

I have what you might call a love-hate relationship with Tom Hayden. I consider him to be brilliant in many ways, and this helped him in the early days of the civil rights, antiwar, and student movements. On the other hand, in his recent book (*Reunion: A Memoir* [New York: Random House, 1988]), Tom cited a meeting in Washington, D.C., in which he had been invited to discuss the North Vietnamese with Ambassador W. Averell Harriman. Tom described a meeting which included only him and Ambassador Harriman. For whatever reason, he neglected to mention that I was also at the meeting. This was surprising because I was first contacted by Ambassador Harriman, and it was I, not Ambassador Harriman, who invited Tom to attend the meeting. I invited Tom because I was aware that he represented a constituency that differed from mine and that he was likely to contribute to the meeting. I imagine that his error was largely an error of memory, and I hope my stories in my book *From Yale to Jail* do not include similar errors.

Several years ago, I participated in a retrospective seminar on the Vietnam War hosted by Hofstra University. Tom Hayden and I were panel members. President Nixon was invited to deliver concluding remarks at the conference. We didn't know up until the last minute whether or not he would attend. Finally, Nixon notified those running the conference that he didn't plan to show up at any conference that had Dave Dellinger, Tom Hayden, and Frances FitzGerald (author of *Fire in the Lake: The Vietnamese and the Americans in Vietnam* [Boston: Little, Brown, 1972]) on the same platform.

Jane Fonda thought the world of Tom Hayden when she first met him. She thought he was the smartest person in the world. In effect, she became a disciple of his, attentively sitting at the feet of the master. I think the worst mistake Jane made, even worse than posing with uniformed North Vietnamese troops at an antiaircraft battery, was the negative comments she made about returning American POWs. She was sincere but inexperienced and expressed attitudes that did not represent her best self. She has expressed regret about making those comments. Incidentally, whenever I was in Cuba or Vietnam, I always refused to pose alongside anyone in a military uniform. I did not think it appropriate and felt also that if I had done so, it would have been misinterpreted.

The day President Nixon left the White House, I had dinner with Tom Hayden and Jane Fonda in Santa Monica. While I was there, a reporter called and asked Jane for her opinion on Nixon's departure. She told us that she always put her foot in her mouth at such times and therefore told the reporter to call back in twenty minutes while she considered what to say. As a result, her comments were probably not as quotable as the reporter might have liked. At the dinner table, Jane spoke of how effective the peace movement had been and how it had been so successful in ending the war. She said she believed that one of us, and I am sure she meant Tom, would some day be president. Her view, I thought, was a naive perception of the role and power that leaders of the peace movement would exert in peacetime American politics.

About a year ago, while lecturing in metropolitan Los Angeles, Jane invited me to dinner with Ron Kovic and director Oliver Stone. This took place after her separation from Tom. During the dinner, Jane got me aside and took pains to reassure me that she continued to be concerned for the cause of peace and justice. I told her that I knew her before she met Tom Hayden and knew how very much she was concerned with these issues and was unlikely to change her views or abandon such concerns, even after she and Tom were divorced.

Walter Rostow, one of President Kennedy's [and President Johnson's] advisers, was a classmate of mine at Yale during the Depression. He was always trying to get me to join the Communist Party, which I refused. Rostow was a cool, calculating individual, colder than Tom Hayden, who appears to have just switched sides when he saw it was to his advantage to do so.

I once attended a dinner party in Brooklyn attended by: Michael O'Neill, publisher of the New York *Daily News;* Frances FitzGerald, the author; William Bundy; and myself. The host, whose name escapes me, was very talkative and monopolized the dinner conversation. Frances became very upset and told the host he had a distinguished group of guests who had a lot to offer but that he would never learn what they thought because he was denying his guests the opportunity to express their views. She told him to shut up. The dinner conversation became more animated after that.

6

Hugh Manes

Hugh Manes traveled to North Vietnam as a member of an investigating team sponsored by Bertrand Russell and later testified before the Stockholm War Crimes Tribunal about the destruction he observed in North Vietnam. In our interview, Manes described the effects of U.S. bombing on the Vietnamese population and its environment. I met with Manes in his law office, located in a high-rise building on Wilshire Boulevard in Los Angeles, California, on November 16, 1990.

HUGH MANES: I am an attorney, and I have been an attorney since admitted to practice in California in July of 1953. My major field is criminal law and constitutional law litigation. In 1966, I had occasion to go with my family around the world, and when we wound up in London, I met the then secretary to the Bertrand Russell Peace Foundation, Ralph Schoenman. He told me what his organization was doing about the war in Vietnam, their activities, and their opposition to that war.

I was, of course, opposed to the war, but I wasn't deeply knowledgeable about it at the time. But when I came back here, I did become active in the beginnings of an antiwar campaign. As a matter of fact, we did legal studies. When I say we, I mean members of the National Lawyers' Guild, here in Los Angeles, became involved in researching the constitutionality or unconstitutionality of the Vietnam War.

We found that our involvement violated some of our treaties, not the least of which, of course, was the United Nations Charter, which limited transgression into the affairs of other countries by any other nation, and the Charter was a treaty that's the law of the land. We also investigated the legality of the divided Vietnam because the Geneva Convention that had originally created separate zones was never intended to result in a North Vietnam and a South Vietnam. It was simply intended to serve as a transition for the ultimate unification of the country under the only leader that at that particular time was thought to have the support of the over-whelming number of people, and that was Ho Chi Minh.

We found that our involvement not only abridged our own treaties and the United Nations Charter but indeed also transgressed the spirit and letter of the Geneva Convention, the accords that were reached at that time following the French defeat at Dien Bien Phu. . . . I spent many hours in the international law library at UCLA, trying to research the trea-ties, various documents, State Department papers, and various other mat-ters. A group of us paralleled our activities and ultimately came out with a document that we sent to Sen. Wayne Morse of Oregon, and he read that document, ultimately, on the Senate floor and made it a part of the *Con-gressional Record*.

I went to Vietnam in 1967 to see whether there were any unconstitu-tional acts being committed by the United States government against the Vietnamese people. I was asked to be a part of a team. [In our group], there was: Joe Neilands from the University of California at Berkeley; . . . Dr. John Takman, a medical doctor and director, Child Welfare Board of Stockholm; Axel Hojer, another medical doctor, also from Sweden; . . . the Swedish delegate to the UN World Health Organization; and a senator from Italy. Unfortunately, none of us spoke Italian, and he didn't speak anything but Italian, so we had a little difficulty with the communication there, but he was a very nice man, an older man. . . .

Many of the international laws against certain types of weapons were incorporated into our own laws by way of treaties or by other means. Our military forces had military rules that precluded use of cer-tain types of tactics as well as weapons. Our purpose, therefore, was to see if there were violations of these international norms, international law, by the *way* the war was being fought, as much as by the fact that it *was* being fought by the United States. . . .

I went to Paris, and that's where we met other members of our team, and they sent one team ahead of us, by a week or so. We were the second team to go in. Before we left Paris, we were educated or trained or what-ever you would call it as to what we were to look for, the kinds of weap-ons that they thought we would be expected to see. A Frenchman, who spoke very good English, and we were told, a weapons expert, and [either] . . . involved in Algeria or . . . an ex-soldier from Vietnam [gave us] . . . some kind of sense of what we could be expected to see. Actually, . . . I don't think we were ever in an area where anything that he described was visible to us. . . .

We left Paris, and en route to Phnom Penh, we landed in Tirana, the capital of Albania, to take on fuel. [Although] Albania was forbidden to foreigners, our plane was able to land there, I guess because of our mission. We had Chinese with their little red books on our plane. I got hold of one of those books. I still have it. I'll never forget. When we landed, a number of the Chinese got off to go to the "lav," and I looked out and saw that one of them had dropped a little red book. I thought to myself that he had dropped his thoughts. We were there for about two hours. I think I counted twenty-one fighter aircraft, all covered, on the landing strip.

We went on to Phnom Penh, and on our plane was the Prince, Sihanouk, who invited us to his palace for dinner that night, and we went. We did not see Prince Sihanouk, but we did see his prime minister. We had a nice chat in which he invited us, if we were skeptical, to go to the so-called Ho Chi Minh Trail [and] he would show us that there was no such thing. From Phnom Penh, we went to Vientiane. We arrived there at dusk. We flew into Hanoi at night, and it was kind of scary, but we made it.

We were particularly concerned with antipersonnel weapons, particularly with a large canister that opened up and dropped what were called "guava" bombs, which contained about three hundred fifty cast-iron balls, about an inch and a half in diameter. These would touch any kind of a surface, even a twig of a tree, and explode, shooting out cast-iron pellets. . . . We found them in fields and on farmlands, we found them near hospitals, we found them in areas which were primarily rural, which were primarily residential, in other words, . . . where the civilian population was. And they were found with sufficient frequency that we concluded that there was a pattern of dropping these antipersonnel bombs deliberately into civilian populations to upset morale and to cause havoc. And of course, many of the victims we saw were children, women, and older persons. Most of the young men were off fighting, I suspected.

I was there for three weeks. My visits were to perhaps four or five different provinces of the northern part of Vietnam. I had extensive talks with people, leaders, and the people who lived in various areas, as well as the leadership of the government. I met Ho Chi Minh. . . . I brought back a tape recording of his statement with which he greets the American people, and he says, "Allo, this is your Uncle Ho speaking" [laughter]. It was a remarkable tape, and they played it over the air with a background of coffins draped by the American flag. That was Channel Four . . . the local television's response to Uncle Ho.

[Our visit with Ho Chi Minh] was the crowning part of our whole trip. To meet this great man, who had fought all of his life against tyranny and who had rallied a huge following, was a great honor, as far as I was concerned, and I never felt any differently about it. I learned that there were over sixty different dialects and dozens . . . of different groups of peoples within Vietnam . . . the Hmong people, the Hill people [and other] . . . diverse cultures within this country. That became difficult for us to really grasp in such a small land. . . .

[The saddest part of the trip was] seeing primarily the wounds, the devastation in Vietnam. Seeing the destruction. Much of Hanoi was rubble while I was there. . . . After we left, whatever remained was also made into rubble, we learned later. There was a great deal of difficulty for the Vietnamese to get medical supplies and getting medical technicians. . . . We learned that the Vietnamese had sent some of their skilled people to the Soviet Union for medical training and had come back, and for the first time in the history of these people, there were medical doctors and medical personnel down at the village or the regional level. We saw hospitals, some of them totally destroyed, we thought deliberately. . . . We would come into little villages a day after they had been hit, and . . . still smoldering. Seeing old people crying and weeping, seeing children dead and the like. It was very, very difficult to see these sights and not be terribly moved.

We stayed overnight in various places . . . principally Hanoi. . . . There were about four different occasions when American planes flew overhead, when there was an air raid in some part of Hanoi. . . . On one occasion, we could hear falling bombs in some part of the city. I was scared to death. . . . In the Reunification Hotel where we were staying . . . when the sirens started going off, everybody would head for the shelters but . . . everybody would walk. Nobody would run. Nobody wanted to show that they were scared to death [laughter]. It became sort of a trial or ordeal of making it to a shelter before the bombs began to fall and not run there, but we did it [laughter].

I never went to a POW location. I did not want to. . . . I know I was at at least one and possibly two press conferences that the Vietnamese held while we were there, and I had no problems in making statements about what I had seen and about the way I felt, but I never broadcast as such any statements abroad. . . . I remember seeing Graham Greene [the British author] briefly. I did see some Cubans and other nationalities. I don't remember seeing any other Americans. There was another French team (the Democratic lawyers' group) that went not to Hanoi but went on . . . to Haiphong and did some studies there. . . .

When I left for Vietnam, the United States, I think it was a day or two before, had for the umpteenth time denied that we were using the lazy-dog bombs, which were the canisters that dropped these three hundred and fifty antipersonnel guava bombs. On the day that I came back, with pictorial and physical evidence of their use in Vietnam, strangely enough, the United States government announced in Washington, "Yes, we do use them, and we have been using them for some time." . . . I had evidence of Navy lettering on the canisters and other evidence, but I suspect that they knew that we were going to expose the lie at a press conference, which we did. So they jumped the gun. . . . The war, we found, . . . was fought by unconstitutional methods, and by methods that violated international norms and standards. . . . I think the whole war was one big deception. I think that it was fought with lie after lie, with the sole purpose of attempting to maintain an economic foothold on that part of the world. . . .

We were not greeted with enthusiasm when we came back. I spent a year campaigning against that war actively, speaking wherever I was asked. I think one of the most difficult speaking appearances was in Santa Barbara, where I faced a very hostile audience. It had to be in 1967 or 1968, after I had made the trip to Vietnam. There were . . . a number of parents of servicemen who had died, and they kept saying, "Are you telling us that our children have died in vain?" . . . I said, "No, sometimes the lessons of history require the extreme penalty for some of us, but I am speaking out so that others will not die."

Contemporaneously, . . . I spent a lot of time, as did many of my colleagues in the profession, counseling young people who were being drafted for this unholy war about their rights with respect to Selective Service and counseling those who already were in the military as to their rights to withdraw from the service if they found that it was beyond their conscience to subscribe to the war any longer.

[At home], a group of us initiated the first two ads against the war to appear in, so far as I know, southern California, certainly in the Los Angeles County area. We raised the money and paid for those ads in the *Los Angeles Times*. One of them was a letter by [Lewis] Mumford, at the time protesting the war and its significance. And then we followed that up with another ad against the war and solicited contributions to make this a permanent operation. . . .

Following the appearance of those ads, I went to Sweden, along with many, many other persons, to testify [November 1967, in Stockholm] before the Bertrand Russell Peace Foundation Crimes Commission, . . .

about what we had seen in Vietnam and what we had found by way of our research.

I want to state parenthetically that I have fought in World War II, that I have been wounded in action, and that I didn't feel any discomfort whatever in playing this role because I had performed my job when I was called upon in a war that we were involved in that was justified and which we did not seek and attempted to avoid, but which was brought upon us. . . .

I prepared a statement following my return in which I recorded in detail all of my observations in every village throughout the three weeks we were there, including our visits throughout Hanoi itself. And of course, I submitted that as part of the documentation [which appeared in the book] *Against the Crime of Silence.* . . .

The attorney general attempted to place us [the National Lawyers' Guild] on the list [of subversive organizations], but . . . the Court ultimately held that that could not be done because he had never held a hearing and he never did hold a hearing, and so, therefore, we were never on his so-called list. . . .

I went to San Francisco, and I was part of that huge protest rally. I was involved in many protest rallies here. I lay in front of Nixon headquarters once — in May, during the campaign of '72 — and I fought to be arrested. I was given a citation but was not arrested. . . . Even today, if I were to run for public office, I would be held in contempt and ridiculed because of my involvement in opposition to that war. That can only be so because our people have never yet accepted the idea that that was an illegal, mean-spirited, racist war, and that our troops would refer to the Vietnamese as gooks. As long as you have that kind of thing, the real nature of that war has yet to be learned. . . .

Patriotism is as varied as there are people. . . . It's supposed to be love of country. I rather think of it as a love of humanity, a love of people, a love of the human condition, wanting to preserve the dignity of people and those who strive to protect it. Those who protect that dignity of mankind are the greatest patriots, as far as I am concerned. I do not believe that a patriot can be defined by the flag that he flies. . . .

One person [in the antiwar movement] *does* stand out in my mind. Ron Kovic's contribution as a symbol of those Vietnam veterans who came back with their eyes opened, who found a different Vietnam than when they went there, and who came out of their experience with the courage to warn what was happening. I think he was probably one of the great leaders of the antiwar movement. There were many — anybody who had the courage to risk his or her economic status, to speak out when it was difficult to do that, when there was overwhelming support for the war, those were great, gutsy, leaders.

The National Lawyers' Guild, which furnished many of the lawyers who fought against this war with the law, believing that we are a nation of laws, not of men, contributed to the understanding, to educating the people. How much? I don't know. I can't tell you how effective we were. It's a total picture. I'm not in a position to evaluate that.

NOTE: Manes showed me a dated German pictorial magazine that included a picture of a group of South Vietnamese special forces troops displaying the severed heads of presumably Viet Cong soldiers, with cigarettes dangling from their mouths. In several cases, the soldiers had hold of the hair of a severed head in each hand. Manes also displayed a picture taken of a North Vietnamese rice paddy that contained hundreds of sticks placed in the ground and marked with ribbons to identify the bombing pattern (as noted by Manes) of cluster bomb fragments (allegedly) dropped by U.S. aircraft. The large number of ribbons indicated a highly intensive pattern of bomb fragments.

7

J. B. Neilands

J. B. Neilands, a professor of biochemistry, was a member of a Stockholm War Crimes Tribunal investigative team and submitted his findings to the Bertrand Russell–sponsored tribunal. During our interview, he described the carnage resulting from the air war conducted by U.S. military aircraft against North Vietnam and discussed why he opposed the war. He also related the details of an interview with Ho Chi Minh and spoke of his broadcast against the war over Radio Hanoi. Professor Neilands was interviewed on November 13, 1990, in his office at the University of California campus in Berkeley, California.

J. B. NEILANDS: I am professor of biochemistry here at the University of California, where I have been employed since 1952. In 1967, I visited North Vietnam as a part of the Bertrand Russell War Crimes Tribunal team and collected evidence on the character and mechanisms of the war, which was subsequently presented at a meeting of the organization at Stockholm, Sweden. I was away from Berkeley for two or three weeks, and I was in North Vietnam for maybe a week or a little more. [Our group included] an American from Los Angeles; a lawyer, Hugh Manes; and two Swedes that I remember, John Takman and an older man, Axel Hojer, a former public health official in the government of Sweden.

I was on sabbatical leave in Sweden in 1965 to 1966. In 1965, we had a big Vietnam Day celebration here on the campus at Berkeley, and I thought they should have a similar event in Sweden. One of the young graduate students in the laboratory by the name of Arne Holmgren told me that I should try to get a wider audience, and he knew of a Swedish fraternity that might like to hear the views of an antiwar American. So he arranged for a meeting in Uppsala, and by coincidence . . . that man, Arne Holmgren, is here today, and that's twenty-five years ago. He is passing through Berkeley and is now a professor of physiological chemistry. He's the man who made me come out in public. From that, I received international notoriety and came to the attention of the Bertrand Russell organization, and I was invited to go to North Vietnam.

I paid my own traveling expenses because number one, I didn't think it was right for Russell to pay for this out of his own pocket and number two, I wanted to stay a little bit on the independent side.

I think the motive force in the tribunal at that time was a man by the name of Ralph Schoenman. He was an executive of the Bertrand Russell Foundation, and he arranged for the travelers to go . . . at that time. Schoenman and [Russ] Stetler were part of the war crimes tribunal, part of the investigation committee, and a part of the secretariat. I am pretty sure . . . they visited North Vietnam in 1966 or so.

I was willing to try to find a visa to go there, but Schoenman advised me to have nothing to do with the American embassy, and so I took his advice. I simply went without any sponsorship other than the Russell tribunal. You had to be sponsored by somebody, and Russell's name was magic in that part of the world. We went first to Paris and picked up the other members of the team and then traveled by Air France, ultimately to Cambodia. We stopped in Vientiane before proceeding to Hanoi. There, my passport was xeroxed, and a record of my transit through there was made and handed over to the State Department. That enabled them to visit me and demand my passport, which I never gave up, of course.

One thing I remember quite distinctly was that there was a lot of joking and horseplay up until the plane came out of Vientiane and headed for Hanoi, the war zone. Then there was almost a ghostly silence. People were quite tense. We hit the runway in North Vietnam, and all the lights were out. There were young girls to greet us, but I noticed, when shaking hands, their hands were calloused. They were workers, and they handed us flowers.

We discovered fairly systematic bombing of the civilian population with weapons designed for that purpose. In addition, we [U.S. aircraft] appeared to have systematically bombed their social institutions, the railroads, the public buildings, and the educational buildings. According to the U.S. Air Force [strategic thinking], this kind of campaign was supposed to alienate the population so that they would go down to Hanoi and throw Ho Chi Minh out of office. According to this concept, Ho was a tyrant. He was keeping the people down by subjugation, but it turned out that he was actually regarded as the George Washington of Vietnam. He was a popular figure because he had good, anti-imperialist credentials. He had fought them all his life.

J. B. Neilands recording testimony from a peasant injured by U.S. bombing, for the Bertrand Russell War Crimes Tribunal, North Vietnam, March 1967. (*Courtesy of the War Crimes Commission, DRV.*)

The power of the United States to wreck things became very apparent. We had small bombs, 250-pound, 500-pound, and 1,000-pound bombs. We had napalm, white phosphorous, Agent Orange, Agent Blue, Agent White, and antipersonnel gas: everything from a hand grenade to a Huey helicopter, which carried a thousand pounds of antipersonnel gas.

We visited mainly with the government officials. We traveled at night to the location by jeep. . . . It was probably Russian. Most of their equipment seemed to come from the Soviet Union. We looked around [at the rural locations] during the daytime, always fairly close to underground shelters, and then went back to Hanoi before [the next] daylight. There were quite a number of bombing raids.

We had an interview with Ho Chi Minh and also Pham Van Dong, the premier. We went to see Ho in the palace, and he served us Johnnie Walker Red Label, straight — poured straight out of the bottle without ice, and if I am a little bit incoherent on the details of that interview, that's the reason [laughter]. Ho chain-smoked cigarettes and joked that his doctor told him that he shouldn't be doing that. The amazing thing to me was what a small man he was. You could put your fingers around his wrist, but he had on a military tunic that was pressed and very nice. Ho spoke a little English, although he preferred French. My French is not very good, but the Swedes spoke French with him. Ho described himself as a figurehead. He said, "That's what I am. I'm Uncle Ho."

We were there for an hour. Ho asked me about the antiwar movement in the United States. Apparently, that was very important to them. I told him that I had been traveling for a week or two and that I really did not have up-to-date information, and he interrupted, "Let me tell you about what's happened in New York City." He talked about a teachers' march. He was very sharp, and he had all his faculties.

Ho was very frail. He was a very light person. He was fairly advanced in age at that time, 1967. He seemed to be in quite good shape. We enjoyed visiting with him and sitting there in the palace. I had hoped to get some comments from him. I had a tape recorder with me, but the batteries fell out, and Ho said, "What kind of tape recorder is this?" I said, "It's Japanese," and he said, "This is very bad PR for the Japanese" [laughter]. [Pham Van Dong] was there, too. We were on the steps of the palace immediately after the visit with Ho, [and a group photo was taken].

We asked Ho, "Supposing the Americans bomb Hanoi to a greater extent than what they already have?" At that time, in 1967, Haiphong harbor was mainly destroyed, but Hanoi was not. Ho said, "Well, we'll just go back up in the hills, and we'll keep on fighting."

I can't remember verbatim [what I said on a broadcast I made over Radio Hanoi], but the revelation to me was the extensive use of chemicals. These were not employed in North Vietnam, but they were in the South. . . . You could find canisters of all these different types of antipersonnel gas, and you could find drums of Agent White and Orange and Blue. Of course, when you cut off the foliage through use of these chemicals, then you cut off all the animal life because only plants can trap the radiant energy of the sun, and all animal life on earth is dependent upon the plants. This scorched-earth policy of defoliating Vietnam was a very inhumane way to fight war. It probably was a violation of the Nuremberg principles.

[Although some might criticize me for having broadcast over Radio Hanoi], I would simply respond this way: I am a free agent. We were not in a declared war. I never regarded myself as a traitor. I regarded myself as a one hundred percent patriotic, American citizen. Lyndon Johnson chose to put five hundred thousand personnel in Vietnam. He was a criminal. He should have been prosecuted and put in jail, together with the other members of the cabal, Henry Kissinger and all those people who were involved. I looked upon those people as the real traitors to American principles.

We visited a prison. We saw some air force personnel who had just recently been shot down. I remember one in particular, a gentleman by the name of [Maj. Jack] Bomar, and when I came back here, the first thing I did was to call his parents in Arizona and tell them he was okay. He was banged up a little bit when he ejected. Otherwise, he was in good shape. His parents were mystified by my telephone call because they had received notification from the Defense Department that he was missing. They never got back in touch with me. I gave them my name. They probably were told to stay away from me.

There were some dozen people who went to North Vietnam in small parties of five or six over a period of several months. Later, in 1967, we gathered in Stockholm and presented all of this evidence before the tribunal, made up of people like [Jean-Paul] Sartre. Russell was too old to travel at that time. I think that internationally, [the tribunal] had a very powerful impact. It had a lot of media coverage and so forth. Of course, it was discredited within the United States by publications such as *Time* and *Newsweek*. It did not have a major impact in the United States.

I would say that I paid very light penalties, [professionally, for traveling to Vietnam]. I had problems with my passport. Almost a year after I came back to Berkeley, two agents from the Security Division of the State Department came to my house and asked me to hand over my passport. I told them that I thought it was valid, and if they wanted to dispute that, to please send me a letter stating why it is not valid. After a couple of weeks, that letter came. It said that I had violated a certain law, and I asked Hugh Manes, the Los Angeles lawyer, "What is this law all about?" And he said, "It has something to do with foreign trade, but the Congress has never passed a law proscribing the right of Americans to travel anywhere at their own risk."

So we went to the federal court in San Francisco, and the judge not only revalidated the passport but stipulated that when its statutory life expired, my, quote, alleged trip was not to be used as grounds for failure to renew. Manes was completely successful, and I think that he had done the same thing with his own passport so he knew exactly how to proceed.

The other problem I had here was on the campus. The university took me off the payroll even though I had saved up my annual vacation . . . to make this trip. But as soon as it appeared in the newspaper that I had gone to North Vietnam, phones started to ring here in the Department of Biochemistry, and I was taken off the payroll. My family's health insurance was canceled. When I got back, I had to go and see the dean and get all that reversed. He told me he was only trying to protect the institution. I thought that he should protect his professors. I had only those two minor problems, and believe me, I was willing to pay them. . . . I was part of the Faculty Peace Committee here on the Berkeley campus, and I ran for city council in Berkeley as an antiwar candidate, a serious candidate. Although I got over ten thousand votes, I was not elected. [That was in] 1967. We were trying to carry along the effort by Robert Scheer who had tried to unseat Jeffrey Cohelan, a liberal Democrat in the same mold as Hubert Humphrey and Lyndon Johnson. Cohelan assured us privately that he was against the war, but when it came to military appropriations, he voted for every one of them. So Scheer ran against him under the banner of the Community for New Politics. And here I was, sitting over in Stockholm, reading all this literature, and I thought that this should be carried on at the city level; that there should be an antiwar city council elected. . . .

I've continued to do my biochemistry. I should be more concerned right now than I am. I feel guilty, somewhat. I should be active in Central American and Middle East issues, but one cannot do everything, and you have to live from day to day.

I think that what Americans need to learn is that our military has too much freedom and our political system is too weak and the [military] can manipulate it. The political system is weak because the media are not telling the way it really is . . . and the American public is without adequate information. . . .

Most Americans don't know anything about the background to the conflict in Southeast Asia. I think that is because we are not very interested in other countries. The U.S. is big, and what's news is what happens in the States and from one state to another. We couldn't care less about what happens in Canada and Mexico. I notice this because I was raised in Canada where we had a lot of information from other countries, relatively speaking.

[I have no regrets.] None whatsoever. I am very proud that I spent the money [to make the trip to North Vietnam]. I could have spent it fixing my house or bought a new car. I could have bought some more land in Mendocino or something like that, but there was a feeling in the air at that time, there was pressure from the undergrads and from the colleagues on the campus that one had to do something.

I was born in Canada and raised in a social democratic household, and I have never been a registered Republican or Democrat because I can't see any difference between the two parties. I have changed my politics from social democracy, where you are people-centered, to where I am more biocentrist, Earth First!, a sea-shepherd type of individual who wants to stop development and preserve the natural environment.

This is my adopted country. I'm a naturalized citizen. I like the concept of freedom that we have in this country, which applies even in science because here I can do my own thing in science. I can get grants from the National Institutes of Health, from the Department of Agriculture, and they allow me to hire graduate students and to develop my own program to a much greater degree here in this country than even in Canada. That's why I opted to stay here and be an American citizen, and I think that to participate in political life is very important and I think that is what all patriotic American citizens should do. They should keep track of their politicians, and I believe with Jefferson that the newspapers and the media and how people get their information in a democracy is the cornerstone of the whole operation. . . .

I think [the expression] "my country, right or wrong" is a lot of nonsense. My father-in-law used to quote that to me once in a while. No, I think we have to support them when they are right and do battle with them when they are wrong.

I think that it was people like Martin Luther King who could reach very large audiences [who were most effective in the antiwar movement]. When they came out against the war, they brought with them a lot of church people. And there were some very establishment people who were against the war. I think Robert Scheer brought us into the electoral arena in contesting a liberal Democrat, Jeffrey Cohelan. Those people were very effective. I think Bertrand Russell was effective on an international scale. In this country, he was written off as a senile old crank because "Americans do not commit war crimes. Other countries may commit war crimes, but not the United States." So for that reason, he had limited influence in this country. . . .

In retrospect, the veterans were very powerful. We should have realized this about the antiwar movement within the military at an earlier time because those boys had their ass on the line, and we just thought they didn't know anything about what was going on. Why, later we found out they had their own antiwar newspapers, published on the battleships. . . . We should have given the movement inside the military more credit.

8

Julius Lester

Julius Lester traveled to North Vietnam as a member of one of the investigative teams sponsored by Bertrand Russell's War Crimes Tribunal. Lester described, among other things, the repetitive nature of public assemblies in which he and his traveling companion, Charles Cobb, participated while in North Vietnam. He found contradictions among the Vietnamese: on the one hand, they were tender and delicate; on the other, they could be doctrinaire and manipulative. Lester, a photographer for the Student Nonviolent Coordinating Committee, shot several dozen rolls of film in Vietnam and was particularly impressed with the determination of the Vietnamese to conduct the war. He also admired the beauty of the Vietnamese women and the absence of billboards in their country.

Lester has written books on music, ethnic folklore, black history, and children's stories. Born in 1939, he is a poet and former professor of Judaic studies at the University of Massachusetts, Amherst.

After unsuccessful attempts to interview Lester during my earlier visit to New England, I subsequently received a taped recording from him containing answers to questions that I had posed to him earlier. His comments have been edited, and he has reviewed them to arrive at the narrative that follows.

JULIUS LESTER: I went to Hanoi in the spring of 1967. I was a member of the Student Nonviolent Coordinating Committee and also a photographer for SNCC. The Bertrand Russell War Crimes Tribunal wanted some representatives of the black radical movement to be a part of the investigating teams that were going to Hanoi, North Vietnam, at this time.

The North Vietnamese were claiming that the United States was dropping antipersonnel weapons and bombing civilians in North Vietnam. The American government was denying this. In December 1966, Harrison Salisbury of the *New York Times* was the first American to go to

North Vietnam and come back and say that the United States was dropping antipersonnel devices in North Vietnam, as well as bombing dikes
and other things. This was the beginning, I guess, of the accusations
against the Johnson administration that it was deliberately lying to the
American public. . . .

I was a part of the third delegation that went to North Vietnam. I
went as a representative of SNCC, specifically to take photographs and
bring them back because this was still a time when people seemed not to
believe what was going on. Shortly before we went, Lee Lockwood had
gone and come back with photographs inside the [North Vietnamese]
prisons that were published in *Life* magazine. I remember going to *Life*
magazine before I went to North Vietnam to talk to them about photo-
graphing inside of North Vietnam and what kind of things they might be
interested in, as I was interested in getting publicity for whatever the
United States might have been doing against the North Vietnamese. So I
talked to somebody in *Life* in the photo section, but I never followed up
on that when I came back.

I traveled with only one other person, Charlie Cobb, and Charlie and
I were friends in SNCC. We were very compatible and liked each other.
While we were in North Vietnam, another American came, Conrad Lynn,
a black lawyer, and he was part of a delegation that included a French
woman and an Italian. . . . We went first to Paris and met with representatives of the Bertrand Russell War Crimes Tribunal. We stayed in Paris
only overnight and then flew from there to Phnom Penh and from Phnom
Penh to Vientiane and from Vientiane to Hanoi. I remember the feeling of
flying off into the unknown. It was strange being in Asia. I had never
been in Asia before. I remember sitting on the patio at the Vientiane airport, watching monkeys play on the runway, and seeing Air America
planes come in and take off, just knowing instinctively that they were
CIA planes. I remember seeing them very openly take seats out of one aircraft and put seats in another aircraft, as if they were legitimate passenger
airplanes.

We flew into Hanoi at night. . . . It was just totally dark. The plane
landed and stopped, and the door opened, and these soldiers came on the
plane. They asked for our passports, and we gave them to them. Then
they motioned to the door, and I remember walking out into this total
darkness. Then out of the darkness comes this very attractive young
woman with a bundle of flowers in her arms, and she hands me these
flowers, and she hands Charlie some flowers.

We were supposed to be in North Vietnam for only two weeks and we ended up staying a month. The reason was that the plane from Vientiane came once a week on a Friday. On the Friday we were supposed to leave, the plane didn't come, so we had to stay another week. The next week, again the plane didn't come. So we ended up staying two additional weeks. . . .

I did not go to Haiphong. Hanoi was the only major city I visited. We stayed overnight in villages. As I recall, we stayed in guest houses that were hidden. We did not stay in the villages per se, and we did not stay with local people. Perhaps the most harrowing moment of the trip occurred on Easter Sunday, while we were in Thanh Hoa Province. United States warships some miles offshore started shelling. All day this went on. Periodically throughout the day, U.S. jets would fly over. I remember sitting in the outhouse and suddenly hearing the sound of the offshore guns or bombs from the jets and thinking that I didn't want to die while squatting over a hole in the ground in an outhouse in North Vietnam. It's very strange to be an American in a country and to watch U.S. planes fly overhead and drop bombs. It was very strange that Easter Sunday in that village, wherever I was, in Thanh Hoa Province. I guess it was the Seventh Fleet. I don't remember.

Just to hear the shelling all day was a very, very strange experience. Later that same day, I believe it was, we were in jeeps traveling along a road when U.S. jets came over, and we were forced to lie in a ditch. I felt like I was definitely on the right side because certainly, what was going on just seemed absurd. It seemed absurd to see American planes dropping bombs and I'm in this ditch, [and] there was nothing obvious around there that was military whatsoever. No bombs fell nearby, and I was not aware of any immediate danger. However, a month after I was there, a Western visitor was killed in a similar episode.

Whatever other provinces I was in, I really don't recall (if I ever really knew where I was). We visited primarily in the countryside, villages that had been bombed, and a certain number of us were shown bomb craters in the middle of villages. We visited a hospital, and I recall meeting a napalm victim and being very affected by that. Specifically, beyond that . . . I honestly don't remember. I took about fifty rolls of photographs. Probably every place I visited is documented in the photographs, but I don't remember the places.

Basically, the people we saw were ordinary people. I was a folksinger, and I had my guitar. That was certainly a way to break

Julius Lester walking away from a bombed structure, North Vietnam, spring 1967. *(Courtesy of Julius Lester.)*

through language barriers. Everywhere I went, I would be asked to sing, and I would sing songs from the civil rights movement, and I would also sing the blues. I would explain that the blues were the feeling you got when the somebody you loved was away from you. It was certainly that for a lot of the women — since most of the people we had contact with in audiences were women and older men, who understood the music instinctively, even though they did not understand a word of the blues. Even after the lyrics were translated, they did not make any sense to the Vietnamese. They certainly understood the feeling that was there.

I remember that near the end, we visited the palace. We didn't meet Ho Chi Minh, but we met Pham Van Dong, the second in command in North Vietnam at that time. We met him, and that was in a delegation of Europeans, and I can't remember if there were others. We had our pictures taken with him. I don't remember anything about that particular meeting. The Vietnamese were very skilled at propaganda, and I certainly became inured very quickly, hearing about the U.S. imperialist, capitalist aggressors and all of that very stilted language.

Right to left: Julius Lester, Charles Cobb, and an unidentified Frenchman. The Frenchman is examining what appears to be an air crew member's oxygen mask, North Vietnam, spring 1967. *(Courtesy of Julius Lester.)*

What struck me about the Vietnamese people and the contact that I had with them was their determination to resist. It was clear to me, very quickly, that there was no way the U.S. was going to win the war because of the determination of these people. And that was just extraordinary to see. For example, in Hanoi, one-person shelters had been dug into the sidewalks, and they were spaced every ten or fifteen feet, along all the major streets. . . . The people's resolve not to have daily life disrupted certainly was evidence that the United States could not have won unless they basically had leveled the country, which the United States was not willing to do at that time.

I did not see or visit any other Americans while I was in Hanoi. Felix Green, the British journalist, was there. We spent some time with him. What it was that struck me was how isolated the people were. They had never seen black Americans, and so that when Charlie and I would walk down the streets in Hanoi or in a village, crowds of people would follow us. Sometimes, we would look behind us, and there would be a couple hundred people following us in total curiosity. There was nothing malicious in it, and it was rather amusing, really. The interpreter sometimes would have fun with them, and he would ask people, "Where do you think they are from?" And people would say, "Russia. Poland. Cuba." And they would be quite stunned to hear that we were Americans. People would want to touch us, to touch our hair, and a couple of times, we saw Afro-Vietnamese children, children who were the offspring of the Senegalese soldiers who had fought with the French against the Vietnamese after World War II. It was very, very strange for both the children and us, strange for us to see these children with very dark skin coloring and Vietnamese features. Certainly, it was very strange for the Vietnamese kids to see somebody with their own skin color. But we didn't have the opportunity to talk with any of those kids.

I was surprised at how beautiful the country was. I remember this one morning in Tan Huoc Province, on these muddy roads, and seeing these terraced fields in the morning fog, and women working, planting rice, standing in the mud. The physical landscape is one of the most beautiful places I have had the privilege to see. That surprised me. . . .

It was my first experience with socialism. One of the things that I liked about it was that there was no advertising, and that was really striking — to walk around and see billboards that dealt only with either hog production or the war effort. There was no advertising for cigarettes and liquor . . . and I wasn't being titillated and stimulated and coaxed into buying this or the other. I found that very cleansing, to be in a country where there was no advertising.

I was surprised by the beauty of the women, the women and their extraordinarily long hair. Women had hair down to their heels, quite literally. And the women were quite coquettish, and even though there was a language barrier, they would flirt in a very innocent kind of way. I was also surprised by men carrying purses and walking down the streets holding hands and that kind of male camaraderie, which one does not see in the West.

There was the persona of great gentleness with the people. On the other side of that, which I was surprised to see was . . . I remember one Sunday, Mother's Day, in Tan Huoc Province, being in this little village, in the middle of nowhere, and watching a man beat a bullock with a hammer because the bullock would not move. Maybe that is normal, the only way to get a bullock to move. Maybe bullocks are so thick-skinned and dumb they don't feel it, but it seemed pretty cruel to me. Underneath the gentleness, I had the feeling that there also was a corresponding negative side. . . .

What I heard basically was propaganda. The propaganda did not surprise me. I had read it in American leftist publications before I left. Perhaps what I heard that surprised me were the personal stories of people whose villages had been bombed. And the napalm victim, particularly talking about how he was still in pain from the napalm and how napalm functioned in terms of depositing whatever it is underneath the layers of the skin so that for years afterwards, one could be in pain.

I guess one lesson that I learned was . . . how can I put it? Communist countries are very controlled countries, and the Vietnamese had difficulty dealing with me and Charlie after a while because we tended to be much more laid back. We were not really ideologues. Let me give some examples. Wherever we went in Vietnam, there was this ritual we went through, which was that we went someplace and some representatives of the village or the factory or the school, whatever it was, would get up and make a long, flowery speech about being "so glad that our American friends have come to see what the United States was subjecting us to. We are opposed to the American government and not the American people. We pray that you will welcome them."

They go through this long spiel, and then they would sit down, and then, of course, one of us was supposed to get up and give the same stuff back. We didn't want to. We hated doing that. Charlie refused after a while, and I was left to do it. Not to have done it would have been a shocking breach of manners and what have you. This dialogue ritual pretty much drove us up a wall. They didn't like for us to sit with our feet on the furniture. I'm used to flopping down in a chair, slumping down, and putting my feet up on the coffee table or something. They got very upset whenever I would do that.

I do not recall what I ate [while in North Vietnam]. I decided it was safer not to ask. I do recall that the food was quite good, both in the villages and at the hotel. In the villages, the food was traditional. At the hotel, one had a choice between Western and traditional. The Vietnamese would put on elaborate banquets of French cuisine the night before guests left Hanoi. These were six-, seven-course meals that went on for hours, and the food was absolutely extraordinary. The best French food I've ever had. The Vietnamese seemed to relish these meals, too, as if they had fond memories of the French. Since I stayed in North Vietnam two weeks longer than planned, I had the pleasure of being treated to three of

these incredible banquets. Besides the banquets, however, the daily food
was wholesome and good but not elaborate. The other thing I remember
about food in the provinces was always being offered bananas, a fruit I
don't like, but I ate them out of courtesy and found them quite good.
Maybe that had something to do with the fact that they were indigenous
and perhaps fresher.

I did not return directly to the States. I went from Hanoi back to
Paris for two weeks and then to Stockholm for the Russell War Crimes
Tribunal and then to Paris and back to New York. The tribunal did not ask
for a report of any kind. I attended the tribunal but was not called upon to
"testify" about what I had seen in North Vietnam.

Six months after I got back, I got an invitation to go to North Korea,
and I turned it down. Even [though] going to North Korea would certainly have given me the opportunity to see a country that very few people from the West had ever seen. I knew that North Korea was far more
controlled than North Vietnam and [that] I might end up in jail in North
Korea. One thing I learned was that I didn't want to go to another Communist country. I did go to Cuba after I came back from North Vietnam,
but Cuba was much more culturally to my taste. The people were much
more laid back in Cuba than they were in Vietnam.

My experience of socialism was that I didn't fit because there is not
much latitude given for individual expression in socialism. It convinced
me that socialism was a good idea in terms of trying to eradicate poverty
and [working toward] the common good, all those things in which I certainly believe. However, I would have a hard time under socialism
because I would have to subjugate my individuality to the common good
and that's something which I am unwilling to do. Beyond that, I don't
know that the trip to Hanoi influenced me in any way. . . .

What I set out to do was to take pictures and to see. I came back, and
I wrote a couple of articles for a couple of publications about my visit. I
certainly talked about it a lot and about what I had seen. What I set out to
do was to come back and to tell the truth as I saw it, as I experienced it. I
think I did that. I think all the people who went to Hanoi over time created a cumulative effect, and I think it was an effective protest. I think
[my trip] was effective. My opposition to the war, [however,] was
expressed primarily through writing. I was never one to attend or speak
at demonstrations.

Going to North Vietnam afforded me the opportunity to see for
myself and not be dependent upon what the government was telling me

or what the Vietnamese were saying also because the Vietnamese were certainly pouring out the propaganda day and night. I went in, able to see for myself. I think my going there was in the best interests of the United States, in the sense of asserting the freedom to travel and to make up my own mind.

No U.S. government official encouraged me to travel to Hanoi. . . . I went because it was a once-in-a-lifetime opportunity to see a country that was at war, to see a country that very few people, very few Americans, had been to. I went out of personal curiosity. I did not go out of feelings that others went for, which were more political. My reason for going was that it was an unparalleled opportunity. I could go, and I could take pictures. It was an opportunity that I simply could not pass up. I did not encourage other Americans to visit Hanoi. I was very careful not to become a mouthpiece for the North Vietnamese or for the Communists or for the NLF. I wanted to go to see, but I did not want to be used. So that meant trying to walk a line and to find where the place of my own integrity was.

I never responded then [to those critical of my trip]. I don't respond now. It was certainly my right as an American citizen to go to North Vietnam and do what I did. And I was very careful about what I did. The Vietnamese asked me to make a tape which they could broadcast to black troops, and I refused to do so. I refused on several grounds. It certainly would have been an act of utter hubris to have done that because black troops did not know who I was and could care less. I also felt that making such a tape, asking American soldiers to put down their guns or what have you, would have been treasonous and that while I was opposed to the war, I certainly did not want to do anything that would be interpreted as being a traitor to my country. I was not opposed to my country. So I refused to make the tape.

What I did do was to make a tape of singing songs, freedom songs, and I felt that that was fine, that that was within the bounds. I had already made a record by that time, and it was no different than if the Vietnamese had gotten hold of a copy of the record and played it. But beyond that, I did not do what, for example, Jane Fonda subsequently did. I don't criticize Jane Fonda for that, but that is simply not something that I would have done. So to those who were critical of my visit, I would not have any response. I am quite comfortable with having made the trip. . . . I neither experienced criticism [nor] paid any price for my trip. I think this may be due to the fact that I did not make an effort to publicize my trip. I wrote one or two articles about North Vietnam and published some photographs, but these were more cultural than political.

I think we [the American public] sentimentalize the Vietnam experience, and I don't think that we have ever expressed real sorrow or regret about that misadventure, and I do think it was a misadventure, as opposed to the recent war against Iraq, which I happen to support . . . [I] thought there was no alternative but to go in and to stop that aggression. But Vietnam had been one country until 1954, when it was divided into North and South, and my feeling about that was that it was no different than if somebody came and divided the United States and suddenly said that there were two United States.

The war accomplished nothing. Of course, there are those who argue that the United States did not prosecute the war fully, and that's true, but I think that's also a reflection of our own lack of clarity as to precisely what the devil the war was about. Iraq was clear to me, but for Vietnam, it was never clear to me as to what was supposed to be done. I don't think we have learned anything from the Vietnam experience. I do not think the American public understands the origins and history of our involvement in Vietnam, and I think that's because the American public doesn't read. . . .

From what I saw of the Vietnamese, I don't know that they needed any encouragement to fight on. From what I saw of them, my sense was that they would have fought to the last child. The other side of it is that . . . the Vietnamese did a better job of presenting their side of the war than the United States did in presenting its side. The United States got outpropagandized. . . . Don't blame that on those of us who went to Hanoi. Perhaps the United States was outpropagandized because the United States was never clear as to what it was doing and why it was doing it. The . . . policy was not clear, and the rationale for the policy was not clear. The Vietnamese rationale was much more clear — that they were defending their country, and it's not hard to relate to that. I am not going to take responsibility for prolonging the war and increasing American military casualties. That responsiblity is not mine. I do not have such power. I really think that [to believe that] is a good example of the ways in which we, as a country, have not taken responsbility for what we did in that war. . . .

I think that I had the expectation that Vietnam would become a more open society. It has become, if anything, a more repressive society, and so that has been disappointing to me. . . .

About the boat people and what they say, I don't have any alternative but to believe them. Why would I not believe what they say? And the things they say, I guess, are certainly an example of the other side of the Vietnamese which I tried to talk about before in terms of something under the sweetness and the persona of gentleness which the people projected. I don't doubt what the Vietnamese boat people are saying. And that's sad. That saddens me that the government has gotten so repressive.

I don't think my feelings have mellowed. My feelings are less anti-American now. I do a course on the sixties, and in my courses, I am getting children of Vietnam War veterans. So it's like I am seeing the war in the next generation. I'm seeing children whose families were destroyed by the war, whose fathers came back from Vietnam [as] potheads or addicts or alcoholics, and families broken up, so that my feelings about the war have, I guess, a more rounded dimension, and I really feel for these children. So feeling for these children, I have an empathy for the men which was not there before. That doesn't change my political evaluation, but my students have humanized the war in a way that was not present before. . . .

I have not read the things that I wrote about the war in twenty years. I would have to sit down and read them to [determine if there is anything I said then that I now regret]. I don't think so. I was bitterly opposed to that war . . . [but] I don't have any interest in reading what I wrote twenty, twenty-five years ago.

I don't have a definition for patriotism. I am an American. I really like being an American. I am not opposed to everything that my country does. Like I said, I was certainly in full support of Operation Desert Storm. Patriotism to me does not mean that I have to be always supportive of the policies of the government. My patriotism is not diminished at those times when I am opposed to certain policies. I am very much an American.

Dave Dellinger was probably [the most effective individual in the antiwar movement] just because of Dave's organizing abilities and the ability he had to mobilize and hold disparate organizations and individuals together.

9

Betty Boardman

Betty (Elizabeth Jelinek) Boardman told of her 1967 ocean voyage in a ketch named the *Phoenix,* traveling from Hong Kong to deliver medical supplies to the North Vietnamese port of Haiphong. Boardman, a Quaker, was anxious to convert her beliefs into an action that demonstrated that some Americans cared about the welfare and health of the North Vietnamese just as much as others were concerned for the South Vietnamese. She discussed the role of the Quakers in the peace movement and the sometimes critical reaction at home to her trip to North Vietnam. Boardman previously wrote about her trip to North Vietnam in *The* Phoenix *Trip: Notes on a Quaker Mission to Haiphong* (Burnsville, NC: Cello Press, 1985). Our interview took place in her home in Groton, Massachusetts, on October 4, 1990.

BETTY BOARDMAN: I went to North Vietnam in 1967 with a group of Quakers sailing from Japan on the yacht the *Phoenix.* We spent eight days in North Vietnam: six in Hanoi and two in Haiphong.

I left Madison, Wisconsin, on the first of February in the middle of a snowstorm. The weather was terrible. All the airports in the area had closed the day before, but a couple of runways opened up in time to get me out on schedule. I went from there to the San Francisco Bay Area, to the home of Phil Drath, one of the crew who had already gone on ahead to Japan. His wife, Marjorie, entertained me and invited me to a meeting with a group of people who had supported her husband in his two campaigns for Congress. These friends gave five thousand dollars to me to carry to Japan to help pay for the medical supplies we planned to take to Vietnam. And a woman in Philadelphia sent me a check for five thousand dollars, asking me to convert it to traveler's checks and carry it to Vietnam, which I did. Some people gave very large sums.

A group of people from around the country had been meeting and corresponding to decide on doing *something*. My husband, Eugene, who was a professor of Asian history at the University of Wisconsin in Madison, and I had been working that year for the Friends's [American Friends Service Committee (AFSC)] committee on national legislation in Washington. I had known some of the group years before and was excited that someone was trying to develop a project which would make Americans think and talk about the indecency of the war.

It was an ad hoc group called A Quaker Action Group [AQAG]. The service committee felt they could not take on this project because the U.S. government would probably object. The AFSC is a very large organization with lots of programs and a big budget, and they couldn't jeopardize that. So an ad hoc group was a much better idea. As a matter of fact, the Treasury Department froze AQAG's bank account twice. That was really all they did do.

We couldn't get visas. Our passports were not valid for traveling in North Vietnam. It was printed right on the passport, "Not valid for travel in China, North Vietnam," and so forth. And your passports can be lifted. Just a year later, one of the Quakers from Madison, Joseph Elder of Madison, a professor of Indian studies and sociology, carried medical supplies to North Vietnam with a validated passport, however, which I thought was interesting.

People wrote to the Vietnamese [requesting approval for our trip]. People in the Quaker movement had worked in Southeast Asia and in Indochina in years past. The American Friends Service Committee, for instance, has done seminars in some of these countries. We got a lot of names of people in Cambodia and Vietnam, and somebody in our group wrote to them, but we got no response. Then, after we were actually at sea, a telegram was sent to Hanoi saying that the group was on its way and asking what plans were there for us to enter the harbor. Well, that got a response.

The Vietnamese sent another cable back, saying, "It's much too dangerous. We can't be responsible for your coming. It's very nice of you to think about bringing us these medical supplies, but please leave them at a neutral port, and we'll come pick them up." Well, that wouldn't satisfy what we wanted to do. We wanted to meet them. There was an idea that the Vietnamese were less than human beings, that they were gooks, like dogs, that you can "off." You can kill 'em; it doesn't matter if their children are burned alive. There was a real carelessness, CARE-LESS-NESS, about that among Americans, and we wanted to come back with proof that these were indeed human beings with feelings and love for their children. We also wanted to make a gesture to them of friendship, [to demonstrate] that all Americans didn't hate them and didn't want them dead. Those were some of the ideas.

When I was ready to leave Madison, I announced at my Friends meeting that I was leaving a week and a day later. A friend of mine, John Hunter, a newsman on the *Capitol Times* staff, was sitting behind me, the first time he ever went to a Quaker meeting. He came up afterwards and said, "Let me break the news tomorrow." I said, "Oh, you can't do that. I'm supposed to have a press conference on Saturday, just before I go, and not before then. I have to get to Chicago to get my Japanese visa, and I have a bunch of things to do that I won't be able to do once you break the news; I'll probably never get a visa."

He said, "But if you call for a press conference on Saturday, nobody will come. Why would they come? But if I break the news on Wednesday, you'll be crammed; everybody will be there." And that's exactly the way it worked. So I got permission from Philadelphia to let him break the news on Wednesday.

We did not use our passports to go into Vietnam. AQAG requested validation in Washington of our passports for travel to Vietnam, and we requested validation in Tokyo and Hong Kong but were refused all along. So we went without it. We didn't miss an opportunity. We didn't want anybody to say we hadn't tried. So at every opportunity, we tried to get our passports validated.

More importantly, we needed to have the approval of the Vietnamese. After their negative response to the announcement of our imminent arrival in Haiphong harbor, it was decided in Philadelphia that one of us should fly to Bangkok, meet Carl Zietlow, who would fly out from the East Coast, and then go on to Phnom Penh, Cambodia, together and negotiate with the Vietnamese representative there. I was chosen for that role because the others couldn't be spared. Carl, who spoke French, had wanted to participate in the project but hadn't caught up with us yet. So from Hiroshima, where we had sailed the *Phoenix* from Tokyo harbor through three days of storm and two days of idyllic cruising through Japan's Inland Sea, I flew back to Tokyo and from there to Hong Kong, Bangkok, and Phnom Penh.

The Vietnamese representative gave us permission to enter Haiphong harbor with the proviso that we not tell anyone we had that permission. A couple days after I got back to Hong Kong, the *Phoenix* sailed in, and the press descended on us. I have always cringed at this scene, where a reporter asked me, "Did you get permission in Phnom Penh from the Vietnamese?" And I said, "No. I don't know what you are talking about." My crewmates were very angry with me about that. "You lied." I didn't know what to do. People have told me since I should have said, "No comment." But no comment means yes. I couldn't do that. That's a sore spot in me.

The *Phoenix* was a ketch. A ketch is a particular kind of two-masted yacht with the rear mast in front of the steering. On a yawl, it's behind. The captain was Earle Reynolds, an anthropologist, who now lives in California. The first mate was Bob Eaton, a young man of twenty-three. He had already refused to be drafted so he was looking forward to a term in jail, which he did get when he got back. Last I heard, he was working for an agency in Washington, and I have a feeling they sent him off into Southeast Asia again. He and his wife and their three or four little children have been in Southeast Asia most of the time since 1967. I haven't seen him since we had a minireunion in San Francisco about seven years ago.

Horace Champney, from Yellow Springs, Ohio, a psychologist, was the oldest of our crew. He was sixty-one at the time of the trip and was the person who thought of using the *Phoenix* and inviting its owner, Earle Reynolds, to join us. Horace died early in September 1990. Ivan Massar, a professional photographer, lives in Concord, Massachusetts. Phillip Drath, a carpenter-contractor-politician in San Rafael, died six or seven years ago. Carl Zietlow, who now lives in Burnsville, North Carolina, was the youth secretary of the AFSC in the Chicago office at the time he joined the project. Earle Reynolds's Japanese wife, Akie, came along as far as Hong Kong.

[At that time], I was forty-nine; I had all of my [six] children. My youngest two were nine and eleven. And the others were either in boarding school or college. Two were still in Scattergood School, a Quaker boarding school, and the other two were in college. Both Phil Drath and Earle Reynolds were older than I. When we were in Misaki harbor, a part of Tokyo harbor, we had to move the boat to the boatworks where it was going to get a new mast. Horace was standing in the middle of the deck, and the wind was blowing his white hair, and he said, "This is what I lived sixty-one years for" [laughter]. He was lovely.

The camera crew got aboard in Hong Kong. The cameraman, Bill Heick, was a filmmaker from Mill Valley, California. The head of the movie project was Dick Faun, who had a contract with the Canadian Broadcasting Corporation to make a documentary of our trip. [All were Americans] except for Akie Reynolds. I had no money at all [to make the trip]. A Quaker Action Group bought my ticket. I made 208 speeches the first year after I got back. And wherever it was, in a church or public hall, the hat was passed. Anything beyond my immediate expenses for the lecture tour I sent to Philadelphia, and ultimately, I paid back my plane fare. But some of the people had their own money.

[The Vietnamese paid none of our expenses.] Not at all. They didn't even want us there, really. They were very lovely to us when we showed up, and they didn't shoot us out of the water as they might have if we had not made the arrangements. I didn't [consider the trip hazardous]. Some people in the group did. Dick Faun, for instance, was very nervous about the whole thing.

We landed in Haiphong, the seaport for Hanoi, and stayed there almost twenty-four hours. We arrived at the wharf sometime after midnight, and we left about 10:00 P.M. the next day, driving through the night. The bridges, which were just pontoons, boats, and planks, were disassembled and dispersed during the day, so all travel was at night.

Haiphong harbor was under attack when we were coming in, and an American plane was apparently shot down. A lot of people were hurt that night; we saw them in the hospital the next week. The first or second day we were in Hanoi, we were talking to a group of Vietnamese when we had to get into an air-raid shelter. There's a funny story about that. We discovered after we were in the shelter that the people who belonged there were on the porch because there wasn't room. We big Americans filled it all up. We didn't know what to do with our heads either because the ceiling was about a foot too low for us. At that point, we discovered that our hosts didn't have any place to go. So we decided to go out and join them as a plane went zooming by, just over the treetops. Earle Reynolds had his head out of the shelter and called back to us, "Don't worry, it's ours." We all just died laughing because it wasn't ours. It was theirs. But it's a good example of what happens to a person's point of view. When you are on the ground and you're being bombed by someone, that's the enemy. It doesn't matter which country he represents.

I didn't know what to expect. I had no expectations when I went. I felt there would be more people living the way they live in Cambodia, in houses raised up on poles, but I didn't see that. We visited several hospitals and saw a lot of terrible wounds, including a little girl who had her spinal cord cut by shrapnel, and that really wrenched me pretty much. We saw a little boy who was blinded and his arm made useless, a baby who was injured in utero, and a lot of people who had been injured by American arms.

We talked to a lot of people, all kinds of people, government officials and cooks and people on the street. We delivered the medical supplies, which were antimalarials, antibiotics, bandages, syringes, supplies. Nothing elaborate. Just the usual thing you find at a clinic. They were packaged for clinic use, not for individuals. We brought ten thousand dollars' worth of those supplies, which were selected and packaged by the doctors of Hiroshima because they knew what kinds of things were especially needed.

We went to a small village where the men were all gone. They had a woman mayor, and some women were working in the fields while others took care of the children; all the jobs seemed to be done by women. When the women came in from the field, I was impressed by the obvious caring for each other, the joking, and the loving kind of camaraderie between them, which is hard to find in this country. We don't work together. I know neighbors and others who work together. But this was different. This was on another level of caring that I hadn't ever experienced. That was a surprise. We asked the Vietnamese what they would like us to do: "Should we send some carpenters over to rebuild your houses? Do you want a medical clinic to be built? Do you want us to send or bring something? What do you want us to do?" They said, "No, just go home and do something about your own country." So [when I returned home], I told people that. This is where the trouble is. Right here.

Julius Lester was there and a couple other people. There were journalists. I didn't see any other American journalists. They were from everywhere else in the world, though. That was an interesting thing. We thought that Vietnam was all closed off. It was just closed off to us. We are the ones who closed it to ourselves. But the rest of the world was there. There were Japanese, Bulgarian, and Romanian reporters and people from everywhere. It was incredible.

We [departed from Vietnam] in the ketch. That was when Dick was most nervous. When we got back to Hong Kong, he told me he was sure that as soon as we got out of sight of land we would be sunk, and it would be blamed on the Americans. Isn't that something? That never crossed my mind. I tend not to be scared in most physical situations. Socially, I'm pretty paranoid, but I trust people's decency. They might cheat me, but they're not going to shoot me.

On my way home [from Vietnam], I went to London, and at one point, there was a demonstration going on at Trafalgar Square. I went up to see what they were doing. Somehow, I got to talking with a girl. Then she came to see me at the Friends International Center where I was staying. She said she and a group of other people were planning to go to Vietnam to put their bodies between the fighting men, and I was absolutely aghast. I was *appalled*. She said, "But that's what you did." I said, "No, we didn't do that. We did something quite different." But that idea did go through our minds at the very first, when we talked about it, when we asked ourselves, "What can we do?" That was one of the ideas tossed in, but it wasn't that kind of a war. There weren't lines [of battle]; you could get bombed. These looked like headstrong kids that might just try to do it and I wanted to discourage that. "Get a different idea, because that one really was not too good."

When I came back and landed at Madison Airport at the end of this trip, my husband was there, and a hundred or more people crowded into the airport, and my husband hung way back. Finally, he came up to me, and some of the people were walking along, saying, "Can you talk to our church at such and such? Can you do this?" And he said, "No. She's home. She's not going to do it." I said, "Gene, I can't do that. I can't." And he said, "You've been away. Now you are home." And he thought I was through. "It's all over." No. It wasn't all over. And I worked my tail off for another year. Then all of a sudden, just exactly a year from that May first when I came back, it was the first day that I didn't have an appointment or a speaking engagement ahead. Some more came, but just occasionally.

I think from a strictly patriotic point of view, [the trip] probably was inappropriate. But I don't believe in that kind of patriotism. There are more important things. We all just happen to have been born into this particular country. But that doesn't put our consciences at rest. We still have a larger loyalty to the human race, to the world, even to animals, in general, than just to one country. I just don't believe in that kind of patriotism. And *we* attacked them; after all, they didn't attack us. *We* divided their country; they didn't divide it.

I don't know what there was to defend [about our trip to North Vietnam] from our point of view. I don't think we had any argument. It's turned out that we were right. We antiwar people were right; the government was wrong. We thought so then. It's been proven since. There are still some hard-liners in the Pentagon and in the government who claim that with a little more money or more something or other, they could have won. What would they have won? My private opinion is that the U.S. was looking for a foothold on the continent of Asia, someplace to work from. It may have been tin and antimony. I don't think that it had anything to do with how one group of Vietnamese was treating another group of Vietnamese. We don't care about that ordinarily. We don't care how people treat each other. Only if oil, antimony, tin, or copper [are involved].

If I believed "My country, right or wrong," then I probably wouldn't have done it. But I don't believe that. I think my country was wrong. I think that as a human being with a conscience, I have to do the best *I* can do, not just the best that Mr. Nixon or Mr. Johnson thinks is best. I've got as good a conscience as they do, and mine counts, too.

I think things were being done in our name by the government that a lot of people were uncomfortable about, but *nobody* was really talking about it, and I think the most important thing we did was to open up the discussion. It happened. In my town of Madison, there were a few peace groups. We had a vigil, we wrote letters, but nothing else happened. We were influencing a person or two, but not many. We went to Washington and talked to our congressmen and our senators, but nothing happened. And then when I came back to Madison, as a matter of fact, when I *went*, it just tore the place apart. The town stood on its ear.

I was on the front page for two solid weeks, every single night, when I got home. Every paper had a story. People could not ignore it. They had to talk about it. The churches all began having seminars on the war. For instance, I was invited by a small group of people up in Wausau, Wisconsin, to come and talk. They weren't sure that they could get more than a few people together because it wasn't really the kind of a town that had many peace people in it. I had made a rule for myself that I didn't care how many people were going to be there. If anybody wanted me to come, I would go. I didn't care who it was or what they wanted. I was going to talk about it. This was part of my job. So they called me some weeks ahead, and I said, "Sure, I'll come." It was going to be in one of the churches.

They put a notice in the paper that Betty Boardman of the *Phoenix* was going to come up there to talk, and people were invited. The town flipped. The minister withdrew his permission to have the meeting in his church. Then I had many telephone calls from Wausau. "Well, we don't have a place to meet now. Do you still want to come?" "Oh, sure." Pretty soon, the head librarian of the city's library called the planners and said,

"This is a public building, and as a public building, we can't deny any-body who wants to make a speech." So the meeting was scheduled at the library.

When I arrived that night, they had a hundred chairs set up. They were full and out scouting around the town, trying to find more chairs. That was a wonderful meeting. I hardly had to talk at all because the town was *dying* to talk. There were people who thought I was a traitor, there were people who thought I was absolutely right, and they got to talking to each other, and yet, it stayed decent. They set up a peace orga-nization there that night, which functioned for the next ten years. I didn't have to do anything. I was a catalyst. That's all I was. And that was won-derful. As far as I am concerned, that is the most important thing we did. But we couldn't have done it without having been controversial. We had to be outrageous, and actually, what we did was pretty outrageous for the time.

I had been an ardent Democrat, and I remember standing up and making not a speech but venting myself at a Quaker yearly meeting in Illinois on the subject of how everybody *really* ought to belong to a politi-cal party, that it was important to get in on decision making at the local level. Then I went to Vietnam, and I came back. I knew all the Democrats; I knew the senator; I knew local officials. Madison, Wisconsin, is a won-derful place. The government is right there. You are a part of it, and you don't hesitate to pick up the telephone and call the governor, if you want to. You can do it.

I went to a Democratic county meeting. They were very good to me at first. They invited me to speak to the Wednesday luncheon club when I first got back. It was crammed. Then somebody introduced a bill into the state legislature that would prohibit people from carrying medical sup-plies to North Vietnam on sailing boats. It was just as stupid as that. It was so pointed. So I had to go and speak to that hearing. Then I went to the Democratic meeting, and I wanted them to take a position against the war. They all told me how wonderful they thought I was but then said, "Now, we really have important business to do. We can't waste any more time." I just left. I never went back to a Democratic meeting. They had important things to talk about.

I did *all* I could. I'm sorry now that so much time has gone by and that I haven't been active and kept up. But at the time, I couldn't have done another thing. I thought I was doing all I could do before we went to Washington in 1966 because I had written letters and held vigils. And then when this wonderful opportunity came, I threw myself into it.

There were some ineffective, blundery kinds of things I did. I remember that first press conference before I left, after John Hunter broke the news on Wednesday and I had a press conference on Saturday. A woman said, "I think you're protesting and calling it something else." As if protesting was a bad thing, and I didn't catch that right away. So I made some mistakes like that. I got angry toward the end of that year, too. There was one man, a Captain Bollenbeck, who had been in a world war. I've forgotten which one. He had never been in battle, but he'd made a career of being a veteran. He had an organization, and he followed me all over the state. I was safe if I was out of the state, but if I made a speech anywhere in Wisconsin, he was there.

And he always stood up and asked the same question, "Had we asked to see American prisoners?" The answer was, No. We had intended to, but just before we left, something came out in the paper that the State Department had asked a Quaker group going to Vietnam to look into the condition of American prisoners. They hadn't asked anybody anything. It was a pure, one hundred percent lie. And we never would have got into Vietnam if that had been true. And that was how I answered each time. And he would stand there and look around at all the people and smile, as if to say, "See, I've got her in a corner, again." And finally, I got mad. After about twenty-five times down the road, I finally said, "Captain Bollenbeck, please turn up your hearing aid." Isn't that awful? I regret that I lost my cool. I decided I had enough; I was pushed too hard. I hadn't been home, I hadn't watered my own plants, I needed a break.

[Subsequently], a group of us got together. I can't quite remember how all this happened. The New Left political convention was meeting in Chicago in 1967. It was the year before the Democratic convention of 1968. The New Left was all kinds of people, every shade you can imagine, from out-and-out Communists to people who were really liberal Democrats. They were trying to put together a new movement that would express what most of them felt. I went to the convention, and I got to know people from Madison whom I had barely known before. We formed an organization called The Wisconsin Alliance, an alliance of farmers, workers, and students. It was a socialist, populist group. It lasted for ten years, and those were the best ten years of my life. The alliance died of too many interpretations of what we were about.

We didn't have officers. The chair rotated. Every time we had a meeting, we had a different chair because everybody had to learn how to do it. And it was great. It's really hard to run an organization like that, but if you ask me what I think is an ideal organization, it would be one that teaches everybody how to run it and doesn't have any elite hierarchy. It's a little hard to get the work done, although Quakers do it quite well. They work pretty much on that principle. The clerk, meaning chair, usually rotates about every two years. Everybody is supposed to take a job, and we make decisions by consensus, and that takes a long time. In that way, you get a lot of issues talked about instead of just voting.

The [meetings] usually have an agenda. Some meetings try doing it out of silence, and the issues come up when somebody's moved to bring them up. That's a little too slow. Usually, we have an agenda, and people talk about the matter. The clerk looks around when the conversation ends or sort of dwindles off and says, "Well, I get the feeling that people like this idea. Is there anybody here who doesn't like it?" It's done more or less that way. But if you get into a hot argument, and people are really snapping back at each other, which you are not supposed to *ever* do, then somebody says, "I think we need a little silence." But generally, you don't answer people back, ever. If you do, things are out of control or at least the person is.

Every so often, somebody says, "Well, the peace people called the GIs baby-killers and stuff like that." Now I won't say that I don't believe it because people have told me that it really happened, and so I have to believe it. But nobody *I* know in the peace movement would do such a thing because we all felt the young men called up to go to Vietnam were just as much victims as the Vietnamese.

I guess I have a little hard feeling, still, about the fliers, because they were all volunteers. But I feel really bad about the draftees. They were used so hard, and they've suffered ever since. I know my husband suffered from World War II. I think things happened to him that changed him forever. He was an island-hopping marine, a language officer. He was right there all the time, and I think it destroyed certain things about him. He was damaged by it. And I'm sure the Vietnam veterans were damaged, at least that much, probably more.

People [from other countries] aren't that much worse off than the people in this country who've given up. . . . And I'm not sure the reasons are too different. Are those who live in a poor neighborhood, have been poor all their life, *really* poor, short of food, don't have an education and can't get one, and don't know how to read, and there's lots of people like that — are they better off with a rotten job?

[I think back to] what South Vietnam was like with the American Army there, lots of cash and cars. There were no privately owned cars in the North when I was there, just military cars and a couple of limousines that took guests around. In Saigon, there was a lot of money, a lot of *brothels*, which they didn't have in the North. They already had re-educated those women and given them other jobs.

The cultures [in North and South Vietnam were] different just because of the occupation by the Americans and the money and the kind of consumer goods they brought in. People from the North didn't have any consumer goods. They were poor people. They had enough food. They had rice; they had vegetables and fruits; they didn't have very much meat. To bring those people in the South into the system [after the war] must have been a tremendous challenge.

I don't know how the Vietnamese could have integrated Saigon and that area into the kind of orderly society that the people of the North were used to. That really was a very organized and orderly place. But everybody ate. Everybody's children got taken care of. Everybody had clothes. They weren't very good clothes. They were cheap. But they all had them, and nobody had anything fancy, nobody. How do you teach people who have been riding motorcycles, driving Oldsmobiles, and living high on the hog? I'm sure [the boat people] were one hundred percent from South Vietnam. I don't think any of them were from the North. They simply weren't willing to live the restricted, the poor life that there was.

Look what we did to Vietnam. We have added to their poverty by our embargo. We have ruined their economy, such as it was. I am of two minds about [resuming trade with Vietnam] because I think that when we go into a country and give it our goodies, we corrupt it in some very major ways.

I know the [Vietnamese] were capable of horrible things, but to a large extent, everybody took care of everybody else; when the road was bombed, everybody just left what they were doing and went out and shoveled the dirt back. The children all were cared for. [At home], I always had to rustle around and find a babysitter. And if I couldn't afford a babysitter, I didn't have one.

I liked Vietnam. I liked their society, and I was anxious about what would happen when the war ended and America poured in its largesse. Look what we did in Japan. We did it in Germany, and we did it in all kinds of places. To a large extent, it was corrupting. And this was an agrarian country. I hated to see it happen. On the other hand, nobody had any right to starve them out. We ruined their fields. You couldn't look out a car window without seeing bomb craters all over.

[The American public was] lied to, publicly, in the newspapers, and on the TV. People who they should believe, their government representatives, lied to them. The Gulf of Tonkin incident: a pure lie. It didn't happen. And yet the American people bought it, and why not? Who do you believe if you can't believe your government? Well, I don't believe my government. I don't believe anything they say. I've got to have it verified by somebody like Noam Chomsky, somebody I respect, before I believe anything I hear from Washington.

[To me, the greatest deception of the war was] that somehow we had business there. We didn't have any right to be there at all. It was none of our business. It didn't have anything to do with us. We supported France when they were trying to hang on to the place, and when they lost it, we connived with France and with Japan to divide the country. We just messed with their lives, unmercifully. The Vietnamese had a right to govern their own country, the whole country. When they went into the South, they weren't invading it; that was their country.

I think there was [a common bond among those Americans who went to North Vietnam]. I think there was a repugnance for the kind of war that it was and the fact that our country was waging a war against these poor, poor people, not unsophisticated people but in a material way, very poor. I think I have never heard of anybody going there who wasn't impressed with how good their society was. We certainly had no organizational contact with most people. We may have known some of them, but they all went for pretty much the same reason, antiwar or anti–*that* war, at least.

I probably feel at least as strongly [today about the war as I did then]. I know more than I did at the time. I was pretty frantic. I was frantic because I thought it was all wrong from a simplistic point of view that one ought not to kill people. I didn't really know the history of Vietnam, and I had no idea why we were there. It couldn't have been good. I studied a whole lot. I learned the history [of Vietnam], and if anything, it has made me feel more strongly. I don't think about it as much as I did, of course, because a lot of time has gone by and *my* circumstances are so different.

I had to think more deeply into some things that I hadn't before. For instance, when Carl and I were in Cambodia, after we had done our business and gotten permission to enter Haiphong harbor, we sat back in our chairs with the two Vietnamese representatives who were there and chatted a bit about things. One of those men said, "I really feel sorry for

Americans because they have such a despotic government." And I said,
"Oh, no. We don't have a despotic government. No. It's really very good
to us, and we don't have any problems. It's bad for you, but it's good for
us." And Carl said, "Betty, think about the Indians. How much is being
done for the poor people? What's being done for the blacks?" . . .

Larry Scott was the person who was most important to *me* in shap-
ing *my* ideas [about the war]. I thought everybody ought to be good to
everybody else. That was the basis of my political ideas. I was on the
Executive Committee of the American Friends Service Committee in Chicago for a long time. Larry Scott was the peace secretary then. I really sat
at his feet. He's the one who started and ran for several years the protest
against the biological warfare materials made at Fort Dietrich in Mary-
land. People stood out in front of that place for years. Later, Larry was
active in the antinuclear desert actions. Larry died in an accident about
three years ago in Arizona.

[Although Larry exerted the greatest influence on me], I don't think
there was one person [who could be said to have been the leading figure
in the antiwar movement]. I think there were a whole lot of people for a
whole lot of different reasons. There were Catholic nuns; there were all
those priests; there were Quakers; there were Unitarians; there were all
kinds of people, and we had a hard time being *heard* at first, but gradually
it opened out, until there were a lot of people. And then, just plain old GI
Joe, even him, but mostly just the kids on the campuses were extremely
important.

SDS trained a lot of people to start thinking. I think anybody who
got the American people thinking about what was going on and talking
was very important. I think the Wisconsin Alliance was very productive
in Wisconsin, and there were other alliances that were offshoots. There
was one in Northern California that I think is still functioning. There were
offshoots from the alliance in a lot of places. The Nebraska Alliance. Fort
Collins, Colorado, had a great peace movement. There are many people
who are very active.

There was always something in Boulder, Colorado. Boulder was a
sort of smaller Madison, but Fort Collins was surprisingly active. They
had something like fifty courses, such as "Protest Movements in Literature," scattered throughout the university [Colorado State University]. I
spoke to a [class] in the English Department when I was out there. Every
department seemed to have a couple of peace courses that had been
tucked in. Very healthy.

[The events of 1967 remain vivid in my mind.] I have trouble with names, but I did get through the whole crew of the *Phoenix* without any trouble. I'm beginning to forget things; I've forgotten the names of the Vietnamese, but I remember the incidents.

[The worst mistake the U.S. government made was] getting into it. And then not having the courage to get out. Lying their way in. Each president seemed to get us in deeper. The Gulf of Tonkin was as bad as anything because it was so blatant, such a lie.

It was a very important experience for me. In personal ways, too. It did things to my family that in some ways were bad and in other ways were good. It taught me more about myself. I had never thought that I really knew very much or was very smart or had very many skills. I could do anything but be sharp. I didn't think I was. But I found out that I did all right. I was the only woman on the crew. There were some handicaps there. There were a lot of times that I didn't know what was going on because the men talked among themselves and didn't remember to include me. That was a handicap.

But all in all, with all the skills they had, I did all right. My child-rearing skills and family management skills were pretty good training, and I could do anything they could do. I had to learn though. For instance, the first time I made a speech, I nearly died. I thought my heart was going to just drop right out. It got easier, easier, and easier. And that's all it is. Experience. Women don't generally have it, and it was very good for my ego to learn that I could do things too, that I was OK.

10

Bill Heick

Bill Heick, a professional cinematographer, accompanied Betty Boardman on the voyage of the *Phoenix* to Haiphong harbor in North Vietnam. Heick had actively demonstrated against the war at home and saw the voyage of the *Phoenix* both as a professional opportunity and as a means to express his pacifist beliefs. During our interview in his Mill Valley, California, office on November 12, 1990, he described the logistics of the trip and the mixed reaction that greeted his return.

BILL HEICK: I think we left in February 1967. There were eight altogether. Dick Faun and I were responsible for making a movie of the project, and the Quakers were very chary about who did the shooting on this project because they didn't want one of the networks to get in there and then do their own philosophizing about the trip. I was acquainted with one of the leading Quakers out here, and I had made a film for them on the rebuilding of churches that had been burned in Mississippi. The Quakers had a project that was taking carpenters from the North down thére, and they rented a house where these carpenters stayed. Each day, they went out and rebuilt from the ground up the churches that had been burnt down.

So through making that film for the Quakers, they knew me and felt I would give them a sympathetic treatment in the film. The film was sponsored by the Canadian Broadcasting Corporation [CBC]. Dick Faun was a sort of director, and I was the cameraman. We were gone about a month, and I think we were in North Vietnam almost two weeks.

Betty Boardman was a moderating element on the trip. Quakers tend to be very argumentative among themselves. They don't compromise, which is a virtue, but sometimes in close quarters, where you don't compromise, they get to be kind of strained, to put it gently. And so there were lots of arguments, discussions we should say, and some of those show up in the film. We had conferences aboard ship, and each member of the crew expressed his [or her] views. . . .

The skipper, Earle Reynolds, had been protesting the testing of nuclear bombs in the South Pacific. He had his boat, the *Phoenix*, built in Japan and then sailed down into the test area, where he was boarded and arrested. He was then taken back to Honolulu and put on trial. He won. He was not convicted of the charges the Navy brought against him. So he had a history of using that yacht for protest purposes. I am not sure whether the Quakers went to him or he went to the Quakers to plan this trip to take medical supplies to North Vietnam.

Earle Reynolds had worked for the government as a physical anthropologist, and he was assigned by the government to go and observe the damage and effects of the bombing of Hiroshima and Nagasaki in Japan. He was so distraught at what he found that it started him on this protest of nuclear testing, which eventually led to his making the voyage of the *Phoenix* to North Vietnam.

There were six Quakers, and I'm sort of a Quaker, and Dick Faun was not a Quaker. Faun had been in Hollywood and heard about this voyage. Somehow, he got in touch with the Quakers, and they sent him to see the Canadian Broadcasting Corporation. Between the Quakers, Dick Faun, and the CBC, they worked out an arrangement.

Dick Faun and I flew from San Francisco to Hong Kong. The yacht was loaded in Japan. The six Quakers sailed down to Hong Kong. That's where Dick Faun and I boarded. We bought foodstuffs and supplies. The medical supplies were all loaded in Japan. After loading up with fuel and supplies in Hong Kong, we sailed south to get around Hainan Island. It would have been a short trip if we had gone north of Hainan Island, but the Chinese wouldn't let us go through that strait, which would have been a short cut. It took us six days to get to Haiphong. . . .

As we were sailing up through the South China Sea, the U.S. Navy sent search planes out, and we'd see two or three of them approaching. They would come right down and swoop over the mast. Every day, they did this patrol, to check on us. Then the big Huey helicopter, the 105, came. It had big doors that opened, and we could see their photographer standing in the doorway shooting pictures of us, and so we shot pictures right back at 'em [laughter]. That was kind of hairy. We didn't know whether they would board us, tow us back to Hong Kong, or what. But they didn't do anything but note our position and our progress. They never responded to any radio communication we made.

The food got pretty rancid after we were out three or four days; the bread got moldy, and a lot of canned, potted meat wasn't very tasty, but I liked it. I got hungry, and it all tasted good to me. Some of the Quakers were used to eating a little better, but there was nothing they could do about it.

Earle Reynolds did everything as far as running the ship. He had an old sextant, and that was his sole source of direction. Navigation was strictly by celestial navigation. He used the sextant whenever he was in doubt where he was. He had a compass and his sextant and that was it. No radar or anything like that. At one time, going past Hainan Island, he wasn't sure where he was. There was a heavy cloud overcast. We could tell he was very nervous. He was checking the charts and kept a watch out in all directions. He didn't want to get too close to Hainan Island due to the warning he had received in Hong Kong about their radar-aimed guns. Their radar would pick up an unidentified ship, and they would shoot it. With the heavy overcast, we had no access to the sun for getting a direction so that we could pinpoint our location.

We had an arrangement with the consulate to report in every night at midnight. We would send out a signal to the consulate's call letters. They wanted that so that they could officially know where we were and know that we had not run into harm. We sent out those messages every night at midnight but never got a response or acknowledgment.

Just by necessity, we sailed twenty-four hours a day. At night, we had to keep a sentry, a watch out the bow of the ship. The Chinese junks sail through those waters with no running lights, and they're out all the time. So we had to beware of crashing into one of those unlighted junks at night. . . . [However,] we passed them . . . without incident.

Horace Champney was somewhat of an astronomer. We would lie on the deck. One person would watch for the junks; the rest of us would look up at the stars, and Horace would tell us what we were looking at because he knew the constellations and all the significant stars. It was an interesting way to pass the time. When we arrived at Haiphong harbor, it was around four in the evening [March 27, 1967]. They sent a patrol boat out with a couple of marine-type personnel, and they came aboard and suggested we wait until after dark. It would be safer. So we gave them a spaghetti dinner and waited until dark. Then they escorted us in through the marker buoys. As we were going in, there was an American air raid on Haiphong. [Surface-to-air] missiles [SAMs] were shooting up in the air. We did see where it looked like a plane got hit and went crashing down. The SAM missiles are heat-seeking, so we made sure there was no heat aboard the boat.

They escorted us in, and we got into the port of Haiphong about ten or eleven. There was a huge crowd, and the women all had bouquets of flowers and gave a bouquet to each crew member. We got all of that on film. They were very hospitable. They put us up in a hotel for the night, and the following night, the main Quakers were taken in these big Russian GIM cars to Hanoi. GIM stands for some longer words, but the common usage is a Russian GIM. They're big, fat cars. They look like the Buicks of the 1950s, when everything was all puffed up, the way that cars looked, even here.

They traveled at night so they wouldn't be visible in case there were bombing raids. They could get through at night without any difficulty. There were several rivers to cross, and the North Vietnamese had made their bridges floating. In the daytime, the bridges sort of hinged and were brought back under the willows and things on the riverbank so they wouldn't be seen. Then at night, they would roll them out and use them for transport.

We stayed at first in the Reunification Hotel, a big, nice hotel, sort of French-style. The North Vietnamese people took care of all our expenses while we were in North Vietnam. They took us on tours around the countryside to villages that had been demolished. We went to hospitals. We had meetings with their State Department people and just talked in general about the whole war. . . .

Nobody could have survived the bombing of the village of Phu Ly that we saw in the film. It was just obliterated. When all those villagers heard the planes coming, they left the village for the woods nearby and just waited until it was over. Then they would go back and try to pick up the pieces and get on with their lives.

Everybody was doing something for the war effort. On the drive at night from Haiphong to Hanoi, we saw crews of women and children with bicycles. They had bags on these bicycles and carried as much as five hundred pounds of dirt in these bags to fill up the potholes in the highway between Hanoi and Haiphong. They worked all night to repair the damage of the daytime bombing.

I think we shot about ten thousand feet [of film]; the total footage shot . . . would amount to ten hours of unedited footage, and then we got film from the Japanese of the war scenes. There was one air raid while we were there, and we shot a little bit of footage of that, but the big fire scenes [in the film] were shot by the Japanese.

In Hanoi, we sort of had free run of the Canadian embassy. Canada maintained their relationship on an official level with North Vietnam. We would drop by the embassy and talk to the people and get news from the States. They would get some of our newspapers, and we would read them to learn what was going on. Canadians were very sympathetic to the North Vietnamese cause. I think they [the Canadians] are less paranoid about communism. For instance, Canadians have a good relationship with Cuba, and I think it's the same situation. They don't look upon communism as the scourge that the U.S did, and therefore they maintained friendly relations with Communist countries. Canadians make a big thing of going to Cuba on their vacations — because we're not allowed to go there. . . .

We were at some government building [when] it just happened. The [Vietnamese] paraded him [an American POW] by, and we filmed him without comment. . . . His burns looked fresh. We didn't find out much about him at all other than he paraded by us, and we filmed it, and that's all. . . . We wanted to see some [other POWs], maybe talk to them, but we didn't have an opportunity. The English writer Graham Greene was there with two American technicians doing a story on North Vietnam. He asked us if we would shoot an interview of him talking to a North Vietnamese, and we shot that for him.

The plan, according to the Canadian Broadcasting Corporation, was to get the film back, fast. They suggested that we fly from Hanoi to Cambodia and then to Hong Kong and then back here. The North Vietnam authorities said, "No. You came on the boat. You really should go back on the boat." They sent us back to Haiphong, and we boarded the boat and sailed back to Hong Kong. All the Quakers except Earle and Akie [his wife] and Dick Faun and myself flew from Hong Kong back to the States. Earle and Akie sailed back to Japan. I think they were living in Japan at that time.

[The film] was sent to Vancouver, I think through the Canadian consulate in Hanoi. I guess the CBC representative in Vancouver took over and got it back to Toronto. I guess the film was edited in Toronto, and Dick Faun pretty much wrote and narrated the script. [The film, *The Voyage of the Phoenix*, appeared on Canadian TV] probably six months [later]. Phil Drath, a Quaker, took this film and toured campuses all across the U.S., and I'm sure he had a big impact. After he got back, he ran for Congress. He didn't make it, but he made a lot of speeches about the war on the campuses. The Quakers paid his expenses, and he ran the film and then conducted seminars and answered questions.

The . . . trip was supposed to be illegal, and none of the passports were validated. When I got wind of the possibility of going on the trip, I wrote to the consulate in Hawaii and said I was a journalist and that I was going on a journalistic trip to North Vietnam and would they validate my passport? I sent my passport, and about a week later, I got my passport back with a letter saying, "Your passport has been validated for travel in North Vietnam." And so I was in the clear, but the rest of the Quakers and Dick Faun weren't. When everybody got back, their passports were confiscated.

[They did not confiscate mine] because they couldn't find me. They didn't know where I was. The State Department sent two FBI agents out to my house. They called up and asked if they could come up and see me, and I said, "Sure. Come on and see me." I had a neighbor who's a lawyer, and I suggested that he come and sit in so that he could hear what's going on and I would have a witness. The two FBI guys and my lawyer came, and we sat there and talked. The agents kept giving me the line, "If you cooperate, we can go easy on you, if you tell us about the other six Quakers." Since I had a validated passport, I knew they couldn't do much to me even if I didn't cooperate. I gave them evasive answers or no answers at all, and nothing came of it. All of the passports were returned to the Quakers. They gave up the idea of prosecuting them.

At the time I went, I was making movies for Bechtel Corporation, a big, worldwide engineering company. When I got back, the trip was covered by the newspapers, and my name showed up frequently as one of the crew members. People down at Bechtel were reading it, and their clients were not sympathetic to the Quakers' cause so that Bechtel was getting static. I was known to a lot of their clients because I made movies for Bechtel for some of those clients.

So when I got back, the word came down, and I had to go see Steve Bechtel. He wanted to talk to me because this was a serious matter. So I went to see him, and it just happened that I had taken my passport and the letter I got from the consulate in Honolulu. He questioned me about the trip and asked if I had checked it out with my superior at Bechtel before I left on this trip. I said, "Yes. As a matter of fact, I told my boss what my plan was, and he said 'Don't tell me. I don't want to know anything about it. I don't want to be responsible for giving you permission to go.'" I recounted all of this to Steve Bechtel and showed him the letter stating that I had permission to travel in North Vietnam, and so he was satisfied that I had not violated U.S. laws, so that everything was all right.

Bechtel did a lot of work for PG&E [Pacific Gas and Electric], and I would have to deal with some of the PG&E PR people. They would really sound off at how wrong I was to go off on this trip, but it didn't last and was soon forgotten. . . .

I am a member of the Explorers' Club of New York, and they have a meeting in San Francisco, a dinner, and then entertainment. They decided one night to show *The Voyage of the Phoenix* as part of the entertainment for that evening. The Explorers' Club has a lot of retired colonels and military people. We showed the movie, and there really was a furor. They stood up and protested and called me a traitor. An associate of mine, Richard Phinney, also worked at Bechtel as a movie producer. We made documentaries together. He was a member of the Explorers' Club and was at the meeting. Both of us really took a beating from half of the Explorers' Club. They just got up and swore and called us traitors and everything. [However], I am still a member in good standing of the Explorers' Club. . . .

I was always in the peace marches. I always went to the protests. Generally speaking, protesting all sorts of things, like the HUAC Committee, the House Un-American Activities Committee. I thought they were un-American. It was McCarthyism. Just un-American. It was not in the tradition of the founders of this country. I was against the war at the very beginning, and I was against it throughout, and when it ended, I was glad it ended. I was not too disappointed about the way it came out — that the Americans left. Had the Americans prevailed, I don't think it would have ended. I had a strong feeling that the North Vietnamese people were going to continue until every one of them died, women and children included.

To a pacifist, there is no just reason for fighting. You have to come to an understanding through some other reasoning process. The Quakers at no time encouraged anyone in North Vietnam to keep fighting. . . . They wanted both sides to stop. The intention of the Quakers going over there with medical supplies was humanitarian. . . .

[I would define patriotism as] the last resort of scoundrels [laughter]. Take the example of Earle Reynolds, [however]. He sailed into the South Pacific to protest the nuclear bomb testing. He was accused of being unpatriotic in doing that. The French continued testing. [Secretary of State Dean] Rusk and the other administration officials protested that. If Earle Reynolds was unpatriotic for protesting the nuclear testing, what does that make Dean Rusk and his associates, protesting the French testing of nuclear bombs? . . .

Let's clear that up. It's patriotic to protest something that is wrong and ultimately proves to be wrong. The fact that at the moment of the protest it appears not to be wrong is not a valid reason for not protesting. When it eventually turns out to be wrong and you protested, your original protest was a patriotic thing because you were protesting against something that eventually proved to be a wrong action.

[My feelings about the war have] certainly not mellowed. I went back and observed that monument [the Vietnam War Memorial] in Washington. All the veterans that come back there are saddened. They are really in a depressed state. And sometimes, I wonder to myself if they are depressed at the fact that they were over there scattering napalm and bombs and using these torches, squirting them into hutches, and calling every North Vietnamese a gook? That's all forgotten in our surge to honor the Vietnam fighters (the U.S. military that went over there), but there were atrocities committed every day. People would be appalled if they were presented [with the details of those atrocities] today. I think part of the problem with Vietnam veterans is that they must feel a lot of guilt for what they did.

11

John Pairman Brown

In 1967 the Reverend John Pairman Brown traveled to a peace conference in Bratislava, Czechoslovakia, and then on to North Vietnam as a member of a group that included Tom Hayden and Rennie Davis. There he saw teenaged Vietnamese girls who operated an antiaircraft machine gun, (and whom he believed had shot down an American plane) use a model airplane made of bamboo in simulated target practice. Reverend Brown believes that three factors combined to force the withdrawal of U.S. troops from Vietnam: (1) Congress, which cut off appropriations in support of the war; (2) the Selective Service system, which reached out and drafted America's youth, much to the dismay of their parents; and (3) the nightly network television news broadcasts of battle scenes from Vietnam, which caused viewers to question the rationale for U.S. presence in Vietnam.

Before our interview began, Reverend Brown mentioned that while he was in Hanoi, he was given a rose for his wife, Emily, by Premier Pham Van Dong. Reverend Brown was interviewed in his home in Berkeley, California, on November 13, 1990.

THE REVEREND JOHN PAIRMAN BROWN: I was invited [to go to North Vietnam]. You can ask, why did I accept? Because I thought it would be a good idea to see the other side. We are told that we should get along well with our enemies. Actually, most of us are not very good at it. [I was an Episcopal priest at that time.] I guess once, always. I am [still] in good standing. I had come to the seminary here in Berkeley after returning from several years in the Middle East at the American University in Beirut. I had just gotten fired after, to all intents and purposes, being promised tenure. I was personally in a very vulnerable position, so all I could do was just swim with the tide. I was working with the Episcopal Peace Fellowship [EPF]. [Later], I became the West Coast field staff person for

Clergy and Laity Concerned. I personally delayed the rollout of the B-1 bomber for about three minutes down in Palmdale [California]. The B–1 rollout occurred on October 26, 1974. The *New York Times* had a story the next day in which I marginally figured. . . .

We somehow mysteriously had shown up in Bratislava, which is the head of Slovak resistance now to the government of Prague. Some of the American organizers had hoped to get the Vietnamese Buddhists there, but the other Vietnamese parties were less than interested in that. But there were delegations from the National Liberation Front. At the conclusion, they [the North Vietnamese] said they would like to invite some of us over there. So seven of us ended up going there, myself and the six kids.

I think I can say, with respect to myself, that I considered Tom [Hayden] to be one of the kids. [The members of the group were] Tom and Rennie [Davis], Norm Fruchter, Carol McEldowney, Vivian Rothstein, a black fellow whose name I do not recall [identified by newspaper reports as Robert Brown, a journalist], and myself. Carol McEldowney died, I believe, in a fiery automobile crash in the Midwest.

In Prague, I had to get a cholera shot, and it was in the middle of something which was exactly like [Franz] Kafka's castle. It was the most enormous establishment. My guide got me all the way to the middle of it, and he said, "All right, now, you'll get out again very easily." And I had visions of spending the rest of my days in that fearfully bureaucratic labyrinth in Prague, never getting out again.

I think Dave Dellinger had more to do with the Bratislava conference than anybody else. I know Dave did. The conference was not really billed as a protest but as a chance for us to meet the other side. In fact, we didn't protest; we met the other side. Dave and a few others were, as far as the Americans were concerned, very much in charge. Dave had an extremely mixed bag there, and every once in a while, some then-hotheaded young man who has since, in many ways, joined the establishment and who shall remain nameless here [in response to a direct question, Brown would neither affirm nor deny that he was referring to Tom Hayden] would endeavor to have a briefing, or raise the level of our consciousness, or something like that. But it really didn't take very well.

On the trip [to North Vietnam], we didn't really have any group dynamics. That may seem hard . . . to believe. The two girls were pretty much off by themselves. The four young men — I think they had some real arguments (probably [about] politics, of various interpretations), but they pretty well patched them up. I don't know. I was so far out of their league, in a different league from them. Well, no question but what our party had a leader. After five minutes, however, he totally gave up on me.

[Our trip to Hanoi was a spur of the moment affair.] Naive as I was then and naive as I doubtlessly am still, I think I had a vague, realistic impression that we were precious guests, guests that they wanted to take very good care of, so I expected to be taken care of. Well, it was evident from our contacts in Bratislava we would be honored guests and that we would be very preciously guarded, and so we were.

They wanted us there because they had a good story to tell, and they wanted their story told. They had a really good sense of public relations. Considering that the reaction of the American people was totally different to this war than to any other previous war, I must say that the Vietnamese showed remarkable acumen in figuring out that there was a wave of populist discontent and getting their message out on it.

We proceeded [to Hanoi from Bratislava] in a little old Soviet-made Czech jet, which plopped down every few hundred miles because it was running out of gas. We dropped by Beirut, proceeded across the Middle East and India, and ended up finally in Phnom Penh. From Phnom Penh, we took the regular plane over and back. We stopped off at Vientiane. There were Air America planes, the CIA's airline, taking off and landing, all the time, from Vientiane. I think they had [Air America painted] on them.

Coming back, we went to Hong Kong and thence across the Pacific. I had never been in Southeast Asia before. It was totally new to see a delta rice-growing economy. . . . They had put down these drainpipe air-raid shelters along the road with frogs in the bottom. But we were too big for them, and our Vietnamese friends lay down on top of us [during an air raid]. It was my old outfit. [I had served in the] Army Air Corps, as it was. I had the solid rank of a staff sergeant. I was one of those who got off because I had a higher education. I had studied aerodynamics at graduate school before I was drafted, so they sent me out to the Technical Service Command at Wright Field in Dayton, Ohio, working on the problems of transonic missiles.

[We were under air attack] just once. There were air-raid warnings, however, at the hotel where we stayed. . . . We were out in the paddies again. We visited an antiaircraft gun. It didn't seem to me much more than a heavy machine gun that had a crew of three young ladies. I should guess they were about nineteen. I've got a picture somewhere of us visiting with the young ladies. One of them had made a little bamboo plane. And they would tie the plane at the end of a long fishing rod, and one of the girls would go out and wave it in front, and the other would sit on the seat of the machine gun. I don't know whether she controlled it herself or whether the third young lady controlled it. They would follow the bamboo plane in the sky for hours on end. I think they had shot one down, actually.

We visited a classroom, and the students made a clear distinction between the peace-loving American people and the Washington administration. The lesson in the context of which I doubt we could have gotten an independent opinion. I have no reason to doubt, however, that the North Vietnamese were pretty solid behind the war effort. They had been fighting Western imperialists for a long time. They beat the French, and I believe they believed they were going to beat the Americans.

That's one of the really bad things the French and the Americans did. We turned the Vietnamese into a somewhat militaristic nation, although I am sure they had tendencies in that direction. We saw big, camouflaged, Soviet antiaircraft missiles. They were on big trailers, and just once or twice, we saw some barrage balloons, evidently holding up steel netting. But pains were taken not to show us those missiles and their trailers. . . . It was a mistake when our cavalcade of jeeps went by the missiles. We were meant not to see them. I think there were a few Soviets at the hotel, but I'm not actually certain. It was a very mixed batch of neutrals and what have you at the hotel. . . .

Once we were asked, while in North Vietnam, what our peasants thought about the war. There was a long silence. We responded that we had no peasants. There was never the slightest pressure put on us to make any statement, to write anything, to tape anything. . . . I'm sure if I had a tape recording of conversations in that intentionally very artificial setting that the Vietnamese set up [when we met with the American POWs], I would cringe at it, but I'm sure I have blocked it out. I just feel embarrassed thinking about it. I've done worse in other situations. I didn't feel that we were being trapped into making any commitments that we would later regret. I suspect that some were or some may feel that they were, but I didn't feel that. I wrote some stuff which was printed in the *Christian Century* when I got back. Well, they edited it so fully that I could disclaim anything that was in it. I haven't looked at it for years, and I'm sure that if I looked at it, I'd find a lot of rose-colored glasses in it [laughter].

We didn't have any options when we were over there of saying anything other than what we did. I was perhaps more of a doctrinaire pacifist than what I am now, but it would have been perfectly ridiculous of me to tell them to come to terms with the Americans, and I didn't.

If the Ho Chi Minh Trail had been a four-lane highway, we would have bombed it out of existence in fifteen minutes. It wasn't. It was a constantly shifting network of jeep tracks. . . . We did have a little jeep trip at night on something that felt like the Ho Chi Minh Trail. It would have been indiscreet of me to have asked for it to be identified more precisely. . . .

How can I put this correctly? [pause] They were very nice people, and I don't think that we were shown any Potemkin villages [false-front structures intended to deceive]. I don't think so. Naturally, they put on the best face, but it did gradually come over me that — and maybe not right away — but that the facilities of somebody who was there as a guest of the management for finding out the true state of affairs were somewhat limited. They trotted out the one Protestant minister in residence. He wore a black shirt. . . . He looked like a Protestant minister. It looked very funny on the Vietnamese scene. I believe he had the party line.

We had trouble getting out of Hanoi because the plane was having a problem. So one day, they absolutely ran out of things for us to do, and our guide was really beside himself. He was a great admirer of Agatha Christie. So finally, he said, "We will go see a film animations studio." It was rather boring, but they presented this great Vietnamese presentation to us, and they said, "We all have unbounded admiration for that greatest of American artists, Walt Disney." I shouldn't ever consider that a moment of humor. . . .

[In] the antiwar movement, against the war in Vietnam, beyond the shadow of any doubt, Martin Luther King Jr. [was the most effective individual]. Unquestionably. It's really sad to see all the people jumping on him after his death. I am sure he did have a lot of mistresses. All this business about the plagiarism and his Ph.D. thesis is something that everybody else does. That business is just absurdly blown out of size. His relations with women were very complicated. It corresponded with a very deep psychic need on his part, but just think where he came from. Out from that privileged situation of the black clergy on whom the black community was totally dependent. He broke out from that. He saw what Gandhi was doing far away, but he translated it. He built the civil rights movement; he brought it up to the point of success, and then he put all of that behind him and said, "Furthermore, we've got to say something more." It's just astounding.

[The most effective antiwar organization was] the U.S. Congress. No. Actually, it was the Holy Spirit of God and the U.S. Congress. The opposition to the war in Vietnam was triggeredby the TV shots of GIs and helicopters burning villages and the Selective Service system reaching into American homes. But the actual organizing wasn't done by Clergy and Laity Concerned, which I worked for, or any such organization but the rain coming down from heaven and watering little local coffee groups that sprung up like mushrooms all across the land. That's what I mean by the work of the Holy Spirit.

The [antiwar] organizations, almost to a man, were counterproductive. The reason that Congress cut off the funding [for the war] was because their constituents told them to, and they were not being deceived. They saw that we were not winning and that it was time to pull out. . . . The organization [that] really brought an end to it was the Selective Service system because the Selective Service system reached into every living room in America. And it picked up the kids. It was just on the verge of picking up my boys, but it didn't quite. Not merely all the black mothers and grandmothers in the ghetto, whose kids joined the army to get a leg up on life, but middle-class moms and dads, whose kids got drafted, whose kids didn't claim some kind of conscientious objector status but duly went and duly went along. They said, "What kind of a war is this that the kid is in?"

The other organization was the silver screen [network television evening news]. They all watched the silver screen. They watched the silver screen, and they saw what was going on, and they said, "I don't think Johnnie ought to be doing that." It was little pockets of resistance springing up all across the land, just like mushrooms after rain, that no organization had the faintest thing to do with bringing into being. The organizations co-opted those little ladies' coffee klatches. But what happened perfectly spontaneously all across the country was what did it, and the organizations just came along afterwards and claimed the credit, [but it was] the Selective Service system and the silver screen and the U.S. Congress [that were most influential in ending the war]. . . . What happened in My Lai came out fairly soon, fairly fully. The communiqués from the front, right up to the end, said, "We're winning; we're winning." But for that to qualify as a deception, the people would have to be deceived. Congress wasn't deceived. I don't think that Americans were.

If you go over to the United Methodist Church in south Berkeley tonight, you will find a bunch of folks sleeping around it. A lot of them are Vietnam vets with bad paper [dishonorable discharges from the armed services]. Some of them are Vietnam vets with good paper [honorable discharges]. I think people agree that there's been almost a total failure of any real effort to rehabilitate them back to society. It was bad enough after other wars. People didn't want to hear about Vietnam. They didn't want to even see any Vietnam vets. So they are only marginalized all across our society, and if people know that, then it's almost too late to do anything about it.

The Vietnam War . . . was a horrible mistake. Winning it couldn't possibly have done any good. The conduct of it has had very bad effects upon our society. [It is similar to a] part of Roman law called *damnosa haereditas*, in which an inheritance consists entirely of debts rather than assets. And it [the Vietnam War] carried on the bad pattern of the Korean War, by which the president of the United States had come to feel himself empowered to declare war by not declaring war, by just conducting it and never taking it to the Congress. It's cut a big wedge right down the middle of American society, which is far from ended. I'm still estranged from a bunch of my in-laws. It seems like a pretty small world to me.

The nation as a whole, peace people and militarists, have accepted as their own the Vietnam War Memorial in Washington, which was designed by that very clever Oriental young lady. It's a national shrine. Nobody would dare deface it. It's sacred to all sides. The Vietnamese knew that, too. They didn't have anything against the GIs. They shot at them, and they blew them up, but they knew that the GIs had been drafted; they knew that they were still predominantly blacks and Hispanics and poor people, poor boys.

It might be good for us not to overwhelm them [the Vietnamese] with tourists in the immediate future. It passes my understanding about how completely we've adopted the Japanese, and the Japanese have adopted us. I was in both Hiroshima and Nagasaki, and all our hosts, the church people, the Buddhists, according to their stories, were so glad to have Americans come and visit with them. I don't understand what's going on in Japanese minds at all. I think they are rather exceptional. I should think that the Vietnamese might feel just a shade of awkwardness at having a whole lot of Americans around. Maybe I am wrong, I don't know.

12

Anne Weills

Anne Weills went to North Vietnam in 1968 and returned to the United States with three American POWs. During the five weeks she was in North Vietnam, she traveled around the countryside, sometimes with the POWs, while waiting for the U.S. State Department and the North Vietnamese government to agree on the format of the POWs' release. Although only in her twenties, she visited with Prime Minister Pham Van Dong and toured what could be labeled the North Vietnamese "banquet circuit," making speeches and meeting individuals from all levels and sectors of North Vietnamese society.

Weills participated in student protest movements against the Vietnam War across the United States. In our interview, she described her experiences in some of the demonstrations that became violent. Former wife of *Los Angeles Times* reporter Robert Scheer and companion to Tom Hayden during the Chicago Seven trial, she spoke frankly about her antiwar activities and of the radical Weathermen group. As a student activist, she had believed that political change probably would occur only through violent means. She and many other individuals her age crisscrossed the United States during the war, networking with others, primarily on college campuses, to express and demonstrate their solidarity against the war. Weills described the efforts of the Vietnam Day Committee of Berkeley, California, to prevent the passage of troop trains through Berkeley, as well as a confrontation between student demonstrators and the police that escalated into violence and death. She also expressed doubt that the U.S. government would ever admit to error with respect to Vietnam. Weills, an attorney, was interviewed in her Oakland, California, law office on Wednesday, November 14, 1990.

ANNE WEILLS: I first went to Vietnam in 1966, with my husband [Robert Scheer]. He was a reporter and editor for *Ramparts* magazine. We went to do some investigatory work. We were in Saigon and did a lot of interviews. Then we were in Cambodia for a month and attempted to interview [Prince] Sihanouk.

I guess [my interest in Vietnam is connected with] my generation. My husband was very active in the antiwar movement, too, actually both husbands. In fact, [Robert] Scheer just had an article published in the October issue of *Playboy*. I hate the fact that he writes for *Playboy*. But it was an editorial, it was on Vietnam, and it was on normalizing relations. Bobby [Scheer] is incredibly busy.

Let's see, I was a student in Paris in the early sixties — '62, '63 — and learned French through reading *Le Monde* and as a student there. Vietnam was still very much a French topic of conversation because of Dien Bien Phu. When I was in Paris, Algeria was the struggle, but there were all these analogies to Vietnam. I came back to the U.S. in 1964, through a series of incidents, events, whatever. Bobby knew about Vietnam. He was researching for *Ramparts* magazine, for [Warren] Hinckle [former president and editorial director of *Ramparts*], this thing on Tom Dooley, how the U.S. got involved in Vietnam. He wrote a pamphlet for the Center for the Study of Democratic Institutions in Santa Barbara. We were the only people we knew who really knew anything about Vietnam. I helped research a lot of the stuff that he did for the magazine and for this pamphlet. So between '64 and '74, about ninety percent of our existence, which may be an exaggeration, was spent waging against the war.

Bobby and I first did all of this research and writing. He did most of the writing. Then, with a lot of other student radicals at Berkeley, we organized this Vietnam Day Committee. We didn't see ourselves so much as radicals, but a lot of us had come out of the civil rights movement. We had been active in that, and then [President] Kennedy started to send troops. It became more and more of a public U.S. strategy to get involved in Vietnam. Troop trains were going through Berkeley. Our first activities, as the Vietnam Day Committee, were trying to stop these troop trains from the Oakland Army Terminal coming through Berkeley. We had demonstrations down at the railroad tracks, stopping troop trains. Then, in 1965, we actually organized more politically, and then Bob ran for Congress in 1965. In 1966 we went to Vietnam, as well as Cambodia, as journalists.

In 1967 there were a lot of national organizations developing around Vietnam. We still had our local Vietnam Day Committee. We had a series of huge demonstrations. In one of them, we encountered the Hell's

Angels. One of the first demonstrations (actually, this was funny) was outside this building. If you look out the window of my office, Telegraph Avenue runs all the way to the Berkeley campus; it's like a straight line to the campus. We marched from the campus all the way down here to this building because Jeffrey Cohelan was the Democratic congressman at that time.

Cohelan, a so-called liberal, supported LBJ. He was one of these Democratic hawks. This was a VDC kind of demonstration, not one of the more legitimate mainstream demonstrations against Cohelan, and we, a couple thousand people, marched up to this building.

That takes care of 1964, 1965, and 1966. Then in 1967, I had a child. There were a series of demonstrations in the Bay Area. We were sort of developing this national movement against the war. I was one of the titular leaders, so-called, [of the demonstration]. But women, of course, didn't get recognized in the same way. We used to make jokes about meetings, how at a VDC meeting there typically would be twenty or thirty people. A female would get up and say, "I think this is a good tactic. We should do this. This should be our strategy." And then silence. "Sit down." The next person, male, gets up and says exactly the same thing. He would receive applause and cheers. Women were very much leadership, in terms of doing the work, both in the VDC and Scheer's campaign for Congress and in leading some of these demonstrations and taking great risks, when it got to be more violent. [However], we didn't get much media recognition. We had a huge "Stop the Draft Week," a series of demonstrations here. The federal reservation, as it is called, is just a couple blocks away from this building, and that's where they would bring in all these young draftees and put them on the buses. Joan Baez led one which was nonviolent. We had another one which was more militant, hundreds of people arrested, and some people injured by the police. Then there was a huge series of trials of the leadership of "Stop the Draft Week," of which I was chair of the committee. It was conspiracy to riot and the usual charges involved with demonstrations. They all got off.

In 1968 we organized for the Democratic [National] Convention. I went to Vietnam right before the convention, in August 1968, for almost five weeks. I saw [Ambassador] Averell Harriman in Paris before we left. He thought we were going to go and seduce and trick all of these poor POWs. They actually greased our whole trip. There were three of us: Stewart Meacham, head of the Asian Division of the American Friends Service Committee; Vernon Grizzard, a draft resister from Boston, who was the head of the Boston Resistance; and myself.

In Vientiane, we saw the U.S. ambassador, William Sullivan, who ended up in Teheran during the hostage crisis. He's been around. I remember coming into the airport in Hanoi, and it was after the bombing. There was a cessation of the bombing, and they were meeting in Paris. It was relatively quiet. There was one bombing while we were there. We happened to be at the Cuban embassy at the time. We all went to their underground bunkers or whatever they were. Actually, there were very few problems during that August of 1968.

We were in Vietnam for five weeks because the U.S. and the North Vietnamese couldn't agree how these POWs [Maj. Fred Thompson, Capt. Joseph Carpenter, and Capt. James Low] would return. We were coming from Hanoi to Vientiane, and the U.S. wanted the POWs to be taken from Vientiane by military airplane to Andrews Air Force Base in D.C. And the Vietnamese, who were releasing these people as a gesture to the American people, in terms of showing their humanitarianism towards the pilots and their desire to end the war, wanted the POWs to go via commercial airlines back to New York and then give a little speech. And then they would give the POWs over to the military. So, Harriman and the Vietnamese warred about that for three or four weeks. At one point, the North Vietnamese even considered putting us on a flight to Vladivostok that would have returned us through the Soviet Union.

[Meanwhile], we traveled around with the POWs. They would take the pilots with us out to the countryside, and we would go to the Zoo [a North Vietnamese prison to which American POWs were confined]. We were allowed to be with them for long periods of time, to interview them, to hang out with them. It made them feel better because we went to the prison where they were when we first got there, and they were released to our custody by the military, by these generals. That was one prison. I saw one other prison while I was in Hanoi. I'm not even sure which [POW prison] was which. I was only twenty-two or twenty-three when all of this was going on.

In hindsight, why didn't I tape-record all of this? Why didn't I take notes? Stewart took very good notes and wrote up a lot of reports for the State Department and for all the different agencies which were interested. He was more mature and is now deceased.

The pilots didn't get to go too far with us. We went to Ha Long Bay and Haiphong without them. We saw a lot of North Vietnam during those five weeks. We went to the South through Vinh and some of the cities that had been seriously demolished. We went almost to the DMZ [demilitarized zone]. We went all the way to the Chinese border.

We traveled. Low talked about when he was shot down. He was also a pilot in the Korean War. I think he was an ace fighter pilot who had this huge reputation. He was an ace MIG-attacker or destroyer. He was flying from Udorn, from bases in Thailand, and bombing North Vietnam. He was shot down over Vietnam, literally by a woman, an older woman. She was a militia woman, an antiaircraft person in her little village.

Low landed and looked around and could not believe that these were the people who are waging this war. He was taken south, towards the DMZ, by cart and different forms of transportation to Hanoi. He went on and on about how he could not believe that such a primitive political economy and society could be waging this incredible war. It caused the American pilots, over a period of time, I think, to have extraordinary respect for the Vietnamese because they had managed to be so successful.

We had these long interviews with the pilots, particularly Low, who had become very cynical about the machinations of the U.S. because he knew about the role of the CIA. He knew in great detail what they were doing in Thailand and in a lot of these more subversive, sort of counterinsurgency strategems. So I said to Stewart, "I want to tape these guys." Stewart said they didn't want to be taped. I said, "We should tape them anyway." Stewart said, "No. Can't do that." Vern and I acted more like we're working for the Vietnamese, and Stewart was more your upright American. So that state of mind was that if we had loyalties, they definitely were more for the Vietnamese than to the United States. I think that was our state of mind at the time.

[We saw no other Americans.] No. Actually, not. In the hotel, Thong Nhat, the hotel for all the foreigners: great food, French and Vietnamese, but no Americans. At one of the museums, I remember seeing names of several Americans who had been there before us, signing in and stuff.

I have some pictures of us at a meeting with [Pham Van Dong]. . . . We spoke with him for about an hour and a half. He was very philosophical and intellectually interesting. He covered a lot of ground, not just the war with the United States. He talked a lot, as I recall, about the peace talks in Paris and how they were going and their struggles to end the bombing and what their strategy was, tactically — how they would do this and the U.S. would do that. They went into such great detail with us. In hindsight, that was pretty amazing since we weren't government leaders.

But it's funny how they treated us as very serious people in the United States. I was a leader in women's liberation which, to them, was somewhat suspect, although also a leader in the antiwar movement. So we reflected a lot of constituencies in American society on which they put a lot of weight because within the United States, we were sort of their, however they perceived it, their fifth column or whatever. We were clearly helping them end the war through our struggles in the United States. They treated us with great respect. I met some generals who were in charge of the prisoners. I have their names. I met the head of the National Liberation Front, [Gen. Van] Tien [Dung], who was in North Vietnam then. I met Cuban ambassadors. We met some high-ranking Eastern European officials. They'd take you to these banquets, and you would give a little speech. The foreign ministry people would all give speeches. I was interviewed by the *Hanoi Daily*.

I think Stewart felt [awkward at times], being older and being less politically active and activist than, say, Vernon and I. Plus, Stewart was less radical politically. We were out there, fighting in the streets, and he was an administrator and more tied to the State Department, even though he was in the AFSC. We had some struggles with him, actually, over how to deal with the pilots. We saw that if we were going to take leadership in the world, in terms of a certain political moral authority, it would be from the Vietnamese. I had no qualms at all. I felt empowered in a certain way and also exhilarated by the fact that I could have this relationship, that I could have these conversations. In a way, we could be considered, I guess, traitors or whatever.

I've never seen the cohesion within a society that I saw in North Vietnam [in 1968]. It was extraordinary. We would be in groups of people, say highly sophisticated leaders from the foreign ministry, generals. This would be one group. Then we would be with a chauffeur, a translator, and maybe a student, and sometimes we would travel with these groups. Within the Vietnamese themselves, despite differences in age, in status, and I am sure culture, background, the things that we weren't even aware of because they were too subtle maybe for us to perceive, the way that people dealt with each other with such a high degree of respect and unity seemed incredibly warm, respectful, and supportive. It was just the way that they communicated with each other. I was so struck by this sense of high purpose and unity and everybody committed to the greater good, I guess is the way to put it. It was extraordinary.

In 1969 we just warred for most of my youth, a good chunk of it, anyway, about Vietnam. So I think that's why, particularly for me, [my] trip to Hanoi [influenced me] very profoundly. We were not particularly ideological but saw ourselves as sort of revolutionaries, socialists. It was not very precise. We went from a period early on of being reformers and then radicals, and then, at a certain point, we became (more like 1969) more like revolutionaries because we didn't see society responding to this horrible crime that we saw being perpetrated on the TV every night. We just couldn't stand it. We were going crazy in all kinds of ways because it just so oppressed us.

[Did I encourage other Americans to go to Hanoi?] Oh yes. And still do. You should understand that it was considered a great honor to be able to go to Vietnam, for us in the antiwar movement, [and] to meet Mme [Nguyen Thi] Binh . . . in Paris. These were our heroines and heroes because we didn't have too many domestic models of these righteous, courageous sort of people. We had internalized, I think, that the Vietnamese were right and the U.S. was wrong, although, in retrospect, we were very simplistic in some of our politics. Anybody who had the opportunity to go to Vietnam was just so excited and jumped at the chance. It was not common. There was a war going on, and you could maybe get a seven-day pass to go into South Vietnam as a tourist, journalist, or whatever. Seven days and you're out, unless you had State Department or military kind of privileges of some kind. So to get to go to North Vietnam. Wow. The Vietnamese were very selective and did not invite or bring in very many Americans.

Dave Dellinger and the National Mobilization to End the War in Vietnam, the "Mobe," as we used to call it, [arranged our trip to Vietnam]. That was the group, although the State Department paid for a bunch of it because they had a contradictory feeling about us. They wanted us to go. They wanted these pilots back. They wanted to debrief these pilots. They wanted to know what was happening to the POWs and, I'm sure, a lot of other things. They wanted us to go. So they put us on the plane; they'd take us to the ambassador [in Laos]. I don't know exactly how it broke down financially, in the end, but I know the State Department facilitated a lot. The ICC [International Control Commission] flight that went from Bangkok to Vientiane, Vientiane to Hanoi was paid for, I think, by U.S. moneys.

[When I returned from Vietnam], I did some television in New York and San Francisco with the *Dick Cavett Show*. Victor Borge, the pianist, was one of my fellow panelists, and he thought I was just horrible. This was all on TV. The old arguments about Vietnam, North Vietnam, the war. He thought I was, I guess, very unpatriotic, although I don't know if he is even an American.

There was that suspicion that we were brainwashed, that we were just agents of the North Vietnamese, but as I pointed out earlier, we were not brainwashed, and we were not agents. But the way we thought about the war and about the way we thought of the whole of the United States, we, in some ways, probably were. I remember debating a congressman from San Mateo County who had been in the Korean War, a very moderate, liberal Republican. We had this somewhat extended debate. I got a lot of positive support because a lot of people felt that our discussion was complex enough so that he wasn't so one-sided, so pro-Nixon, and I wasn't so extreme. They felt it was a very interesting and reasonable discussion. I got baited for being, I suppose, a Communist or a radical. We thought we were patriotic. You see, that's the great irony. I remember being told, "If you were a patriotic American, you would be supporting our boys in Vietnam." I said: "Are you kidding? We're the ones trying to stop the troop trains. We think no Americans should go to Vietnam. We think it horrible that Americans are dying. Why do you think we are crying every night when we watch the TV and sort of tearing our hair out as to how we're going to stop the war?"

It was just horrible for us because these were our peers, our brothers and sisters. My younger brother got a deferment for some nerve damage in his leg; first he had a student deferment, then he had that deferment. But my father, a conservative Republican, thought that my younger brother should go; it would make a man out of him and all that. Of course, I'm sure he would have died, had it happened. . . .

You have to realize that we live in northern California. If you think of regions of the country, the Bay Area in particular has always been a tolerant, relatively progressive, enlightened area. We started early demonstrating against the war. By the time I went to Vietnam in 1968, we might not have been in the majority, but there was a lot of support for our views, even though they might have been on the cutting edge.

I went back to Vietnam in 1988. My older son was an exchange student at UCSB [University of California, Santa Barbara]. UC has an exchange program with the University of Thailand. He was a foreign student at Chiang Mai, which is an extension of the University of Thailand. We visited him, and then I took my youngest son to visit Vietnam.

I retraced all my steps of twenty years ago when I had gone to North Vietnam in 1968 to bring back the three Navy pilots. I was going through a drawer the other day. I found pictures of all my pilots; we were on the plane, saying good-bye to North Vietnam. We brought back a major and two captains. It was interesting to go back twenty years ago to Hanoi and to Haiphong and Ha Long Bay and see what I had seen twenty years ago. The horrible thing was that it was worse than it was in 1969. We were there for about two weeks, from December 1988 to January 1989. We went to the New Year's Eve party that the Australian government gave at their embassy in Hanoi, which was great fun.

Returning to Hanoi was sort of like Rip Van Winkle. It was like everything was older but exactly the same. More decrepit. The airport was exactly the same, except falling apart, not having been painted, kept up, or maintained in years. The poverty was just incredible. The people were poorer in 1988 than they were in 1968.

As it turns out, we were there during a massive inflationary period where the government had basically restructured its economy. I don't know all of the particulars, but there was a big shift in the way they organized their economy. Basically, it's because they don't have money, because there's been no trade, and because there's been this horrible austerity for twenty years or even longer. . . . When [President] Reagan came in, it was hard-line, anti-Vietnam. They've basically been starved. The U.S. embargo has been very effective. The U.S. kept all the Western European countries and Japan and ASEAN [Association of Southeast Asian Nations] from trading with Vietnam. The South, however, is economically much better off than the North. It has all the infrastructure (the telecommunications, the roads) left by the Americans. Historically, they operate in a much more capitalistic context, in which markets seem to flourish and are more successful economically than the North.

The North is depressed. People in the streets were depressed. There were feelings of anxiety and despair and undercurrents of real hostility toward the government. Disillusionment with the political system was profound. It was almost as if those characteristics of the national culture that enabled them to win the war and to be so powerful and so unified against the United States were not compatible with a nation at peace.

There is incredible austerity at home because they don't have trade with the West. Certain Japanese companies have come in, and there is limited development and manufacturing. Some trade is developing, but this is all very recent. In fact, it was just beginning in 1988. The *Indochina Digest* chronicles a lot of the new trade relations and agreements that Vietnam is developing with both Asian countries and Western European countries, basically the EC [European Community] countries.

The government took us to an outlying area of Hanoi, to a pagoda. There we saw poverty to the extent that children were begging. There were even signs of malnutrition in some of these children, and these are just beautiful children (those eyes), but you could see it with their bellies. It was so difficult for me to deal with because I felt that but for the United States, this would be an incredibly prosperous country in Southeast Asia because the Vietnamese are very self-disciplined and hard-working. For me, as an American, I was crying half the time because we made war against these people for reasons that, really, don't make sense in my mind.

What's so horrible is that when you go back, you see that not only have we waged this war but then we starve them. There's all these quotes of Henry Kissinger and Deng Xiaoping of China, meeting and talking about how they were going to bleed Vietnam white and use U.S. dominance over the IMF [International Monetary Fund] and the World Bank and all these international economic agencies that give loans to developing countries to basically block Vietnam's development. And they have been successful. It is pitiful.

[When I returned to Vietnam], you saw dissension. You saw disillusionment. It's been how many years of war? First the French, then the Americans, and then the Cambodian civil war. It's like a war weariness. Of all the ideals that they felt might be realized after the war, none of them (at least economically) came to fruition. They were starved. Postwar, they were already weak because of their investment in the war. Then came the economic embargoes of the West and their reliance upon the Soviets and the Eastern Europeans who gave them considerable economic support. It's sort of like not thinking smart.

They built huge industrial plants for Vietnam that did not fit their economic superstructure or infrastructure at all. It seems as if a lot of investment was wrongly invested, so that it didn't have the proper kind of effect in terms of helping the economy develop. There was this sort of falling from grace, a sort of disillusionment, a cynicism. These young people could care less. The images of the heroes and heroines of the war against the Americans, which were very real in 1968, 1969, 1970, and early 1970s, had faded, and there was nothing positive in between to bring the younger generation in to play a very positive [leadership] role.

In 1974 and then in 1979, they invaded Cambodia for a number of reasons, one of which was that Pol Pot was massacring Vietnamese civilians on the border. But then they've been at war again. They left Cambodia in large numbers last year. They lost almost as many as the Americans lost in Vietnam, almost sixty thousand Vietnamese, fighting the Cambodians, fighting Pol Pot and the Khmer Rouge.

I am so disappointed in the postwar political leadership. The great irony for me is that the government that led this struggle to win the war against the United States as a political leadership, postwar, has been terrible. I think they have failed just miserably to take advantage of the moral authority they had internationally after the war, to organize a sort of counterpolitical struggle against the United States around this embargo. They had a lot of friends internationally after the war, and the U.S embargo was illegitimate and wrong. I think they should have organized against it. Instead, they put all their weight with the Soviets and the Eastern Europeans, relying upon them for economic development, and then because of the changes in the Soviet Union and Eastern Europe, that aid is now being cut off or diminished considerably or as the Soviets are doing, treating Vietnam as any other capitalist trading partner. I think it's true not only in Vietnam. Underdeveloped countries, in order to fight colonialism or imperialism or whatever, are constantly at war and develop a political structure more suited to war. But after the war is over, they don't know how to operate in peacetime. They aren't really economists, and they lack the political leadership to create a more democratic, economically viable society.

I read, I do keep up with this. There are, as in every culture or society, a lot of internal contradictions within the [Communist] Party itself. When we were in North Vietnam in '88, '89, I had an interview with someone in the justice ministry. He was in the foreign ministry when I met him in 1968. Swan Wine is his name. He gave us a very in-depth interview. I was with a group of professors from the United States, who were traveling with another group. He was incredibly critical of the government.

Swan Wine feels, as do others, that there is this old guard, like in China, rigid, hidebound, an oligarchical group that refuses to give up power, who are antidemocratic, authoritarian, and patriarchal, who just don't know how to give up power to this younger generation. And then there's a younger generation, relatively speaking, in their forties and fifties, who want to democratize, who want to liberalize, both politically and economically, but have not been allowed to. In fact, at the National Assembly in 1987 and 1988, the government finally agreed to economic liberalization in terms of more free markets that would take government out of a lot of areas of commerce they had formerly totally controlled and dominated. But they are still holding back on political liberalization.

There's been an intense struggle within the National Assembly to do this. There's the younger generation of politically progressive Vietnamese in the Communist Party (very analagous to China and what happened in Tiananmen Square) who want to liberalize and use the best of what they consider to be socialism and integrate it with the best that they see in capitalism and then create this new model for development. But the old guard has resisted and, ironically I think, help[ed] the most reactionary, the most backward Vietnamese. It's an alliance of the hardest line in the government and the most conservative sort with the reactionary Vietnamese because I don't think the hard-line wants liberalization. They fear they are going to lose their power. In the last few years, they have deported friends of Vietnam, people who worked for the Mennonites internationally, and a lot of nongovernmental organizations that aided countries in Indochina because they were bringing in bourgeois, liberal newspapers and bringing in foreign ideas.

The old guard within the Vietnamese Communist Party feels that if it allows liberalization, Vietnam will be like Eastern Europe and that they will no longer exist; they will be out of power. And that fear of being out of power has led to increased political repression in the last few years, beyond what was the case three or four years ago. But the power struggle within Vietnam, I suppose, is healthy. I just hope the good guys win.

[Looking back on the sixties], we weren't particularly self-critical in that period. We were very self-righteous. That really characterized our sense of ourselves because we were waging the war against the war. I think tactically, when we got into this Weathermen politics, we got into fighting the police as the agents of the government because we couldn't get to Henry Kissinger. So we carried out the warfare in our streets, through these demonstrations and riots or whatever. It doesn't seem right to treat the police as agents of the government, but in fact, that's as close as many of us would come, and we certainly wrote letters and fought with our representatives to do something. I think we operated in those ten years or so at every level conceivable, in terms of trying to impact policy and change policy.

I wasn't [a Weatherman], but I was living with Tom Hayden from 1968 to 1971, and I was in Chicago during his conspiracy trial, and I worked with "Weather People," as we called them, and was involved in some of those demonstrations. During that period, I defended a lot of their politics, within a political context. The Weathermen attacked a lot of the rest of the movement for not taking up the gun and taking up the fight in this more militant and more aggressive way. I was part of that "tendency," as we used to call ourselves, different groups and stuff.

There was a period of about a year, 1969, I would say, where we went through this whole fight with Peoples' Park [in Berkeley]. That was something which we really created and thought was very valuable. And then they took it away from us. Reagan was the governor of California. He was ideologically the total opposite. He was making war on us. They were strafing the university with tear gas, and we were students. Hayden and I and a bunch of us were close to being killed that day in May of 1969. We were right near where James Rector was killed in Peoples' Park. They were throwing tear gas canisters at us, and we were throwing them back. Then the second group of county sheriffs came up and shot around the area where we were and killed this man who was on the roof.

All these events radicalized us, consistently. I remember at the end of that Peoples' Park, they brought in the National Guard. They were in Berkeley (troops, machine guns, and tanks), in Berkeley. We just became increasingly alienated and radicalized. The Weather People started doing these bombings. They were against banks, against institutions like that, nothing too profound. We were just at our wit's end. Whatever works [laughter], we're going to try. Just on that, I think some of our tactics got a little off the wall. In hindsight, they were less than effective, and also what they did was isolate us from the broader antiwar movement.

I don't quite agree with this, but a lot of my peers from the movement felt that the Weathermen and the most radical tendencies within the antiwar movement basically killed the possibility for an ongoing national organization. It sort of resulted from that period. Weathermen killed SDS, and SDS had been the framework that brought together all these students and all these people. There's a big debate in certain circles around that question.

Interestingly, as a woman, and this goes to the women's liberation movement, which came later in the sixties and early seventies, I think we had a somewhat different way of organizing, a different way of articulating our position about Vietnam. I think if women had taken on more leadership, although this may be very idealistic, we might have softened a lot of the edges of the movement, which might have then made it more inclusive versus this more hostile, kind of aggressive character that I think it had, particularly towards the end. I don't know.

I see a lot of analogies to [Vietnam in] the Persian Gulf. . . . Here we have this huge intelligence community, the NSA [National Security Agency], the CIA, all the different agencies of the government, and look at the abysmal job they do in terms of intelligence. [There have been many] criticisms of the CIA in terms of the Soviet Union, how the CIA was predicting this huge, powerful Russia, this economic force that was going to do us in, and since [Leonid] Brezhnev, since the middle seventies, the Soviet Union has been falling apart. Now we're seeing it obviously falling apart.

I think that the reasons we [the U.S. armed forces] went into Vietnam were illogical and weren't consistent with reality. Any investigation of Asian history would have found that the Chinese have had hostilities with the Vietnamese forever, continuing to this day. Right after the Vietnamese invaded Cambodia, the Chinese invaded Cambodia because the Cambodians, the Khmer Rouge, were their allies, and they wanted to destabilize Vietnam. They don't want a Vietnamese-dominated Indochina. If only we had done our homework.

Our politics, our military aggression, is based on really fraudulent historical and political analysis. We made grievous kinds of errors that caused countless numbers of Americans to die or be maimed. . . . Besides all those Americans killed, in Oakland today, we have homeless Vietnam vets; we have an extraordinary number of Vietnam vets who are dysfunctional because of that war.

I don't want another generation, this generation, of young people to suffer, to go to Iraq, to die. For what? If it [the threat] is articulated and real, like the Nazis were, in terms of their invasion of Europe and Eastern Europe, of course we should go to war. We have to defend democracy in the world, but I think that's not the case with Iraq and certainly wasn't the case with Vietnam.

The greatest deception of the war was that somehow, if we didn't go to war with Vietnam, there would be all these Vietnamese on the coast of California, trying to destroy our society. I guess it goes to the heart of this fear of communism. Interestingly, we grew up in this Bay Area. My first political act was fighting the HUAC, which had come to San Francisco to investigate all these communist labor leaders. We thought the whole thing was a joke. I don't know exactly how we came to think that way.

As kids, we didn't internalize at all the anticommunist ideological baggage that came through J. Edgar Hoover, the McCarthy period, and post–Second World War. It all seemed silly and absurd, to demonize a country, an ideology. You just don't demonize it, characterize it, and deform it to fit your ideological bent. Although, I think, ironically, we did . . . [demonize the United States] in the late sixties when we [the antiwar activists] became more ideological, political, and made some of these errors in the reverse. We also, I think, idealized the Chinese and the Cubans and the Vietnamese. They were the heroes. But I think to assume that Vietnam was a threat to the security of the United States was absurd.

[Misunderstandings about the war] go to the underpinnings of the Cold War because that's the reason we went to fight in Vietnam, as a continuation of the Cold War. I don't know who said this, but basically, "war is political aggression that's taken to a military level." We had been fighting with the Soviet Union and their allies since the war. I think Vietnam was seen as just an ally of China and then the Soviet Union. We're going to stop the spread of communism by any means necessary, and I think all other errors or deceptions flowed from that.

We [the antiwar activists] never bought it, and I think a lot of the American people who trust their leadership had bought into this anticommunist hysteria or nonhysteria, thinking, "Yes, we're good; they're evil." "The evil empire," as Reagan described it. So if you characterize something as evil, then the Viet Minh and Viet Cong become the evil communists. And you dehumanize them, and then you can make war and kill them.

I'm not sure [that I would have done anything differently], except to have done more and to have done it better because I think we did get somewhat isolated politically because we became so radical politically, ideologically. As we became more antiwar and more anti–the U.S. government, we became more identified with the revolutionaries of Cuba, China, and Vietnam, and I think as we became more doctrinaire, politically, ideologically, we then alienated ourselves from your more typical American who might, for obvious reasons, have been against the war. We sort of isolated ourselves.

It's hard [to say which individual in the antiwar movement was the most effective] because I know a lot of their weaknesses, having been pretty closely linked to a lot of them, but Dave Dellinger strikes me, maybe because he started out a pacifist, remained a pacifist, and probably still is a pacifist. He was always a more stable, sane element and also consistently a leader, although older than most of us. He was just a very strong role model and a very good leader. He was very ethical and principled in a way that a lot of the leadership of the antiwar movement individually were not, like some of the conspirators in Chicago — for example; the Yippies, Jerry Rubin and Abbie Hoffman (although Abbie was brilliant). Abbie was fantastic. His suicide was truly a suicide. Some people suspect more conspiracy theories, which I think are ridiculous.

I guess SDS, with some qualifications, [was the most effective anti-war organization]. SDS was never much of a West Coast group. We had a series of coalitions in the Bay Area, which involved all the antiwar groups, the women's groups, the environmental groups, and minority groups, to varying degrees. These coalitions totaled maybe ten thousand but were able to organize demonstrations of up to two hundred thousand people at Golden Gate Park against the war. Some groups obviously were much broader than others. Those coalitions had different names, but the National "Mobe," for example, was basically a Midwest, East Coast coalition of antiwar people, groups, and organizations. On the West Coast, we had our own. We had the Vietnam Day Committee that went on for about four or five years. Then we started organizing more in the communities and formed the Community for New Politics. But if I wanted to pick one in that early period, which was very critical for the development of a national antiwar movement, I would say probably SDS. The SDS would come out here and hook up with us, and we were organized in these other formations. The networks were incredible. We had what you might call an international youth network, with SDS being the basic infrastructure, which would hook up to every antiwar group at every campus. All the Cal-UC campuses were a part of the network. This network was hooked up to German students at German universities. We had contacts in Japan, all through Western Europe, England, and Australia. I haven't read much about it in any of the books. There aren't too many books on the sixties yet.

Danny the Red [a young radical from Germany] came. He talked to us. These Germans would come through Berkeley, and we Americans would go to France, or to England, or to Germany. And we had money. That was another thing I think is not dealt with. In the sixties, I think they say now, the dollar was worth four times as much as it is now. And there was a lot of fat. There was a lot of prosperity. There were a lot of government programs. I guess there was all that poverty money, although that didn't affect us.

I can remember, we just had a lot of money, and a certain percentage of us had trust funds. I had a trust for school. I would go to school for six months, and then I'd drop out for six months to do political stuff, and then I'd go back to school for six months [laughter], and so I was a professional student, I'd say, for five or six years. You'd get a ticket from your mother to go somewhere or go do something, and instead, you'd go somewhere else. That was the period when *Ramparts,* for example, was funded by heirs and heiresses, who had considerable estates that they had inherited. In the late sixties, early seventies, a lot of that same group of young, wealthy people gave their money to foundations, or they would create foundations, which basically distributed their income or their wealth. In that early period, the prefoundation period, people would say, "Oh, great idea," and give you all this money to do something. We had a lot of freedom to travel. With or without an organizational structure, we were this network where everybody was traveling and communicating. It was like, "Have briefcase, will travel." People just traveled. We went all around the country, talking.

After the invasion of Cambodia, there were about twenty-five thousand people from around the U.S. at Yale in New Haven for a conference on the Black Panther Party. Bobby Seale and Ericka Huggins were on trial there for the murder of some agent who had been killed. We had just come to give them support and have this rally. That happened the same day we heard the announcement about the U.S. invasion of Cambodia. This was May 1, 1970. Everybody just went crazy. All of the speeches. Everybody started organizing. We organized this kind of an assault on all the eastern seaboard campuses, in just about every major university and college in the East. . . .

There were networks within networks. SDS was a chunk of it, but everybody working together, and everybody's network intersecting with everybody else's. And so within a few weeks, we organized this huge march on Washington, in which I think there were maybe three hundred thousand people. We just had this amazing communications system. It wasn't formal in the sense that people think of organizations and formal structures. It was very informal.

[If we had then the computers we have today] . . . oh, wow [laughter]. It would have been amazing. [The networking] would have been to the fiftieth power and more than what we managed to do then. It's true because this was all telephone calls and letters and a lot of traveling and personal communication. I think Americans are particularly inundated with electronic media. I have a twenty-two-year-old and a twelve-year-old, and I see generational differences even between them, in terms of their intellectual interests and pursuits and how they receive and develop information. The younger one is much more media-focused. I know there's a plethora of books on Vietnam, and a lot of them excellent books, but in terms of this younger generation learning the lessons from Vietnam, in the state of California, there are no history textbooks that really do give it more than a few paragraphs. At UCSB, when my older son was a freshman, they started a course on Vietnam. It actually came out of the Religious Studies Department, and overnight, it became the most popular class. Eight hundred kids. It's packed every semester because these kids know their parents went through that period, and they know what an upheaval it was, and they know how controversial it was and still is in some ways. They want to know about it. So the hunger is there.

Society has done a disservice in terms of really instilling the lessons in these kids, but I think it's because we haven't come to terms with it ourselves. The powers that be, the political and intellectual leadership in the mainstream of this country, haven't come to terms with it. So until that happens, you can't formulate the analysis to put in the textbooks because no one has unity as to what that should be. Although some of us do [laughter].

13

Madeline Duckles

Madeline Duckles traveled to Hanoi with Ethel Taylor and Cora Weiss. They visited schools, saw an underground factory, met with three American POWs, and talked with Premier Pham Van Dong. At a musical concert she attended, a soloist presented his wooden flute to her as a gift for her son.

Duckles described how moved she was by the suffering of the civilian population of Vietnam and how she has worked to bring seriously wounded Vietnamese children, primarily from South Vietnam, to this country for medical treatment. She was interviewed in a private dining room in the Men's Faculty Club of the University of California, Berkeley, California, on November 13, 1990.

MADELINE DUCKLES: I have worked with Women Strike for Peace, the Women's International League for Peace and Freedom, and as a volunteer with the American Friends Service Committee. We were concerned with the war long before the general public. As early as the Cuban crisis, Women Strike for Peace met to discuss the United States presence in Vietnam. I also worked with the Committee of Responsibility, an organization which brought war-injured Vietnamese children to the United States for medical treatment who couldn't be treated in Vietnam and who, after treatment was completed, were returned to their familiies. On the . . . very human level, it was a terrible, terrible war. As I dealt with the Vietnamese children we brought here for treatment, it became very clear that since all the able-bodied men were fighting in Vietnam, on one side or the other, the people in the villages were the old men, the women, and children. The burden of the bombings and most of the suffering fell upon them. Essentially, it was a war against children. Not since the Massacre of the Innocents had there been anything like this. Through this work, I became much more interested and knowledgeable about the history of Vietnam.

I accepted the invitation to go to Vietnam with great eagerness because we women felt that we were not at war with the Vietnamese women. One group, the Women's International League for Peace and Freedom, in fact, signed a peace treaty with the women of Vietnam, ending the war with Vietnam, certainly among us women. It was really our sense of idealism about what democracy ought to be, particularly its foreign relations, which led those of us in the antiwar movement to oppose that war, to try to come up with positive solutions, and led us to go to Hanoi during that time. [The trip] cost thirteen hundred dollars, and I borrowed a hundred dollars from thirteen people [laughter], and then I paid it back. A few people said, "Don't bother." My husband and I put in some of our money because it cost a little bit more than thirteen hundred dollars. But it's nice to have thirteen friends from whom you can borrow a hundred dollars.

We went to Phnom Penh and then to Vientiane, where we took an International Control Commission plane to Hanoi [in December 1969]. The ICC plane flew only every two weeks during a specified two-hour interval. All bombing and antiaircraft fire were supposed to stop during that time, so that if the plane was delayed, it didn't fly. It was a small, light plane. It was a harrowing flight. The plane had been shot at not long before. A Polish diplomat had been killed, I believe.

Hanoi was still in a blackout. When we landed, all the lights went out, and there were no lights that we could see on the field. We just landed blind, and the earth came up to meet us with a jolt. The few automobiles on the road from the airport into the city traveled with very dim lights. On street corners, there were little clusters of lights. At first, I thought they were candles, but actually they were very tiny kerosene lanterns, miniatures of the kind used on trains years ago in my childhood in the country. People were gathered on the street corners, sitting around, talking with one another. There was no electricity at night because of the blackout and the fear of the bombings. I came to admire the Vietnamese people tremendously because in the midst of all this hardship (and I was so depressed while I was there, with such a feeling of sadness and despair that this should be going on), they could laugh, make jokes, and provide entertainment for us. It was amazing. I can't imagine myself doing that in such circumstances.

Life began early in the morning, before dawn, usually with music. Loudspeakers on telephone poles played, I suppose, patriotic songs. In the city, many people carried little baskets, which looked like wastebaskets to me, containing chickens, and the chickens would cluck. The only other sound was the sibilant swish, swish of bicycle tires on the damp streets.

The Vietnamese people speak very softly. As a tall American woman among these small and graceful people, I often felt like a cow among butterflies, what with the Vietnamese women wearing their *ao dais* [long, dresslike garments, similar to Indian saris] and these large American women beside them. I always had to bend down to hear them speak because they spoke so softly and gently. One of the people we met described the bamboo as the symbol of Vietnam, which was gentle and bent with the wind but was strong. It would grow in any climate, in any soil. You could bend it, but it wouldn't break.

It was a devastating experience to be there during the war. As one man (I think he was editor of the paper) said to us, "When you can put a man on the moon, why do you come to bomb a country such as ours where the principal means of transportation is the bicycle?" The resiliency of the Vietnamese people in time of war was astonishing. They were able to cope with this terrible bombardment and hardships and the evacuation of people from the cities to thatched huts in the countryside. Even the Conservatory of Music survived in that fashion. Heaven knows, the Vietnamese had been fighting for nearly forty years. . . .

[While we were in Hanoi], a special meeting was arranged for us with three American prisoners of war. We talked with them, and we brought home a lot of letters to their families in the United States. That was really one of the things we most wanted to do. We had a lot of pictures taken with these prisoners of war, for us and for their families. We wanted the war to be over so that they could all come home. The Vietnamese said, "As soon as American troops withdraw, we will send all the prisoners of war home." It took a long time before that happened. But they did.

We went to Haiphong and to the countryside in Hoa Binh Province. We saw shipyards; we saw manufacturing, such as it was; we saw some work going on underground, in caves; we went to Ha Long Bay in the northern part of Vietnam, which was once a great resort for the French. There are about fifteen hundred little islands in Ha Long Bay. We went out on that bay, up near where the first American plane was shot down. We went out in a little launch and drank soda pop. It was as if we were on a holiday, and the Vietnamese women and men were laughing and telling us about the countryside and telling us amusing stories. Two of the young women had been fighting and had just come back on leave. Yet somehow,

American prisoners of war, Markham Gartley, Paul Brown, and William Mayhew, meeting with Cora Weiss and Madeline Duckles, Hanoi, December 1969. *(Courtesy of Madeline Duckles.)*

they had a poise of spirit that enabled them to put the war aside and act as if they were receiving guests in a comfortable, social situation.

The dragon features prominently in Vietnamese art. I was asked what I would like to see. I said jokingly, "I would like to see a dragon." They had told me that on one of those islands, there lived dragons. The day before we left, two young women came from *Women's Press* to interview us, and they brought us a gift, a dragon made out of a buffalo horn.

While we were there, the National Theatre was closed and so was the ballet, the singing and dancing troupe. So they arranged a special concert for us in a home once lived in by the French and which perhaps was an embassy at one time. There were singers, musicians playing traditional Vietnamese instruments, and performers of various kinds. A tenor sang, and there was a magnificent musician who played the bamboo flute. He had played this flute all over Vietnam and particularly in Vinh Linh. Vinh

A street scene outside a public office in downtown Hanoi, December 1969. *(Photo by Madeline Duckles.)*

Linh was right on the parallel which divided North and South Vietnam. This area had been bombed so often that the people lived underground. They had even developed some kind of skin disease from not getting enough sunshine. Underground, they had schools and a hospital, and they took their livestock out at night to graze. I said, "Why don't they leave?" The Vietnamese looked at me in astonishment and said, "But this is their home." You don't leave your home.

This young man who played the flute so beautifully (and played it for the troops) had learned all the bird calls to play his flute for the people in Vinh Linh so that they would know that, somewhere in Vietnam, the birds still sang. After this concert, the only instrument I really recognized other than a piano was a cello. I went backstage, just as I would here, to talk to the musicians. I talked to the cellist about my son who plays the cello and also spoke to the flute player about my son who plays the flute.

Downtown Hanoi, December 1969. *(Photograph by Madeline Duckles.)*

He had a piccolo which he had got from Europe. The piccolo was hard to come by. We talked about my son's flute instruction and the pieces he played. The Vietnamese said, "A bamboo flute is easy to make. Take this one home to your son."

My son has the flute. It is very hard to play. When I came home, people said, "Oh, you've been propagandized. They told you only what they wanted you to hear. They planned it all." But there were so many spontaneous gestures, like this one. Nobody knew I had a son who played the flute or that I would hear a flute player.

We had a meeting with Pham Van Dong, the premier of Vietnam. This man had tremendous strength. One felt this. He spoke in French. You could see he was just seething with anger when he said, "You have seen for yourself. Our cities have been burned. Our forests destroyed. Our people maimed. Why have you come to do this?" We had no answer. We had a long interview — nearly an hour or more. We asked questions. What about the peace? I think it was then he said, "When the war is over, then the problems begin."

Madeline Duckles, Cora Weiss, and their escorts visit the ruins of the Nam Dinh textile mill, December 1969. *(Courtesy of Madeline Duckles.)*

[Why would the premier take time out to talk to] three American women? I don't know. But when I got back, could I see a congressman in Washington? I could see my own, I could see Ron Dellums, but that was it. Nobody wanted to talk to us. Nobody really wanted to hear about it, but because we had brought letters from the POWs and because that had gotten quite a bit of publicity, we were interviewed by the press and invited to appear on television.

On our return flight, two weeks after arriving, it was shortly before Christmas. All of the people in the embassies were going to Hong Kong to rejoin their families or going to Bangkok on leave for the holidays. Some Vietnamese were also on the plane, going off to Bangkok or elsewhere. The plane was overbooked, and nobody would get off.

We didn't take off. There were tremendous arguments going on in the back of the plane in Vietnamese and in French. The pilot said that if they didn't fly within their prescribed time limits, and their two-hour period was being eaten into, they would be shot at, and he would not fly. Nobody would get off, and we were trying to shrink ourselves small in our corner of the plane so that we wouldn't be put off. It looked as if we were going to spend Christmas in Hanoi, away from our families. They began unloading the baggage. Abruptly, a Canadian, very nobly, made the sacrifice of getting off the plane so that the plane could fly. I don't know who that man was, but I'm eternally grateful to him.

I think many people undoubtedly regarded [my trip to Hanoi] as a traitorous act, that I was consorting with the enemy, and again and again, all I could say was, "They were not my enemy. The Vietnamese are not my enemy." I worked very hard at getting people on television programs when they came back from Vietnam. We tried to educate our people. I had hoped many people would go because I thought that the more people who went, the more the message would get out about what this war was really like.

I think some of my neighbors concluded that I was a Communist [laughter], and one of my husband's colleagues was heard to say, "What is Madeline thinking of? What will she do to Vincent's career?" And my husband said, "What does he think my career would have been without her?" [laughter]. There was a lot of that. And when I would speak at a church or someplace, there was always somebody who would criticize me. Even during our television interview, I was asked if I were a Communist. I didn't mind saying that I wasn't, but I didn't like the question. I wish I had the courage to say, "I refuse to answer." And then everybody would have assumed I was a Communist.

[The Committee of Responsibility has] brought back eighty-seven children, I believe, most from South Vietnam. Two paraplegics are now in Berkeley, and both have gone back home to visit; two are here who were orphans: one a girl living in Los Angeles, who had a great deal of reconstructive facial surgery, and one in Pham Thanh, about whom a wonderful documentary film has been made. It has been shown in Berkeley and will appear on national public television. It's called *Thanh's War*.

Among the children we treated, the paraplegics had it rough. I'm trying to think when we brought the last ones back. Nineteen seventy-three, I think, was the last. They all came in on a space-available basis, on a medevac [a U.S. Air Force medical evacuation] plane. I met all the children as they arrived at Travis Air Force Base, about sixty miles from Berkeley. They were treated in Texas, New York, Los Angeles, Boston, Seattle, and in North Carolina — wherever we could get hospital beds and doctors. Services were volunteered, beds for what we could talk the hospitals into reducing in price. Other agencies from other countries treated war victims, primarily those who were napalmed, but I have no documentation on which countries, besides Switzerland. Only the Quakers gave humanitarian aid to both sides, and the American Friends Service Committee always sent somebody with that aid because they don't want it used for military purposes. I correspond with one of the children in Vietnam, and I see the three Vietnamese in Berkeley very often. . . .

When it comes to cultural exchanges, we should recognize that we have a lot to learn from the Vietnamese. We always think of ourselves as this Lady Bountiful giving to these poor people. They have ways to teach us, first of all, about inner strength, about enduring hardship, about family relationships, about gentleness, and about living with one another. The Vietnamese children who came here for medical treatment had been physically injured; they had been psychologically injured; they were separated from families; they had lost families; they came to a whole new culture and experienced cultural shock beyond belief. Despite all of this, not one of them was falling apart. Not one had psychological trauma as we understand it. In their background was a family solidity, a solidarity that gave them tremendous strength.

I learned a lot in the course of dealing with these children because they were in foster families while they were convalescing. After two days, the foster family wanted to keep them. Partly, they wanted to save them, but we are possessive, so possessive. The Vietnamese could let them go. They didn't have that kind of grasping. And yet they gave them strength. In this whole business of raising children, we have a lot to learn.

[My life] was changed in a sense of an obligation which I didn't feel before to those people whose lives we had destroyed and whose country we had damaged so severely. If you were there now, as I was in 1987, you'd see the defoliation, which led to soil erosion, flooding, and so forth. I was in Hanoi for about a week. I didn't have time to go elsewhere. My original plan was to go from Hanoi to Ho Chi Minh City and from there to Phnom Penh and then Vientiane, but I wasn't able to do that.

I wanted to go back and see what progress had been made since I had been there. Progress has been very, very slow. They haven't managed their economy well. They tried, after the war, to follow the Soviet model, and it wasn't successful. Now they've embarked on a much more free market economy, and they realize that, for them, this is going backwards. I wish they had a little more political liberalization, but they are so afraid of economic instability, they are so close to the margin. They are perhaps the fourth poorest country in the world — after Ethiopia, Bangladesh, and Cambodia.

When I was in Hanoi, this last time, I was taken to visit a school, a kindergarten, and here were about thirty or forty little children. There were almost no toys, no play equipment, no crayons, no paper, no cutout books, none of these things. The children learned songs and so on, and I said, "They have nothing to play with." And someone said to me, "They play with one another." . . .

I'm sorry that they kept that many people in the re-education camps that long. I think that was a great, great mistake. In a sense, I can understand their problem because at the end of the war, there were almost a million South Vietnamese in military service. After the [Central] Highlands fell, they simply began to go berserk. There were a number of subversives left around, trying to overthrow the government. Also, it was just as if you woke up one morning and — the economy of the South was based on American imports — it was gone overnight. They didn't know how to deal with these people and just put everybody in so-called re-education camps.

We never have acknowledged use of Agent Orange and its effects upon the Vietnamese people. We are reluctant even to accept that it hurt our own people. And then you have [Adm. Elmo] Zumwalt's son, who was a victim of it. And Zumwalt justifies it, saying he never regretted doing it. It was the right thing to do. And so if you have this ideology, I think, you constantly live with the rationalizations that justify it.

The missing in action [MIA] issue, I think, is a terrible hardship on the families. I think anybody who has seen that terrain knows that the missing in action should be declared dead long since. Nobody ever thinks how many Vietnamese are missing in action, and they are in the hundreds of thousands. . . . The Vietnamese, if anything, feel more strongly than we do about the graves of their ancestors. You must find a way to bury, and people go back at Tet, always, to the graves of their ancestors. It's a very important part of their whole life and being. . . .

The work to be done is to prevent war. I don't think it's beyond the capability of American minds to resolve conflict. If we build a bridge, we get the best engineers, the best geologists, the best technological advice. Yet when we have a human problem to solve, we don't bring in any of these people. We go back to the caveman era. Who's got the biggest gun? Who's got the biggest club? We've got to do it differently, and we have this capability to do it differently. . . .

I think Martin Luther King was one of the great ones, and he spoke out against the war in Vietnam. He said, "Peace and justice are a single

struggle." And I think that's a great statement. I think people in prominent positions who took a stand, like Ramsey Clark, were very courageous. And the women, we women, I think, we were outstanding. There
were a lot of women. We were the first ones to do this.

Women Strike for Peace [is still active] in some areas: Washington,
D.C.; New York; Berkeley; and in Seattle, it's very strong. In Washington,
D.C., we have a legislative office that does a lot of good lobbying. A major
issue for both the women's peace organizations to which I belong is ending nuclear testing. If we end nuclear testing, we could end the making of
nuclear weapons. Glen Seaborg [formerly with the Atomic Energy Com-
mission] of this university is one of the strongest supporters of that. And
Owen Chamberlain, a Nobel Prize winner, also is strongly behind us to
end nuclear testing.

At one point, there was a group called the Jeannette Rankin Brigade,
a group of about five thousand women. We went to Washington from all
over the country to protest the war. Jeannette Rankin was there. She voted
against World War I and World War II. We wanted to stage a sit-down in
the Congress and have all five thousand of us women arrested. Jeannette
Rankin said she wouldn't participate if we did that because we would be
breaking the law, and she didn't want to do that. So we didn't do it. But it
would have been a great thing if five thousand women had been arrested
at the Capitol.

I went to that demonstration. We had some big people there. The
people from the East Coast don't think we on the West Coast function, but
we do. We had a great demonstration, about five hundred thousand in a
polo field in San Francisco at Golden Gate Park. That was our biggest
demonstration. [It was] in the early seventies. About the time we were
having the big ones in Washington, D.C., and New York.

In 1965, while [I was] with my husband who was on sabbatical in
Italy, the first bombing of North Vietnam was announced. There was a
tremendous demonstration against the bombing of cities. It meant much
more to Italians than it meant to Americans. About thirty thousand people demonstrated in Florence. I was asked to speak in the Piazza Strozzi.
This was in my dossier with the FBI. I took liberties with Shakespeare
(and how subversive can you get?) and used these lines:

What is a man if the chief good and the market of his time
Be but to *war* and sleep? A beast, no more?
Sure, He that made us with such large discourse,

Looking backward and before, gave us not this capability
And God-like reason to fust in us unused.

Shakespeare didn't say *to war*. He said *to feed*. I had an interpreter, and my speech was brief. What I said that was considered dangerous was that in the United States, there were demonstrations in many cities protesting the bombings. The United States embassy in Rome, however, claimed the United States population was totally behind the war effort, and that was the contradiction. . . .

A political scientist on this campus, an acquaintance of mine, has said, "The trouble with you women is that you overemphasize emotive factors," meaning human life. And if we are not about human life, as a country, as a people, as policymakers in Washington, then why do we exist at all? I'm convinced that there is no future in war or violence and that, as the Quakers say, the way to peace is peace.

I think it takes a real American to seriously consider the American beliefs on which this country was founded. The trouble is we never finished that revolution. . . . When I say we should finish that revolution, I am referring to the fact that decisions are not made by the people, and I'm not sure the people we elect really represent us. We should be dedicated to the common welfare, the common good, but we are not. I think the American Revolution was fought for justice and equality, which doesn't exist, not racial justice, not social justice.

14
Ethel Taylor

Ethel Taylor traveled to Hanoi in 1969 with Madeline Duckles and Cora Weiss, who also were members of Women Strike for Peace. Her trip to Vietnam was shortened to one week because of an ear infection. Taylor related incidents of ridicule and ostracism she experienced on her return from Hanoi. She also discussed her role as an activist against nuclear testing and the Vietnam War. A co-founder of Women Strike for Peace, Taylor spoke of the war and its effects from the standpoint of a mother who was radicalized by what she perceived to be a government out of control. She described how difficult it was for her and others to dress up in conventional women's attire of the time (tailored suit, white gloves, and hats) and then lie down on sidewalks in protest against the war.

Taylor is a sculptor. The interview took place on October 13, 1990, in her Bala Cynwd, Pennsylvania, apartment.

ETHEL TAYLOR: [I traveled to Vietnam in] late December of 1969, [along with] Cora Weiss of New York and Madeline Duckles of Berkeley. [I paid for the trip] personally. We were invited by the North Vietnam Women's Union to discuss the setting up of a clearinghouse, the Committee of Liaison With Families of Servicemen Detained in Vietnam, in this country for the transmission of mail and packages from prisoners of war and their families and vice versa. This was because the Vietnamese did not abide by the Geneva Convention on prisoners because they said this was not a declared war [and that] the United States, by bombing them without provocation, was committing a criminal act. So the POWs were not even called prisoners of war by the Vietnamese; they were called war criminals.

I guess this was the most significant thing that I have ever been involved in, to be part of this plan which would notify parents, wives, and children that their sons, husbands, and fathers were still alive or were not alive. Before I went, word got around to the prisoners' families that I was going. I received hundreds of letters from families asking if their kin were alive because they didn't know. There was very little information from Vietnam about whether they were or not. When I went in '69, there were families who hadn't heard from their sons since '64, when they knew they were shot down.

There was a family out in my area who contacted me because their son was shot down in 1964. This family was really instrumental in notifying all the families in the area and also as far as California that I was going. And I came back with thirty-six letters. It almost sounds like a television situation. I came back at Christmas with these letters for families who had no idea whether their sons were alive or dead. And I was able to call them and tell them that their sons were alive and that I had letters from them which I was putting in the mail right away. [This was their first indication that their kin were alive.] I received wonderful letters from them. Of course, there were all these other families who had sent letters for me to take to Hanoi, but I had no information for them. But it was really a unique experience to be able to do this, and Cora, Madeline, and I really felt specially blessed to be able to do this.

The family that lived in my neighborhood whose son was shot down in 1964 didn't know if he was dead or alive. In addition to thirty-five other letters, I was able to bring back a letter to them from their son. They were so thrilled and grateful that they promised when their son came back they would have a big party and their son and I would stand together receiving guests. It never happened! When their son came back, he would have nothing to do with me because he was convinced that the peace movement lengthened the war. He wrote a letter to the local newspaper expressing that view, and I responded with a letter to the editor debunking that position. I wrote that the POWs, due to their imprisonment over all those years, had no idea what the feelings of the American people were and how sentiment changed to an antiwar position as the war dragged on.

[Their son] felt the peace movement's activities lengthened the war. He didn't know that during the presidential campaign of 1964, Lyndon Johnson was quoted as saying on August 12, 1964:

Some others are eager to enlarge the conflict. They call upon us to supply American boys to do the job that Asian boys should do. They ask us to take reckless action which might risk the lives of millions and engulf much of Asia and threaten the peace of the entire world.

Moreover, such action would offer no solution at all to the real problem of Vietnam.

Despite [making] this statement, upon winning the presidency, Johnson immediately sent fifty thousand more young men to Vietnam. Nixon became president, claiming he had a plan to end the war, and four years later, with fifty thousand American soldiers dead, the war ended on the same terms that could have ended it four years before. I say now and I said then that the administrations lengthened the war, and the peace movement tried to stop it. . . .

We went to Paris and stayed there for a few days, meeting with the Vietnamese, the head of the delegation in Paris of North Vietnam, and Mme Binh, who was head of the National Liberation Front delegation. Paris was the best place to start to go to Vietnam, meeting with the Vietnamese. . . . They briefed us about what we would find in North Vietnam, how we would go, and the technicalities of the trip. We then went to Cambodia and Laos.

We went up and down [by air] to Athens, Tokyo, and Ceylon. I think we went to Cambodia from Ceylon. I'm not quite sure. There was a lot of going down and coming up, which was deadly for an ear infection. Tony Bennett sings: "I left my heart in San Francisco." I left part of my hearing in North Vietnam.

[We flew into Phnom Penh and] stayed at a hotel overnight. Because of my infection, I started to run a high fever in the middle of the night. Cora, always the dependable one, somehow located a doctor. He happened to be Vietnamese, and he knew the Vietnamese women wanted me to come to Vietnam. He gave me a lot of medication and wired the Vietnamese women that when I arrived, I should go right to bed. The next morning, we left for Laos. I was groggy but determined to go on with this adventure into the unknown. In Laos, we made a connection with the International Control Commission plane, which took us from Vientiane to Hanoi. It was a rough ride in a somewhat primitive plane.

We arrived in Hanoi at night. We landed by the light of two headlights on a truck. When we landed, the door of the plane burst open, and we were immediately surrounded by soldiers with flashlights. When we disembarked, we were met by our Vietnamese friends whom we had met previously at conferences in Canada and in France. It was like a homecoming. They brought flowers. I never thought I would see these women on their own turf. I'm only five feet tall, but with most of the women, I felt very tall. They practically lifted me by my elbows and sort of carried me to a car.

They took us to the chalet where we were to stay. It was a shabby relic of the French occupation. They got me into my nightgown and put me to bed. The whole thing was like a dream. Then the door opened, and this vision of a woman in a long white dress came in with a hypodermic needle that looked to me about a yard long. She said, "Doctor calling," and injected me with vitamin C. I remember thinking that my friend Linus Pauling would have approved. I fell asleep, and that was my first night in Hanoi. A truly remarkable experience.

I arrived in Vietnam with an ear infection, which was exacerbated by the long flight and the many landings and takeoffs. I managed okay but decided to leave a week early because flights in and out of North Vietnam took place only once a week, and I was fearful that my condition would get worse, which it did. For all the time I was there, the women couldn't do enough for me. Because of the antibiotics I was taking, I didn't have much of an appetite, but they tried to titillate my appetite with delicious food. I'm sure that they didn't eat the kind of food they served us. When I didn't seem tempted by Vietnamese food, one night they announced they had made a "bifstake" for me. The next morning, Cora and Madeline left on a two-day trip to the countryside. Although I wanted to go, the Vietnamese would not allow it. But before they left, the Vietnamese women sent them to a beauty parlor. They wouldn't let me go because of my infection. When Cora and Madeline returned, they looked like two bubbleheaded astronauts. The "bouffant" had hit Hanoi.

I did not meet with [any Vietnamese officials]. Cora and Madeline met with officials of the government during the week after I left. I did not [see any of the American POWs]. Cora and Madeline met with three or four prisoners after I had departed. We were driven around in chauffeured limousines. I believe they were the only cars on the road. Everyone rode bicycles. One day, the women took me shopping. When I got out of the car, a crowd of people gathered. They were very quiet. I didn't know whether the quiet was threatening or questioning. From the midst of the crowd, a woman with a baby in her arms walked toward me. She put the child in my arms. I was so very moved by this gesture. To me, it meant that it was the children we must protect from war.

I was most impressed with the people. The people. They had the patience of people who have been invaded by one country or another for hundreds of years and who have overcome. They separated the American

Ethel Taylor and Madeline Duckles at a nursery school for children of women in higher education, December 1969. The children had previously attended a school located in an underground bunker that also served as their home. *(Courtesy of Ethel Taylor.)*

people from the American government and seemed to have a very warm feeling towards the people.

We visited a kindergarten class of little kids who had just recently come aboveground after a long siege of living and learning underground due to the bombing. They swamped us with loving attention even though there was a big poster on the wall with a drawing of Uncle Ho running after Americans with a hatchet. The country was drab and colorless, but the people were warm and caring, not only about us but also about the American people generally.

I met a woman who asked me a question that really boggled my mind. She asked, "What do American mothers tell their children if their father is killed in Vietnam?" She said, "Here in Vietnam, it is not difficult. My husband was killed in the war, and I told my child that he died defending his own country." And it made me wonder, what does an

Madeline Duckles, Cora Weiss, and Ethel Taylor meet with Vietnamese women, December 1969. *(Courtesy of Ethel Taylor.)*

American mother tell her child? That he died defending the United States, which is ten thousand miles away from Vietnam? So I have wondered about this often. . . .

I learned about the My Lai massacre from Vo Thi Lien, a twelve-year-old who had eighteen family members tortured and slaughtered in front of her. One hundred ten babies, women, and old men were slaughtered at My Lai, and William Calley, at his trial, said, "It was no big deal."

I heard things in Hanoi which stretched my credulity. It was only when I got home that some of it was verified. I listened one afternoon to a man from the Peace Committee of the National Liberation Front describe the terrible birth mutations which they attributed to the chemical defoliant 245-T. When I got home, I read a statement by Nixon's scientific adviser, who admitted that in a laboratory test, rats injected with 245-T gave birth to a preponderant number of deformed babies. Subsequently, an order was issued to cease using this chemical, but it was later disclosed that the order had not been carried out.

It wasn't until Congressman [William R.] Anderson and his delegation, during a visit to South Vietnam, exposed the Lon Son tiger cages in the early 1970s that the American people knew that these obscenities existed. I heard testimony from Mme [Khanh] Phuong who had been held as a political prisoner under [Ngo Dinh] Diem. What sickened me more than her description of the torture (the pouring of lime into her eyes, nose, and mouth) was the damning fact that this prison was visited regularly by an American adviser, sometimes accompanied by his wife, who lived in a nearby villa. [The] adviser . . . saw the horrible conditions but said and did nothing. Mme Phuong told me that the one thing that will always be imprinted on her mind is that she was kept handcuffed, and that the handcuffs were imprinted "Made in USA."

The only contact I had with [our] government was when I left Vietnam and arrived in Laos on my way home. I was met by a State Department official who was accompanied by a doctor. The official said he understood I had been ill. I really wondered how he knew that. He offered the services of the doctor. I thanked him but told him that my problems had been taken care of adequately by the Vietnamese doctors.

My next contact with the government was when I returned home. As you can imagine, I was news for a while. I was having a press conference in my home when I received a call from the Pentagon. A Colonel Works called to commend me and the other women for the wonderful job we had done. He asked if it would be all right if one or two Defense Department representatives came to see me just to get my feelings about things. I replied that it would not be all right because to me and to most of those in the peace movement, the enemy to peace was not in Vietnam but in the White House. I certainly didn't want to be in the position of seeming to give information to government officials on anything in Vietnam. I was glad to hear that the Pentagon approved [of] our actions, even it was for just a short period of time. Shortly after, families of POWs were asked to refrain from dealing with our Committee of Liaison, even though the transmission of mail and packages depended upon our committee.

[The State Department didn't take away my passport], but they kept an eagle eye on me. In my FBI dossier, which I received through the Freedom of Information Act, there are a number of pages devoted to my getting my passport renewed. There is an "urgent" wire to the Washington FBI which noted my passport number and the day I received it. They noted that the Passport Office advised that there was no record of my having requested State Department validation for travel to Vietnam. They were right, I didn't ask permission.

I was amazed that I was such a hot item to the service clubs when I came back from Vietnam. The first to invite me, an Optimist Club, was very cordial. It became known to other clubs that I gave interesting talks on Vietnam. I received invitations from Lions, Rotaries, etc. There were frightening incidents, like being hit over the head with a heavy stick while demonstrating outside "Re-elect Nixon" headquarters. But the worst kind of experience was when people were afraid to talk to me because they were fearful that their peers would think they were soft on communism.

My last speaking engagement to clubs was devastating. When I started to speak, men in the back started to shout and scream, "Hanoi Hannah." It was taken up by practically everyone; it was an experience I was to have on other occasions. In the audience were a priest, a prominent businessman, and someone I knew slightly. As I left, I met them outside, and they apologized for the behavior of the group. I asked them why they didn't defend me on the inside, and they admitted that they didn't want to incur the wrath of the Rotarians. I wrote to the program director who had invited me and said how saddened I was that Father so-and-so and the others were afraid to defend me. He sent back a scathing letter in which he said he had questioned them, and they denied talking to me outside.

Another time, I was invited to speak at a church to commemorate World Peace Day. I didn't know anything about the church, but when I arrived and met the minister, he informed me that I was in John Birch territory. The chairwoman announced that after I spoke, she would escort me to the back of the room, and I would receive people who wanted to speak to me. I started to speak, and, as if by signal, one row after another stood up and walked out, just like at a funeral. I kept on speaking, and when I was through, protocol prevailed, and the chairwoman escorted me through the empty church to the back of the room. No one was there.

I started to leave, and a woman dashed out of the women's room, put a piece of paper in my hand, and dashed out. When I got into my car, I read it. It said, "My name is so-and-so; my phone number is so and so. I want to know more about Women Strike for Peace, but I was afraid to ask you in front of the people." This was what was more frightening than any other kind of abuse. The government had been successful in their anti-communist zeal to put fear into people and to alienate one group of citizens from another.

[My trip to Vietnam] was the most meaningful experience of my life, besides having children. I had been in the peace movement for a long time and was exceedingly committed to the cause of peace and justice. But this experience was beyond that. We carried our opposition to the war to the land our government called "enemy," and we found friends. Our ability to make connections between POWs and their families was an extra bonus.

That this trip and my other activities might be considered treason by proponents of the war did not concern me. I was sure that right was on our side. I only learned later, through my FBI files, that there was continuous consultation between a federal attorney in Philadelphia and the FBI about whether I should be tried for sedition because of my open support of draft resisters. After two years of such correspondence, the case was dropped.

[My opposition to the war at home] was certainly a learning experience for me about myself. I was a middle-aged, middle-class American woman who thought I would live out my whole life without seeing the inside of a jail as a prisoner, and there I was, locked up two times. At the time, it seemed easier to get arrested than not get arrested . . . to do things that were a little drastic than not to do them. There were so many times where it was absolutely essential that I put my body where my mouth had been. Going to Vietnam was a natural sequence because it was important to have credibility. It was important for me to go to Vietnam to see for myself and to meet all these people myself, to see what they were thinking, and see what the devastation was. And I did.

I remember one instance. At that time, women were wearing hats and gloves, white gloves. And even if we weren't active in Women Strike for Peace, we would have worn them because that was the style. But wearing hats and white gloves was a political statement because it encouraged women who saw us on television or saw pictures of us in the newspapers to look at us and say, "They're just like me. They're not wild-haired radicals." They identified with us.

There I was in my hat and my gloves in the paddy wagon. We arrived at the jail, and the back door opened. I was first. I looked down. There was about a five-foot jump with no steps. I stood there in my hat and white gloves, waiting for the policeman to come and help me down. And I waited. The policeman came and said, "Jump, sister." So I knew my life had changed and was on another track. And that was what we did. We seemed to put aside fear. My basic philosophy was, "What can they do, hang me? Electrocute me? What can they do to prevent me from defending what I believed to be the right thing?" And it wasn't terrible; it was just unusual. One thing led to another.

[I was arrested] twice. [Each time, I stayed in jail] overnight. Something that happened in the second arrest is and has always been a mystery to me. The arrest was the result of the Capitol sit-in. The next morning, we appeared before a judge for arraignment, and he set a date for trial later in the summer. As we were leaving, a federal marshal stopped about six of us, including myself, and took us into a ladies' room and handcuffed us to a pole and left us there. A few hours later [without explanation], we were released.

I think I did as much as I could do. I could do all that I did because I had the full support of my husband and children. I'm sure there are things I could have done more effectively, but I don't think I could have been any more involved than I was without being a basket case.

It's not easy to be a patriot. It's not just Fourth of July, fireworks, and the American flag. It's not including a statement against abortion in the Pledge of Allegiance, which is being considered in some areas. Being a patriot sometimes can mean being very unpopular because sometimes you have to go against what is conceived by most people as being patriotic. Patriotism is being against the policy of your government when you think the government is wrong. No "my government, right or wrong" for a patriot. I think that I and all of the people who acted and demonstrated against the war in Vietnam were the patriots. Trusting a government without asking questions is a dangerous thing to do. A patriot asks questions.

I think that if [the American people] had immediately understood the genesis of the war in Vietnam, they would have immediately opposed it, but by the time people realized what was going on and where Vietnam was, we were totally committed. They didn't know the history of Vietnam, a country which had fought off invaders for more years than we have been a nation. They didn't know that we financed eighty percent of the French Indochinese War, and when the French were beaten, we stepped in. It has always seemed incomprehensible to me that we destroyed a country ten thousand miles away, killed untold numbers of Vietnamese, caused the deaths of fifty-eight thousand Americans and who knows how many wounded and scarred in an effort to eradicate communism.

They [the American people] did not understand the horror of the war even though they viewed it on television nightly. They were lied to by presidents. False body counts were given out so as to show how victorious we were in killing the enemy. It seems almost inevitable that in every generation, there has to be this bloodletting. It's a terrible thing that each generation's young have to worry about what kind of war they will be involved in. It seems that as far as government is concerned, it's so much easier to increase a defense budget than to cut a defense budget. The peace dividend we thought we would get when communism stopped being the enemy is now being eaten up in another war-threatening policy [the war in the Persian Gulf, Desert Storm].

So many times, the question is asked, "What is the lesson of Vietnam?" To many, the lesson learned is that "in the event of another war, go in quickly, destroy the enemy, and get out, using all the power needed to do the job." The late and unlamented, by me, Gen. Curtis Lemay said, "Let's bomb 'em back to the Stone Age." That was one lesson learned. Then there was a muddled position, heard so many times: "I'm against our involvement, but as long as we're there, we've got to win." Going to war should be a last, not a first, resort. If our country is attacked, then we have no option but to react militarily. But 1941 was the last time our country was attacked, and since that time, we have been involved in four wars and seem to be heading for number five. Despite a rotting infrastructure, homelessness, and a gargantuan deficit, billions are spent on wars of questionable purpose. I'm fearful of what George Bush means when he speaks of a "new world order." It sounds like more of sticking our nose in places where it doesn't belong.

The thing that maddened me most [during the Vietnam War] was that Congress completely gave up its constitutional power. Just as now, in the Middle East, they were willing then to abdicate their power to presidents who lied and connived because they couldn't admit to the powerlessness of power. My senator [Richard S. Schweiker] at that time was very gung ho about the war, but despite that, we were able to talk about it. Years after the war, when a group of us met with him on another issue, he said of me to the group, "Ethel taught me a lesson. She taught me that communism is not monolithic, that Vietnamese communism is nationalism and not part of an international communist network." That was very satisfying to hear, but later, he went on to run as the vice presidential candidate with Ronald Reagan in 1976 in the primaries. He didn't ask my opinion on that move.

The most misunderstood aspect about our involvement was why we were there. We shored up one corrupt and repressive government after another. We supported these "democratic" leaders in order to stop communism from spreading. What haunts me is the fact that we supported tyrants from Diem to [Nguyen Van] Thieu, to [Nguyen Cao] Ky. We stood with oppressors against their own people in the name of anticommunism and participated in the most heinous acts. Massacres, burning of villages, dropping prisoners out of helicopters, and the defoliation and destruction of a country. In many areas of the world, we have supported fascist regimes against what we called "communist aggression." After the French left Vietnam, Ho Chi Minh presented his people with a declaration of independence which he modeled after ours because he was an admirer of Jeffersonian principles. I wonder what Diem, Ky, and the other "democratic leaders" or even John Foster Dulles for that matter thought about Jeffersonian principles.

I also have a great deal of difficulty with the MIA issue, although I have tremendous sympathy for the relatives of MIAs. I can't see, however, that it is the responsibility of the Vietnamese to locate all of the remains. They did not provoke the bombing of their country. Recently, a Vietnamese doctor visited the United States and was asked about the MIAs and what the Vietnamese government was going to do about it. He answered with a question, "Is the American government going to help us find our three hundred thousand MIAs?" The Vietnamese are willing for

U.S. teams to come to Vietnam, where they would work together to search out remains. This is already taking place. I think this is fair.

No, I do not mean to be callous at all. I've had heartrending contacts with MIA families. I understand deeply their need for some tangible evidence of their loved ones. My problem is with the government's hints that assistance or recognition of the Vietnamese government depends upon the Vietnamese producing all the remains. . . . When I spoke to American parents of pilots who had been shot down, who were either missing in action or were POWs, many of them said the same thing, "He loved to fly. Being a pilot in the air force gave him this opportunity to fly. He certainly was against the killing, indiscriminate killing of people, but this was his job, and he loved to fly." Unfortunately, his love of flying caused the death and destruction of a country.

I think it is necessary also to remember that these pilots would not have been killed or missing if the United States had not involved us in a civil war, ten thousand miles away, which was not our business. After the peace talks concluded and the POWs came home, there was a campaign afoot that POWs still remained in Vietnam. Nixon and my own Senator [Hugh] Scott were spreading false information around. They compared the situation with the French departure from Vietnam. They said that there were French POWs remaining. I wrote to the French embassy, and I asked Ambassador François Bujon De L'Estang if this information was true. He replied, "I want to emphasize that we do not consider that there were prisoners who were never returned, but soldiers who were killed or disappeared in unknown circumstances." . . .

The secret war which Nixon and Kissinger carried on in Cambodia [revealed] a government with contempt for the people and a secret agenda for continuous killing for a cause which was not ours. A real job was done on the American people, and except for a few brave souls, Congress let it happen. When the peace movement attempted to expose these things, they were mocked, derided, and told to go back to where they came from.

I think Richard Nixon and Henry Kissinger were war criminals. For them to be treated as elder statesmen and be consulted on talk shows feeds the peoples' conception of that war: If these men were so honored that Henry Kissinger was awarded a Nobel Peace Prize, then what was done couldn't have been so wrong. At the very least, [however,] Nixon should have been impeached, and Henry Kissinger should have been held accountable in a public forum for the treasonable acts he committed.

Vietnam, to me, is a symbol of flawed government; I'm talking about our government. So my anger and indignation is still directed at Vietnam-thinking which goes on, even as we speak. The Vietnam War was a war not only against the Vietnamese but also a war against the American people. That war is not over. It's the war that keeps on giving. Thousands and thousands of Vietnam veterans are ill, mentally and physically, because of that war. Agent Orange may be responsible for illnesses in their children. It's like the atom bomb dropped upon Hiroshima, the fallout from which is still affecting the third generation of Japanese. Vietnam was like bacteriological warfare. It infected all of us. I just hope that there won't be a post–Saudi Arabian syndrome and then a post–somewhere else syndrome. The lesson of Vietnam has not been learned, and that's what prevents much mellowed feelings on my part.

When John Foster Dulles [secretary of state under President Eisenhower], without consultation with the Vietnamese, handpicked Diem, who had helped the French suppress the independence movement, to be prime minister of the Republic of Vietnam, I was sure we were on the wrong side. Ho Chi Minh, who helped the U.S. in the struggle against the Japanese, was certainly more fitting as an ally than the corrupt, cruel series of dictators we supported in the South. I maintained this position throughout the war and was even more certain after I met the Vietnamese. But my basic purpose was to get the U.S. out of Vietnam and leave the settling of the problem to the Vietnamese.

We were told by the North Vietnamese that when pilots, whose bombing had destroyed villages and children, were shot down, the villagers would have killed them but for the interference of the soldiers. Some POWs said they were tortured. I have no reason to doubt that they were. The U.S. bombing of North Vietnam, the defoliation, and the U.S.-sponsored cruelty and destruction in the South defied rules of war and conventions. Our presence in Vietnam was the trigger that unleashed the destructive forces on both sides.

[Resumption of diplomatic relations with Vietnam] is long overdue. In World War II, the Japanese attacked our country, and the Germans attacked our shipping, but after the war, we started building them up until today, they are two of the most powerful nations in the world. We were not attacked by Vietnam, but nevertheless we destroyed their country. The fact that we did not win that war has something to do with our reluctance to do the right thing. There is movement now, I believe, toward some kind of recognition and, hopefully, rebuilding assistance.

There are many reasons why the [Vietnamese] boat people were so anxious to leave: they wanted to escape re-education camps, they wanted a better life, or they were afraid because they had supported the U.S. . . . [The boat people and re-education camps] have not [caused me to] re-evaluate my position toward the Vietnamese government. When the U.S. took over after the French had been defeated, I became involved because I was opposed to my country interfering in a civil war in another country, thousands of miles away. As I learned more, I was convinced that the United States, a democracy that was the result of its own revolution against oppression, was on the wrong side.

[The single most effective antiwar organization was] Women Strike for Peace, of course. [We were effective] because we got involved early on. As early as 1964, a delegation of Women Strike for Peace met with Vietnamese women in Djakarta. We were a crisis-oriented movement. All over the country, we were a familiar sight on the street, with leaflets and petitions. We initiated draft-counseling groups. We openly supported draft resistance. We saw [those young men] as our sons. I had a son of draft age, and fortunately, he did not go. But it was always a threat, and it was a personal motivation.

We had about eight to ten thousand members across the country. I was national coordinator of Women Strike for Peace for, I guess, fifteen years. [Women Strike for Peace] was founded in Washington in 1961. I was the organizer of Pennsylvania's Women Strike for Peace. We have within this year, [however,] closed down our national office in Philadelphia and continued with our national legislative office in Washington, so that I am more emeritus in Women Strike for Peace than the active member I once was.

After the war ended, Women Strike for Peace went back to our original purpose for being, which was "End the Arms Race, Not the Human Race." We came into existence under that slogan, demanding a nuclear test ban treaty. Scientists informed us that the fallout from the Soviet and U.S. tests [was] harmful to our children's health through the food they ate and the milk they drank. It was like the polio scare before [Jonas] Salk and {Albert] Sabin. Our demands were against both the U.S. and the Soviet Union. In 1963, a partial test ban was established which still permitted underground testing. So after the war, we went back to the struggle for a comprehensive test ban as a first step to disarmament. But the Defense Department had not been sleeping during the war in Vietnam vis-à-vis the continued creation of new and exotic weapons.

[Members of Women Strike for Peace] met with Vietnamese women in Montreal and Toronto in 1966 or 1967. In 1968, Women Strike for Peace organized a conference of women whose countries were involved in the war in Vietnam. It was in a château on the outskirts of Paris where Australian women, Vietnamese women from North Vietnam and the National Liberation Front, Japanese women, and our delegation met for five days.

What was so significant about that meeting was that as we were leaving, the peace negotiations were starting in Paris. Of course, we didn't know it would be a long, long time because there was about a year's discussion on whether the table should be round or square. But we left with the feeling that if only they had the spirit and the humanity of the women whom we had been meeting with, they could have been out of that meeting in three days.

Through the Freedom of Information Act, we received, albeit reluctantly, information which, to our amazement, notified us that we had been under surveillance by the intelligence units of the army, navy, and air force, as well as those of the Department of Defense and the State Department. Only the marines didn't keep an eye on us. This can only mean that we were effective indeed.

In June of 1975, the "Report to the President by the Commission on CIA Activities Within the United States" was released. Nelson Rockefeller had been commissioned by President Ford to chair this commission. The purpose was to determine if the CIA had violated their charter by instituting surveillance upon domestic organizations. And they had! We learned that the CIA paid women agents one hundred dollars a week to infiltrate our organization. We also learned, as a result of this investigation, that the CIA had been opening mail we received from abroad. We instituted suit against them. The suit was against not only the CIA but also against a myriad of defendants, including Kissinger, [former director of the CIA, James] Schlesinger, Western Union, and Globe Communication. We lost the suit, except for an out-of-court settlement by the CIA.

On November 20, 1980, Women Strike for Peace received a check for five thousand dollars. A paltry sum perhaps but a tremendous morale builder for us. We applied that money toward our campaign to abolish the CIA. Poetic justice?

Jack Anderson [a syndicated investigative reporter] wrote in a column that the dossier on Women Strike for Peace was nightstand reading for President Johnson. We chained ourselves to the White House to protest funding of the war. We had a sit-down in the Capitol, which resulted in about fifteen arrests. As mothers, aunts, or grandmothers, we identified early on with the Vietnamese women and always in the open, except in the case of Djakarta, where we feared we would be stopped if it got out. I am so proud of the women of Women Strike for Peace, all of whom believed that the enemy to peace was not in the rice paddies of Vietnam but in the White House. We acted upon that belief. . . .

[To put Jane Fonda in perspective], she was an internationally known figure with a tremendous career. [She was] in a hostile environment, which this country was for the most part, in the beginning and the middle of the Vietnam War. She took a tremendous risk. And I think she took the trip to Hanoi because she felt very, very deeply about the issue. I don't know that it damaged her career, but it certainly made her a figure of derision in this country with people who were gung ho about the war. I admired her tremendously. There were a lot of things that she said in the beginning that I wasn't so excited about. But I knew from my own knowledge that this was a learning experience for her. She felt very deeply about the issue but was exposed too quickly on the national media before she had the historic facts nailed down.

[Among those who protested against the war], it's hard to separate the individuals from the peace movement as a whole. Some people were better known than others, but altogether, people gave of their time, strength, health, money, and comfort to band together to try to stop the war. Two men I consider heroic but not of the peace movement per se were Sen. Wayne Morse of Oregon and Sen. Ernest Gruening of Alaska. They were the only two senators who had the guts and the morals to vote against the questionable Tonkin [Gulf] resolution, which really unleashed the terrible military power on North Vietnam. I knew Senator Morse, and he always said that if President Kennedy had lived, he would have withdrawn American advisers from Vietnam. Who knows?

15

Cora Weiss

Cora Weiss visited Vietnam five times between 1969 and 1978. Her 1972 trip created a sensation in the United States because the North Vietnamese and the U.S. government publicly debated the conditions under which Weiss and seven other Americans would accompany three American POWs back to the United States. While the debate raged for several weeks, Weiss, the other members of her party, and the POWs toured the North Vietnam countryside. Weiss also traveled to Paris to meet with representatives of North Vietnam and the National Liberation Front. Her personal, unofficial discussions were intended to publicize the peace terms sought by the the North Vietnamese and the NLF and to demonstrate that formal negotiations could succeed and that the views of both sides to the conflict, not only those of the United States, should be considered. A member of Women Strike for Peace, Weiss was liberal in her politics. She had extensive contacts among those who shared her views and worked vigorously through her networks to recruit travelers for trips to Hanoi.

Weiss discussed how she and others, through the Committee of Liaison (an organization that she and Dave Dellinger created), coordinated the travel of Americans to Hanoi so that each month, for a period of three years, a group of three Americans routinely traveled to Hanoi with letters for the American POWs and returned with mail for their families. I interviewed her on October 7, 1990, in the living room of her Bronx home.

CORA WEISS: I went [to North Vietnam] three times during the course of the war and twice afterwards. The first was in December 1969. The purpose of the trip was to extend an offer on behalf of the antiwar movement in this country with a nongovernment organization in Vietnam to exchange mail with prisoners of war and their families. As a result of that trip, I brought back the first names of the American pilots who were known held (as the Vietnamese said, detained) in Vietnam. . . . And I brought back the first big batch of mail. They wanted me to hurry back before Christmas. I wanted to stay there to see more, but they, a committee called Vietmy, insisted that the mail be delivered before Christmas. *My* in Vietnamese means "American." Vietmy was the Vietnamese-American Committee. It was a committee of what we would refer to as NGOs, nongovernment organizations, but very close to the government, obviously. [Their] job was to relate to the American peace movement [and] what was going on in this country on behalf of their country. So one might say they were quasi-official. They were official enough to be able to accept my offer, but they were unofficial enough so that I could not be accused of negotiating with their government. . . .

Women took this initiative. We were three women from Women Strike for Peace: Ethel Taylor from Philadelphia; Madeline Duckles, who still lives in Berkeley; and myself. We had met Vietnamese women in Canada on July 4th of that year, and that really started our relationship with the Vietnamese people. It was their invitation that took us to Vietnam in the first place. It was because Vietnamese women invited American women that I was able to make this offer on behalf of the broader movement. Then we set up a committee called the Committee of Liaison With Families of Servicemen Detained in Vietnam. A quick phrase, the committee for POWs, essentially. The Vietnamese shortened our name to a cable address, which was COLIAFAM, Committee of Liaison With Families, COLIAFAM. The word *Co* in Vietnamese means "Miss." Frequently, I would walk around in Vietnam, and people would say to me, "Oh, Miss Liafam."

It was a cooperative effort. Dave Dellinger and I were co-chairs and initiated the committee; Dick Barnet was on it, and so was Richard Falk from Princeton. I think there were no more than six of us altogether on the board. I became the executive director and ran the office. It was all done on a shoestring. It lasted from the end of 1969 until 1973, when the pilots were returned. Our purpose was the exchange of mail. And we did it every single month for three years, with one exception. The reason we couldn't do it that one month, they [the Vietnamese] claimed, was because of bad weather. I remember I always thought that it was political weather until I went to Vietnam once and discovered that the weather can be very, very treacherous, and indeed it was bad weather. But every single month for three years, I sent three people with mail from the families of the POWs to North Vietnam, and they brought mail back from the pilots.

That mail established the list of POWs. [Secretary of Defense] Melvin Laird always said, "We don't know who's there, and they are keeping the names from us." We made every effort to encourage the Vietnamese to give us complete lists. Another very positive thing that we did was to negotiate an increase in the amount of materials in a package that a prisoner could receive. Until we went, the prisoners were entitled to packages from home on Easter and Thanksgiving or Christmas, two or three high holidays in the course of the year. And many of them weren't getting it at all because nobody in this country knew who was actually there. So it was hit and miss.

A lot of MIA families were sending these enormous packages, not knowing whether there was a recipient at the other end. But until then, the packages allowed were small, just shaving equipment and toiletries, essentially. As a result of our first trip, we increased the package size from seven to eleven pounds, I think, and increased the number that they could receive in the course of a year to every other month and increased the goods that could be sent. So they got playing cards and pocket books and scissors and things beyond shaving cream.

The problem then, of course, was that the U.S. military got into it. They tried to take advantage of this and told the families not to deal with us in New York but to use another route, which the military claimed was secure. The route called for families to send their packages to some U.S. post office box in Europe. Whereupon, some of the packages apparently were opened and secret spying material was inserted. In Vietnam, we saw Colgate toothpaste tubes or wrappers of Wrigley's chewing gum with materials, parts, and wires to put together radios and communication equipment. As a result, the Vietnamese said to us, "Look, we're not inviting you to bring packages in so that we can be sabotaged. So unless the package comes through your committee, it doesn't come." And that was the beginning of certain conditions that were established. We worked very hard on behalf of American families. We were very concerned to see that they got their mail immediately, that there was no delay.

I remember when Bob Scheer, now an editor of the *Los Angeles Times*, went over. He insisted on taking the mailbag to Los Angeles with him, and I kept saying, "You've got to get it to me," so that we'd get it to the families very quickly. So there was a delay of a few days. But we were very fastidious about it. We kept very careful lists, we kept very careful records, and we did not want to get into the propaganda game of saying they are withholding this or that. We were not going to be used either by the Vietnamese or by the American families and the American government. We were simply providing a direct humanitarian service.

[In] August of 1972, I spent two weeks in North Vietnam. I was one of a group of seven, consisting of David Dellinger; the Reverend William Sloane Coffin; Prof. Richard Falk of Princeton University; Associated Press reporter [and winner of the Pulitzer Prize] Peter Arnett; the mother of POW Mark Gartley; Olga Charles, wife of POW Norris Charles; and myself.

In October 1973, I went to Vietnam with Don Luce and Prof. Sam Noumoff of Canada. We were the first Americans to go south into the liberated zone of Quang Tri from the North . . . when the war was still on. It was the first liberated province of South Vietnam. We had to cross the Ben Hai River, and it was flooded, and there was no way we could get across. They kept delaying and delaying. I was very concerned because my husband was at home with three kids, and it was a five-week trip. In the process of waiting to get across the Ben Hai into South Vietnam, we had to be entertained or diverted or kept occupied in some other way. So they took us up to the China border. That was quite extraordinary because the only five towns that the United States did not bomb in all of Vietnam during the entire period were those five towns along the border with China. The Chinese, of course, invaded Vietnam after the U.S. left and bombed these five towns. We saw where Ho Chi Minh hid in a cave during the French war. And we saw the border traffic with China and a tremendous amount of trade back and forth without visas and passports. In any event, that was an extraordinary trip.

My fourth trip to Vietnam was in August of 1976. Peter, my husband, and I went together. We drove in a van with an open thirty-gallon drum of gasoline to gas up on the way because there were no handy Exxon stations on the route. That was the first time Americans crossed from the North into the South after reunification. I think unification was August 1976, and we were there within days after they voted for unification. That was a long, hot drive.

My fifth and last trip was to the South of Vietnam in March 1978, when I worked for Church World Service. We went to what was just then begun to be called Ho Chi Minh City, with ten thousand tons of wheat from American farmers.

[Getting to and from North Vietnam] was very, very difficult; . . . We carried a copy of the Constitution and the law books in our coats in case Pan American [Airways] objected. I think [my husband Peter bought] the first ticket that said New York–Hanoi of any ticket that was ever written in this country. It was difficult. For example, on the 1972 trip to bring the prisoners of war home, we went on SAS [airline]: New York, Cope [Copenhagen], Bangkok. Travel inside Indochina was managed by the ICC, which was run by Poland, Canada, Hungary, and Indonesia.

The ICC ran little, tiny old pieces of equipment which took off [laughter] by the grace of God. And you had to wait in Bangkok and get in line. And there was a lot of bribery involved. People were desperate to get on that plane. And that's the only plane that you could use to get to Hanoi if you were in Bangkok. So UN personnel had to use that, and UNICEF was going in, and the UNDP [United Nations Development Program] was going in, and personnel from countries that had diplomatic relations with Vietnam were using that. We're talking about nine, twelve, or eighteen seats. And it ran only three times a week. So we're not only dealing with a country that's ten thousand miles away but which also was virtually impossible to get to.

Most people did not want to do the New York–Moscow, Moscow-Hanoi route. There was another route, the Bangkok-Vientiane-Hanoi route. That was the ICC route. So I've done it all. But in 1969, you couldn't pick up your telephone and call the travel agent and say, "Book me to Hanoi." It was just much more complicated than that. There was no relationship. And there still isn't. Air France goes into Saigon, Ho Chi Minh City. But then it was a little difficult. Coming out, we came out Air China in 1972. Hanoi to Peking, Beijing. And then on an Ilyushin Aeroflot, Beijing-Moscow, and then SAS from Moscow to Cope and New York. That was a bit of a trick. We made it. Don't pick a country that's hard to get to, if you want to go to war. . . .

We were eyewitness reporters to damage, to what in fact was going on. One of the purposes, aside from the citizen diplomacy role, included facilitating other people going. I had to make sure that there were three Americans every month going with mail, and so we combed the country for people to go and carry mail. It wasn't always easy because it was quite dangerous. I've spent many a day and many a night in a fallout shelter. It's not quite like the fallout shelters in this country that we built against possible nuclear air attack. These were holes dug in the sidewalks, usually full of rainwater and other living things. The bomb shelters were awful. They were horrible. But it's what saved the population of Vietnam.

Nothing justifies carpet bombing. Nothing. That is just not a justifiable act. That is a genocidal act. You cannot just go and wipe out whole bodies of people. Let them have their own civil war if they want. That's what they had in the first place. Let them have a war of economics. Let them have a war at the ballot box. But that doesn't justify bringing in thousands of American soldiers and their equipment and everything that that means culturally.

Our purposes in going [to Hanoi] were: (1) to facilitate the mail, (2) to enable others to go as eyewitness reporters and to be citizen diplomats, and (3) to see what was going on because so many times, we didn't get any news in this country. First of all, we got no news from North Vietnam because American journalists were not exactly roaming around North Vietnam. American journalists were at the Roxy in Saigon and in the field. So one of the important purposes was the eyewitness reporting. We traveled at great length throughout North Vietnam to achieve that. I went to the northern border, I went to Hanoi and Haiphong after the Christmas bombing in 1972, and we went throughout the southern regions. I have photographs of our trip that are incredible [with respect to] the nature and extent of the damage. We're talking about civilian damage; we're not talking about military targets, just whole towns obliterated by the bombing.

I've never been in a war before. I was an American child witness to the Second World War. We used to knit caps for American soldiers and give them coffee at the railroad station when they went off to war. We collected remnants of soap and used toothpaste tubes. That was the closest I'd ever come to a war. Korea was very far away, and I had no involvement in that. In Vietnam, I was on the field with the victims of my own country's bombing. Frequently, I had to hide from my own country's planes. That was the eyewitness reporting. For example, after the My Lai massacre, which Seymour Hersh so vividly described, I met with two children who were survivors of My Lai and whose stories I took down verbatim. It was very horrifying for me to hear the nature of the destruction of that village, which included women and children. Later, I visited My Lai and saw the ditch where women and babies huddled and into which Lieutenant Calley ordered his soldiers to shoot.

I remember coming back from my first trip, and the Chicago Eight trial of Hayden, Hoffman, Dellinger, and the others was on. I was a witness at that trial for Tom Hayden and tried to describe to the judge what I had just seen and heard in Vietnam. Of course, that testimony was stricken from the record. But those were very life-remembering experiences. So you don't want to go to war quickly in the Persian Gulf right now, when you know what war is about. . . .

I remember a kind of amusing moment when we were in a jeep at about two or three in the morning. We had to travel at night all the time during the war. We were traveling to Phat Xiem, where a huge Catholic cathedral had been terribly bombed. All of a sudden, Bill Coffin, who had been with the CIA as a military liaison, spotted a silver streak in the sky. He knew it was a plane. It probably was not a Vietnamese plane. All I can recall is that first I was in the jeep, and within a second, we were in a bunker. Everything had stopped. The driver and the Vietnamese logistics people had just moved us bodily into bunkers. And the Vietnamese started singing to calm our anxieties and our fears. I kept saying, "Shhhh," because I was afraid the pilots could hear us. It's odd what you do in times like that.

I'll never forget meeting a young woman who was brought to her wedding on the shoulders of another woman because her feet had been blown off by land mines. . . . You remember things. You can't forget them. . . .

When we sent Americans with mail, they went to visit American prisoners of war in the prison camps and traveled through Vietnam. We always sent three. Now, you can say that that's a Christian magic number. But I think it was because it was just easier to have a small group. There would either be one man and two women or two men and one woman. In any event, Ron Young and Trudi Schutz got married, partly as a result of their trip to North Vietnam, or at least they got to know each other better.

Tom [Hayden] and Jane [Fonda] got to know each other pretty well on that first trip. On their second trip, they were encouraged to have children. I remember that. And at one point, they actually took a child to Vietnam. Their first kid's name was Troy, which was originally spelled Troi, named after the young Vietnamese who gave his life blowing up a bridge in the South. They left Troi in the North while they traveled South. By the time they got back, Troi had been toilet trained, something that every mother would envy, instant toilet training. Well, that was kind of funny. There were a lot of domestic fallouts. . . .

On each trip, in 1969 and in 1972, I visited with other POWs, took pictures of them which I brought back for their families, and also brought reports back. One guy, [U.S. Navy Lt. William J.] Mayhew, was shot down with [Lt. Markham] Gartley, and Mayhew stayed behind. Gartley came home with us in 1972. Later, I went to Mayhew's wedding. And then there were other guys from the Hanoi Hilton, as it was called. Yes, we met with a number of them. But then we also met with Vietnamese victims.

American POWs Markham Gartley, Paul Brown, and William Mayhew, at a meeting with Cora Weiss and Madeline Duckles in Hanoi, December 1969. *(Courtesy of Cora Weiss.)*

And so we saw both. Before we brought the three men (Gartley, [Lt. Norris] Charles, and [Maj. Edward] Elias) home in 1972, we [the Reverend Harry Bury, Olga Charles, the Reverend William Coffin, Dave Dellinger, Prof. Richard Falk, Minnie Gartley, and Mary Anne Hamilton] traveled together with them [in North Vietnam] because when you bomb North Vietnam, you don't really ever get to see the country. You see it from a bomb shoot. So before we left, we traveled around a bit to see what Vietnam looked like.

[Although critics might say we were used by the North Vietnamese], *use* is a two-way word, in a sense. We could be using them; they could be using us. But in the end, three men were reunited with their families, and more news was found out because these three guys debriefed for days on who was there, what the conditions were like, and so forth. So it was useful to the American government to have them back. We brought back

Ceremony at which three American POWs — Lt. Norris Charles, Maj. Edward Elias, and Lt. Markham Gartley — were released to a group of Americans that included Dave Dellinger, Richard Falk, and Minnie Lee Gartley, who are shown together in the lower left section of the photo, Hanoi, August 1972. *(Courtesy of Cora Weiss.)*

more mail. A propaganda coup for them, perhaps, but the thank-you by the United States was the Christmas bombing. Don't forget that. That was Henry Kissinger's thank-you for releasing three men. The pilot's release was a statement by the Vietnamese that said, "Here's an offer. Want to talk? Let's talk. Here's a gesture." They kept looking for gestures to make, and they were all spurned. And Kissinger bombed the daylights out of Vietnam after that. . . .

I had my hands full with this. The Americans who went represented a variety of organizations, from the Quakers to the Mennonites to even Vietnam veterans. Barry Romo was a Vietnam veteran. He was the first to go back. That's an extraordinary story. Barry went with Joan Baez and Michael Allen. That was during the Christmas bombing of 1972. That's very early for a Vietnam veteran to go back to Vietnam. But since then, Vietnam veterans have been going in droves and building medical clinics

A group photo taken at the Vietnamese embassy in Laos, August 1972. *Rear, left to right:* Dave Dellinger; the Reverend William Sloane Coffin; Cora Weiss; and Richard Falk. *Front, left to right:* Vietnamese counselor; Olga Charles, wife of POW Norris Charles; and Minnie Lee Gartley, mother of POW Markham Gartley. *(Photo by Peter Arnett.)*

and rebuilding villages. I don't know that that's happened in previous wars. There is a need, as part of the Vietnam syndrome, to see what you did and try to have some recovery. It's both recovery for yourself as well as rehabilitation for the village. So you try to help understand what you did and why you did it. So Barry essentially started, one could say, the return of Vietnam veterans. . . .

I was in Women Strike for Peace, and as their representative, I was elected national co-chair of the Mobilization Against the War in Vietnam, which ran a huge rally in Washington on November 15, 1969. That was a turning point in public opinion on the war in Vietnam. So it was from my role in Women Strike that I was able to participate in other activities, but that was the only organization I belonged to. . . .

I guess decency and justice came with my genes. I've always participated in efforts to improve the quality of life and to create an atmosphere of decency, to prevent conflict here as well as abroad. . . . I was quite active in the civil rights movement. I was Martin Luther King's national treasurer in the Gandhi Society for Human Rights, which was his fund-raising arm for much of the work that he did.

My husband and I played hosts to kids who did fieldwork in the [U.S.] South in SNCC, the Student Nonviolent Coordinating Committee, and that was a very burning-out experience, a difficult experience. After a year in the field, they could get a week in the country, and we would take them to our home in the country in the summer, and they would recover from their experience. Those were usually young black kids from the South. That was an interesting experience because the community that we lived in never had young black kids living there before. This was in the early sixties. And these kids had never been in the North before, so it was a good experience on many levels.

[I traveled to Vietnam despite obligations of family because] sometimes when you do things, you don't examine why you're doing them. It just feels that it's the right thing to do, and if you've got the capacity to do it, you do it. It never dawned on me that bombs would be dangerous. I never thought that I was going into a seriously dangerous situation. When I think about it now, I wonder if I would ever let my own children do what I did. It was crazy, I guess, looking back on it, because it was very dangerous. But my marvelous husband learned how to change diapers and cook dinners. And we had a lot of nice young friends who came and lived with the kids and with Peter.

I remember when I went to Paris to make the arrangements for the POW release, Frances FitzGerald [author of *Fire in the Lake*] came with her boyfriend and stayed in the house to help take care of the kids. That was a nice babysitting job on Martha's Vineyard; that wasn't bad. But there was a lot of support. I guess I realized that this had to be done because if the war was going to be fought over the POW issue, then that was the issue we had to deal with in order to end a wrong war that had absolutely no legitimacy morally or legally; we had to end it as quickly as possible. There were thousands of American kids coming back in body bags. That was inexcusable. To stop that and to stop the thousands and tens of thousands and, finally, over a million Vietnamese from being killed. You do if you're called; you'll serve. . . .

We refused to have the Vietnamese pay for [our transportation costs to and from Vietnam], not that they offered or that they could. Everybody had to raise their own money. It was a twenty-four-hour flight, and it's ten thousand plus miles away. As I recall, even then it was close to two thousand dollars; maybe in the early days it was fourteen or fifteen hundred dollars. But it was never cheap. People did everything. They even sold cupcakes. If you had to have a bake sale, you did it. People scrounged. It was very important. And everyone recognized the importance, and so there were a lot of contributions. But it was not funded by any government. . . .

It was because of my value system that I got involved, and that's a value system that very much supports peace and justice. I must say that after seeing some of these pictures of the patients that I've sat over and interviewed and the families of the dead and dying and missing that I'd been with, I'm more adamant than ever that conflict be negotiated and not fought militarily. I don't know that I could say I'm a pacifist. I'm certainly a nuclear pacifist. I've never examined thoroughly other forms of pacifism, but in a nuclear age with sophisticated equipment, it's absolutely essential that people not go to war anymore. And I think that experience, for me, probably made that indelible.

I never was in this to support the Vietnamese government. I'm trying to prevent the war in the Persian Gulf, and I'm not supporting any government. The Vietnamese have gone through a very horrible time after the war. They may have won a war, but they lost a victory, in a sense, because of the embargo, because the United States has refused to recognize them. There has been no trade, and the United States kept telling its allies not to trade with the Vietnamese. The Vietnamese have been in very, very bad shape economically. And they've hurt. They've hurt hard. The United States never fulfilled the agreement that we wrote with Vietnam in Paris, the Paris agreement, which called for healing the wounds of war. So they always thought they were going to get a billion dollars, perhaps three billion, whatever, money that they could easily use and they never got. So they hurt, badly.

I had no expectations of the [North Vietnamese government]. I have talked to them about feelings of discomfort that I've held, that they didn't share their intelligence with us about the Cambodians, for example, about the Khmer Rouge and Pol Pot. They didn't let us know the nature of their true relationship with China, and just recently, I received an apology for that, which I find rather amazing. I'm overwhelmed right now, actually, that the foreign minister of a country would apologize to someone for not being totally forthcoming during the war.

But they claim that they: (1) did not have terrific intelligence on these two issues in their early stages, and (2) really hoped upon hope that the tension with the Khmer Rouge and with the Chinese could be settled amicably because Vietnam was one country that did not particularly, for good reason, want to get involved in a war again. Their desire for a peaceful solution apparently overwhelmed their willingness to express to Americans what they knew about the genocide that was going on in Cambodia. . . .

I'm sure the United States not only [alleges that the Vietnamese have violated the terms of the peace agreement] but makes many more charges, including the fact that the Vietnamese have not uncovered the last MIA. Of course, the fact that Germany has not uncovered the last MIA, nor Korea. . . . In no war has the MIA issue ever been settled finally. They also made charges about withholding Amerasians. The charges and countercharges are enormous. I'm not here to sit in judgment of who violated what. But the U.S. needed every excuse it could find to prevent it from giving postwar reparations to Vietnam.

We've never lost a war before. It was beyond our capacity to acknowledge our loss and also pay for it. I think enough time has now gone by. It's fifteen years, and I think it's time now to recognize Vietnam and to open the trade routes. After all, look at all the other changes in the world. Moscow and Washington, who hated each other for forty-five years, which led to the biggest arms race in history, are now in bed together. Iran and Iraq fought each other for ten years and now are dealing with each other. Enemies make strange bedfellows.

Why did the U.S. go to war in Vietnam in the first place? I don't think you can get an answer from any student in America today. I doubt it. Was it tungsten? . . . [President] Eisenhower, as I recall, valued the resource of tungsten in Vietnam, which we needed. And we thought that if we were to lose Vietnam to the Communists, we would lose a resource. It's very interesting because perhaps somebody might one day write that tungsten was to Vietnam and the war with the United States what oil is to the Persian Gulf and the war with the United States and that we are indeed at war to protect our trade routes.

Very frequently in conflict, people forget the reason for the fight. But that was a ten-year, not fight, but war, in which not only thousands of people were killed, over a million in Vietnam, but a whole culture was turned inside out. A whole society was turned on its head. The period of the 1960s and early 1970s witnessed one of the most extraordinary changes in American society. For years, families, fathers and sons, either supported each other or turned on each other over the issue of whether to fight. It wasn't just a question of changed hairstyles but a whole culture that changed.

There's now an expression in society about whether a person seems to be "sort of sixties." If you're "sixties," it says something about the nature of your attitude or your culture. In any event, the point is that people have forgotten why we went to war, and the reason why we continued to fight the war seems to have changed during the course of the ten years of the war. Because at one point, the war began to be fought because of our POWs. We had to stay fighting until we got them back. Well, that wasn't the reason to go into war in the first place, was it? . . .

Wars are normally fought or justified to us because our security is at stake. The question is, "How was our security at stake [in Vietnam]?" I don't think Americans understand why we went there or what it was all about. I don't think the kids who fought there understood why we went there. There is the expression "to keep America safe" or "to keep America safe for democracy" or "safe from communism." You know, the Vietnamese were never planning to come to the United States to take our country. There were plenty of other Communist countries in the world with whom we were trading.

I just don't think the war was understood at all. I may be wrong, but I guess only the polls will tell. Go around and speak to people in the street who didn't go to Vietnam, who simply paid their taxes, and ask them why they think it was fought. I bet you'll get a lot of different answers or maybe a lot of "I don't knows." But we do know that one of the reasons it was fought, apparently, was to help develop a new level of weaponry, antipersonnel weaponry, which had never been used before, new equipment for which Vietnam was the testing ground.

Every time Congress was asked to vote another shot in the arm of money, there were always headlines the night before that would say, "VC Offensive." And that was to encourage Congress to vote more bucks so that the arsenal just began to bulge, and endless amounts of money were put into the supply lines for the Pentagon. There were constant warnings that the Communists were coming and that there were Viet Cong offensives, whether or not they happened.

One deception was plain, the accuracy of news reporting. Earlier I mentioned the Roxy. That was a famous hotel in Saigon where they used to have what they called the "five o'clock follies." At five in the afternoon, the military would brief American journalists. There were two kinds of journalists in Vietnam. There were the Peter Arnetts who went out with Charlie Company and risked getting blown apart at the front, and there were a few of those. Then there were others who just went to the five o'clock follies. A lot of reporting was done based on materials handed over by the military.

One of the prisoners we brought home in 1972 was a recon pilot, a reconnaissance pilot. His job was to do body counts. He could make up anything and did, according to him. So there was just a lack of accuracy.

I don't blame a lot of [the boat] people for leaving Vietnam. Some apparently are now going back but not very many. And there are many who go home to visit. It's good for remittances for the families that stay behind. We see in Kuwait what happens, for instance, when you lose remittances. A change in regime threatens a person's way of life, or he perceives it that way. And it probably did. If you were a successful capitalist doing well in the South who was now being told that you were under new orders and new regulations, you wouldn't like it, and you would want to send your kids abroad. Well, that's true in many, many countries, isn't it? Soviets leaving the Soviet Union, for example, doesn't justify the United States invading the Soviet Union. My husband came here to escape Hitler from Austria in the 1930s. Change of government, change of economic way of life, and change of lifestyle will change peoples' views about whether they should stay where they are.

Something has to happen to try to stop the movement of refugees in this world because it has become a very serious item. There is an incredible population shift going on. It results in "brain drains" for the countries that they leave, which is not healthy for future trade relationships. Some of the smartest, most wonderfully creative people in the Soviet Union have been leaving. That's not good for us as Americans because then we're going to have fewer enterprising people to trade with in the former Soviet Union in the end.

[With regard to allegations of mass executions after the war], anything is possible. [However], if you don't know, you can't say. Peter and I went to a re-education camp in South Vietnam. It was an effort on their part to do something with the people who opposed them in the war and who were responsible for part of the destruction in South Vietnam. As victors, they couldn't let the opposite military just keep walking around on the streets without some kind of action, I guess, much as we had the Nuremberg Trials in Germany after the Second World War. Whether or not they handled that right — I'm sure many researchers and historians are going to look into that.

But rather than execute a lot of people, they did put tons of them into these camps and then released them. And many of them were let go to go to the United States. So I'm not sure about that, postwar executions, mass executions. I'd like to look into that.

I'm not sure I could give a handy definition of patriotism. Doing what's good and what's right, supporting life and not death, and bringing people together instead of keeping them apart. That sounds pretty good to me. And paying your taxes all the time. I never withheld a penny.

One or two months after I came back with the first mail from the prisoners in November 1969, Congressman Benjamin Rosenthal, the Democrat from Queens [New York] (he has since died), brought me to Congress and, in an extraordinary ceremony, declared that this was the height of patriotism, to risk one's life. I'm reluctant to mention it now because it seems a bit much. But he described risking one's life to do something (we didn't have to do it) which enhanced the quality of life for the prisoners and their families and allowed the government to know more than they were able to know otherwise as the height of patriotism. [Even] George McGovern, for example, likes to refer to me as his grass-roots patriot.

[To claim that our trips to Vietnam prolonged the war is] giving the antiwar movement an awful lot of credit. I can't believe that a band of citizens had that much power, really. The North Vietnamese had a goal, a united Vietnam. The Americans had a goal, destroy Vietnam. We weren't going to either change those goals or lengthen the war. What we were trying to do was shorten the time of the destruction of the war. I don't think these little visits encouraged the Vietnamese in the least. . . .

Time and age does mellow, but it doesn't weaken your resolve to still support right and justice. . . . If we had to rely on one individual, we'd still be at war. The beauty of the antiwar movement was that it was such a patchwork of classes and races and ages and people. There were the singing crowds, the Joan Baezes and Judy Collinses; all the music; and Phil Ochs, whom I remember most warmly. That created a whole new musical culture. Music was terribly important in reaching people. There were the Vietnam veterans themselves who came back. There were housewives. There were my colleagues in Women Strike for Peace who would go around with banners that said, "Not my sons, not your sons." We wouldn't give our sons to war. There were young mothers who went around with banners saying, "Children are not for burning." I don't think you can put your finger on any one person.

Women Strike for Peace got started as an organization against the testing of nuclear weapons in 1961. It took an internal struggle and many discussions before we moved the focus away from nuclear testing. Women Strike was effective because we were mostly all young mothers in the 1960s and housewives. I was not working full-time then; I was working full-time in the peace movement.

We were very creative and very innovative. We tried to see [Secretary of Defense Robert] McNamara, and he wouldn't see us. He closed the doors of the Pentagon for the first time in history. We just stood there and took off our shoes and banged our heels on the door. I thought that was terrific. And it got some attention. We tied ourselves to the fence of the Executive Building next to the White House to protest the war and try to see the president. And we were willing to go and visit the Vietnamese. We created the concept that all women are sisters. When the U.S. government wouldn't let the Vietnamese women into the United States, we went to Canada to meet them. When the Canadians tried to bar our way, we negotiated our way in. And we'd never done anything like that before.

Once we actually lay down in front of the Dow Chemical Company building on Park Avenue because they made napalm or the ingredients for napalm. We lay down on Park Avenue in our coats and suits and put signs on our bodies, "I'm a dead Vietnamese; I'm a dead Cambodian." We did things that I guess we never thought we had the capacity to do but which under the First Amendment to the Constitution and because this is a democratic country we had the right to do; and we exercised our constitutional rights. We also had some creative genius, I must say [laughter].

[Women Strike for Peace] was the beginning of peer-group organizing. The lawyers organized. Peter [Weiss] was active in that. And there were medical groups, the Committee of Responsibility. There were different groups that formed for different purposes. . . . Very few [peer groups formed] during Vietnam. Most of them have formed since Vietnam, but the origin was in the Vietnam War. I think they were formed by their own people. For example, if you were a professor and didn't want to join a general organization and deal with all of the issues, you would form "Professors Against the War in Vietnam," which indeed happened.

I have only one regret. I was going to save this for my own book. There was a demonstration in Central Park where a group of people wanted to burn their draft cards, and that would have been an act of civil disobedience. I was not very keen on civil disobedience because I thought it would drive away the mainstream of the population, which included myself and which we desperately needed to affect public opinion. In retrospect, as the leader of that demonstration, I should not have denied

[them] that [act of civil disobedience], and perhaps that would have moved things a little faster. I may have been wrong, and I'll go into detail when I write my own book, if I ever do. I don't have any other regrets. Maybe I ought to, but I don't. . . .

I can't remember most of the things I said. I hope that I wouldn't regret having said them. . . . I thought that [Jane Fonda's broadcasts over Radio Hanoi] were an unfortunate mistake. I don't think that there's anything illegal . . . or immoral [in] broadcasting on the radio as long as you're honest and not broadcasting for the purpose of enhancing one side or the other. But knocking prisoners or accusing people of lying seems just ridiculous. . . . That was very unfortunate. It didn't help. But I think she has said that herself at some point. . . .

If you're a decent person, you don't like lies, and to the extent that the government lied in order to perpetuate its war, one can't support that. And to the extent that the government decided to pick on Vietnam and permitted a war which was not necessary, you can't support that either. When government is good, you support it, and that's why we have elections to try and achieve good government. One can't knock government as an institution, but certainly one can knock it when it doesn't behave properly.

16

Noam Chomsky

Prof. Avram Noam Chomsky traveled to Hanoi in April 1970, after being told that it was urgent that he go. Upon arriving in Hanoi, he learned that he was wanted primarily to lecture at the Polytechnic University, which he did. Chomsky also spent a week in Laos and determined that a reported North Korean invasion of Laos was false.

Chomsky expressed dismay that the U.S. press failed to report accurately on the depth of the destruction and the scope of the killing in Cambodia. He was particularly irate about the deception committed by the U.S. government during the war and the failure of the media to accurately report the extent of the destruction being inflicted upon civilian targets in North Vietnam by U.S. bomber aircraft. He suggested a hypothetical reporter's account of the American Revolutionary War in language similar to that used to describe the Vietnam War. Professor Chomsky, who actively supported resistance to the draft, also expressed outrage and despair about a system of government that is unwilling to admit error and in which lying by government officials and political leaders is systemic. He believes that prosecuting the Vietnam War was a crime for which top U.S. government officials should have faced criminal prosecution.

Professor Chomsky, born in 1928, has taught and lectured in Europe, Asia, and the United States. He is the author of several dozen books on semantics and political affairs and has received international awards and recognition for his scholarship. Books that he has written related to Vietnam include: *American Power and the New Mandarins* (New York: Pantheon Books, 1969); *At War With Asia* (New York: Pantheon Books, 1970); and *Culture of Terrorism* (Boston: South End Press, 1988). Professor Chomsky also wrote the forward to *Prevent the Crime of Silence: Reports From the Sessions of the International War Crimes Tribunal* (London: Allen Lane, 1971); and his article "From After Pinkville" was included in *Ecocide in Indochina,*

Barry Weisberg, ed. (San Francisco: Canfield Press, 1970). Professor Chomsky is a member of the faculty of the Department of Linguistics, Massachusetts Institute of Technology, Cambridge. The interview took place on October 5, 1990, in his campus office, located on the second floor of a dated, barrackslike structure.

PROFESSOR CHOMSKY: [I traveled to Hanoi] once, in March of 1970. I was in Hanoi for a week. I was in Vientiane for a week. [I traveled with Douglas Dowd and Richard Fernandez.] We knew each other. We had no other affiliations other than various connections. We were all involved in resistance to the war. [I was] one of the founders [of Resist]. I was involved with lots of other organizations, the American Friends Service Committee, the War Resisters League. I guess I was actually a member of the International Confederation of Disarmament and Peace, which was based in London. I was officially a member of Resist. There were lots and lots of other groups with which I was associated in one or another way.

The invitation [to go to North Vietnam] was transmitted to me by Cora Weiss, who was involved in regular contacts with the Vietnamese, and where she got it, I don't recall. I can't remember the name, but I know that after I received the invitation — I had received many such invitations, but this invitation came from a friend who said that there was a sense of urgency behind it, and so I should really try to do it. Immediately after I got the phone call with the invitation, I got a call from the State Department who obviously intercepted the telephone communication . . . just expressing their willingness to help and to expedite the trip in any way they could and so forth. Who the caller was, I don't remember. The only visas that we needed, as far as I recall, were from the Laotian embassy in Washington. I paid for [the trip] myself.

I couldn't say who [else] went, actually. Some of the people who went are personal friends, Howard Zinn, for example, who went at least once, maybe more, and Dan Berrigan. Some of the people I sort of knew. We had associations: Staughton Lynd, Tom Hayden, others I probably didn't know. . . . But there was nothing coordinated, as far as I knew. I don't know if I either encouraged or discouraged [other Americans to go to Hanoi]. It was hard for me. I was in the middle of teaching. . . .

I only discovered the purpose [for the trip] when I went there. Although I had often been asked to come, I had not done so because I was very busy. This time, what I was told was that it was something very urgent [and it was] very important that I go. I didn't know what the urgent thing was, but I thought I'd see. The urgent thing turned out to be they wanted me to lecture at the [Polytechnic] University. In fact, much of the time I spent there, I spent lecturing at the university, talking to people in various fields that I had any acquaintance with. One of the reasons for the timing was that that happened to be a lapse in the bombing. And they had been trying to maintain a university system in the jungles. And now they were moved back temporarily, into the remnants of the Polytechnic University in Hanoi. Much of it was destroyed by bombing. But there were still remnants of buildings. They were bringing people back in during this period when the bombing was not going on right there. And they were trying to reconstruct something. There were very few Americans or Western intellectuals who they could bring in to lecture.

I mainly lectured on my specialty for hours and hours, lectures on anything I knew anything about to everybody around. I remember one day, I went seven hours straight, lecturing on linguistics and related fields. I also did other things, of course. But the only thing that was at all nonroutine, not a programmed trip, was this, so I assume that was the urgent reason. I was surprised to learn about the level that they had been able to keep up in academic work and intellectual life under these grotesque conditions.

I got to areas in the region, Thanh Hoa Province. We traveled some but none of the areas of intense bombing. Although I knew abstractly what it was like, it is different when you see it. So in a sense, what I knew abstractly, I saw at firsthand. Some things about the intensity of the bombing of civilian areas surprised me a little because they hadn't really been reported. For example, in Thanh Hoa City, a large hospital had been completely obliterated and there had been some mention of that, but the claim here was that had happened in the course of bombing military targets. But it was transparent that that was false. The hospital was in the middle of a settled urban area which was not bombed. It was quite a distance; I can't recall offhand, but I would say it was a few miles before you got to the nearest possible military target. So it looked as if the Thanh Hoa hospital was targeted.

There was one bridge, called the Ham Rong bridge, which the United States had been trying to blow out. There had been villages nearby, and they had not yet got the bridge. Later, after we left, they got it with smart bombs. I don't know how many sorties had been aimed at it, and everything in the region was absolutely flat. You couldn't even see the remnants of villages. In fact, the hills were already shaved off with bombing. A little hill was all that was left of some mountain. The devastation was striking. Traveling through what was left of the highway, you could see B-52 pits from the bombing all over the place. Plenty of devastation. I had sort of known it generally and wasn't surprised in that sense.

[While in North Vietnam], I saw Pham Van Dong, who was prime minister. I didn't [see any Americans while I was there]. The two people who were with me did. They went to see prisoners.

It is claimed that there is something in the FBIS, which I think stands for Federal Broadcast Information Service, a government record of [alleged foreign broadcasts], that attributes something to me, claiming it was broadcast over Radio Hanoi. But I have no recollection of that. The only thing that I can imagine is that comments we made at some meeting somewhere were also broadcast. Or it may be a fabrication or misattribution. It is possible that it may have been a statement I made at a public gathering of some kind somewhere that was recorded. Or there may be some other explanation.

[The trip remains vivid in my mind.] In truth, very much so. I also spent a week in Laos. There, I learned a lot that I didn't know and that the American press corps didn't know and that is pretty much out of history. In fact, there I did a lot of research in that week. I found out a great deal and also published a great deal and brought back a lot of material that the press was at that time suppressing and which still is known only to specialists, which I sent off to Senate committees and other places. If I went back [to Vietnam], I would do it for two reasons. For one thing, to learn, as always. And for another thing, probably to do what I did the first time, lecture at the university.

If I had more time, there were things I wanted to do very much and that I didn't do and then nobody ever did but that they were willing to let me do. In particular, what I wanted to do very much was to go into northern Laos. Northern Laos was, at that time, the target of maybe the most intense bombing in history. It was later exceeded by the U.S. bombing of Cambodia, but that was two or three years later.

I had spent a good deal of time in Laos, interviewing refugees from those regions. This had been mostly suppressed by the U.S. media. A little trickle here and there, but they were basically suppressing the facts. And I made a big effort to find out what they were, and I did get a lot of material from refugees. They told me in Hanoi that it would be possible to get me into the regions from which the refugees had come, but it would have been a long business. It would have been probably at least a couple of weeks' trip through the jungles and back roads and trying to avoid bombing and then maybe a week there and maybe a week back. I would have very much liked to do that, but I couldn't figure out a way to take off the time. If I had been able to go back, that's what I would have done.

I would have very much liked to have gone down to the southern part of North Vietnam, below the twentieth parallel where, according to the few people who did go — John Pilger, a respected Australian journalist, and others — it was basically turned into a moonscape, and I would have liked to verify just what happened down there. A few others went down to those areas. Mostly, we were confined to the area around Hanoi which was heavily bombed. . . . To get farther away took time because there had been so much destruction that it was a slow trip. And I didn't have the time.

I didn't set out to do anything, so therefore, I can't say that I accomplished what I set out to do, but it was very interesting to me. First of all, as I say, in the Laotian part, I learned a lot and found out a lot that was basically unknown or else suppressed. In the North Vietnamese part, I didn't learn very much that I didn't know. I was able to do what they wanted, which was lecture, and I was happy to do that.

I would say that the major impact [of the trip on me] was probably Laos . . . because that was largely new to me. I had not realized the extent of the savagery of the American attack, aimed specifically at civilians, with no possible military concern, until I did the research in Laos. And although I had been very critical of the press, I had no conception of the level of deceit that the press was involved in until I went to Laos and saw it firsthand. . . .

Of course, the government deceives, but that's their business. They are in the business of lying. You expect governments to lie. Every government. Why should they tell the truth? The media on the other hand, I can't say that I ever had any particularly starry-eyed view of them. But I was surprised by the level of deceit that I observed and the level of refusal to look at the facts I observed. I think even the American embassy in Laos was surprised by this. In fact, I know they were. Just to give one minor illustration, there was a standard story at the time, which is still in all the history books, that there were fifty thousand North Vietnamese troops in Laos, and at the time that I got there, there had just been a speech by President Nixon saying that the North Vietnamese had sent seventeen thousand more troops, that it was an invasion of Laos. As a result, the whole press corps was in there.

Everybody flew into Vientiane because there was this big North Vietnamese invasion. When I got there, the first thing I discovered was that every journalist there was laughing about it because they knew it was a fabrication. The reason was that the day of the Nixon speech, they had all attended the "five o'clock follies," to pick up the news. You go to the American embassy at five o'clock, and they tell you what you are supposed to report. And they had the standard briefing from the bored military attaché who gave the same briefing and had been giving it every day for a long time. They never heard of any North Vietnamese invasion, and then they turned the radio on that night, and Nixon was announcing a North Vietnamese invasion. So of course, they knew it was a total fabrication, but they all reported it anyway. One journalist who I found — I checked when I got back — [was the] head of *Time-Life*, did report it. But he put it down at the end of his column. He had a joke that the initiated could understand, saying, "This is a fake." But basically, the press just reported what they knew to be a lie. I was interested in pursuing that further. So I started asking what's the evidence for the fifty thousand North Vietnamese troops, and nobody knew.

So I figured, well, I'll go to the American embassy and see what the evidence is. So I went to the American embassy in Vientiane, and I asked to talk to the political officer, and there was a guy named Frank Murphy, and he was very friendly and affable, and I said I'd like to see what kind of documentary evidence there is about the North Vietnamese in Laos. So he was very happy. He said I was the first person who had ever asked. Nobody had ever asked. Everybody else just scribbled what they were told. He took me to a room and gave me all kinds of documents, Rand Corporation reports, intelligence reports, and so on. And I spent a fair amount of time going through them. They were very interesting, and I took a lot of notes. It turned out that according to their evidence, there was one battalion of twenty-five hundred troops in Laos. That's it. The rest of the alleged fifty thousand troops were old men carrying bags of rice on their shoulders to places that were being so heavily bombed that they couldn't farm.

Any American reporter could have found that out. But none did, and none wanted to know, just as none wanted to go to the refugee camps where you could find the stories of what was going on inside Laos. If you wanted to find out what was going on in the bombed-out areas, you go to refugee camps, thirty kilometers outside of Vientiane, where at that time, there were about twenty-five thousand refugees who had just been flown out by the CIA — their mercenary armies swept through one region, and they had fresh stories.

I spent twenty or thirty hours during the week I was there just taking refugee interviews, and one reporter, an American, went with me, a young stringer for the *Far Eastern Economic Review* who occasionally would get something published here. One or two reporters went on their own for a half hour or an hour and picked up a little information. But basically, nobody wanted to know. It's much easier to sit in the hotel bar in Vientiane and go to the American embassy to get the official news, and it sort of went on like that.

During the one week that I was in Laos, I met a member of the royal Lao government, the minister of rural affairs, a wealthy landowner. This is the government that we supported, that we installed. I had a long interview with him in which he described to me why he basically hoped that there would be a victory by the Pathet Lao, the guerrillas. He said that this would be terrible for him. He was a wealthy landowner. They'd probably get rid of him, and who knows what, but it was the only thing that could possibly save Laos, and he was a nationalist and he wanted the country saved. And he went on at length about this. I asked him if I could use the material. He said, "Sure," but not to identify him, just identify him as an urban intellectual. . . . No journalist ever found such a person.

I met Pathet Lao cadres that were underground in Vientiane, including some who were working undercover, others who were there on sort of R&R [rest and relaxation]: sort of sneak into the town to get away from the bombing. I ran into all sorts of things. Nothing remotely like this ever appeared in the press, and very little of it is in history books. It's not that I was a great journalist. It's just that it was immediately in front of you, if you bothered to look. It's not the worst case; it's the typical case. The heaviest bombing ever was the bombing of rural Cambodia, about three years after this, which exceeded the bombing of northern Laos apparently.

It's pretty hard to put figures on this, but [the bombing of Cambodia] was one of the [tragedies of the war]. The bombing had been very heavy. [From] about January to August of 1973, the bombing really reached a peak of intensity, which was hitherto unknown. It was bombing in inner Cambodia, peasant areas. That's basically what sort of created the Khmer Rouge. It led to such a legacy of peasant hatred that the Khmer Rouge recruited very widely at that time, as we know, and became a major force. That bombing drove maybe a million people into the city. The American reporters were there in Phnom Penh, and across the street there were a million refugees.

Sidney Schanberg [reporter for the *New York Times*] was there. Dith Pran, his assistant, was there. In order to find out what was going on in inner Cambodia, they didn't have to take a trek out into the jungle to find refugees. All they had to do was cross the street. And you could answer for yourself the question of what happened. I've done it. I went through and published something about the record of their reporting during that period. Sidney Schanberg had a long story in the *Times* virtually every day but no refugees. There is a sentence here and there about refugees, but basically, he was avoiding it. That's the wrong story. Dith Pran wasn't interested. Dith Pran didn't care what happened to the peasants of Cambodia, as he demonstrated at that time. They were being massacred, and he never cared enough to ask one of them what was going on. It was when he and his friends were attacked later that he got upset, which is not surprising.

Sidney Schanberg's record is just disgraceful. He was the main *Times* correspondent, and he totally avoided this topic, the major topic. If you look at movies, like *The Killing Fields,* you will notice that it starts with an American bombing of a Cambodian village. And that's the one case that Sidney Schanberg reported. Why did they report that one case? Well, because that case was a mistake. They bombed a government town by mistake. And after all, anybody can make mistakes, so that you can report. And they described all the horrors, the people torn apart, and so on and so forth. What about the bombings that weren't mistakes? What about the time when they hit the target, they hit the village that they wanted to hit? Those you don't report because that's the wrong story. We could say the same about Vietnam, and it goes on right through today.

How much reporting do you see today about the people in Vietnam still dying from chemical warfare poisoning? Thousands, if not hundreds of thousands, are affected, and certainly thousands [were] killed by U.S. chemical warfare. They are still dying. You still find the deformed fetuses of newborn babies in hospitals. How much reporting have you seen about that? Wrong story. It's the wrong story. We don't want to know about that, and therefore, we don't report it. . . .

I had no expectations particularly [of the current Vietnamese government leaders]. I think they've done a pretty rotten job, and I frankly thought they probably would do better, but I had no special expectations. My position at the time, and I wrote it at the time, was that the United States was in effect turning the whole of Indochina over to North Vietnam, and the reason was — as I wrote at the time, right after I came back from that trip — I said: "Look, what's going to happen is one of two things. Either the United States will just wipe out the whole place or else the North Vietnamese will take it over because we've destroyed every popular force everywhere else."

We've destroyed the South Vietnamese, who were the worst victims of the war. It was obvious to me that we were destroying the Laotians. I assumed that we would destroy Cambodia. I didn't predict the Khmer Rouge, and I said probably the North Vietnamese who were tough and disciplined will be able to withstand this, so the end result will be they will have everything because we've destroyed everything else. And I think that's close to what happened. . . .

Whether we should restore diplomatic relations, I can't answer. That's kind of an understatement. . . . What we should do, we should have Nuremberg trials for ourselves, and we should pay them reparations. If somebody asked me, "Should the Germans renew diplomatic relations with Israel?" I'd laugh. The Germans should give reparations to Israel, and the United States should give reparations to Vietnam. We owe them. We can't pay for what we've done, but we killed several million people, we wiped out three countries.

[Does the American public fully understand the origins and history of U.S. involvement in Vietnam?] Certainly not. In order to even get a minimal understanding of it, you'd have to be willing to carry out a major research project. The government has no interest in telling the truth about this or basically any other matter, and the media are basically servants of power. It seems true of everything that happens right in front of you even today. If you want to understand what's happening in the world today, you aren't going to find it out in the media.

The U.S. version [of the Vietnamese boat people] is that they are mostly economic [not political] refugees. That they are fleeing from unbearable economic circumstances and from repression. How do you account for that? Let's ask other questions. In 1776 there was a revolution, somewhere. After that revolution, about four percent of the population fled, fled in terror, during the revolution and afterwards. Boat people were fleeing from Boston in the middle of winter. They were going off to Nova Scotia and dying in the snow, writing back terrible letters about how they had escaped from these maniacs and so forth.

Four percent of the population of Vietnam would be about two and one-half million people, considerably more than the reported number of boat people would make it — the recorded numbers are underestimated undoubtedly because many died — so let's say roughly comparable to the percentage of the population that fled from the American colonies. While there is no comparison, the people that fled from the American colonies were fleeing the richest country in the world with unparalleled advantages. But they were afraid. And George Washington wasn't Pol Pot. After revolutionary upheavals, somebody lost. Revolutionary wars are civil wars. The U.S. revolution was a civil war. It was about as much a civil war as the Civil War was. Our revolution was a civil war.

If we described our Revolutionary War the way we describe other countries today, here is the way we would describe it. We would say that there was a group of local terrorists, led by a thug named George Washington, and they were working with the French. The French had most of the military force. There was a French-English war going on, and in this area, the English were driven out by the French with the assistance of some local terrorist forces who were terrorizing the population, after which there was a huge flight of people in terror, including a lot of the black population, because they knew what was in store for them. Plenty of American Indians couldn't flee because they had nowhere to go, but they knew they were going to be targeted next by the genocidal goals of the winners.

And that's essentially what happened. So the terrorists won, thanks to the French fleet and the French army. That's the way we would describe it if we were describing it the way we describe some other country. It would be distorted, of course, but that's just to say that what we say about everybody else is distorted. If you ask about why people fled from Vietnam, they are plainly fleeing from one of the poorest countries in the world, a country that was totally devastated by war, which has had virtually no recovery, in part due to the very repressive and incompetent regime. Many are fleeing from repression which is harsh, not on a scale of what we've seen elsewhere but very harsh. That's the story.

I have been looking to see if there is any evidence [of a bloodbath after the war]. There is no evidence for it. There are some people who claim that. . . . Karl Jackson, who is an Asia specialist at Berkeley, if I am not mistaken, has written a few things claiming there was a bloodbath, but virtually nobody has backed that story, so far. Whether he is right or not, I don't know. In fact, everyone was kind of surprised at the lack of such a response because it's pretty typical after such a war. For example, in France after the Nazis were expelled, there were tens of thousands of people slaughtered, and as far as we know, nothing like that happened in

Vietnam. Maybe it did. Maybe some evidence will come out and show that it did.

[I believed I was acting in the best interests of the United States] when I was opposing the war. When I was organizing resistance, I was acting in the best interests of the United States. Of course . . . it depends upon what you mean by the United States. If the term *United States* refers to the government, then, no, I was not acting in the best interests of the government, nor would I ever choose to do that because I don't regard the people as slaves of the state. If you ask whether I was acting in the best interests of the American people, yes, sure. We had no business being there. We were involved in aggression. The best interest for them was to get out of the aggression.

Patriotism is service to the people, not to the state. [The expression "my country, right or wrong" raises the question] What do you mean by my country? By my country, do you mean the state, or do you mean the population? If you mean the population, well, sure. You kind of care about the population. If you mean government, no. Government is usually an enemy of the population. Anybody from Thomas Paine to Thomas Jefferson up till today could tell you that.

If [it is alleged that my trip and others like it prolonged the war], it's kind of an odd criticism for a number of reasons. For one thing, the activities I was in — the main reason I never went [earlier] was because I thought what I was doing here was much more important. Now, what I was doing here was working against the war. Now, I presume that working against the war here encouraged people there to continue to fight on, so if the criticism was to have any validity, it should be directed against what I was doing here, say, giving talks against the war and so on. So the proper way to formulate the criticism would be to say: "Everyone in the United States should shut up. If the U.S. government decides to attack another country, we should goose-step on command. If the United States carries out genocide, no matter what it does, we should goose-step on command because otherwise, it will encourage other people over there to keep fighting." That's the criticism. In other words, the criticism could be expressed by a Nazi or a Stalinist but not by anybody else. And for that reason, I don't even bother responding to it. So, for example, let's take the analogue. Suppose that some Nazi in Nazi Germany criticized the people who were opposed to the Holocaust or people who had been opposing the Nazi attacks [saying], "Look, you're just encouraging the Americans and the British to fight on. You're prolonging the war. More Germans are

going to die." Can you answer that question? Can you even get the words
out of your mouth? . . .

I started [my opposition to the war] much too late. I've written about
this often. I never really got seriously involved until about 1964, beyond
the petition-signing stage. And that was much too late. By . . . that time,
we probably already had killed a couple hundred thousand people,
which is not a small number. We were serious. We'd been bombing South
Vietnam for two years at that time. So it was much too late. Sure. After
that, I don't think I did near enough.

I am sure that there were lots of things that I said that were probably
misleading or wrong. There must have been. How could there fail to be?
But the main thing, by a long shot, was that I didn't do enough. . . . The
most effective [antiwar] people were people who were unknown to history, as is usually the case. So young people mostly, people who were
organizing locally, people involved in resistance, those are the people
who got everything done. People like me couldn't have done anything if
there hadn't been local people all around doing the basic work.

I don't think there was any central organization [opposed to the
war]. This is the United States. I think the most important things that happened were local, and it was usually local groups. They sometimes had
affiliations, but the affiliations were pretty thin. It's kind of like the activities against the U.S. wars in Central America in the 1980s. There were
actions going on all over the place, and I think they were very effective.
The interactions were extremly thin. The United States is a very depoliticized society. We don't have a political life. But it's a very free society.
Very free, but there's no politics. The result is that what happens at the
national government level is virtually divorced from the citizenry.

On the other hand, the population is involved in all kinds of things,
and the state does not stop them by force because it doesn't have the
power to coerce. You have this kind of odd combination of a society
which is free, very free by comparative standards. Police can't come in
and stop us from doing what we are doing. On the other hand, it's very
depoliticized, in that it has no political parties, it has no political participation of any real significance, and most of what happens is [that] the
media are very much dominated by the same state-corporate interests.
The result is that most of what happens is through churches or informal
networks or something that is outside the framework of the mainstream
political system. . . .

[It's] not our political system [that I esteem; it's] our society. That's
something very different. A free society but basically a nonfunctioning

political system. That's probably the main reason why people don't vote, and if they do vote, they vote against their own interests, as the polls show. The votes are mainly a mode of ratification of decisions made elsewhere, and I think that's the way people [essentially] look at the government. That's the way the founding fathers intended it, incidentally, but that's another story. That's why they were so afraid of democracy. . . .

[The passage of time] has intensified [my feelings about the war] for two reasons. For one thing, because I have learned more, naturally. Material has come out since then. Not much. But some has come out. And secondly, the way in which the war has been treated here and still is being treated is an example of such extraordinary cowardice and hypocrisy that it simply intensifies my feelings. Take, say, the Agent Orange discussion. Right now, there is the issue of [whether we] should establish relations with Vietnam. What's impeding those relations?

If you look at the government pronouncements and the media and even most of the publications on the Left, you'll see that what's impeding our granting diplomatic relations to Hanoi is humanitarian issues. Namely, they have not yet dealt properly with the humanitarian issues, the main one being the fate of the Americans missing in action. That's the only real humanitarian issue left open.

In other words, we attack a country, we kill several million people, we wipe the place out, we carry out chemical warfare, we leave the place littered with bombs from which people are still dying, we carry out extensive chemical warfare with hundreds of thousands of victims, and after all of this, the one humanitarian issue is whether they are forthcoming about information about American fliers who were shot down bombing them. That's the only humanitarian issue left. You'd have to go to Nazi Germany to find that level of cowardice and viciousness. And that's virtually one hundred percent of articulated opinion in the United States. Nobody can see this.

We talk about Agent Orange. American veterans suffer from Agent Orange, and people worry about that, and they should. But American veterans were subjected to a very small amount of chemical warfare. South Vietnam was the main target of our attack. We attacked South Vietnam and then the rest. South Vietnamese were subjected to very intensive chemical warfare. Does anybody care about them? Have you ever heard one word saying that we ought to do something for the victims of chemical warfare in South Vietnam? No.

When we talk about Saddam Hussein carrying out chemical warfare, we're outraged. We should be outraged. It's outrageous. Have you heard anybody say that there's another country that carried out chemical warfare in the recent past? And, in fact, is now saying that the victims of that chemical warfare, and that was only a small part of it, are guilty of moral flaws or moral crimes because they are not helpful enough to us in recovering the bodies of the pilots shot down? I mean, this is surreal. I can hardly see how people could imagine such a scene.

Imagine a scene where an American president, Jimmy Carter, the most pacifistic of American presidents, gets up in public, and he is asked in a press conference, "Should we, I don't know what, do something with Vietnam?" He says, "No. We shouldn't because," he said, "we have no debt to Vietnam because," he says, and these are his words, "the destruction was mutual." The destruction was mutual. In other words, Quang Ngai Province looks just like New York City. He says that, and nobody bats an eyelash. What that tells you about our country and the educated classes within it is startling and indescribable. And all of this, if anything, has only intensified my feelings of opposition to the war and to the political culture from which it grew, which reigns. . . .

We should have diplomatic relations, trade [with Vietnam]. We owe them a tremendous amount. Contrary to Jimmy Carter, the destruction was not mutual. Sure, we should try to do something. We can't pay for what we did. But we could do something for it. Even the Russians, for example, are able to say that what they did in Afghanistan was a terrible crime. They're able to say that. We don't have anywhere near that amount of honesty. We are so hypocritical that we can have front-page headlines in the *New York Times*, as they did, saying, "Russians admit that they were wrong in Afghanistan." That's fine. Now let's have an editorial in the *New York Times* saying we attacked South Vietnam and wiped the place out and that was wrong. I'll wait for that day to come. I'll never see it. . . .

As far as Vietnam is concerned, my feelings were expressed rather well . . . back in 1965 [by] David Shoup, who was then commandant of the marines, and I think soon fired or left. He gave a speech somewhere or other in which he said, "The best thing we can do for the people of Vietnam is to get our bloody, dollar-crooked hands out of their affairs." I think that is basically the answer. That's the best thing we could have done for the people of Vietnam. After that, they'll make their own mistakes, and their own mistakes are ugly and unpleasant and rotten and so on. But it's their mistakes. If you look around the world, you find the same thing. We've got enough of our mistakes that we can worry about.

There is no reason to believe that our intervention in any other country is going to be anything but harmful. That's the historical record, and it's to be expected. Intervention is carried out for the purposes of those who intervene, not for any other purpose. And it's only going to be a strange accident if that turns out to be beneficial to the ones who are targeted for intervention. That's why . . . the principles of our legal system and treaties that we have signed . . . say that the threat or use of force in international affairs is illegal, and is a war crime. And I think that's right, and the changes that should come about in our society are a recognition of this.

We should live up to our own — the laws aren't bad. There is a lot that can improve them. But the legal system does incorporate principles, general principles which are valid, like the rejection of force, the subordination of any activity to UN authority, and so forth. We should live up to that. We should also be willing to look at ourselves in the mirror, without lying to ourselves, and ask what we did and what we do and why we did it and so on. If we can get to that point, we will be able to be a positive force in the world, and we have a long way to go before we get there. . . .

[I believe that] everybody [who was] in a leadership position [in our government should have been subject to a Nuremberg-like trial]. . . . When I say Nuremberg Trials, I don't mean to suggest that they should be hanged like the people at Nuremberg were hanged. Part of the reason for that is that (here, we have to be a bit cautious) Nuremberg itself was an act of extreme hypocrisy. If you look back at the war crimes trials . . . they had to invent what constituted a war crime. This was ex post facto. They were not trying the Nazis and the Japanese for things that were listed as crimes but that they were inventing as crimes. It was already a question whether ex post facto criminal prosecutions were legitimate. But let's grant that they were.

There is no doubt that the Nazis, in particular, were unique, so something was required. Then comes the question of what counted as a war crime. How did you set up that legal structure? How did the American prosecutors decide what was going to count as a war crime? When you look back at the record, which I have done, you discover it was quite simple. A war crime was defined as any crime that they carried out that we didn't carry out. So, for example, bombing of urban areas was not considered a war crime because we did more of it than they did. It was considered a legitimate defense at Nuremberg for a Nazi war criminal to put up testimony saying the Americans and the British did it too.

[Grand] Adm. [Karl] Doenitz was certainly a criminal, a war criminal. His defense included putting up as a witness Adm. [Chester W.] Nimitz, the U.S. naval commander, who testified that the United States had committed similar crimes. So, therefore, Doenitz was free of these crimes. Admiral Nimitz didn't go on trial. It was just that Admiral Doenitz was free, and in general, if the Nazis could show that we had done the same thing, that was not considered a crime. Now, that's farcical. A crime is a crime, not a crime that somebody else commits. The whole Nuremberg structure was based on farce, and therefore, we shouldn't honor it.

When you go over to Japan, it gets even worse. The Tokyo trials were just a grotesque travesty. Gen. [Tomoyuki] Yamashita, for example, was hanged because of atrocities carried out by troops of his in the Philippines at a time at the end of the war when he had no contact with them at all. There were no communications. They were just around the Philippines somewhere, and he was off somewhere else. He was hanged because of their atrocities. By those standards, the whole American army command should be hanged.

The whole structure of Nuremberg was victor's justice. It was not justice. Nevertheless, putting aside the hypocrisy, there were valid principles there, and those principles should be . . . applied. I don't think that the criminals who carry out war crimes, right up to today (for example, the invasion of Panama, which was a war crime), I don't think that those people should be hanged, but I think there's every reason why their crimes should be revealed and why they should suffer what people should suffer if they've committed serious crimes.

NOTE: Professor Chomsky, in a follow-up letter dated January 18, 1993, responding to an initial draft of the Preface in which I found little to choose between the folly of the war as it was pursued by this country and the treatment of American POWs by the North Vietnamese. He wrote:

> Suppose you read somewhere in the Russian press, pre-Gorbachev, that "the Afghan war should not have happened. Twenty thousand Russians did not have to, and should not, have died." What would your reaction be?
>
> The Afghan resistance who we were supporting were, in fact, a gang of terrorists, drug-runners, and thugs, as you can see by the way they are destroying what remained after the Russian onslaught (facts which lead to no outrage here, in contrast to the far milder

actions of the North Vietnamese after 1975 — in fact, a comparison to the Khmer Rouge would not be outlandish). They treated captured Soviet prisoners with barbaric cruelty, and in fact invaded Russia itself, killing and destroying.

Suppose that you read in the Russian press, pre-Gorbachev, that "It's difficult to reconcile the barbaric behavior of Afghan jailers against . . . which was the greatest wrong." Do you really have problems answering the question in that case? A close friend of mine was a partisan leader in the early forties. He described to me how downed Nazi pilots were sometimes flayed alive by villagers. There was barbarism on both sides. Do you have difficulty determining which was the greatest wrong? In the first case, the Russians wouldn't have regarded the analogy as fair; after all, they were defending Afghanistan against terrorists run by the CIA in a noble cause, however in error. The Nazis would have had the same reaction.

NOTE: To clarify some of the comments he made in the interview, Professor Chomsky also noted:

the "deception" of the government and media, and unwillingness of the government "to admit error," were and remain the least of my concerns; in fact, "admitting error" is almost meaningless, in this case. What particularly "outraged" me was exactly what particularly outraged me when the Russians invaded and devastated Afghanistan: not the fact that the Kremlin and *Pravda* deceived people (who cares?), or that the government was unwilling "to admit error" (it would be worse if they did "admit error" when they had in fact committed grave crimes; in fact, unlike us, they did finally concede the crimes). What outraged me in Vietnam was the U.S. support for French colonialism, its takeover of the South in violation of the Geneva agreements and establishment of a vicious terror state that killed some seventy thousand people under Eisenhower, the outright aggression against South Vietnam launched by Kennedy when the violence couldn't succeed in controlling the domestic population, the later escalation of that aggression and expansion of it to all of Indochina, and the monstrous crimes against humanity, in the technical sense, conducted in the course of these war crimes, in the technical sense (since 1962; before that, it wasn't technically "war crimes" in the sense of international law, but rather the standard kind of wholesale international terrorism that we engage in in Central America and elsewhere). The dockets would be full, by the standards of Nuremberg. There was no "error" to admit, any more than in the Kremlin. And the "deception" was a pretty minor flaw in comparison with such actions as targeting B-52 attacks directly on villages, to select one war crime at random.

17

Peter Weiss

Peter Weiss, an attorney, traveled to Hanoi with fellow lawyer Morton Stavis at the invitation of the Association of the Bar of the City of Hanoi. Weiss also went to Florence, Italy, and Paris, France, on separate occasions, in unsuccessful attempts to improve communications between North Vietnam and the United States. He discussed the legal actions he initiated to oppose the war, including a lawsuit he filed against the U.S. government to stop the bombing of Cambodia, which he claimed was illegal. Weiss was distressed about a popular notion in Washington that the war could have been won if properly pursued, a concept that ignored the idea that the war should never have been fought in the first place. At the time of the interview, Peter Weiss was associated with the law firm of Weiss, Dawid, Fross, Zelnick, and Lehrman, of New York City, and the Center for Constitutional Rights. He was interviewed in the living room of his Bronx home on October 7, 1990.

PETER WEISS: I had two contacts with the U.S. government before visiting Hanoi. In 1965, while in Europe on a business trip, I got a call from my old friend the mayor of Florence, Georgio La Pira. He called me about eleven o'clock at night in Strasbourg and said, "You've got to come to Florence tomorrow." And I said, "I'm going home tomorrow." He said, "No, it's absolutely essential."

La Pira thought he had a peace feeler to communicate. He had heard from his friend Amintore Fanfani, who, at that time, was foreign minister of Italy, what he and Fanfani thought was a significant advance in the Vietnamese position on negotiations. So I changed my plans and went to Florence the next day and spent about four hours with La Pira and came back and communicated this to a number of people in our government. The principal message was that the North Vietnamese were ready to talk, which was not all that new, and the subsidiary message was that if we were going to bomb Hanoi or Haiphong, all bets were off. Ten days later, they bombed the oil installations outside of Haiphong. That was the reaction of the U.S. government to that message.

When I returned to New York from Florence, I wrote a memo which I delivered personally to Arthur Goldberg, then our ambassador to the United Nations, and to Jonathan Bingham, then my congressman. I delivered additional copies of the memo to McGeorge Bundy, national security adviser to President Johnson, and to Senators J. William Fulbright and Robert Kennedy.

On another occasion, Dick Barnet and I went to Paris to meet with Mme Binh. The purpose of the trip was to clarify the NLF's negotiating position. We wrote a piece in Paris that appeared on the front page of the *New York Times* the next day. When we came back, we went to see Helmut Sonnenfelt, Kissinger's deputy at the time, and reported on our visit with Mme Binh. My first trip to Vietnam was in 1970, and I think it was the first organized lawyers' trip. Lawyers had been on trips to Vietnam as members of the peace movement, but this was specifically at the invitation of the Hanoi Bar Association.

When my colleague Morton Stavis, who went with me, and I came back, we gave a talk at the Association of the Bar of the City of New York, and I still have the poster upstairs. It's called "A Visit to the Association of the Bar of the City of Hanoi." They were our hosts for the trip, and we met the leading legal personalities in Vietnam, the chief justice, the head of their bar association, and the equivalent of what we would call the attorney general. . . .

Mort Stavis and I, who were in this delegation of two going to Hanoi, had our tickets written from New York to Moscow to Hanoi. That probably was the first time anybody wrote a ticket like that since the beginning of the war. And we expected a certain amount of flak from the personnel at JFK [International Airport]. So we came equipped with a bunch of law books, which we thought might have convinced the attendants at the Pan Am counter that we were justified under the Constitution. But they never raised the question. They just looked at the tickets and gave us our boarding passes. Pan Am was flying to Moscow, and then we took an Aeroflot to Hanoi. Moscow had direct flights to Hanoi. There was just one change of planes. . . .

One of the purposes, I think, of the Vietnamese in inviting us there was to expose us to the findings of their War Crimes Commission, which, at the time, was headed by Col. Ha Van Lau. We spent almost a whole day with him and with his staff, and they brought in some of the victims of the bombings, napalm victims, and so forth. I think they figured that a lawyers' delegation would be an appropriate group to communicate that kind of information. . . . It appeared quite clearly to me that [the United States was acting in violation of international law in Vietnam].

On the day that we left Hanoi, after about an eight-day stay, we were awakened at five o'clock in the morning by what sounded like heavy artillery fire. This was at the hotel in Hanoi, which, at the time, was not a war zone. We didn't know if it was bombing or what it was. They came at seven o'clock to pick us up and take us to the airport, and it was clear that something was going on. It took even longer than usual to get across the pontoon bridge over the Red River, about two and one-half hours. There was an air of excitement, but they never told us what had happened. We didn't find out until after we were out of Vietnam that it was the Son Tay raid. . . .

In 1976, my wife, Cora, and I . . . traveled from Hanoi down to Ho Chi Minh City. We went almost the entire length of Vietnam, about two-thirds of it anyway. . . .

I was active during this period in a group called the Lawyer's Committee on American Policy Towards Vietnam, which managed, considering its small size, to get a fair amount of attention in the press. We developed the thesis, with documentation, that the United States was engaged in Vietnam in what, under the Nuremberg principles, would have been called a war of aggression. That's a question which frequently was raised in American courts during that period and which almost made it to the Supreme Court. At one time or another during that period, five justices of the Supreme Court voted to take a case that would have ruled on that question, but they never got enough of them together on one case.

It seemed kind of esoteric to people at the time, but then the legal questions raised about the conduct of the war led to enactment of the War Powers Act in 1973 because a lot of people in Congress felt that, while they weren't terribly interested in questions of international law, they had been suckered into going along with the war through the Gulf of Tonkin resolution. . . . The War Powers Act tried to implement the war powers clause in the Constitution so that this kind of presidential war wouldn't happen again. At the time, it was really a burning issue in Congress. But the legal aspect that played into the movement against the war was the question of how the war was being fought: carpet bombing, napalm, search-and-destroy missions, the killing of civilians, My Lai, and so forth. That got an awful lot of people very worked up about not wanting to be a part of it.

I don't think any war has ever been fought in which both sides have complied with the rules of war. . . . I could probably name some instances . . . where the North Vietnamese also violated rules of war to some extent, certainly in the treatment of the prisoners. The fact that they kept thousands of people in detention camps for as much as ten to fifteen years obviously was a violation of basic human rights, the rule against prolonged detention without a trial. And there undoubtedly were some executions in the course of the war. But I, as an American citizen, felt that my primary responsibility was to call attention to the violations we were engaged in. . . .

My opposition to the war wasn't based on what kind of a society I wanted to see in place in Vietnam. It was based on the fact that I thought we had no right to be there interfering in what was essentially not a civil war but a revolution that I think was justified against the regime in South Vietnam, which was a murderous, oppressive, and a human rights violator regime. The decision to [deploy U.S. armed forces] . . . into Vietnam seemed to me to have more to do with what you might call psycho-history, more than anything else. That is, the people who made the decision to go in felt that this was a matter of establishing the credibility of the United States, but they didn't really see it as a military objective. But by the time we decided to escalate, Vietnam had become the cutting edge of the Cold War. Any place where the other side, which was perceived as the mortal enemy, made an advance, we had to step in and stop it. I don't think it would've been any different if it had arisen in Africa or in Latin America. It was not a fight against the North Vietnamese. It was a war against the people who we perceived were pulling the strings in Moscow. . . .

All of us live in overlapping circles of community: the family, the town that you live in, the state, the country, the world. I don't think it's right to pick out one of those, namely, the country, and say your loyalty to that takes precedence over everything else. Loyalty should be defined in terms of, How do you best function in that community? What can you do for that community? . . .

I'm old enough to have been through two cataclysmic events of the twentieth century: World War II and Vietnam. I find it difficult to separate out of my mind the fact that part of my family died in the Holocaust in

Europe at the end of World War II. Somehow, by the end of the century, this world is going to have to find a way to solve its problems without committing the kind of mass crimes that were involved in World War II or in the Vietnam War. The answer to a problem is not to kill hundreds of thousands of people in the most brutal way conceivable. And I still feel that way very strongly about both of those wars.

Before the Vietnam War, I was very active with the American Committee on Africa. It was basically an anticolonialist group that I helped to found in 1954. [I have been active] on human rights, both here and internationally. I was chairman for a while of the Manhattan-Bronx Council of the New York State Commission Against Discrimination, so I was interested in questions of racism.

Generally speaking, I have some sense from somewhere about what's right and what's terribly wrong, and I'd like to be on the right side of things. I may not always be correct about what's right and what's wrong, but I do have some fairly strong feelings about that, together with the feeling that one of the things that's wrong is for a citizen lucky enough to live in a democracy not to do anything about an issue he perceives to be wrong. . . .

I don't think there were too many people who were more influential or more effective [in the antiwar movement] than [my wife] Cora. But there really were a great many others. I don't think you could pick out one person. [Former Congressman] Al Lowenstein, in his way, was very effective. He probably had more to do with [President] Johnson's decision not to run again than anybody else. Tom Hayden, in his good days, was very effective.

What distresses me about the experience of the Vietnam War is that so little is known about it today. And that so few lessons of the Vietnam War have been learned. One of the lessons that Washington seems to have taken away from the Vietnam War was not that it was the wrong war fought in the wrong way but that it could have been won in a different way. You hear a lot of talk about surgical strikes. But as somebody said to me the other day, talking about the situation in the Gulf, "If you're going in for a surgical strike, you'd better make sure that the patient doesn't sit up on the table and punch you in the face." I wish, however, that the lesson that we had learned from the Vietnam War was that, given the unbelievable destructive force of modern weapon systems, another way must be found to resolve conflicts.

18

Irma Zigas

For Irma Zigas, like many of the other Americans who journeyed to North Vietnam during the war, the trip was the most moving experience of her life. Opposed to the war, she organized and managed a counseling service in Long Island, New York, to assist young men who wished to avoid the draft, as well as draftees who hoped to avoid a combat assignment in Vietnam.

Zigas provided a memorable account of her successful effort during the 1980 Democratic National Convention, in which she and Gold Star Mother Louise Ransom arranged for Fritz Efaw, a draft evader who spent the war in Canada, to be nominated as vice president of the United States. Zigas is now associated with the San Francisco Museum of Modern Art. She was interviewed on November 12, 1990, in her San Francisco apartment.

IRMA ZIGAS: We all left from our home cities and met in Los Angeles. We left in October 1971, on a Pan Am flight that made every stop from Hawaii to Okinawa. It must have been a mail run that finally ended up in Hong Kong. We stopped there overnight and then the next day, took a Royal Air Lao plane to Vientiane, arriving after a memorable six-hour flight. We left Vientiane Airport the next day and flew to Hanoi on a Russian jet. When we finally arrived, we were exhausted and nervous.

There were three of us: Amy Swerdlow, a professor of women's studies; Willie Barrow, a minister; and myself. Amy Swerdlow was with Women Strike for Peace. She was a writer and used to write our monthly magazine. Willie Barrow was from Chicago and had worked in Operation PUSH with Jesse Jackson. She was a very articulate woman. She is still organizing in Chicago, to the best of my knowledge. I had organized the antidraft and counseling service for Women Strike for Peace. We all had different points of view and different perspectives of what we were involved in, different aspects of organizing people and bringing back a message. . . .

The [Vietnamese] Women's Union extended the invitation. I guess Cora [Weiss] was the focal point, and she organized it through them. I had, in 1968, gone to an international peace movement conference in Paris [attended by] women who were involved in peace issues around the world. Then there was a conference in Toronto where we also met with the Vietnamese Women's Union. At that time, an invitation was extended to us to go to North Vietnam. We had to decide whether we would really be able to afford it personally. It was a very expensive trip . . . there were risks involved [and] . . . family obligations versus our commitment to what we were doing. It was a long, stretched-out siege deciding, Was our commitment there? What was the risk? How much was it going to cost? And would we be able, if we returned, to talk about it?

It was a memorable and frightening experience, going to a country that was at war. As Americans, we had never experienced war firsthand and didn't know what it would be like to be bombed or to be under siege. The thought that we were in a place that was being bombed and in a state of war was actually mind-boggling to me and my colleagues. We were very frightened. Before we left, our children were convinced we would never come back. They knew about the war and were convinced we were going to die. We certainly tried to make them feel better, but we weren't certain either.

We were committed to trying to bring an understanding of what was going on in Vietnam and felt that the reason for the war was not clear. We felt that we, as activists in the peace movement, were very much concerned about the future of our country and as mothers who were concerned for our children. That we really should find out and speak about what was happening in North Vietnam when we returned. We took mail, medication, and packages from their families to the POWs. I personally carried thirty pounds of mail, medicine, and packages. It never left my side. I slept with it until I turned it over to the Women's Union representative in Vietnam to go to the POWs. [We also carried mail from the POWs on our return.]

Our most memorable experiences were: the sight of Hanoi, which looked like a suburban area totally gutted and bombed — we couldn't believe it; the children; the respect we saw people had for one another; the total determination of the people. Their determination was such that, when we returned, we felt there was no way we would ever defeat these people, short of bombing the country into total oblivion.

The most amazing thing was that we learned as people, who came mostly from middle-class backgrounds, what it was like to see people struggling to survive and to achieve personal dignity, which is what they really wanted because they had been colonized by so many different countries in the past. The fact that they felt that they now had the right to do certain things for themselves and not have babies in the field, that they could now have them in a clinic, was the most startling aspect of the trip.

We had to travel by night. We did travel by day during a lot of it. In Hanoi, there were a couple of air-raid warnings, but there was not any bombing that I knew of. We went to Haiphong. I don't remember the names of all the villages, but we did go out of Haiphong. We went along the coast and were into the mountains somewhere. There was no bombing directly that I was aware of, but when we were driving from Hanoi to Haiphong at night, we had to stop and go into the ditches. I am not sure why. We were never told. . . . Either there were flights coming over [or] they weren't sure whether there was bombing, and we had to be quiet. We had to sit there. I remember they had prepared cold eggs. I was sitting there, and it was the most delicious egg I had ever tasted, but I was a nervous wreck [laughter].

When we were in an area somewhere near Haiphong or in that general vicinity, we visited a couple of peasants' houses. They were up on stilts, I remember, and we had tea. They took us outside, and there was a grave of a downed flier who apparently the local militia had shot down. They showed us the grave, and they gave us the guy's dog tags and we brought them back. We didn't announce it when we came back but gave them to . . . someone from the Pentagon. And until the day of the end of the war, they never told the family that the guy was dead. We checked this out. We know that until the end of the war, this man was listed as missing in action because I know who it was.

They said [the reason his family was not informed was because] it had to deal with the fact that civilians had gone to Hanoi, had brought back dog tags of a dead American flier, and I guess there was a lot of politics involved . . . that if an American peace worker could notify the government that a guy was dead, why, this was a no-no. Rather than let them know the guy was dead, they kept him as an MIA until after the war. I have no comment on that. . . .

When he [the Vietnamese peasant] gave us this American pilot's dog tags, I asked the family, "Why did you bury him, and why do you tend the grave, and why are you doing this because it's the enemy? They are shooting at you." And I wanted to understand it. They said that someday the war was going to be over and that they hoped they could be friendly with the Americans and that they were not going to consider the dead flier anything but a human being, and therefore, that's why they did that. It was a little bit disconcerting, coming from America where there's always a lot of this "them and us."

It was thought-provoking to hear somebody talk like that. They said that they didn't feel that the Americans were the enemy; the governments had to make peace. And that was a learning experience, I have to say. Whether it was propaganda or not, it was certainly thoughtful. It had a lot to do with a change in my thinking, in many ways.

The most amazing thing [about the Vietnamese] was that they are very political and well organized. They talked about their long history, their struggle against the Chinese, and how they overcame Genghis Khan. They have a long history of fighting for independence. In a very primitive little house, they spent a great deal of time documenting the American peace movement. They had posters, buttons, leaflets, and things. When I saw that, I just burst into tears.

They felt that the peace movement was going to end the war. Obviously, they placed a great deal of importance on it. [But] we felt so powerless. These materials served as propaganda for the people who came in to see the museum. It was the way the Vietnamese government showed their people there was support for them. We requested to see Americans, and when we first came, we told them what we would like to do. We gave them a list, and they were startled that we wanted to see Americans, and they said they would take it under advisement, but we never saw them. When we were in Hanoi, we decided that we wanted to try and visit Beijing. We went to the Chinese embassy and asked if we could have a visa. We figured, "My God, we're in that part of the world. When would we in a million years ever get to go there again?" At that time, the Chinese were trying to get seated at the UN, and Women Strike for Peace had lobbied to have China seated. We thought we could try to talk with the women in Beijing. We went to the Chinese embassy in Hanoi and requested a visa, and they turned us down. I remember speaking to the official. We said: "We really would appreciate speaking to the Chinese people because we have been working so hard to see if we could get Mainland China represented at the UN. We feel it would be very important. It has been twenty years, and hopefully, we would be able to exchange information."

He said, "We have waited twenty years to be seated, and we can wait another twenty years." It was so indicative of the philosophy of the Chinese to refuse us. But when we got back to Hong Kong, we found out that the reason was that Kissinger was in Beijing on a secret mission.

We came back on a Canadian plane from Hanoi into Vientiane and from Vientiane to Hong Kong [and then by] a Pan Am plane. When we were in Vientiane, we knew there were a lot of CIA government people there, and they would say, "There's the peaceniks." It was kind of an odd, nerve-racking experience, to say the least. And the Vietnamese would not allow us to have Hanoi on our passports. So they gave us a separate visa.

[Our trip] wasn't intended to be a protest against the war. I didn't personally see it that way. I really felt it was a continuation of a person-to-person, people-to-people contact. I feel that the Vietnamese women and the people whom I met felt the same way. We felt it was a way of learning, of educating and keeping contact because the people were not the enemy. We felt that it was very important to continue understanding what was going on, and hopefully, we could have an impact upon our government and make them understand how we felt.

One couldn't encourage people to go to Hanoi. You really had to be invited. You couldn't say, "Hey, I want to go," and call your travel agent. My recollection was that an invitation really had to be extended. They were very busy trying to survive the war, and having delegations come in and out was an extremely trying experience because they felt responsible for their lives. While we were in Vietnam, it was quite obvious that there was a lot of concern for our well-being because they knew that we supposedly were "illegally" in their country. Our government knew we were there, but it was sort of sotto voce. But they were very concerned for our well-being, and we had to drive by night. It really was very trying for them because [of their concerns for our safety]. . . . I'm sure they would have liked more [visitors] if they could have afforded it or dealt with it.

Would I recommend people to have gone as an experience? Well, it changed my life, totally. I felt that my value system changed, and my understanding of human beings changed. It was a turning point in my life because of what I learned there. I had a greater understanding and a greater respect for human beings. I was a pretty good middle-class housewife in Long Island, and being exposed to what I had seen and the fact that people survived, and the rigors of living in such an undeveloped country, and the dignity and humanity that these people had was quite a learning experience for me. What you learn is that certain things aren't as important as others, materially and otherwise.

I couldn't live there. It was a different form of government than what I am used to, and I am sure that survival in those conditions would be difficult. I don't know whether I would feel the same as I do as an American visiting. I certainly had a great deal of respect for these people and understood why they were doing what they did, which I never would have if I didn't go there, and I spent the year trying to tell people about it.

[At that time, I was the mother of five] children from eleven to twenty. . . . I was involved with Women Strike for Peace and with the whole issue of the atom bomb and the radiation in the atmosphere and just continued my activism. When it came to Vietnam, I became very involved in the antidraft and the GI movements. That was my particular responsibility: organizing and helping to educate families, young men and women, and everybody about the war. And that those who refused to be inducted should not be vilified and should receive family support and set up counseling procedures so that they could understand what they could do with their rights.

[Women Strike for Peace] wasn't really membership; you didn't join up and sign a pledge. You made contributions. . . . The national office was in Philadelphia. There were chapters in all the five boroughs, and I used to go into the New York City office. Then we organized one in Long Island, the Great Neck Women Strike for Peace. We organized the Long Island draft-counseling service in my basement. It was basically contributions. . . . We had chapters around the country. We worked in coalitions with other women's groups who had peace on their agenda as well.

It was not an easy row to hoe. I was vilified, called a communist-lover and a pinko. Some of the things my children endured: "Hey, your mom is a red. She went to North Vietnam." The kids were really put into the position of having to defend me, which, in a way, was a dialogue — some was, and some wasn't. My kids were vilified, but I felt we learned a lot. My children learned a lot. I learned a lot. We have more respect for people and for each other. I don't think [my children were ever physically abused]. . . . It was more verbal. Or they were shunned. Barry [my son] and I used to go at it. He thought I was too radical. He was in high school and considered himself a little less radical than I was.

I didn't lose any friends, but certainly, most of the people that we were friendly with, all of us more or less agreed (they all felt the way I did) on the war. We had neighbors who were very civil, but if they got to talking to me about the war, you just couldn't deal with it. It was a middle-class neighborhood. They would say, "Oh, bull, you're off again doing your own thing. You are just a commie," and so forth.

I went to schools, mostly. I spoke to groups, other women's groups. I spoke with anybody who would have me speak. The majority of the speaking was either at colleges or high schools. I even went into some grade schools. We brought back a lot of artwork. I also brought back musical instruments and books. I spoke about the life there, the people, and what their history was because very little was being taught in the schools at that time about North Vietnam or Vietnam in general. It was basically educational. I spoke also about what I saw and my feelings about what I saw.

I went into kindergarten; I put on my Vietnamese dress, and I brought musical instruments which I encouraged the children to touch; I brought pictures of the Vietnamese children and showed them the kind of music they play. Some of the musical sounds were very hard for me to deal with because they are very high-pitched and different. It was a different culture. It was dealing with people on another level. I became hopeful that if I could speak to people, answer questions, and have give-and-take, that was enough to keep up my morale. Even though it was long and exhausting, that's what kept me going. . . .

I continued my work through the year Carter was elected. After that, I was traveling with my husband because he thought we would be moving to another part of the world. Then we came out here to San Francisco, and I was active as a volunteer with various groups.

One of my best friends, Louise Ransom, lost her son in Vietnam. She and I were tremendous co-workers on the amnesty issue, one of the things that was an offshoot of it, a continuation of our activity after Vietnam. We talked about when the war ended. How were we going to deal with the people who didn't go, either the AWOLs, the GIs that left, and the people who went to Canada or abroad? Louise lives up in Vermont at the moment. She came from a Dutch Reformed background. Her oldest son, Mike, was killed, and she said he died for nothing. And then, as a Gold Star Mother, she came out against the war. She really had an impact.

Here she was, saying, "My son died in vain." We worked together until 1976, when we actually felt our work was almost completed. At the 1976 Democratic [National] Convention, when Carter was nominated, we had mapped out a campaign to have a young draft resister nominated for vice president, addressing the nation and the convention on prime time and making a speech against the war. His name was Fritz Efaw. Louise and I were with the National Council for Unconditional Amnesty, which was a coalition of groups. We organized this campaign and brought in

Fritz, who was under indictment in Oklahoma for draft resistance. He had lived in England and was with Americans Abroad, and was nominated as a delegate to the convention.

The reason this is so fascinating is because this is a logical conclusion to our activities. How do we have closure? The war was over, and we had all these people whom we had encouraged and supported, who were really all over the world, and we wanted amnesty. We were lobbying the candidates for amnesty. The long and the short of it was that we got people around the country to sign a petition putting his name in nomination for the vice presidency. We knew what the rules of the convention were. We followed them according to Hoyle, and we were going to have him nominated.

Every politician in the country was trying to be the person to nominate Fritz Efaw when they heard what we were doing. Now, you have to understand that we were dealing with people who had been in Canada, very radical, GIs who had gone underground, and this was a coalition effort of people who finally were going to have a national platform. It was the most amazing thing. We had Ramsey Clark knocking on our door, asking whether he could nominate Fritz Efaw, and we had the greatest joy of our lives saying, "Mr. Clark, you indicted this man. How could you even ask to nominate him for vice president?"

Suddenly, here we were. Louise Ransom, the Gold Star Mother, nominated Fritz Efaw, and Ron Kovic, the Vietnam vet, seconded the nomination. We had these petitions ready to go to Robert Strauss, the head of the Democratic National Committee. And we went up to him and said: "We are now at the point where the war is over. Mr. Carter is going to be nominated. The rules of the convention say that other people can be nominated for vice president. We are going to nominate Fritz Efaw, who was a draft resister, who was a duly elected delegate to this convention as a representative of Americans Abroad."

Strauss said, "Absolutely not. He's too young."

So we said, "What about Julian Bond?"

I said, "Okay, you don't want us to nominate Fritz Efaw? We'll nominate Gold Star Mother Louise Ransom. She's old enough, and we have enough names."

"Oh, no. Okay. You can nominate Fritz Efaw."

So we said, "Fine. Thank you." We said, "We want Louise Ransom to put his name in nomination."

He said, "Okay. And who's going to second?"

I said, "Ron Kovic."

He said, "Absolutely not. We don't have any ability to get a wheelchair on the podium."

I said, "Wallace was just on the podium talking about some issue. You're telling me you can't get Ron Kovic's wheelchair up the same ramp?"

He said, "Well, they've taken it down."

I said, "Well, we have four vets who are willing to hold him up by the elbows."

"Okay, you can have Ron Kovic."

So it was the prize of all of our experiences. It was almost as if our job was finished when Louise Ransom nominated and Ron Kovic seconded the nomination of Fritz Efaw for vice president of the United States in the middle of the Democratic National Convention, prime time. Mayor Daley said, "Shut up everybody and listen." We could see him on television quieting people down. It was like we had come to some sort of closure.

[The reaction to the nomination] was great. Great. It was a huge display. Efaw turned down the nomination, of course. The interesting thing was that his name was Fritz Efaw, and the headline in the newspapers the next day was "Fritz Nominated." It was Fritz Mondale [laughter].

I haven't spoken to him [Efaw] recently, but we kept in contact for a while. Of course, he had to go back to Oklahoma under the indictment. I think it was thrown out. I'm not quite sure what exactly happened. He is now teaching in Tennessee, and Louise Ransom and I are in constant contact. The last time I saw Ron Kovic was at the Democratic convention here in San Francisco. I've written to him.

Louise has . . . always been very involved in veterans' affairs. In fact, she was working for the state of Vermont on veterans' issues. And then she organized a prison project because a lot of the vets were getting into a lot of trouble. And she's still actively involved with them.

I think the [American] people have learned more [from the Vietnam War] than the government, considering what is going on in the Mideast right now. One would hope that the Vietnam experience had been indelibly impressed on our lawmakers, our government, and the people, and I feel that it has had quite an impact. Of course, one never can bring back those who died there. One hopes that their families can adjust to it. I would expect that they hope that it is not going to happen to somebody else. It has hurt a lot of people and seriously scarred our national psyche, but I feel that, in the long run, it will have been a learning experience. Hopefully, we will keep our heads about what is going on in the rest of the world and not repeat the experience.

I think, because of the impact of the Vietnam vets and the Vietnam Memorial, that the issue is now being talked about. The schools have to bring the war into the curriculum. I don't feel that people really understand why we got into the war or how we got into the war. Most people don't know what the Gulf of Tonkin resolution was or what it meant. It's interesting to hear a lot of the news commentators comparing what's going on in Saudi Arabia now, talking about Vietnam and the Gulf of Tonkin and the fact that we didn't have a declaration of war and we had to learn from it. That's why I feel the war has had an impact. The responsibility many of us have is to continue to understand the history of the war.

I don't think [the war] was well documented in the press. I think it was a television war. I don't think the government was honest about what was going on. Americans are pretty patriotic. They want to believe what the government tells them. And I think the government wasn't telling them the truth. That's very hard, and it has made people suspicious and jaded. There have been a couple of good books about how our involvement came about, but there hasn't been any real understanding of how we got in.

There is no reason not to [lift the embargo against Vietnam]. It's crazy. What are they not doing? I just don't understand it. . . . Of all the things I learned, I feel that a quote of Ho Chi Minh I heard in Vietnam applies, "There are no permanent friends, and there are no permanent enemies; there are only permanent interests." When we were in Hanoi and talking about Ho Chi Minh, I did not realize that Ho was an ally of ours during the Second World War. American pilots wore a flag on their flight jackets which they showed if downed in Vietnam, and there was no problem of safe conduct.

They showed us one of those flags from the Second World War, and then they showed us a flag the pilots wore who were bombing them. There were two different messages. One said, "I am an American. Take me to my embassy." The other one was entirely different. [That is, pilots in both of the conflicts wore the same American flag on their flight uniforms: during World War II, the Vietnamese would provide sanctuary to downed American pilots, who were their allies against the Japanese; during the Vietnam conflict, downed American pilots, who were now enemies of the North Vietnamese, were taken prisoner.] It kind of hit home: one minute, we are friends; the next minute, we are enemies. And it was the interests that was what it was all about. I tell it to my kids; I tell it to everybody. It's true.

I had never really given any thought as to what their internal government was all about [either then or now]. That was not what I felt the issue was. From what I hear, things aren't terrific, but that depends on what terrific is. Does everyone have to have a democracy, or is it whatever their form of government happens to be? It's the same thing we are saying about what's going on in Eastern countries. If I were living in Vietnam, I might feel differently, but living in America, it's a hard thing to say. When we were in Vietnam at the time, they were fighting for self-determination, dignity, their culture, and so forth.

They did not have those things when they were colonized. Whether they have it now, I don't know. Obviously, when you had people in the South who were used to a different way of life than those in the North, obviously there are going to be problems.

[To say whether my trip was in the best interests of the United States] is an arch way of putting it, but I felt that as an American, hopefully if I came back, that I was doing a service in being able to get another point of view across as to what was going on. Obviously, my government didn't think so, but on the other hand, sotto voce, they supported it.

I didn't think it [the trip] was unpatriotic. I felt that as an American, I was doing the right thing. It was my right as an American, and I felt that was what America is all about. I felt that the government was wrong in prosecuting the war, and as an American, I had a right to protest it. Whether going to Hanoi was an illegal act, the government, nevertheless, was quite aware I was going. All the prisoner-of-war stuff, the vitamins we brought in, the mail we came in with — that was not unknown to the government. Even though it was going through the families, the families had a line right to the government, and they knew that we were bringing mail, packages, and so forth in and out. It was not a courier service, however.

[I would define patriotism as] honoring your country by exercising all of the rights given to you under the Constitution. I don't feel that [the claim that the travel of Americans to North Vietnam lengthened the war] is valid. From my observation there, I felt the Vietnamese would have continued prosecuting the war to the last person. Whether the peace movement allowed them to feel that there was hope [or not], I don't feel that was the reason that they continued the war. The reason they continued was that they were not going to give in until there were negotiations by the Americans, in some way or another, and they were using every tool at their disposal to achieve that, as the Americans were on their end. When the interests said it was over, it was over.

[My feelings about the war] certainly haven't mellowed. The situation in the Mideast brings it all back. It is intensified. What's going on with our government at the moment brings it all back. I sort of put the whole war experience in a memory bank, and it was just kind of there. I don't think it has mellowed. I'd say, if anything, it has intensified. . . .

There were just so many wonderful leaders [in the antiwar movement], all of them from various constituencies. . . . They really did a great job in getting the message across. I feel that a lot of the young men who refused to go had a great impact on changing thoughts and views about the war. I think that Martin Luther King had a great impact because he was so visible, and when he came out against the war, that had a great deal to do with many people listening to the peace movement. . . . The full-time, committed pacifists like Dave Dellinger, who really are against all wars, were a great learning experience for me.

I think it was all the coalitions of everybody working together. Just the fact that they were even able to agree on certain issues just to get together and get people out against the war. That was really the biggest thing, just the unanimity of getting large numbers of people to speak out. It was a coalition effort. There were groups that had been at it longer than others, like the War Resisters League and the Friends Service Committee, or the ACLU [American Civil Liberties Union] (which had always been issue-oriented). And Women Strike for Peace had been around earlier. But it was their ability to coalesce that had the biggest impact.

What did we learn from the war? It keeps flickering in my mind, with the way that the government is going on in the Middle East. Have we really paid attention? Are we listening? Are we remembering? Do we have to bring this up again? It's a very frightening experience to think about it and to have so many hundreds of thousands of troops. For what? For a barrel of oil? What is it really all about? Have we not learned? That's frightening to me.

NOTE: Zigas provided additional information about her draft-counseling activities in a letter that I received dated March 19, 1991:

The Long Island Draft Information and Counseling Services started in 1967, at a meeting of Women Strike for Peace in Great Neck, Long Island, New York. The idea of forming the counseling service was in response to the increase in the numbers of people being drafted due to the escalation of the War in Vietnam. Women Strike for Peace put together a group of volunteers to counsel and educate young men as to their rights under the Selective Service system.

The American Civil Liberties Union, the Fellowship of Reconciliation, the American Friends Service Committee, the War Resisters League, the Central Committee for Conscientious Objectors, and all the major religious peace groups spoke to the first twenty volunteers. These men and women were trained in the highly technical and complicated law of the Selective Service system as well as military law and what rights if any people had once they were in the military.

The training took several months of work, meeting in the evenings once or twice a week until the counselors felt knowledgeable and the trainers felt the counselors were up to snuff. The volunteers were all working people who volunteered to do this counseling in the evening. The bond was that they were all opposed to the U.S. involvement in Vietnam. The Long Island Draft Information and Counseling Service opened its doors at the Ethical Humanist Society Building in Garden City, Long Island, in 1967, on a Tuesday evening with fifteen counselors and a support group of twenty-five others who staffed the center: did the scheduling; answered the phones; comforted tearful, young men, their parents and friends; dispensed coffee and tea; and handed out relevant literature. The service soon expanded to three nights a week, and more counselors had to be trained. They were so busy that many of the counselors saw these people at their homes. The number of counselors grew to fifty.

In addition to the counseling, many members of the counseling service and Women Strike for Peace went to demonstrations in support of men who were refusing induction, to trials for draft resisters and GIs who disobeyed orders. In all, the Long Island Draft Information and Counseling Service was active till the draft ended. Thousands of young men were counseled and supported. The impact of the service was far-reaching. It served as a model for others around the country and continued to do GI counseling until the end of the Vietnam War. In fact, the service briefly came alive again during Desert Storm, preparing itself in case the draft was reinstated.

19

George McT. Kahin

Professor Kahin provided a clear, insightful account of the origins of the Vietnam War, as well as the inertia in the U.S. government that kept it going. Kahin's prime research interest before going to Vietnam was Indonesia. He still regrets the opportunity cost of time spent on Vietnam that diverted his attention from more intensive study of political processes in Indonesia, particularly President Suharto's succession to Sukarno and the ensuing bloodbath in which hundreds of thousands of Indonesians died, not all of whom were Communists. Kahin went to Vietnam believing that he could help the U.S. government clarify the conditions for peace sought by the North Vietnamese. His attempts as a facilitator were ignored by the U.S. State Department, and he was unable to obtain cooperation from the U.S. media, which were reluctant to antagonize President Nixon.

Professor Kahin has written two books concerning U.S. military involvement in Vietnam: *Intervention: How America Became Involved in Vietnam* (New York: Alfred A. Knopf, 1986) and *The United States in Vietnam*, with John W. Lewis (New York: The Dial Press, 1967). Kahin was born in 1918 and has been associated with Cornell University since 1951. He was a sergeant in the U.S. Army between 1942 and 1945 and served in the European theater. The interview was conducted in Professor Kahin's office, 104 McGraw Hall, Cornell University, Ithaca, New York, on October 2, 1990.

PROFESSOR KAHIN: I was [in Vietnam] twice: 1971 and 1972. I think it was September or October. I went there as an individual. . . . The first time, I went there because I wanted to establish what the actual negotiating position [of North Vietnam] was. I was encouraged by Senator [J. William] Fulbright to do this and report back to him and also by Senator [George] McGovern, whom I knew. I had worked with both of them beginning in 1965. There had been a thing called a national teach-in. I was the one who was supposed to debate McGeorge Bundy. He didn't show up. Not because he was intimidated but because there was a U.S. invasion of the Dominican Republic, and he was suddenly called on to go there.

My acquaintance with these two senators began just after that. In 1971, it was clear to me and to a number of senators whom I had been working with that the Nixon administration was obfuscating the actual possibilities for negotiating [a peace settlement] and the actual negotiating stance of the PRG [Provisional Revolutionary Government] and the Hanoi regime.

So I went to find out. I was able to get in on my own. I went in through Laos. I hadn't expected I would necessarily be able to go in, but I was talking in Vientiane to the top representative of the Hanoi government in Laos about the negotiations and possibilities, and I remember we discussed the plan of Clark Clifford [who succeeded Robert McNamara as secretary of defense in 1968], which had just been floated. He asked me what I thought of it, and I could see some problems with it. He was quite interested that I could see these problems. He said, "You really should go and talk to our people." At the time, I couldn't arrange it right away as I was planning to fly to Rangoon. He said, "When you get there, check in with our embassy." I did. And so I was able to get a visa to go into Hanoi. I went in through Vientiane.

I took my wife with me. This was a period when there was no bombing. It was September 1971. So, their chargé d'affaires in Vientiane having been encouraged by the people in Hanoi to let me come in, I went in with the announced purpose of learning what their negotiating position actually was. I had previously visited South Vietnam a number of times, first in 1961. Earlier in 1971, I had again been spending some time in South Vietnam, and of course, an election was coming up, the first presidential election since 1967, and there was some hope that this election might be a reasonably fair one, and Duong Van Minh, who had been the nemesis of the U.S. for a long time, seemed likely to win against Thieu and Ky if the election was reasonably fair.

Remember, Duong Van Minh led the generals that threw out Diem. And then we, particularly elements in the Pentagon and [Gen. Paul D.] Harkins [head of the U.S. Military Assistance Command in South Vietnam], got rid of him at the end of January of 1964 because he indicated that he wanted to explore negotiating possibilities with the enemy and that also he was opposed to bombing the North. There were a number of other lesser reasons why he was ousted. He had been exiled for some

George McT. Kahin; Audrey R. Kahin; Col. Ha Van Lau, chief negotiator at the Paris peace talks for the Hanoi government; and Prime Minister Pham Van Dong meet in Hanoi, August 13, 1971. *(Courtesy of George McT. Kahin.)*

time. Now he was back. And he was running, and he had a lot of support, particularly from the Buddhists and some of the progressive Catholics and other antiwar elements. And I ascertained that when I was in South Vietnam. This was important because as a consequence, he was encouraged to run. And there was an interaction here with the new "seven point" negotiating program announced by the PRG, which was supported, of course, by Hanoi in its negotiating stance. The PRG, Provisional Revolutionary Government, was the new name for the NLF, National Liberation Front.

If the election had been held honestly, Minh had a good chance of winning it, and he would move toward a negotiated settlement. That was very clear. That's why the people on the other side were interested in him because they thought that a moderation in their negotiating position, as represented in the "seven points," could encourage elements associated with Minh and make feasible an accommodation that would serve the interests of both sides, both North and South Vietnam.

I mention the PRG's "seven points" because it relates to what I discovered when I was in Hanoi. I was fortunate enough to spend several

School damaged from U.S. air raid of July 4, 1972. *(Photo by George McT. Kahin.)*

sessions with Ha Van Lau, who was the chief negotiator on the other side and the one on whom Pham Van Dong, the prime minister, relied. So I talked to him and also with Pham Van Dong. This was in order to elicit in as much detail as possible what their actual negotiating position was, to ensure that there was a prospect of a position on their part that would fit with these elections that were occurring in the South. Duong Van Minh's willingness to run encouraged them to moderate their negotiating position. So we had several days of talks with Ha Van Lau. My wife could take shorthand. At the end of each session, my wife would type up the notes she had taken and show them to him that evening, and he would go over them, and then he would give them to us the next morning with his [amendments] and corrections, so that by the time we were through and he checked with Pham Van Dong, the prime minister, we had a pretty clear idea of what the negotiating position really was. And as a matter of fact, when we were through and saw Pham Van Dong, he said, "Yes, the record you have established in these interviews is exactly right. This is

Vuong Xuan Ba, 38, and his sons, ages 6 and 4, in an underground hospital near Thai Nguyen, recovering from wounds suffered in an air raid of September 22, 1972. During the raid, his wife and two of his other children were killed. *(Photo by George McT. Kahin.)*

our negotiating position." It was appreciably different from what the Nixon administration was telling the American public and the Congress.

Consequently, as expected, I prepared a long memorandum for Senator Fulbright and sent it back to him, and he tried to use this as leverage on the State Department but not to much avail. The interesting thing was that the administration was so anxious *not* to give the impression that there was a possibility for a reasonable, negotiated settlement that it took this memorandum and leaked it to a columnist named Joseph Kraft. And he came out with a column, which badly distorted the substance of my report. He said that even this fellow with the dovish inclination, Professor Kahin, had come to conclude that the negotiating position was just too tough to make any settlement possible.

It wasn't what I said, of course, at all. It was selectively leaked, and it was garbled and doctored, which I think helps to illustrate why it was so very hard to move towards negotiations when the administration was reluctant. It had its own reasons and found it easy to spurn the real possibilities that existed for a negotiated settlement of the war.

Inside a cave north of Thai Nguyen, North Vietnam, September 27, 1972. George McT. Kahin (*extreme right*) meets with Lt. Gen. Chu Van Ten (*seated across from Kahin*), Hanoi's first minister of defense. (*Courtesy of George McT. Kahin.*)

Remember, this was the time of Nixon's southern [U.S.] strategy. He was courting the southern vote, and there tended to be a greater disposition towards a more militant policy in the South. That was part of it. There were other reasons, and he was playing his China card; he thought he could induce China to apply leverage on Vietnam that would benefit the U.S. So that's one episode.

Then there was a second episode. That was the next year. That time, there was bombing, so I went by myself to Hanoi, again through a route from Vientiane. This was the time when Nixon had resumed heavy bombing. I have a file of pictures that I took then of the extent of damage, not just around Hanoi but in Hanoi itself, the main hospital, workers' quarters, schools. This was the time when the American public was being assured that we weren't hitting Hanoi. We were. And I spent a fair amount of time in bomb shelters during this period. I think [I spent] about eight days in the North this time.

When I was there, a CBS correspondent named John Hart had been to Haiphong to see how effective the American blockade and the bombing were. He was very envious because I had been given permission to go up toward the China border. The reason they permitted me to go was because I had an abiding interest in their policy toward minorities. I wanted to see how they were being governed up there. But at the same time, of course, it gave me the opportunity of seeing pretty clearly whether the blockade was working or not, whether the road system had been interdicted, and whether the railroad system had been interdicted. Hart told me he wanted to talk to me when I came back.

And when I went up north for three days, I found that the roads were congested with traffic coming down from China. It hadn't been stopped at all. The drivers drove in the daytime as well as at night. Large trucks, pushcarts, everything you could imagine was coming down from the China border. This meant that the blockade was ineffective. Moreover, the railroad was running, and a pipeline for oil had been constructed, coming down across the border. The American bombing was not effective. Based on conversations I had with some of our pilots, I can understand why. If [as a pilot] you know that down on the ground there are a lot of SAM missiles, precision bombing is not something you are keen to undertake because if you are interested in something really approximating precision, you would have to get down very low and greatly increase your chances of getting hit by antiaircraft fire. Or else you'd have to have one of these smart bombs, and we only had very few of those. As a result, many bridges were still serviceable, and if they were knocked out, there were one or two floating spans moored over in the foliage by the river-bank, waiting to be shoved into place. So they weren't really hurting much as far as transportation was concerned. It was clear that the Nixon blockade was a sham and a shambles. It wasn't working.

I drove up north at night. When I got there, I would go out in the mornings along one of the roads. If you got out early enough, it was usually safe. American pilots didn't start out until about seven-thirty or eight o'clock in the morning, after breakfast. You were also pretty safe at dusk coming back. There wasn't much bombing then. If there was, it was unusual. Probably ninety to ninety-five percent of the bombs were dropped during the daylight hours.

I could go pretty much where I wanted. They took me rather seriously. Maybe because they knew I had some connections with various senators who were opposed to the war. I had also co-authored a book on the war [*The United States in Vietnam*] which they knew about. So they regarded me as well informed, and they didn't seem to be playing any tricks. So I had considerable freedom to go where I wanted. Obviously, there were places I couldn't have gone if I had wanted to, but I did pick places, and I went to them. . . .

Many villages that straddled the roads had been bombed. Early one morning, I passed a village straddling the road. Coming back that evening, I found that most of that same village had been obliterated by bombing, but the road hadn't been interdicted. The bombing was so inaccurate. Because our guys were usually staying up high, understandably, out of a sense of self-preservation, they weren't interdicting roads, and they weren't hitting bridges in the area I traveled through, but they were doing a lot of damage to villages close to the roads. So I asked to see some of the civilian underground hospitals. There were a lot of fresh casualties. There were many civilians, women and children mostly. I took some pictures of them.

To make a long story short, Hart thought what I'd seen was very important. He said, "I'd like to have CBS put you on when you get back." I said, "Fine, I'd be glad to." He said, "What you learned about the interdiction was the most important thing, but the extent of civilian casualties is also significant." So he sent cables to CBS, and they agreed I should be put on their program at their New York studio. I got in touch with them right after I returned to the States, and they said, "Yes, we have been waiting for you. Just sit tight in your hotel room, and we'll get back to you." So I sat tight for almost two days. Finally, they said quite sheepishly: "Look, we are afraid we can't put you on television. We can't explain it to you over the phone. We know that you are an old friend of one of our correspondents, and we are going to send him up from Washington to have lunch with you, and he'll explain why we can't do it." He came up, and he wasn't very happy about things either. We went to a very nice restaurant, but neither one of us was very hungry. He told me that there were two reasons why they were not going to put me on. The first reason was that CBS knew that the American public had had a bellyful of looking at casualties and atrocities and that people would turn off their sets and watch something else. They didn't want to see it any more. [My CBS friend continued]:

So in that aspect of your reporting, they are not interested. But more importantly, they can't put you on because you are going to talk about the failure of Nixon's policy of interdiction and that it isn't working. You are the first person with firsthand knowledge of this. This contradicts what the people looking at this from up in the air are saying and what some of the generals are saying. And CBS is up for the relicensing of its affiliates with the Federal Communications Commission, which Nixon has pretty much packed. And if this is put on, CBS's chances of getting a renewal of its licenses for those affiliates will be at hazard.

So those were the two reasons. There wasn't much one could do. I did write an article for the *Washington Star*. The interesting thing was that they wanted to print it, but they said, "If we print this, we have to have a riposte, a rejoinder. We can't just print it by itself." So they had a fellow who was a speechwriter for Nixon insert a piece alongside. I found this was generally the case. Martin Agronsky had a program. He asked me on it to report on my trip. When I got to the studio, I found he, too, had felt obliged to ask somebody from the State Department. And that was pretty much it. I think the media were rather intimidated by Nixon at that time. So there wasn't a whole lot one could do. I talked to [Senators] Fulbright and McGovern and a few others about this trip. . . .

When I saw Pham Van Dong in 1971, I had chided him in a friendly sort of way. I said, "I think you are unwise, having just those Americans come over who you know are in the peace movement. It's all right. But really, you ought to supplement that by bringing over Americans who have influence who are on the fence, who haven't made up their minds about the war." He said, "Well, perhaps you are right. What would you suggest?" So I thought, and I said, "Well, how about university presidents?" He said, "Fine. And we will get back to you."

That was the background of the second time I went. They had thought I was going to come with some American university presidents, and that was most disappointing because I was given carte blanche to pick out a dozen of them. And I called around to most of the major universities and talked to their presidents. I had backing from our president here at Cornell, who was willing to vouch that I was an honorable, sensible person. We had serious conversations. The upshot was a pattern that was uniform: "Well, we have to get back to our board of trustees about this. I want to consult with some of my senior colleagues. It's a good idea. I can see that it's important for people like us to go and see what is actually going on."

I gave them some assurances that I would take them to places that they thought were important to go to. But in any case, I waited a couple of weeks before either they got back to me or I got back to them. And [the response was], "So sorry, something has come up. I can't manage it." So this was Harvard, Yale, Princeton, Stanford, and others. The president of MIT said he was interested but that first he would have to check with his friend Henry Kissinger and have his approval. I didn't expect he would call back, and I didn't bother to call him again.

I would have gone with them [the university presidents] to Paris and gotten in touch with the Vietnamese embassy there and arranged to go by Air France or Aeroflot to Vietnam, at least to Vientiane and from there on to Vietnam. That's the way I did it, and that's the way it was expected we would come. But I didn't have any contact here. I did this by myself. [Senators Fulbright and McGovern] knew I was going [a second time. They did not request that I go], but I told them I was going, and they wanted me to report to them, which I did do.

[On the second visit], I met people in their Historical and Social Sciences Institute and their minorities office. I didn't meet the prime minister the second time. I saw the foreign minister and one or two other ministers. I was impressed by the fact that in Hanoi, the main hospital, as well as schools and workers' flats, had been recently hit by American bombing. So that aspect was of interest to me, but I wasn't at this time just looking into their negotiating position.

[Minorities appeared to have been treated] pretty well then. I don't think it has been so good after 1978 because some of these minorities straddle the China border and they [the Vietnamese] are anxious about whether they can rely upon some of them, although I think that they are a bit paranoid about that. At that time [1972], they arranged a visit for me with General Chu Van Ten, who had been the first minister of defense in Ho Chi Minh's government and who was himself a Nung, one of the minority groups. It was indicative of their policy then that he was the one that ran what was called the Viet Bac, comprising five provinces along the northern frontier. And he saw to it that I saw what I wanted to see.

It was quite clear that a number of offices in government in this area were filled by minority people, which was a sign that they were being realistic enough then not to antagonize the minorities and try to make all [of the appointees] Vietnamese. They gave the Nung and several other minorities a fair amount of cultural autonomy. They let them have their own primary schools using their own language, for the first years of schooling. I think it was three or four years. And gradually, Vietnamese was introduced into the schools.

I think it was the second time . . . that I overlapped with [a group of Americans] briefly. Cora Weiss, Dave Dellinger, and a few other people came in a body. And I went to one or two cultural events that they were attending. I talked with them, and they had come to accept the release of an American pilot. After they left, I said I would like to see how these people were being treated. And so I requested a meeting with American pilots that had been interned, and they brought [them] together [Professor Kahin met with seven POWs: Capt. Glen Burns; Capt. George Rose, Capt. Melvin Matsui, Lt. Carrol Beeler, Lt. Richard Fulton, Lt. Gregg Hanson, and Lt. Donald Logan; see "Cornell Professor Reports Meeting 7 P.O.W.'s in Hanoi," *New York Times*, October 5, 1972, p. 14]. I have a picture of them. And we talked. I don't know what constraints they were under, but the one thing I was able to do was to get the Vietnamese to agree to let me take letters from these people out. I'm sure they inspected those letters. They didn't want anything to go out in code or anything, but I was able to take letters out to wives and families.

I don't think the POWs I saw, all of them at least, were the same as those other people had seen. There was no way for me to establish whether these were the same men that had met with other visiting Americans or not. Very possibly they were. These people were certainly opposed to the proposition that the bombing was going to free them. They thought that was foolish, and they used some very strong invective.

I was totally unprepared for the fact that Hanoi had been hit, heavily. It was hit inordinately harder later, of course, in the Christmas bombing. But this was in September, the beginning of October 1972. There was fairly heavy bombing during the last few days while I was there. I was in a bomb shelter a good bit. I saw one American pilot being shot down. He was lucky. He had a new kind of parachute that carried him out over the China Sea so he could be saved. And they were aware of that. The extent of destruction of schools, of workers' flats, and certainly the hospital surprised me. Nor was I prepared for the bombing in rural areas. Some villages were off the main roads, and I saw that they had been hit. The explanation I was given was that when the American pilots were returning to the carriers (they could identify carrier-based planes) and the weather wasn't good, rather than jettison their bombs into the sea, they jettisoned them over land.

[Although I considered myself an antiwar individual], I didn't participate in demonstrations. I certainly supported the movement and advances in civil rights in this country, but I hadn't been an activist. I was the person selected in the National Teach-In in 1965 simply because there were so few people that had any acquaintance with Southeast Asia. That's one of the real tragedies of that situation. We needed Vietnam specialists in this country, but the very few who existed were working with government, and they weren't all that good. We hadn't trained people who were really knowledgeable about Vietnam. We had some people who knew something about some Southeast Asian areas. I was the director of the Southeast Asia program at Cornell. But my area of knowledge was largely focused on Indonesia. The tendency of a lot of Americans was to say, "Well, if you know one country in Southeast Asia, you must know it all." And that was crazy. You wouldn't say that about Europe, would you? You wouldn't expect a person who was a French specialist to know much about Poland.

[I haven't been back to Vietnam since 1972.] I haven't been invited back. Well, I was invited to go to a history conference in Hanoi, but that was organized here in the United States by somebody at Columbia. It was a history conference two years ago on the war, bringing Vietnamese and Americans together. The Americans included one who had worked for the State Department in a fairly senior position during the war and others who were academics.

But in 1976, I did actually essay to go back to Vietnam but found that there was some reluctance. They asked, "What is it you want to do?" I said that I wanted to continue to look at the situation among the minorities in the North. I think I mentioned earlier that there was a shift in policy. It's not really a heavily repressive policy, but it is not as enlightened as it was during the war. Then it was very important to get along well with these people because of their strategic positioning in the North adjacent to China, this being the area that Ho Chi Minh's group first freed from French and Japanese control, and these northern provinces constituted the initial base of Ho's operations. Then they had excellent relations with these minority groups.

Ho knew a couple of minority languages; Pham Van Dong knew a couple; they made a real effort to get along with these people. It was incumbent upon them, and they did it then. But this changed somewhat after the war. They developed an overly suspicious attitude toward at least one of the minorities I was interested in along the Chinese border because of their fear of China and the fact that they had many relatives on the China side of the border. And so I was not given permission to go.

[The present Vietnamese government has] been quite a disappointment. One of the disappointments was the way in which the Northern element has treated the old NLF leadership. Members of this group haven't been accorded, it seems to me, the positions in the new government merited on the basis of the struggle that they put up. A few of them have positions of minor or middle-range importance. But, by and large, they have not been accorded the kind of treatment in the new regime that they deserve.

[What do I think of the postwar re-education camps?] I think [that] re-education camps existed, still exist in some places, and that they took in quite a few people. It wasn't an enjoyable life in those re-education camps. But there wasn't any bloodbath, as had been predicted. There were a few executions, a small number of executions, as far as I know. I haven't been on the ground there, so I can't be accurate about that. [What do I think of the charge of the use of poison gas against the Laotians?] It strikes me as phony. They've got along pretty well with the Lao leaders, not the Cambodians, but certainly with the Lao leadership.

[With respect to the reaction of others concerning my trip to Hanoi], it's predictable that you would get some hate mail and that people would write articles that would be critical of the positions that you took. [Did I believe I was acting in the best interests of the United States when I went to Hanoi?] Absolutely. [Did I hope that my trip would help shorten the war and save lives?] It's what I did have in mind. This futile hemorrhaging of lives on both sides, ours and theirs, the enormous destruction of civilian population there. These poor, misled American kids. I talked to lots of them there and here who had no real clue as to what the thing was all about. They had been completely brainwashed. Some of the official army films shown to these fellows at the port of embarkation disregarded fundamental facts. The historical analogies that were drawn were a gross distortion. The misinformation was really very grievous.

[Could serious negotiations have shortened the war?] . . . You have to realize, of course, that if there is a negotiation, it can't be a negotiation where we get our way. It's their country. You couldn't expect a negotiation that would end with the United States still politically controlling half the country. South Vietnam was, in fact, an artificial American construct. We had violated the Geneva Accords when we transformed the demarcation line at the seventeenth parallel into a political boundary. The agreement explicitly enjoined against that.

We wouldn't sign that agreement, but we said we wouldn't upset it. We certainly did upset it. I think most people don't understand that our involvement goes back a long ways. It goes back to the fall of 1945. It was American ships that were bringing French troops into Vietnam. We were financing and providing arms for the French effort indirectly. We were doing it for European reasons. We got into Vietnam not by any Asian gate but via Europe.

We were afraid of the potential of communism in France. France seemed politically critically wobbly then. The Communist Party was the largest party in France. In the election of 1946, they did even better. We were afraid of the outcome in France, and therefore, we supported the French in Vietnam in order to secure French cooperation vis-à-vis Soviet power in Europe and so as to ensure that nationalist sentiment in France did not turn against us and undermine progress towards that objective. Remember that having been humiliated by defeat and occupation by the Nazis, many Frenchmen yearned for a return to France's "grandeur" through the re-establishment of their colonial empire. Note that the French Communist Party understood this and so as not to lose votes during the first two years after World War II, supported France's military reconquest of Vietnam.

One of the big operative factors of our domestic politics was the fact that you had, during the [Sen. Joseph] McCarthy period and right afterwards, the use of the loss of China issue as a club against the Democrats and by some of the right-wing Democrats against their colleagues. It is fatuous to think that China was ours to lose, but that perception was operative in a very signal way on the American political scene. Successive American administrations didn't want to be accused of losing additional Asian territory, even though it wasn't theirs to lose, to Communist control. It figured very importantly in the Vietnam equation.

[My two trips to Vietnam] pulled me away from the areas that I had worked on before. I first worked on Indonesia quite intensively, and it pulled me away from Indonesia in 1965, at a time when there was great turmoil there, and there has been very little understanding of what happened in Indonesia in 1965. There was a major change in government. Over half a million people were massacred. I sometimes reproach myself for not having stuck with Indonesia because that is a situation which is certainly not well understood today. The present government of Indonesia is not about to acknowledge what actually did happen. I think that's true of a number of colleagues of mine in the Asian field who were drawn away from their own specialization because they felt a prior obligation to try to help end the war in Vietnam, especially if they could get to Vietnam and do field research there, to see the actual nature of the situation there.

[Which individual American was most effective in the antiwar movement?] It's very hard to say. There were some congressmen and senators, especially McGovern, Fulbright, [Mark O.] Hatfield, [Harold E.] Hughes, and [Charles E.] Goodell, and later Bobby Kennedy and Gene McCarthy, you could single out. There were organizations like the American Friends Service Committee, the Mennonites, and the Indochina Resource Center which, considering their size and their resources, did quite a bit.

[My feelings about the war are], I suppose, [stronger today] because of what I learned in the research on a recent book I wrote about Vietnam, called *Intervention*. In the process of doing that, it took me about ten years, I took advantage of the Freedom of Information Act. If I have any distinction, it is that I am credited with getting more government documents on the war declassified than any other person, something which I believe is helpful to other people because they can make use of them. In the process of my research, my opinions were reinforced when I saw what had been going on inside our government and the kind of judgments that were made on what kind of evidence. One of the things that surprised me most was that my criticism of Lyndon Johnson was ameliorated because I found the kind of advice his senior advisers were giving him. Bear in mind, these were men whose reputations had been formed during the Kennedy administration. Johnson took them over. He felt insecure in foreign policy, and he relied on them very heavily, and they gave him some very bad advice. Of course, they were protecting their own tails in that case simply because a departure from policies they had already developed in the previous administration could discredit them. This inclined them to keep on the same track, for their reputations would certainly suffer from any serious inconsistency of position. So when they learned more, they did not adapt to the new knowledge. They were just as hawkish, if not more so.

[Were there deceptions during the war?] There were so many. The actual terms of the 1954 Geneva agreements was one; Tonkin Gulf was one. The character of the Buddhists was another. The Buddhists were a potential third force, but we clobbered them. I'm not talking about the first time, when Diem was overthrown in 1963, when we felt the Buddhists were a rational force because they agreed with us. But rather in 1966, when they had won wide, popular support for the removal of our protégés, Ky and Thieu. Then a great deal of American heavy equipment, including many tanks, were turned over to Ky, and he was given

American airlift facilities for use against the Buddhists, to smash them, and those military elements that supported them in Danang and Hue. It was reported, but people don't remember this. Neil Sheehan and others who were in Vietnam then reported what was happening, but it didn't get the audience that it should have. A third force is a tricky term, but there was the possibility of an alternative government led by the militant Buddhists that could have negotiated a decent settlement. Moreover, everything that Nixon got in his settlement in 1973 he could have gotten at the outset of his administration without the four additional years of slaughter and destruction.

[What was the lesson of Vietnam?] I suppose most fundamentally, that other people's patriotism and sense of nationalism is just as deep as ours. If you try to move in and dictate the lives, the polity, the kind of government somebody else has, to push aside the people that they regard as their legitimate leaders, you are going to have a very strong reaction, just as would happen here if somebody tried to do that to us. But it seems to me there has been precious little empathy for the sentiments of other people. We tend too much to look at them through our own prism of national interest. There is not enough effort to understand the way people in other countries perceive their own interests.

[How do I define patriotism?] I think patriotism in a democratic political order, a democracy, enjoins upon a citizen not simply the right but the duty to criticize his government when he sees it going wrong, particularly if it is in his area of specialization and he knows what is going on in the situation and has a clear idea what the facts are and can see through some of the smoke screen and obfuscation that government sometimes is responsible for. This was certainly a clear-cut case of that.

20

George Wald

Prof. George Wald, as a matter of conscience, denounced the Vietnam War in an open forum at MIT, on March 4, 1969, making headlines in newspapers across the country. Wald traveled not only to North Vietnam but also to South Vietnam, where he experienced firsthand the autocratic methods employed by the South Vietnamese government against those who opposed continuation of the war. Wald disputed the account of torture related by an American POW that was widely publicized because he, Wald, had personally met the prisoner while in Hanoi, and the prisoner had spoken well of the treatment he had received. Professor Wald believed that all of society's institutions were vulnerable to corruption. He questioned whether the United States truly had a two-party system because Democrats differed so little from Republicans. Wald also condemned the United States for typically serving as the arms supplier to *both* sides of armed conflict throughout the world. Of late, he spends much of his time and effort researching various religious orientations.

Wald, born in 1906 and a Harvard University emeritus professor since 1971, was awarded the Nobel Prize for his research in 1967. He has received numerous honorary degrees and awards in science and has lectured in Europe, the United States, and Asia. Wald was a contributor to *War Crimes and the American Conscience*, edited by Erwin Knoll and Judith Nies McFadden (New York: Holt, Rinehart and Winston, 1970). The interview took place on the back porch of Professor Wald's summer cottage in Woods Hole, Massachusetts, early in the morning of October 6, 1990.

PROFESSOR WALD: I was invited by the [Chinese] government to visit Mainland China in January 1972. This was a very unexpected invitation. It came quite suddenly, as though I could just leap off that exact week. It came from the Chinese embassy in Toronto, Canada. I was teaching at Harvard and said I'd be very glad to go but I would have to finish my teaching. So that brought me to something like the middle of January. I went to China then for five weeks. When I was in Peking, Beijing, I visited the North Vietnamese embassy and had a long talk with the chargé d'affaires. He wasn't the full ambassador, but he was in charge. I told him that when my visit to China finished, I should really go home, but that if he made it worthwhile, I would go to Hanoi.

I said there were four things that I wanted if I went. . . . One thing was to get out of Hanoi itself and see something of what was going on in the country. The war was still on and all that. Another thing was to be able to visit some American prisoners while there. I [also] wanted to meet significant members of the Hanoi government. So that's three. And [fourth], I said I wanted to get out of Hanoi to make some sort of significant contact with what the war was doing, where the war zone was. He said that was all fine.

I went to Hanoi, and it should be understood that my sympathies in this whole situation were very much with Vietnam. I thought that the spectacle [of American military involvement in Vietnam] — and have said publicly in the States, published it in the speech that changed the whole course of my life [March 4,1969] — was the most disgraceful episode in American history, that is, the whole picture of the most powerful and wealthiest country in the world invading one of the very poorest and weakest countries in the world. It seemed to me very distressing, obscene, in fact. The fight they were putting up, I thought, was admirable. They were being bombed all the time by our planes, and they had no planes. When I did enter a war zone city and town in North Vietnam, the thing they were proudest of was having shot down an American plane. They didn't have any antiaircraft stuff. They just would get out with rifles and pop away. How this happened, how they managed, I don't know. They shot down a fair number actually because coming in to bomb, the American pilots would dive low, apparently.

In any case, I was very sympathetic with the people. I liked Hanoi for its great simplicity. The Vietnamese I found to be a very gentle people, if you didn't come at them with a gun. But the proudest thing in their entire history was getting rid of the Chinese. China had invaded and taken over Vietnam. It's a very strongly nationalistic country. They really love their country. Kicking out the Chinese many centuries ago, that's the biggest thing in their entire history. When you read now that they have trouble with the Chinese, it is a good thing to remember.

All of those things that I asked for [of the chargé d'affaires] happened. Perhaps the most interesting thing was my interview of two American prisoners in Hanoi. They were very different from each other. One of them was an intensely serious person. They were fliers, both of them, and not young but mature men. I had, before entering China, bought in Hong Kong a very good tape recorder, which I had never used, but I had it with me then. I had complete taped records of those two interviews. They were very interesting. The first man had his plane shot down very early on. He had been a prisoner for, I've forgotten now, four or five years. He said of everything that had happened, he used the word, that it had been "correct." He had trouble, isolated for a year, but his treatment was, as he said, correct. He had nothing specific to complain of. I told him that I would be glad to get in touch with his wife and family. I told them both that. If they had a letter they wanted to give me or to just put a message to their relatives on my tape, that would be fine.

The other man who, I think, was a little younger (both were navy fliers, as I recall) [and] had been shot down much later. In being expelled from his plane, his arm was broken. Now, there was something that enormously interested me in both their stories. It was that both of them came parachuting down in the Vietnamese countryside where by then, particularly for the second one, families had lost people, had been napalmed. There was plenty of reason for infinite resentment. The most interesting thing, in a way, that they had to tell me was that having been seen parachuting down, they were found by Vietnamese peasants. Those peasants took care of them and brought them perfectly safely to Hanoi and turned them over to the authorities there.

They immediately saw what had happened to the pilot with the broken arm. He told me a woman doctor had splinted and tied up his arm so that it wouldn't give him any problems on the trip toHanoi. I wondered a little, if I may be forgiven for saying so, what would have happened if a Vietnamese flier who had been downed near, say, Chicago, after endless bombing of the ordinary population, people on the farms, and all that, [if he] would have been as well cared for. These were ignorant peasants. Part of the answer to that question is the North Vietnamese government. From the very beginning, they had said they were fighting the American government, not the American people, and that may have helped.

When I came back, I did get in touch with the wives of both prisoners, and after a time, the men did, of course, come home. I remember, I think, Jane Fonda saying, and it was perfectly true, "They looked like an arriving football team." They were in good condition. Those American prisoners of North Vietnam were well fed and cared for.

Now, this second man, the one with the broken arm, was very interesting because when I interviewed him, his arm was still in a sling. There was a sort of wooden paddle fitted into the cast around his arm, which he said to me cheerfully he had just gotten that morning. Because he was having trouble with his hand dropping and falling asleep, one of the guards had whittled this little paddle out of wood to hold his hand out. He told me that the cast was coming off shortly. The reason I am saying this is that when he came back, he was one of the atrocity cases in the news from one end of our country to the other.

He told an absolutely incredible story about his imprisonment that was given wide publicity, and mind you, this was a month after I got there. This man told the story of what the Vietnamese had done in preparation for either Ramsey Clark or Jane Fonda's visit. One or the other. I have forgotten now. I have all that in notes in Cambridge. What the Vietnamese had done (according to this flier) was to stand him on a table, with the broken arm attached to a hook in the ceiling. Then, the guards would repeatedly kick the table out from under him, so that his whole weight fell on this arm.

That one month after I saw him, he must have been entirely well with his arm all fixed and set. He told this story about the time when his arm was badly broken, when he was brought in. That was torture, which was what it was called. I checked up with the surgery department at Harvard and was told that if anything like that had happened, it would have pulled his arm out of its socket and probably made the arm part at the break. A broken arm could not have possibly survived that kind of treatment and then got well, as I found him, even a month or six weeks before these other people visited him.

So that story went all over the United States, and as I recall, Andrei Sakharov, the Soviet (who incidentally felt that the United States should see to it that they conquered Vietnam at that point; that was the side he was on), wrote with great scorn of the stupidity of that American ex–attorney general, Ramsey Clark, for not realizing why this man spoke well of his treatment, for not realizing that he'd been so severely tortured and feared that if he said anything wrong that he would be tortured again. So this made a great story, and it was false. And in fact, this flier appeared on the program *60 Minutes.*

I called the man who did the *60 Minutes* interviews, who was told this ghastly story of the pilot's torture and told him that I knew that this story was false, and I would be glad to meet that ex–navy flier on his program. "Work it out," I said. He was very interested but then told me that the Defense Department wouldn't permit such an encounter.

So, yes. I did go to a war zone, and there I had another experience that dismayed me and again made me admire the fantastic fight that the Vietnamese were putting up. This was in North Vietnam, where I was taken to a town, the name of which I've forgotten, about eighty-five miles south of Hanoi. It was just a small place but very, very important, strategically, because it had a railroad bridge over a river and just beyond the railroad bridge, a power station.

And through the entire war up to that point, we are talking 1972, American planes had been trying to get rid of both that bridge and that power station but without success. They tried everything. They tried dropping bombs in the river in the hope they would float down and blow up the bridge. I think just as the war ended, they finally got the bridge. Meanwhile, this town, realizing it was a strategic target, was doing everything possible to survive. I visited a machine shop carved out of a deep cave in a mountain. That was a very interesting visit. It was amazing. There were about eight machine lathes used to repair things like trucks and so on, things that they needed.

At a certain point, they gathered with me. We had tea together, and then they said, "Songs are more important than bullets." There was a young woman with an absolutely wonderful voice who sang a song to me about the bridge separating North and South Vietnam and how lovers see each other across the bridge but can't meet, can't communicate. It was quite nice. I visited a hospital there. You understand that these people, knowing that they would be under pretty continuous bombing, had moved schools, hospitals, everything, out into the fields, out of town. And this hospital was just in shacks and in hastily constructed buildings, each one with a great big red cross painted on its roof so that the fliers could see it. . . .

It was Christmas Day. . . . Only a tenth of the North Vietnamese were Christians. Mostly they were Buddhists. But Christmas was nevertheless a national holiday for that godless, communist country. But for our godly, democratic country (you see, everyone was at home for that weekend; Christmas was on either Saturday or Sunday), in any case, on Christmas morning, when they [the American pilots] might well have been at some service, instead, three American flights took off for that town and, ten minutes apart, dropped bombs. The targets (they didn't kill any soldiers), the targets were all civilian. And there I was visiting that hospital. The bombs were not only big, explosive bombs. They had dropped the anti-personnel stuff that just cuts people up. The antipersonnel stuff was responsible for most of what I saw.

There was no time or occasion to put on a show for me. I was just going through this makeshift clinic. There were kids, there was one who [was wounded by an] antipersonnel [bomb] that cut the spinal cord so that she was incontinent, of course, and paralyzed and not able to walk for the rest of her life. There was a small child whose grandfather was holding it. The mother had been killed. It was a pitiful thing, and as for the reality of what I was told, that was perfectly clear and certain because one of the bombs dropped on the hospital was a dud. And there I was, so far from home, reading the tag on this dud bomb that was as fresh as the day it was written and told the whole history of it, which I promptly recorded.

Vietnam was pitted in many places like a part of the moon. [Egbert W.] Pfeiffer [a former University of Montana professor, can] tell all about that. But what we know has been elaborately reported and photographed — the napalm and all that stuff. Terrible. And endless killing of civilians and children. The rule was that every American plane had to get rid of its bombs before attempting to land because landing was a dangerous business with bombs. So if nothing else, you would cast them overboard without aiming.

[No U.S. government official encouraged me to travel to Hanoi.] Certainly not. I came back with a filmed interview with five brand new U.S. prisoners. My god, a guy got on the plane which had stopped just to refuel in Alaska and promptly sat down with me. He was from one of the broadcasting companies and wanted an exclusive. I told him I couldn't give any exclusives. He was planted there just to get to me, to get the film. So I was whisked through customs at New York. I had a whole roomful of press people and so on. I told them everything they asked that I knew. At the end, I was told by a *New York Times* guy, "That was a good interview, but it doesn't have any news." And that was it. . . . I said I wanted [the film interview] distributed. But something crazy had happened. They told me at least that the pictures were there, but there was no sound. So that was never shown.

[Although a government publication may list my name as having broadcast over Radio Hanoi], if I ever got into Hanoi Radio it's news to me. I am saying unequivocally that I never broadcast on Radio Hanoi. I had lots of conversations, but I never broadcast for them.

The next year, I visited Saigon with a group of students to try to stop the war. That was an interesting experience, too. No one stopped an American in Saigon. Now, this was our ally. I was in Saigon for ten days. There were all kinds of peace movements there: a student peace movement, a Catholic peace movement, a women's peace movement. I met them all. All of them. The students were very active, wanting to stop the war. They organized a meeting at which all of these peace movement groups and all of the press would be there. It was originally to happen in a Buddhist university.

I was with seven American students. The most mature one, the one who fitted in in certain ways best, was a law student at Harvard University. He had been in the Peace Corps in Vietnam. He could speak and even read Vietnamese. So he was a very useful person. I was the only older person in the group. And then came this day at which we were to have our big meeting. These Vietnamese students were very formal about having a meeting. They appeared at our little hotel the night before and had drawn up a whole agenda, exactly what and when. This was to happen at the Buddhist university, but they told us that it was possible that that would be occupied, be guarded if the government got word of this. In that case, we were to come to Saigon University itself, and they designated which room.

Saigon, now Ho Chi Minh City, had these little taxis. Each could take only three passengers. There were eight of us. That meant three taxis. So a taxi came down the street. We were afraid we were being watched and were careful. We weren't going to get into any taxis that might be plants. In any case, this taxi came barreling down the street, and we signaled it. And this man from Harvard Law School, who could speak Vietnamese, and I got into it, leaving six people for two further taxis. Well, fortunately for them, two taxis pulled away from the curb just at about that point, and three of our people got into each of them. But they were simply taken off into the blue, taken to the airport area, just taken away. Both taxis were plants. However, in one of the two taxis, there was this big student, a big guy, and he began to kick from the inside, kick the cab to pieces. So the cabbie stopped, and they got out, and pretty soon a taxi came along, which they hailed. But so did a man on a motorcycle, who said a few quiet words to that taxi driver, and once again, they were taken completely adrift.

Meanwhile, we reached the Buddhist university and found it completely surrounded by armed men. The smallest weapons you saw were M-16 rifles. They were all in battle gear and so on. So after waiting about three-quarters of an hour for the others to arrive, and nobody else had appeared, we got another taxi and went to the university. There was our meeting. It was pretty wonderful. It was very well attended. Delegations from all of the Vietnamese peace organizations were there, and the press was there.

There came a point at which the police arrived. That was very funny because the students at this meeting just rose like a wave, rushed to the doors, which had been locked, and slammed, pounded on the doors and cursed out the police so violently that the police decided they better get reinforcements. Anyhow, they went away, and the strange thing was that we finished the whole agenda. As we did so, all hell broke loose. There was not just the police but the security forces, all in battle gear, and they had strung barbed wire all around the neighborhood.

But nobody ever stopped an American in Saigon. And so, there I was with these students, and I'd been told there was no seeing our ambassador, Ellsworth Bunker. . . . I encountered him once before. I think it was at Middlebury College, Vermont. I had been told there was no seeing him, but there I was with students, and as we came into the embassy, there was a marine at a desk, and the students just pounded on the desk and said, "We want the ambassador, and we want him now." And the next thing I knew, we were sitting with Ambassador Bunker. He seemed to be cheered up to have an older guy like myself and a professor at Harvard in the room. He was a tall, handsome, elderly, aristocratic-looking person. He said some remarkable things to me. He said what wonderful things this war was doing for Vietnam. He said, "Why, those peasants used to bring fruit and vegetables to market in sampans. Now they all have outboard motors on their sampans. They all ride motorcycles where they used to ride bicycles. We are doing endless good for the Vietnamese."

What we had to say to him was that the Saigon police had arrested and jailed six Vietnamese students who had come to a meeting with us, and they're the people who concerned us. "We want them released." Bunker said to us, "You wouldn't want us to try to influence the Vietnamese government, would you?" "Yes," we said. "We want those guys out." And, in fact, that's what ended our trip because I had the inspiration of saying to a government representative, "You let those students out, and we will immediately leave Vietnam." That's what happened. We were told when the students were released the next day. We just got out of there.

The only time I returned to Vietnam was to Hanoi, when I was invited to the victory celebration in 1985. The thing I missed was any sign of the Chinese at this victory celebration. And it was curious because during the war, North Vietnam had been greatly assisted both by the Soviet Union and China. I asked about that and was told, "Oh, they're here." They weren't very much in evidence. But the Soviet people were, and the Soviet people had built the equivalent of Lenin's tomb for Ho Chi Minh, which, in fact, was not yet opened. But a couple of days later, I was taken to visit the tomb. And there was Ho Chi Minh looking beautiful and asleep. They had done the same kind of job on his body (the Soviet people had) as they had done for Lenin.

I had some strange and sometimes disappointing interviews with officials of the Hanoi government, officials of the Communist government. One in particular was with one of their top theorists and editor of the official North Vietnamese newspaper. He was a nice man. He surprised me at one point by saying to me, "How are things going on Route 128?" I said, "My God, have you been to the United States?" "Oh no," he said, "but we know all about Route 128." That's where all the electronics in the Boston area [are] spread out. They are not doing well now, but they were doing fine then.

In any case, his views shocked me at one point because he quoted the oft-quoted communist slogan, "From everyone according to his abilities, to everyone according to his need." But he had changed one word. His quotation went, "From everyone according to his abilities, to everyone according to his *work*." That was different from need, and I asked him about it. "Oh," he said, "you see, communism lies ahead of us. We are now in a socialist period trying to get there. When communism really arrives, then it will be need, but now it's socialism, and it's work." I'm virtually quoting him because I remember this very well. He said, "A manager has quite different needs from a worker. A manager needs room, quiet, a relaxed life, so that he can run things. What is the need of the worker? Good health, so that he can produce."

I was a little dismayed by that. I'm saying this because I think I know where I stand, and I don't buy slogans. That was [during] my original visit, not during the victory celebration. I may have seen him again, but I'm not sure. He was a nice man, otherwise. . . .

I paid [my travel expenses for my first trip to Vietnam but] not to the victory celebration. I think Hanoi paid for that. We were a delegation of five people, five Americans. David Dellinger was one of them. When we arrived, my heavens, we were all just dressed any old how because we had been traveling a long time. We arrived in a Soviet passenger plane, and as we stepped down to walk across the field, there was an honor guard in the fanciest uniforms you've ever seen.

I'll tell you one word about the victory celebration that surprised me very much. I had an excellent seat, up front on the reviewing stand. As each military unit, all beautifully uniformed and in fine order, hit the reviewing stand, it broke into the *goose-step*, wonderfully expert, stiff legs out, and slamming down on the pavement, held until past the whole reviewing stand. Great Prussian style.

At that time, I asked to speak with Catholic Church representatives. And indeed, I had a visit then with three priests who were well placed in the organization of the Catholic Church in Vietnam. I asked them, "Well, how is it? You are in a Communist country. How is it?" "Well," they said, "as you know, we are allowed to hold our services, do our things." Then one of them said something that impressed me very much. He said, "Perhaps it is only in a socialist country that the Christian religion can be properly exercised."

A speech that I gave at MIT in 1969 . . . changed the whole course of my life. . . . MIT students and faculty had organized a three-day conference on the misuses of science, and they had asked me to speak on the first day. I had been thinking about these things for a long time. And I wondered if I dared to say what I thought, and finally I decided I would, and I called that talk, "A Generation in Search of a Future." I didn't have any manuscript. I was just talking from a few notes. The next day, the *Boston Globe* called me and asked for a manuscript, and I said I didn't have any, but they found that a radio station had been taping it. So they got the tape and transcribed it and I went down there for an hour and edited it, and they spread it, taking up the whole op-ed page. And then the *New Yorker* published it, and then it went across the country, and then it began to be translated into Italian, Japanese, and so forth. It really got around, and for a while, I got those three weeks of whatever you want to call it, fame, that one gets in the United States.

One day, I had luncheon with forty-four senators in Washington. Nixon was down the hall. It was the first time the president had entered the halls of Congress, just to push something or other. I've forgotten all that. I was on all the talk shows. It was just amazing and something to get over, something you had to get over, being an oracle. Ha. So here I am.

I always was interested in politics, but I didn't have a voice, and perhaps I'm in the course of losing it, and it's about time. And I have another thing that I'm into. I don't think I can stop being interested in politics, and that speech gave me a voice internationally. So, for example, I'll be going to Germany to a conference to speak there. I've been traveling a great deal, over much of the world by now, occasionally connecting up with governments and so on. . . .

We're getting very little news [about Vietnam's government], . . . and I don't have any intimate connections, so I don't really know [how well they are doing]. I would have to go over there to evaluate it myself. My sympathies are with them still. I wish the United States would stop regarding Vietnam as *the enemy*, largely through pique at having essentially lost the war. It's a wonderful lesson to the rest of humanity that (I said that in that 1969 speech) the Vietnamese have a secret weapon: it's their willingness to die beyond our willingness to kill them. I think that's a very, very powerful weapon. I think the most powerful revolutionary force in the world is just the people, unarmed but willing to be killed and refusing to leave the streets.

Because the governments are so far ahead in armaments, there is not much the people can do. It's no longer a time, as in Paris in the nineteenth century, for raising barricades, fighting from behind piles of stones and bedsteads. That doesn't work anymore.

[Does America] fully understand [the origins and history of U.S. involvement in Vietnam]? I think those who have any interest in understanding can well understand. I am very distressed at the present situation in our country. Very much. I think we've essentially lost our democracy. I think the watershed was around 1950, and we are now in the strange position of being the only superpower in the world. And we are running an enormous risk, the possibility of a military coup in the Soviet Union. That would bring back the Cold War in quite different terms from having President [Mikhail] Gorbachev in charge.

I have no great feeling that our country has a wise government, and as for Congress, that's my biggest disappointment, I think, because we have been for some time gravitating toward, and now we're there, a one-party state. The [*Boston*] *Globe* published a letter that I wrote them that began, "I've been a registered Democrat for all of my voting life, but I now regard the Democratic Party as the Democratic wing of the Republican

Party." We do not have an organized political opposition, and without a political opposition, we are not a democracy. So the American people really have no effective say in what happens in the government. It's not a bit healthy, if you've got democracy in mind. It's absolute death. You see, what I fear is that this will catch on worldwide because we are very pleased to see what were formerly Communist governments trying to become democratic and introduce the market economy.

What I fear most is that the United States in its present condition, which I regard as the frustration of democracy, is going to catch on internationally. We've worked out how one frustrates democracy, while still calling it and pretending it's democracy. President Reagan taught our entire public that democracy is the chance to vote in an election. Voting in an election doesn't mean a thing unless there are meaningful choices. And I have asked big American audiences when I was talking much more than I do now, "How many of you have ever had the privilege of voting for someone you really wanted?" No hands go up. That's our American experience: voting for the lesser evil.

[The greatest deception of the war was] that we were fighting to free the Vietnamese people, that we were fighting for an ideal, just as right now we are not yet fighting, thank heavens, and I hope we won't, but we could, in the Near East, for the freedom of Kuwait. The royal family of Kuwait has a personal fortune so large that if we got into the war, they could afford as a family to pay for that war.

[To say that my trip and those of others to North Vietnam lengthened the war] isn't logic. It's propaganda. It's made up by those guys from Madison Avenue who work for the government day and night. . . . I regard myself as a patriotic American (incidentally, almost always enthusiastic for what I find in the American people) but dismayed by operations of the American government which are hard to defend, and I don't try. But I do do what I can, which is not much, to try to change that. . . .

I've just raised the question, "What government in the world would I be proud of?" You see, I think the business of running a just and humane democracy is not a solved problem. And incidentally, in that kind of situation, there are no final solutions because all institutions are infinitely corruptible. *All* institutions, including churches, including universities. My heavens, I had forty-three years of teaching at Harvard, and what a story I could tell. It's very strange, very, very strange. I told the present president of Harvard when he first became president that I thought the principal activity of Harvard University was not education but construction.

And I believe that to be true. The education is an excuse for the buildings. So that's what I feel.

I don't look for perfect government, but I sure would like a government that *tried,* and our present government, I think, is about as corrupt and corruptible as it can be. And the same people are paying for the operations of both political parties. Mr. Reagan sold the American public the thought that something called bipartisanship is an ideal state that displays national unity. But, my heavens, we have only two parties, and if they work together (is my arithmetic wrong?), that makes one; and that's what we've got.

I don't think [my feelings about the war today] could be intensified. I said in that talk in 1969, a long time ago, that I thought it was the most disgraceful episode in American history, and if anything, we're piling on other such disgraceful episodes. Please note something. We can hardly get into an intervention by now in which it isn't true that we, *we,* the United States, has *armed both sides,* both its allies and its enemies. Iraq was armed by us [and the Soviet Union].

[My membership in antiwar organizations during the war was], I think, nothing different from what is now true. That is, I send checks where I think something useful is being done for peace, justice, taking care of children, the poor. I am trying to finish a book. I don't travel as much and don't speak at rallies and so on as I used to. But it's mostly writing small checks because I don't have a lot of money. For example, yesterday, I sent a check to the black man who is running for governor of North Carolina against Jesse Helms. I would love to get Jesse Helms out of the Senate. . . .

I have never been much of an organization man because I like to just think things out for myself. . . . I worked with organizations, but the anti-Vietnam public was very big. Guys who could afford it went to Canada, some of them to Sweden, to escape service in that war, and indeed, the public feeling against it was so strong that Vietnam veterans have a hard time. And I have good friends, very close friends, in the Vietnam Veterans Against the War. It is curious to remember now that John Kerry, our senator from Massachusetts, I think, was the chief organizer and president of Vietnam Veterans Against the War. The government response to all such organizations is to infiltrate them.

I've said so many ghastly things, I would say just in passing that, to my mind, one of the most disgraceful things about our country, the United States, is the CIA. I thought I had already reached a level of cynicism in which I could no longer be surprised. But just very early this year, in the course of a couple of weeks, we learned something so utterly disgraceful I could hardly believe it. First, it was the CIA that fingered Nelson Mandela for arrest in 1962. The whole country knows that this man was jailed for twenty-seven years. And this is not out of some radical publication; this is spread over the American press and comes out of ex-CIA sources that are boastful about it. One of our CIA representatives in Pretoria, South Africa, said he told the [South African] security people just where they would find Mandela, what he would be wearing, every detail. They got him. It's one of the biggest coups we ever pulled off. The CIA operative was in a state of glory.

Second, within two weeks of the first disclosure was something that I remember well because I am old enough to have lived through it. We have behind us a century of genocides. The first one involved the Armenians in 1915 to 1916. I know a lot about them because I function on the People's Permanent Tribunal. I have functioned at times as president on international tribunals, and one of them was on Armenia. But nearly the biggest genocide of the century was in Indonesia, where about three million people were killed in the course of a few weeks. It happened when the Indonesian president, Sukarno, was displaced by General Suharto. Suharto is still dictator of Indonesia.

At that time, for a few days, if you had an enemy, if you owed money to somebody, you had only to say, "Oh, that guy is a Communist." The Communist Party was legal in Indonesia at that time. You could say, "That guy is a Communist" and just go over and kill him. But what we learned a few months ago is that the CIA had prepared for Suharto's coup a list of about five thousand Communists, and day after day, the Indonesian army people would come into the CIA office and check off those on the list whom they had killed and note how many were still to be killed. And they wiped out the Communist Party of Indonesia so successfully that it's never raised its head again. So that's another gold star for the CIA. I remember it well. There was horror in this country with the extent of the killing. But who would ever imagine that the CIA was conducting it?

I would like to say something that I haven't said before because I am no bleeding heart or crackpot idealist. I really do want peace and justice and needy people to be cared for. My present biggest activity involves what is happening to children right now. Where do I get my information? From UNICEF, from the United Nations Children's Fund. In the 1989 report, it reported that something like 40,500 children die per day, *per day,* of hunger and diseases fostered by hunger. That, to me, is such an utter disgrace, I do what I can to stop it.

I wish I could do more or had done more. I am not sure I can, but I haven't even really tried to say those things about the present state of our nation that I have just said. . . . I think I did everything that I could [to oppose the Vietnam War] and, as a matter of fact, at the expense of my scientific work, finally. I was spending nine-tenths of my time on international politics. I have no regrets, however. Now I am on a book, and the politics is being neglected to some degree. But those 40,500 kids per day, dying of hunger, they'll keep me in this.

21

Ramsey Clark

Ramsey Clark's trip to Hanoi received page-one attention in the international press because he had previously served as President Lyndon B. Johnson's attorney general. While in that position, Clark had taken legal action against some of the antiwar protesters. His reversal of position toward the war was greeted with hostility by many. Clark described why he visited Hanoi, his concern for the suffering of the Vietnamese people, and his reaction to the criticism made of his trip. He was appalled at the destruction of civilian facilities he observed in North Vietnam. Comments he made on his return concerning North Vietnamese civilian casualties, damage to dikes, and his perception that American POWs were treated reasonably well were received with healthy skepticism at home.

Clark was born in 1927, served in the U.S. Marine Corps Reserve from 1945 to 1946, and was attorney general of the United States from 1967 to 1969. He currently has a general civil and criminal law practice and also engages in constitutional trials and appeals. The interview took place on October 9, 1990, in his New York City law office.

RAMSEY CLARK: I went to Hanoi and North Vietnam in August, I believe, of 1972. I went as one person in a fairly large international group. I think I was the only American. . . . We traveled together to get there. And then we separated for specific efforts. But basically, we were together during the course of nearly every day, I would say.

I'm not sure we had a title. I can tell you who some of the people were. There was Shawn McBride, a Nobel Peace Prize laureate and former foreign minister of Ireland and son of John McBride and Lauren Conn. McBride also received the Lenin Peace Prize and was the only person, I believe, who won both the Lenin Peace Prize and the Nobel Peace Prize. There was also a Swedish lawyer and political figure, Hans Goren

Franc, who was, I think, still in the Swedish parliament. Another member of the group was a quite famous Danish political leader, Flodie Yacobsen, a scholar and political figure and parliamentarian, who was head of a major segment of the underground during the Nazi occupation. There also was a medical doctor, a woman, from Moscow in the Soviet Union, who had quite a high position. She may have been head of surgery for the Department of Medicine or whatever they call it in the Soviet Union. There was a Swedish television crew. And there were others, but I remember only these at the moment.

[With respect to my purpose in going to Hanoi at that time], I probably divide that into two segments, my personal motivations and concern and the reason for the group. Like many Americans, I had been deeply concerned about the U.S. military actions in Vietnam, our use of sophisticated technology against life, our failure to appreciate their lives as well as our own, our indifference (we'll bomb them back into the Stone Age), and the carpet bombing. So I had been anxious to find a way to express to the Vietnamese people my concern as an American, to show them that Americans didn't uniformly support the war and respected and appreciated their humanity. And I had probably wanted to go and had tried to go for some time. I was looking for an opportunity that would make it possible to get in. On this particular trip, for instance, Don Luce, a person I had worked with on Vietnam and some other issues, such as Southeast Asia, the Philippines, and others, was going with me. We had made arrangements with *Time-Life*. In fact, that's how we financed the trip. I was to take pictures. Don was a picture taker, and I wasn't. Consequently, the pictures didn't come out too good. ABC Radio and Television supplied cameras: a movie camera and a still camera. Don, however, was not permitted on the last plane. He was not cleared either, apparently by the Vietnamese. But it's never been definite. He just wasn't let on the plane when we were finally leaving.

No, [I was not encouraged by our government to make the trip]. In fact, I announced the trip and had a call from the State Department. I think it was William Sullivan. I met with him. He urged me in very strong terms not to go. . . . I'm sure the State Department felt (I don't recall how he articulated it) that an American, particularly a prominent American, showing support for the Vietnamese people in that way would be harmful to our diplomatic and military interests in the region.

We were particularly concerned that summer about the dikes. And there was a widespread belief and repeated speculation about U.S.

destruction of the very intricate dike system that supported the growth, particularly, of rice. It was necessary to control water levels to produce rice. There were a number of Americans that wanted to sit on the dikes, either to prevent their destruction or to show that our commitment was of such a magnitude that if the dikes were taken out by American bombing, Americans would be willing to go with them. Under these circumstances, I felt the strong moral compulsion to go as an American to make a statement, primarily to the Vietnamese.

I was also concerned about our POWs. I had been concerned about prisoners for most of my adult life, wherever they are. And I believed in addressing both the conditions and the release of prisoners wherever it's feasible. And I wanted to meet with U.S. prisoners of war to determine their conditions and to see if some release could be secured because there was no need, really, to hold most of those prisoners of war. They represented no military threat. Our military manpower supply was superabundant compared with a small country like North Vietnam. And they were wartime prisoners. If they had committed an offense, it was in the name of their country, not from personal motivations of greed or lust or violence or something like that.

So those were the basic personal reasons why I went. The international group, I think, was part of an international peace movement that opposed what it considered to be, and I think correctly, U.S. aggression in Vietnam. The group consisted of pre-eminent Western figures and appropriate Eastern bloc figures, although the woman doctor was the only Eastern figure I can remember at the moment. There may have been someone else, but I can't think who it was. And they felt the need and were a part of a regular effort by international peace groups to show the Vietnamese people their concern and commitment to an end of the war.

Don Luce made most of [the arrangements] for me and actually got as far as Moscow. Some of us may have joined in West Europe some place and then flown into Moscow. I don't think we spent the night in Moscow. But I remember clearly on the field that night, they wouldn't let Don on the plane. My impression is that Don arranged transportation for the two of us to West Europe or to Moscow, probably to West Europe, where we picked up an Aeroflot plane, I imagine. And then from Moscow on in we flew, as I recall, to Tashkent, perhaps next to Calcutta, and then Burma. We had to wait for quite a while because of American air activity in Laos. And then we flew on in, in an Aeroflot regularly scheduled flight, as I recall, from Vientiane.

[While in Hanoi], we met with leaders obviously, with Pham Van Dong, judges, and lawyers, because of my background. We met with health officials and visited hospitals. I remember going by Bak Mai. We looked at housing. We traveled some; it was extremely difficult at that time to travel in the day. We did go to Haiphong in the day, although I'm not sure. I know certainly that the Chinese community there felt threatened by Vietnamese attitudes toward it. I went down south by myself on a trip. I wanted to spend some time in villages. I asked to be provided a means of travel. We drove at night because in the daytime anything that moved would be subject to air attack by the U.S. So we'd drive at night, and I spent the night in villages on a couple of occasions where Westerners had never been. Of course, communications were all through translators. It was a fascinating personal experience to see how people were living without electricity and rural conditions, supporting themselves from agriculture and providing a little surplus for the rest of the people. . . .

I think every American had a strong sense of the extent of the destruction and probably of the strong morale of the people, the resistance. I had seen a lot of destruction. I'd seen the destruction of Europe in World War II and Japan. This was urban destruction of cities and all. So I was not shocked by the destruction. You'd see villages that were largely destroyed. Six bombs may have hit near, and twenty other bombs hit nearby. Haiphong had areas that were fairly heavily destroyed. Hanoi had some damage and destruction but nothing like World War II. When you got out into the villages, you really wouldn't sense the war except in the spirit of the people who were working hard and proud of their production, missing sons and brothers and fathers, men who'd been off to war for one, two, three, four, five years, whatever it might be.

I've traveled virtually all my life. Since I was seventeen, I have traveled extensively alone around the world. I was able to move pretty much around North Vietnam wherever I wanted to. The only concern they had would be during air alerts when they had, as a matter of public safety, a very rigid view about what you do in case of an air alert, and that is, you get in a hole. And I wanted to move around during those periods and was generally able to, although sometimes they would just insist that you get in the hole and wait until the alert's over. But I was able to move around and see people. Unfortunately, I couldn't speak to them without a translator, and when I would move around by myself, I would be cut off from verbal communications. But I could see them. And I didn't see anything other than high spirits and firm commitment.

You'd walk through the streets of Hanoi at night, and it was just abuzz with bicycles, like schools of fish on bicycles going around. It seemed like all night long, people were going back and forth to work without lights. You had to be pretty careful where you crossed the street because of the bicycles whisking by. Some would have little dim flashlights, but they wouldn't permit them to have lights that would show. But the spirit of the people was unquestionably extraordinarily committed and determined. . . .

You'd see some attacking U.S. aircraft, maybe a half a dozen times in two weeks. But they'd be at a distance, and while you realized their firepower was enormous, you also realized that you were less than a needle in a haystack, so the probability of getting hit was as low as walking around Manhattan. . . .

I felt that the United States government was tragically wrong in its military actions in Vietnam and that someone who really loved the country had a high obligation to say so and to stand up and to resist. In part, that's what democracy offers, and if conscience will find the courage, you can solve problems in that way. So I felt the highest moral obligation to do what I did.

In personal terms, I found it as satisfying as virtually anything I've done in my life. It was an irresistible moral obligation as I saw it, and not to have done it would have been extremely damaging to me as a human being. . . .

A trip like that is not one of specific objective purposes. You don't intend to sell so many units of a product or sign a contract or achieve a particular result. As I have already said, in personal terms, it was probably morally essential to my character that I do it. When you feel that strongly about something and fail to act, you have to live with yourself. I think not to have gone would have hurt me very badly, so certainly, I achieved it. You find in life that sometimes the hardest things to do are ultimately the most personally rewarding and fulfilling — the most painful experiences. And it was a very difficult experience for me from many levels. It's not something you do as a matter of personal pleasure. I think, although it's extremely difficult for me to measure, that it was respected by many Vietnamese. I think it helped reinforce the recognition that you can't hate another people however violently their government may act towards you. Finally, human nature is the same everywhere. Children, all people, are equal in value and dignity. And I think it helped the Vietnamese recognize that the American people are good people but the American government policy is wrong and that that is what has to be changed. . . .

I had agreed to speak at the American Bar Association in San Francisco. It always meets in early August. I had spent two weeks in Vietnam, and I didn't have time to get to San Francisco to make my speech if I came back via the West. So I headed East. My recollection is that I flew out to Vientiane and then down to Bangkok and from there to Hong Kong and then across the Pacific to San Francisco.

When I got back, I was walking off the plane in San Francisco, and I'd been traveling for a couple of days at least. Because, you know, it's slow going getting out of Vietnam, and I hadn't stopped any place. I made a stop for six hours, but I hadn't found a bed or anything. I came back to Vientiane, and then by the time I got around to Hong Kong and got on a regular flight, it had been probably twenty-four hours already. So I was exhausted. And I walked off the plane. I wasn't expecting anything except to go to a hotel and get some rest 'cause I was speaking the next morning at the American Bar Association. And here was a huge congregation of press. As soon as I got off the walkway, they were sticking bright lights, cameras, and microphones in my face. The first question was, "The attorney general says you may be prosecuted for violation of the Logan Act. What's your response to that?" That was the tone of the press, the major press. The minor press were favorable but very few of the major press. That was the tone of it throughout and for years. I didn't find the public reaction quite the same way. For instance, ABC ran film clips, and I did some hours of tapes that they ran on their radio networks and reran on individual stations. I don't know how many hours there were altogether. But I can remember continuous programming of maybe two hours. And then they cut it down to twenty to twenty-six minutes for a thirty-minute program, and it was played and replayed, and all this generated a lot of mail. And, you know, over the years, I have done a lot of fairly controversial things. But the mail, while preponderantly opposed, had a large segment that supported what I had done and thanked me for it in various ways. It's the type of act that, in a time of high passion, many people react to very violently. I can't say there were more than a half a dozen instances, though, when I met with overt unpleasantness in moving around the country. I was moving around the country all the time.

I ran for the United States Senate two years later here in New York, and it came up. There was some suggestion that the CIA had information that was harmful in various ways. But I don't think it affected the campaign particularly. I was able to secure the Democratic nomination and got about two million votes in the door.

Personally, I don't think [the criticism of my trip has] required any, I'm not aware of any, adjustment or anything. I had opposed the death penalty as attorney general, and the reaction was very similar. I wondered whether the reaction to priests and ministers and rabbis, for instance, who opposed the death penalty would be the same as when the attorney general opposed it. Because when law enforcement or what is perceived by the public as law enforcement opposes an extreme enforcement sanction, the public seems to react in a different way. And this was early, this was in the sixties. But the feel was almost identical with the feel that you got from Vietnam and similar positions that I've taken and things that I've done.

I went to Teheran in the middle of the hostage crisis against an executive order entered by President Carter and was threatened at that time with prosecution by the attorney general. But, you know, I had worked for many years on human rights in Teheran, and I saw their country being destroyed by the hostage crisis and felt again an absolute moral necessity to go. I was being asked by the prime minister and the foreign minister and the UN delegate of Teheran to please come to see if we couldn't find a way to help the countries out of this crisis. The reaction at that time was similar. Although the country was highly unified in its hatred toward Teheran because of the hostage crisis, the reaction wasn't quite the magnitude as the trip to Vietnam created.

I think if you believe in things, if they're important, they will create some hostility. If there is an agreement on them, they're not important anymore because apparently they've been resolved. There's no social controversy about it. So you expect some attention to arise when taking a moral position or an immoral position, as others may see it. And if you try to live a life of principle, you expect that. You don't encourage it because you seek understanding and where that's failed, reconciliation among peoples. But you have to expect some emotional disagreements with strong statements.

[Although some believe that I was deceived by the North Vietnamese with respect to the conditions under which American POWs were held], the first thing you have to address is the enormous propaganda effort of the United States, which is overwhelmingly directed at the American people. You didn't have to propagandize the Vietnamese people. You could hardly reach them by any means of communication that we had. So here's the United States's people saturated with disinformation, misinformation, falsehoods — whether it's casualties, body counts, secret bombings, military activities like the Phoenix Program, and things like that.

The American people are duped by their own government, by a very expensive and sophisticated effort to deceive us. Democratic institutions can't really live with that. The idea of democracy is premised upon an informed public, a public with access to the truth, a public that doesn't have to wrestle with its own government to find the truth. It's not misled or deceived by its own government about the truth.

Just take the Tonkin Gulf resolution itself. What a terrible tragedy. Years later, we had a retired United States admiral who flew the last plane to fly over the Tonkin Gulf saying there were no boats. Those are his words, "There were no boats." And here we are in this huge war with all these Americans committed, and for someone to then say that, a lonely traveler to Vietnam — which is gettin' the hell bombed out of it, whose people are undergoing miseries the American people have never experienced and can barely imagine — to say that you're duped is to miss the big picture. Even if you were duped, how significant can that be in comparison with this enormous misrepresentation of the truth to the American people who were really buying it?

The invasion of Grenada, the invasion of Panama, the bombing of Libya, all of these aggressions that our government engaged in involved intensive misinformation campaigns against our own people, often admitted. CIA Director [William J.] Casey said that the CIA had engaged in an intensive misinformation campaign against Libya to make us hate them. We were being conditioned to hate the Vietnamese people. They're a beautiful people, and they suffered an enormous injustice at our hands.

There's an old saying that "if you do a person an injustice, you then must hate him to justify yourself." And we have to watch that. I don't think I was duped. I think I've been in more prisons and seen more prisoners under more conditions over a longer period of time than practically anyone who ever lived, unless it'd be someone with the International Committee for the Red Cross who spends a professional lifetime of prison visitation. I don't mean to suggest that the prisons were good, and I didn't say so. The men I saw were in pretty good shape, good enough shape to say they wanted to come home and make it morally convincing. But there are prisons all over the world, including the United States, that are tragically inhumane. But I would say to that argument that visitors were duped, "What would you expect them to show, things that were derogatory of their country and their conduct?" How derogatory could it be anyway or would it have to be to justify B-52s bombing people that tried to defend their country with a rusty rifle? . . .

It's certainly a tragedy that a people who have suffered so much would suffer more [as boat people]. I think of Iran. Iran has suffered for generations. It suffered for twenty-five years under the Shah, and after we replaced the Shah, it suffered through this ghastly war with Iraq. And it's suffering to this day. You know, if you'd hope for justice, you would say that there'd be an end to suffering, that there'd be some adjustment to provide some of the enrichment and justice in peoples' lives. Our conduct toward Vietnam since the war has been, except the violence, the direct physical violence, as immoral as our conduct before and during the war with Vietnam was. It's hard for us to imagine the economic effect on a small country like that of all the sanctions that we've applied. So after devastating the country in this god-awful war that had gone on for a generation before we got there, instead of trying to provide some economic aid and means for recovery, some compensation for damage that had been inflicted, what have we done?

Look at the Marshall Plan in Germany and Italy after World War II. Did they inflict fewer casualties on American troops than the Vietnamese? Why this continued hatred and economic war on Vietnam? And then there is this comparison. While we were being told that sanctions wouldn't work against South Africa with its system of racist apartheid, while President Reagan during his eight years was engaged in a romance with racism, supporting the apartheid government there and saying sanctions are out of the question, we are applying these crushing economic sanctions against Vietnam because of our geopolitical interests, disregarding the lives of the people there.

I would love to see Vietnam prosper. I would love to see it live in peace and freedom under governments of its own choice and under international law that protects the fundamental rights of everybody everywhere. But I believe that the United States still has a major obligation to assist Vietnam economically and ought to address the task now. You can call it what you want [either grants or reparations], but it ought to be economic assistance that would help them rebuild their country. It's a desperately poor country.

The gap between the rich and the poor countries in human terms is the great crisis of the planet right now. We have a billion people on earth suffering malnutrition, knowing constant hunger. We have millions dying of starvation worldwide. And still we have the rich countries getting richer and the poor countries getting poorer, and we're going to have more than a billion more people on earth during the remainder of this century, and eighty percent of them are going to have beautiful darker skin, and they're going to live short, miserable lives of hunger and want and homelessness and ignorance and disease and poverty unless we do something drastic. And Vietnam shows you how our hatred inhibits us from addressing these problems, and our greed makes us more interested in our own acquisitions than in the lives of their children. For our own future and good, we need to overcome that. We need to help Vietnam rebuild itself. We absolutely should have full diplomatic relations and economic relations and try to make up for the injury that we've inflicted on a couple of generations of Vietnamese.

[The American public remains misinformed about the nature and the origins of the Vietnam War.] No doubt about it. . . . I had an interesting experience on this subject just recently. I was on a night television program on CNN and they had a call-in. It was on the Gulf crisis, and I was saying the U.S. troops ought to leave, should withdraw immediately. And a Vietnam veteran from San Francisco called. He'd been home now for fifteen years or a little bit longer, and he's just really learning how it was that he got sent over there and nearly killed. And it was all based upon lies. And if he'd known the truth, he wouldn't have gone. . . .

I don't think you can say that there was one single [deception in the war]. . . . Take whether there were boats in the Gulf of Tonkin that particular day, although that had enormous significance. But I think it was the recurrent conditioning of the American mind to believe that the Vietnamese government and people were evil, that they were intent upon conquest and domination, that they had no respect for humanity, and that to kill them was not a sin. Just take the way we treated the body count. We were extraordinarily proud of the body count, these enormous and inflated numbers. We deceived our military generals and admirals over there, too. There's one survey you may recall that showed that out of forty-odd general officers who served in Vietnam, all but a handful said they had been misled about Vietnamese casualties and made policy decisions based upon these deceptions. The consistent deception that we'd killed more than had actually been killed certainly suggested gross indifference to their lives. . . .

The main and most obvious thing that we've learned from the Vietnam War but perhaps not the lesson that we should seek is that we don't want to get caught in a mess like that again. In other words, from a purely selfish standpoint, we found it very painful and damaging, and the pay-off wasn't worth the investment. We don't want to do that again. The suggestion is, though, that if you can have an easy win, if you can knock off a Grenada or Panama or bomb and kill a couple hundred people in Benghazi and Tripoli and get away with minimal casualties, it's okay. The lesson is that we don't want to get caught in a ground war where we have a lot of casualties. The lesson that we have to try to learn is that everybody loses. Everybody loses in these military engagements. You don't win. The lesson is that we should seek to solve these problems on this planet at this time since the technology we have is absolutely disastrous and can lead even now, with what we call the Cold War seemingly over, to catastrophe.

We have to find better ways of solving problems than through force and violence. Yet the United States hasn't done that. Watch the alacrity with which we speed to the Persian Gulf. We can send an enormous force there in a very short period of time and be cheering all the way. Then we get there, and we wonder, now what do we do? Now how many body bags may come home? How did we get into this mess, and was there any other way? But it's too late because our instinct is still — it's more than an instinct, it's a clear government policy that's supported by an instinct — to use force when force can't solve the problems and is extremely dangerous.

Clearly, [the U.S. government hasn't learned the lessons of the Vietnam War]. A thing that we saw in the invasion of Grenada . . . I was down there about four or five days after the invasion . . . was a lesson the government learned: keep the media out. That was as clear as anything. And they kept the media out. Remember Ernie Pyle in World War II sitting in a foxhole next to the GI, with his pencil and pad writing up what this crazy major had just done or what this sergeant did with his machine gun? And that was a real war, so to speak. A hell of a war. And here in Grenada, it's so dangerous that we have to keep the press out for a week. Now, what's that about? What's that mean to democracy? What's that mean to freedom in America? What's that mean to the First Amendment?

It means that the government has found that if it wants to have its way where it's doing something controversial and wrong, then it better keep the press out. But we also have this terrible national psychology that, somehow or other, we had failed in Vietnam or we had failed tragically. But our failure was not in failing to win militarily because to have won militarily would have cost millions of lives, and who could possibly call that a victory? But we had this sense of defeat, and therefore, we had to have some military victories.

President Ronald Reagan objectively wanted military victories to make America proud of itself again. Go out and kill a few foreigners to show we're still number one. And that's not what makes you number one. It's what makes you a menace to humanity.

[Apropos my current feelings about the Vietnam War], unfortunately, I think human nature, maybe it's just my nature [alone that] requires revitalization. Whether it's urban poverty or whatever it is, if I don't re-experience it fairly regularly, the pain subsides. I think it's probably almost a physiological fact of human nature that unless you're confronted fairly regularly with a very painful matter, you can insulate yourself so you don't feel the pain. Now, having said all that, I find myself making speeches. I made a speech on the Persian Gulf last week, and as I was leaving, another speaker was speaking, and I heard him talking about Vietnam. And I realized that I hadn't mentioned Vietnam. And I wondered why I had failed to mention Vietnam. It wasn't a tactic. I wasn't trying to say, "Well, I don't want to overdo this Vietnam analogy," or something like that. I just hadn't mentioned it, and I guess, in part, it's because it's been a long time and there's been a lot of other violence and a lot of other wars and a lot of other dangers. But the message of Vietnam is profound in the American experience, I think.

There are some historians of the ancient world who believed, as scholars, that the decline of Athens came with its brutal, final assault on the island of Milos, where, after having surrounded the island, they starved it down. It was just a little place. It wanted to be nonaligned, as we'd call it today. It didn't want to favor Athens; it didn't want to favor Sparta in the Peloponnesian War; it just wanted to be let alone. And Athens couldn't afford to have somebody out there let alone. So it surrounded and starved it down, finally invaded, killed the men, repopulated the island with some Athenians and people from client states, and sold the women and children and some survivors into slavery there and elsewhere. These historians believed that finally, the people realized, however subjectively, what they had come to and what they had done. This is the place that we think of as producing Ephideas and Socrates, and here it's destroyed this island and killed these people who were helpless in its power. And that was not just symptomatic; it was causative of the decline and ultimate failure of Athens. Now, that may be imposing a moralistic view on history, but there is something about the human will that's affected by these things.

It's powerful, really powerful, to see Vietnam veterans reacting to the Gulf crisis now. We formed a coalition here on the Gulf crisis. At the first meeting, we had contacted only one veteran's group, Vietnam Veterans Against the War, which I worked with at some length. Five Vietnam veterans and veterans groups, not just Vietnam (World War II, Korean War) groups showed up, and all passionately wanted to act in a way to prevent another generation of veterans and casualties. The Vietnam vets themselves had one line that is very powerful, and that is, "Justice for the last generation of American veterans, and no more generations of American veterans." . . .

It's very difficult to look back [and re-evaluate my actions of over twenty years ago] and unrealistic. It's an hypothesis contrary to fact, which is probably idle to engage in. But there's a general feeling that the most that I can say is that I wish I could have found ways to do more, to say more, and to be more effective to bring the war to a quicker end. The war didn't really end, although a lot of people said that it did, because the economic and the psychological war continued and even continues to some degree to this day, against Vietnam. But at the very least, you'd have to say that, finally, for the first time in its history, the American people, by opposing their own military cause, got to discontinue direct military engagement against a foreign people, and that offers some hope.

It's impossible to judge whether a single trip or all the trips [to North Vietnam] or all the protesting were ultimately positive or negative. I think on a trip like mine, you have to ask whether it created so much passion that it might have caused some increment in support for the war. But I'm not sure that we're smart enough to make those refined calculations. And I don't know where they get you. I know this. If they inhibit conduct based upon conscience to end violence on some strategic theory that if you don't say or do anything, you may not upset the other people, and maybe that's violent — it's doomed to failure. Finally, we have to resolve these things in the tumult of our social organization or disorganization, and you throw in your word and your bite, and chance will determine the outcome.

I haven't [visited Vietnam since 1972]. I would love to go back and then all through the area half a dozen times or more. . . . There've been a number of invitations . . . but I just haven't found an opportunity that seemed to make it important to go at that time. I'll go someday, and I'll look forward to it. I keep in touch with some Vietnamese here and there and very fondly.

We still have endangered Vietnamese here. It's hard to believe, but we've had a number of assassinations in the United States. I went to Washington a number of times for Vietnamese Americans whose lives had been threatened, whose husbands had been killed, trying to get the FBI to provide some incremental investigative effort. And these are all people who were seeking reconciliation with Vietnam, members of the exiled community who, because of their reconciliatory words, are being killed by people who were part of the former government of South Vietnam.

[To sum up], it's awfully important to the soul of America that we never forget our conduct in Vietnam, that we constantly examine and re-examine it, try to know more about it, to determine how it was that we were willing to commit all of this technological violence, all these lives of our young sons and brothers, to a war in that country. We have this fascination with our own Civil War; we love to tromp over the battlefields. There's a lot of militarism in this, actually, but the war we need to examine the most is a war that has the greatest lessons for our national character and for the future of the planet, the war in Vietnam. America can't be policeman for the world. The very concept is antidemocratic, anti–self-determination, anti-independence, antifreedom, antieverything American people say they're for. And yet this police action, so-called, was the major American effort in post–World War II earth to render this international police service. And it was a terrible failure. It caused untold injury and harm at home and abroad, and it's imperative that the American mind never get very far from its inquiry as to why we were in Vietnam and what we hoped to accomplish by military force there as we face the future, if we hope ever to live on a planet that doesn't solve problems by military force.

22

Paul Mayer

The Reverend Paul Mayer, a pacifist, grieved over the devastation he saw in North Vietnam. A portion of his trip to North Vietnam was shown on the television program, *60 Minutes*, using television equipment furnished by the network. Mayer believes that this country has not truly repented for its role in the Vietnam War.

Mayer now lectures at the New York Theological Seminary and is executive director of an organization called the Religious Task Force. He brings together children from war zones, both foreign and domestic, "as part of a healing process." The interview took place by telephone the evening of October 9, 1990. (I had intended to meet with Reverend Mayer in his apartment in East Orange, New Jersey, but was advised by my brother Joe, who lives in Waldwick, New Jersey, that it was not safe for strangers to walk the streets of East Orange at night.)

PAUL MAYER: I traveled to North Vietnam in May 1971 with Margerie Tabankin, president of the National Student Association. Ms. Tabankin has since been active in Hollywood, California, with a women's political group. [Our group included] William Zimmerman, who was a member of Medical Aid to Indochina. Since Vietnam, Zimmerman has been involved in activities related to Central America. There was also a minister, Robert Lecky, who was editor of Clergy and Laity Concerned About Vietnam. . . . I did not pay for my transportation to and from Hanoi. I believe someone else picked up the tab; the tickets may have been paid out of peace movement funds. As I recall, the last leg of our flight was by Aeroflot, at no expense to me.

We were the first group invited to Hanoi after a pause in the bombing. The CBS program *60 Minutes* gave us television equipment for use during our trip. The film later appeared on a *60 Minutes* program. We spent one week in Hanoi, which turned out to be a period of intensive bombing. It was a shock, to be bombed by U.S. aircraft. There were air raids all the time and some rather close calls. The Vietnamese were afraid that we would be killed. We were in air-raid shelters quite a bit, and some danger was involved. We just surrendered to the situation. We stayed at a guest house near Haiphong, where outside the Vietnamese scoured the ground for antipersonnel bombs. The guest house had been bombed shortly before we arrived.

We traveled quite a bit outside of Hanoi, considering that this was a situation which was very acute. We saw a lot of rural villages, a lot of small places, as well as Haiphong. We talked to a lot of people, visited hospitals, schools, and churches. We met religious leaders, the foreign minister, intellectuals, writers, and poets. We visited a lot of people in a pretty grim scene. We met with a lot of government officials. There was a lot of dialogue. The Vietnamese took very good care of us, sometimes embarrassingly so.

We also met with five to six United States pilots somewhere in Hanoi. They obviously were not happy. We tried to give them human support, although, from both a religious and moral viewpoint, I was opposed to U.S. bombing. Several POWs seemed to be changing their position. One of the POWs, whose name was Edison [Miller], spoke out against the war. It was a hard meeting. The trip was arranged through Cora Weiss. I believe we brought mail back from the POWs and called some relatives for them when we returned to the United States. We held a press conference when we returned and discussed what we had seen.

I was a member of the Harrisburg Defense Committee, which spoke out in defense of a group composed of pacifists and priests who were accused of attempting to kidnap Henry Kissinger. I was an unindicted co-conspirator. All of those accused were found innocent of the charge. I worked in the peace movement. When I returned from the trip to Hanoi, I did a lot of speaking to the news media about the value of my trip and not spouting some propagandistic rhetoric. I published some antiwar articles in *Newsday* and wrote a letter critical of American involvement in the war to the *New York Times*. After the trip, I joined a "fast for life," organized with nine other persons, to protest the war. We fasted for forty days. During the fast, which took place in the summer of 1971, we traveled from New York City to Miami, Florida, and Washington, D.C., where we held a vigil at the White House. . . .

I don't believe that this country has adequately repented for its role in the Vietnam War. I am a refugee from Nazi Germany. I left Germany for the United States in 1936, when I was five years old. After the war, I returned to Germany and studied religion. I had very much a sense that the religious community either ignored or collaborated with Adolf Hitler during the war. The German people, after the war, seemed to be suffering from what I would term moral amnesia, attempting either to disclaim that anything evil had taken place or ignoring the fact that it did. In Germany, just as in the United States, there never has been an adequate national penance.

The Vietnamese were brutally punished in the war, and we have a responsiblity to heal. I think that the Vietnamese, since the war's end, would have been prepared to have a less restrictive regime, but the total embargo imposed by the United States has caused them to tighten up their society. On the other hand, if we had truly sought peace and reconciliation with the Vietnamese, I believe they would have had a more open society.

The Vietnam War was really one of the great tragedies in our history. An experience of that nature does not leave a country untouched. It has contributed to the drug addiction of some veterans and homelessness for others. It is a reflection of our failure to learn from the war. Nobody in a position of national leadership has had the moral vision to repent for our failings in the war. It seems to be that, at times, our nation has had messianic aspirations and that a "Rambo" chauvinism drives our national psyche. It is not encouraging. . . .

I don't believe patriotism has a negative value but can be positive if not defined in a narrow, chauvinistic way. Patriotism should include not only a love for one's own country and one's own people but also a belief that we are not better than anyone else and a love for those from other countries as well. To be patriotic means to be involved, even if it means consorting with the enemy. That's what peacemaking is all about. . . .

23

Susan Miller-Coulter

Susan Miller-Coulter, a member of the Episcopal Peace Fellowship, traveled to Hanoi in 1972 with activist Tom Hayden on one of the monthly trips scheduled by Cora Weiss. Miller-Coulter went to Hanoi believing that she and the other members of her group would return with American POWs. Subsequently, they were disappointed to find that this was not the case, and they never learned why the North Vietnamese had invited them.

Miller-Coulter, at the time of the interview, worked as a nurse in a hospice. Her teenaged daughter sat in on the interview because Miller-Coulter wanted her to hear about her experiences and thoughts on the war. The interview took place on October 10, 1990, at a neighborhood restaurant on the corner of 9th Avenue and 23d Street in New York City.

SUSAN MILLER-COULTER: I traveled to Hanoi in 1972. . . . I looked it up in a folder. . . . It was the 4th through the 11th of November. [In our group were] Howard Zinn from Boston University; David Hunter from the National Council of Churches; Carolyn Mugar from . . . a veteran's organization; Tom Hayden; a woman named Jan [Austin, who] was with a publication in Berkeley, and Fred Branfman.

I was employed by the Episcopal Peace Fellowship [EPF], an organization of largely pacifist Episcopalians. In those days it was considered part of the Fellowship of Reconciliation. But I was invited more in my capacity as a member of the executive committee of the People's Coalition for Peace and Justice, which was a loose affiliation of several hundred different antiwar organizations.

The People's Coalition for Peace and Justice paid some money directly [for my travel expenses]. I didn't do any fund-raising, but several people called various large donors who were sponsoring trips like this, so some money was donated specifically for the trip. And then I got some money from personal sources, from family and friends. Going over, we went from Kennedy to Copenhagen, to Hong Kong, to Vientiane, and directly into Hanoi. Coming back, we went to Tokyo, Alaska, and to New York. That was what the travel agency set up. There was no particular reason.

Periodically, Cora Weiss and other members of the Committee of Concern received telegrams from Vietnam asking for delegations to be sent for various purposes. A telegram arrived asking for a broad-based coalition to be sent in. It must have been some time in October, and the telegram didn't say why they wanted us. They wanted a fairly big, representative group. We spent a fair amount of time in meetings debating [why they wanted us to come]. Our best guess beforehand was that they might release some POWs to coincide with the American election, but that turned out not to be the case. We got very strange answers from the Vietnamese, who were pretty inscrutable, about the real reason for the trip.

We had the impression about halfway through the trip that whatever the original reason, they had changed their minds. We never found out what the original reason was. We had gone to the countryside north of Hanoi and visited some installations and villages and some places that had been bombed. When we got back to the city, the trip just dissolved.

[We] talked to the composers' union and the teachers' union and the women's union, and that seemed pretty insignificant and meaningless. When we got back, we decided that they probably had wanted to release POWs or make some statement about where the Paris peace negotiations were, but somewhere during . . . our [trip], they changed their minds and just decided not to do any of that.

We saw six or seven American prisoners in the prison camp in Hanoi. It was a very formal, stilted, awkward sort of meeting. We were given the names and addresses of their relatives in the United States, and we did send messages to all of them when we got back to the United States. We divided up the list, and everybody contacted a few relatives.

One of the things that struck me was something I saw in the countryside. We went to a very remote, rural area north of Hanoi. I saw an agricultural area that had been carpet bombed. All they managed to kill was a bunch of chickens. I saw things like that wherever we went. . . .

[I encouraged other Americans to travel to Hanoi.] . . . We were there in November, and another trip went at Christmas. I was in personal contact with Michael Allen, who at the time was dean of the Episcopal

Seminary at Yale in New Haven, Connecticut. He's now in St. Louis. Michael had already decided to go and came to talk with me about it, I think to resolve his last doubts about whether or not this was a good idea. . . .

I joined the antiwar movement in 1968, right after the death of Martin Luther King, and that was a very life-changing experience for me. The trip intensified my commitment to antiwar activity. I didn't have any doubts about what I was doing because I'd been doing it for too long, and I had read a lot. I was convinced that what I was doing was right. [The trip to Hanoi] gave an added emotional dimension and an added depth of commitment, but it didn't change anything. It deepened things. . . .

[My involvement in protest movements declined after] I left the EPF in 1973 until about 1978, and then when my daughter was born, I pretty much stopped for a while, not out of lack of conviction but [because] the movement was at a pretty low ebb. I was busy being a mother to a new baby, which was an enthralling adventure. I went on peace marches, and I did do some demonstrations but nothing like my former level of involvement.

I expected that the [Vietnamese government] would act quite differently from the way that they've acted. I was shocked and demoralized by the way they behaved after the war. I find myself on the whole agreeing with Joan Baez's opinion of the Vietnamese government's conduct. On the other hand, the government of Vietnam has had very little help from any of the other governments in the world. It's one of the most desperately poor countries, not that that excuses anything.

Although it couldn't have been predicted, the domino theory has been shown to be absolutely absurd. Vietnam fell; nothing else fell, except the entire Communist world has fallen. . . . It was clear from 1973 on that what was happening in Vietnam was certainly not affecting [the] United States's peace and security in any way. . . .

[Our trip] certainly wasn't in the best interests of the United States government. But I think it was in the best interests of helping people to understand the issues and helping more people come to a position where they were against the war and bring the war to an end more quickly, which saved lives on both sides. . . .

Patriotism has become very [much] associated with the right wing and "my country, right or wrong" and people who don't really want to examine issues very carefully, that just wish to uphold the flag at whatever cost. It's perhaps unfortunate that we've allowed patriotism to become imbued with those sorts of meanings. It's basically been co-opted by right-wing political elements. Being patriotic is not necessarily in the best interests of most of the people of this country. I think the government still lies to us. And one of the things that they do is say, "Let's be patriotic," in order to [promote] some of their best interests. And their best interests are not in the best interests of most citizens. . . .

The Vietnamese were committed to keeping that war going until they got rid of the United States. In fact, I think it was the example of the Vietnamese talking to Americans who helped Americans to stand firm against their government's policy. I think that the people who say it the other way around have it backwards. I don't think about [the war] as often, but my opinions are the same. I would certainly do the exact same things over again that I did between 1968 and 1972. [I have] no regrets at all. I'm very proud of it.

I would probably personally single out David Dellinger [as the most effective antiwar activist] because during the period of 1965 to about 1970, David was an absolutely brilliant coalition builder. He traveled the country tirelessly. He was one of the few people who was able to speak to elements of the far Left and keep anybody from the far Left talking with anybody at all from the moderate wing of the antiwar movement. He was always able to place what was happening in Vietnam in the context of where the American antiwar movement needed to go and to explain it to large numbers of people in a way that convinced them to keep up their spirits and keep up the pressure on the government.

Toward the end, the antiwar movement split up, and a lot of very bitter disputes and a lot of factionalization arose, which even to this day isn't completely healed, and that was too bad. But the antiwar movement did succeed in its main aim. Although the principal cause of the ending of the war was the Vietnamese resistance, the antiwar movement played a very significant role in bringing the United States government to the realization that it was no longer worth the social cost back home. . . .

People on the West Coast might have a somewhat different opinion than people on the East Coast, but definitely for East Coast groups, I think that the mobilization committees and the coalitions were important. I have no idea [what these differences were]. I never went to the West Coast. But I just had the feeling there was. That was what West Coastees used to tell us, that we were different.

I think if I had it to do all over again that I would probably be more willing to commit acts of civil disobedience and to commit stronger acts of civil disobedience, which would incur more time in jail. I think that was actually among the more effective things that we did. And if we had done more of that earlier, I think it would've been good. I think it would have helped shorten the war.

[One example of civil disobedience] that I did do was in 1972 or 1973. A bunch of people who were pacifists went out to an ammunition depot in Leonardo, New Jersey, and we sat across the railroad tracks in an attempt to try and stop the movement of munitions. That seemed to make a lot of military people very nervous. They didn't like it at all, and we were strongly challenged. I remember going into court and being told by the judge that if we ever came back again, it was not going to be a mere slap on the wrist, that we were going to be given serious jail time. That was a useful activity because at that point, we needed to let the government know that we were serious to the point of really putting our lives on the line, that we really wanted the bombing to stop.

24

Telford Taylor

Prof. Telford Taylor served as the second chief prosecutor for the U.S. government at the Nuremberg War Crimes Trials. He initially supported the U.S. military role in Vietnam but turned against the war when civilian deaths on both sides reached extraordinary numbers. Contrary to others, Taylor believed the destruction of Europe in World War II exceeded the damage he saw in North Vietnam. He also believed that the bombing of North Vietnam was consistent with conventional military operations, did not violate international law, and was not a war crime. Taylor went to North Vietnam not because he wished to express displeasure with his government but because he was curious as to the nature of the war and because it was convenient for him to travel at the time he did.

Professor Taylor, born in 1908, has received numerous honorary degrees and international awards. He has been a visiting lecturer at Yale, Harvard, and Columbia law schools. Taylor was also a contributor to *War Crimes and the American Conscience,* edited by Erwin Knoll and Judith Nies McFadden (New York: Holt, Rinehart, and Winston, 1970). The interview was conducted at Professor Taylor's Morningside Heights apartment in New York City, on October 10, 1990.

TELFORD TAYLOR: [My trip to Hanoi] would have been in December of 1972, just before the so-called Christmas bombing, which I recall was from December 18 to December 30. [We were there] just about [two weeks]. We came out of North Vietnam just one day before the bombing stopped. I believe we left on December 29.

There were four of us in all. Joan Baez; the Reverend Michael Allen, one of the chaplains at Yale University; and a fourth, a young man, Barry Romo. Mike, of course, was a clergyman. This was the Christmas season, and what he was looking forward to doing with Joan there was that he would preach and she would sing and give them a Christmas celebration. I was interested in other things.

What started this off, probably sometime in November, was that former Attorney General Ramsey Clark telephoned me. He asked if I would be willing to think about going to North Vietnam. The reason he gave for calling me had something to do with a friend of his who was a churchman here, William Coffin. He felt Coffin had been much maligned because he had gone to North Vietnam. He thought that if I went, it might, to some extent, diminish the flak that Coffin had been taking. I don't know why he thought that, and whether I would have gone for that purpose, in particular, I don't know.

But it so happened that Clark's inquiry [was] in November, and [for me to go] in December made it very easy because it was between my law teaching intervals. Therefore, there would be no interruption of the law teaching. At that time, it was before I married my second wife, so I was living alone. Beyond that, I had written a book called *Nuremberg and Vietnam: An American Tragedy* [New York: Bantam Books, 1971], in which I had made some negative statements about the war in South Vietnam but in which I had also said that as far as what I knew about the aerial bombardments in North Vietnam, I saw nothing unlawful about it.

Having said those things and given an opportunity to go to North Vietnam and see what I would see, I was rather anxious to go and see whether what I had said was borne out by what I would find there. Finally, I am a guy who likes to travel and go to places I haven't been before. I had never been to the Far East, no further than the Hawaiian Islands. So I could go, it wouldn't interrupt anything, it should be interesting, and so I said yes. And went from there.

Cora Weiss was the woman at this end who ran the thing — after Ramsey Clark had called me and I had said yes, assuming that it worked out all right. Cora Weiss next called me and said come and talk. I think I had met her once or twice before, I'm not sure. She had, I was told, some months before the Americans started going over there, gone to Paris and met the North Vietnamese who were in Paris. She made arrangements through them for those people who were willing to go and wanted to go. She, for some reason or other, and I'm sure she was right, thought that Allen would be the best person to be the manager in the sense of getting the visas and all those things. So I didn't have to worry about visas or about what hotels we would go to.

The North Vietnamese would be glad to give us the necessary visas to go and come back, and they would put us up while we were there. It was very definite they would not pay our way over and back, but they would give us the visas, and they would also put us in a hotel so that we would be fed and all that sort of thing. I paid for my trip by making a deal with NBC. They loaned me a very fine camera and said that they would be glad to use anything I got that they felt would be helpful. Well, of course, I did. I had written a good many articles for the [*New York*] *Times* from time to time. They simply said that they would be glad to treat me as a stringer. So these arrangements paid for my trip.

I suppose it was Cora Weiss who had put together a great deal of mail for the American prisoners. The so-called reason why we went was that we would carry this mail over and present it to the recipients when we got there. Well, we didn't present it to the intended recipients because most of the American prisoners refused to meet with American civilians such as Jane Fonda and thought we were a bunch of "lefties."

As far as the route we took, we flew first to Copenhagen and slept overnight. We then took a very long, nonstop flight from Copenhagen to Bangkok on a KLM aircraft. We got there in the morning and had lunch. And then immediately, there was a plane, part of an air fleet whose name I can't remember but which, I was told, was actually owned by KLM. We flew to Vientiane and spent the night there. While we were there, we happened to meet up with a *Times* correspondent named [Malcolm W.] Browne, who was married to a South Vietnamese woman, and we had a very entertaining dinner that night and had a good sleep.

The following morning, we took off on a Russian Aeroflot aircraft. Of course, it's not a very long hop from Vientiane to Hanoi. A very interesting thing [occurred] on that trip that I was able to dope out later on. On the airplane, the only other passengers were a group of about twenty to thirty-five Russians, all as alike as two pins. They were in civilian clothes. I didn't know what they were saying. They looked like salesmen, prosperous salesmen. They talked a great deal among themselves, and when we got to Hanoi, they simply vanished. We never saw them again. I'm reasonably certain that those were the Russians who handled and manipulated the rockets. The rockets all came from Russia, and they knocked down sixteen B-52s. I bet those were the Russians or some of the Russians who came in to do that. We landed in Hanoi, and then they disappeared, and this hello group picked us up and went off with us.

We were met by a group of three or four North Vietnamese, one of whom spoke English. Both Joan and I spoke French well enough to cope. I don't pretend to be a very good speaker, but I was able to get along quite well . . . most of the North Vietnamese had been brought up bilingually.

Most of the educated North Vietnamese spoke French well. A lot of them had been educated in France, for that matter. Virtually all the people that I saw there would speak French, and a number spoke English, including the group that shepherded us while we were there.

When we went in, it was three days before the bombing started. At that time, we had planned to stay either one or two weeks, depending upon how things worked out. And we would not have been confined at all to Hanoi. We had planned to go the very next day to Haiphong, but that was the very night the bombing started. So we didn't go, and we never did go anywhere except in the immediate vicinity of Hanoi. I don't believe we would have stayed as long as we did, which was about two weeks, but we couldn't get out until I made arrangements to get out....

This hello party took us around practically everywhere. In the course of it, I spent an afternoon with Vietnamese lawyers. We went into several hospitals and talked to the doctors. We talked to politicians of rather medium status. We did not get at all involved in high-level politics, nor did we see any military people. But Michael Allen, being a clergyman, was much interested in seeing their clergymen, and I went along on those visits, too. So in the course of our visit, we saw quite a lot on that level. A lot of things we didn't see because there had been a large exodus from Hanoi during the early part of the year, beginning in February or March of 1972, because there had been bombing right close to Hanoi and, in one or two cases, in it.

A lot of people were out of town. All the students had been sent away, where I don't know but a long ways away from Hanoi and with them, of course, a number of teachers. When we got there, Hanoi was still at least three-quarters populated, but by the time the bombing was nearly over, it was at least half-evacuated because [of] a very considerable continuing exodus during the bombing. As it was, we [had] only three days before the bombing started, and those were all spent around Hanoi. Just before we started to see something else, the bombing started, and we never went anywhere else.

I didn't see [anything that would indicate air attacks that might be considered war crimes]. I had quite a discussion of war crimes in general with the Hanoi group of lawyers. I should say [however,] that I remember one of the educators who talked to us about education, most of which was not going on because of the evacuation, who said quite bluntly, "You know, we don't think lawyers are very important under present circumstances. Engineers and other people like that would be useful in other ways, yes, but there wasn't very much reason to train lawyers."

All the lawyers that I met there were almost as old as I was. They were well along, and it looked to me as if they were quite sad. The days of Frenchified lawyers in Hanoi was sort of over, and I felt rather sorry for them. They were very gentlemanly, and I had a nice time with them, but there was one division of opinion. They took the view that the bombing *was* in violation of the laws of war, but they really couldn't put any basis for it. . . .

There never were any laws of aerial war like the laws of land warfare and the naval laws. None of those things that happened in the early part of the century for the navy and the army had ever come about as far as the air was concerned. There were no laws of aerial warfare, basically. . . . But even so, I hadn't before seen and while I was there I didn't see anything that I would have thought was unlawful.

The first week I was there, I very much held in my opinions about things because I couldn't really tell too much about what we were trying to do. But it became pretty clear to me after I had been there a week or ten days that we, the United States, were not trying to bash Hanoi. There *were* two or three very bad drops, but it was plain, I thought, and I am quite sure now, that those were the result of navigational errors or some trouble with the aircraft. Most visitors to Vietnam were not familiar with the laws of war and lack of its provisions on air war as distinguished from land and sea. No doubt the U.S. air force was of my mind in the matter. But afterwards, the air force drew up proposed laws of air war, which have not yet been accepted by higher authority. . . .

I was surprised as hell when the bombing started. I had read in the papers that there was a somewhat cool relationship at the moment. Kissinger had come back from France, and they weren't negotiating. There had been some remarks about the possibility of a revival of the bombing, but I rather thought that if the likelihood of bombing was close, I don't believe they would have wanted us to come. We would have been rather in the way. Therefore, I was surprised by the bombing.

That was not new to me because I had been in London during bombing during World War II, and when it started, I said, "My God, I've heard that siren before, a long time ago." Once the bombing began, it was quite regular. I wasn't really surprised except for that.

I was much educated [in Hanoi] with things [Vietnamese] that I didn't know about, and it was very, very enlightening. I must say that I liked the Vietnamese, liked with a qualification that it was quite plain from a couple of things that . . . they would lie and be deceitful if this was necessary for their purposes. But they were very good company, in general. In terms of doing what they said they would do, they did.

I went and talked to the army and the air force when I came back. They said B-52s are very difficult to navigate when they have a heavy load of bombs, and if they got nicked somehow and had trouble navigating, the first thing they would do would be to jettison. And they were of the general opinion that [instances of missed targeting] were probably what they were. Anyhow, there were only three really bad drops in Hanoi. There was quite a lot around us, but there was much more down in Haiphong where they had the boats coming in, cement factories, and other things that would be legitimate targets of aerial warfare.

But the Vietnamese insisted on saying that it was a violation of the laws of war. It wasn't any violation of the laws of war. I don't know [if there were others who would agree with my interpretation]. . . . I don't believe I know any of the others except for an American scholar on Russia, Harrison Salisbury. He had written a great deal about the bombing. There was bombing going on, but anybody who had been in World War II and had been through bombing in Europe and in England would say this was a piddling thing compared to what had gone on there, and nobody then had said that this was unlawful. That was one of the points I made in my book. It wasn't that I meant to say that it was a wonderful thing to do, but there wasn't any law about it, and we ourselves had done much bigger things in this line than what was happening now.

The three who accompanied me didn't know anything about the laws of war. We all got along quite well on the whole, but this was not an area that they got into, so I didn't really meet anybody that raised this matter. . . .

What the North Vietnamese told us at first was that all the prisoners were a long way away from here. That was just a bloody lie. As a matter of fact, the great bulk of the American prisoners were not more than a fifteen-minute walk — right in Hanoi, at the so-called Hanoi Hilton. They were right there. In addition to that, there was another very small group of Americans who were [imprisoned] separately in a place they called the "Zoo," which was sort of on the outskirts of Hanoi. But all of them were right in Hanoi.

As soon as something happened where the North Vietnamese wanted us to meet with the American prisoners, they said, "Oh yes, they are right here, right here." And off we went. It's funny, you know. We were, I think, in the course of a meeting with some educators when all of a sudden, our hello gang came out and said, "Look, there have been some American prisoners who have been hurt by the bombs. You must come and see." "But you've told us that they are miles and miles away." "Oh, no, no. Fifteen minutes." So off we went to the Zoo, whose reason for existence was that it housed those American prisoners who *would* see visitors.

That's a good example [of their willingness to be deceitful if it served their purposes]. To get rid of the whole problem, they would tell us it was too far to go, but as soon as things changed, they would change the tune and the facts to suit the necessities.

I think there must have been in that group called the Zoo somewhere between twelve and twenty [POWs]. Generally speaking, they were not disposed to criticize in any way. But something did happen there. What we had been told was that one of the Americans had been badly hurt by a bomb. There had been one bomb that had dropped fairly near and had rattled things around, and an American prisoner had hurt his hand by something that fell on it. That was all that amounted to.

But beyond that, I was very curious to ask a few questions of them. So I asked the American prisoners, "Where were you when that bomb fell?" They said, "We were under the bed." I said, "Well, that's a funny place to be. Why weren't you in the shelters?" "Oh," they said, "we don't have any shelters." I looked out in the yard and saw a lot of dug shelters. I asked, "What are those?" "Those are the shelters for the guards." So what they had done was make shelters for the guards and none for the prisoners. This made me very angry.

When we finished talking to them, I said to the captain in command, "Why aren't there any shelters for the prisoners?" He said, "Oh, we had some when the bombing was on previously, but we filled them all in." I said, "You didn't fill in the ones for the guards, did you?" He had no answer, of course. I simply got up and went away without saying goodbye. Just got up and left and made it very apparent that this was not to be tolerated. It was very interesting. About six years later, I was invited to Alabama to give a lecture at the air force headquarters down there. One of the colonels there had been a prisoner when I was in Hanoi. I told him this story and we checked the dates. He said, "Two days later, they came around with shovels and other things for us to dig holes for ourselves."

After my little episode at the Zoo, a couple of my compatriots warned me that they didn't know whether my hosts would welcome my presence. As a matter of fact, that worked out well, too, because a few days later, we had one of those conferences where an important newspaperman from North Vietnam talked to us and, without mentioning any names or any particular episode, talked about the fact that they had improved the protection of the prisoners.

[For our return trip], the Russian Aeroflot plane couldn't get in any longer because the first night of the bombing, they bombed the major civilian airport, and although they didn't close it down, they knocked off a good deal of the runway so that the runway was too short to handle the Russian plane. The only plane that was coming in at that time was a twice-a-week plane. It came, I guess from Bangkok, carrying some official international group that was supposed to keep the peace between North and South Vietnam.

They had an old plane that ran back and forth between Bangkok and Hanoi and also between Bangkok and Saigon. But they never got one in while I was there because they didn't have to come during the first three nights we were there, and after that, there was bombing going on virtually every evening. They would sometimes come up while bombing was going on, and then they would not land and go back.

The only plane that was coming in, which I didn't know about until later, was a Chinese plane. Of course, the Chinese border was much closer, and it was just a short hop. After we had been there a week and had two false alarms about getting out, we weren't able to get anywhere else. We'd seen most of what there was to be seen as tourists. We twice went out to the airport to take that international plane back, but it never came in. It got to be well after Christmas, the 26th or the 27th of December, and I decided we ought to get out of there and go home. I should add that although Michael Allen was handling the administrative part of it, I guess that, in general, because I was much older and had a military record and had a legal record, etc., the members of my group pretty much came to me on what we were to do now, etc.

I went then immediately to the North Vietnamese and said that I would like to be introduced to the Chinese ambassador, whoever he was, and see if we could prevail upon him to let us go out on the Chinese plane. We did that. I remember Michael Allen couldn't think whether it would be a good idea for us to get up in rough clothes to show that we were in the hoi polloi or to get dressed up. I said, "Look, these are Chinese. They are very, very much people who want things to be right. I suggest we put on coat and tie." And I was certainly right. The Chinese plane came in on schedule in the morning. There was bombing going on, but they came in anyhow and stayed on the runway, and we got on it and flew to a town called Nanning just across the border in China. We had lunch there.

The Chinese had fixed us all up everywhere, and then we took another Chinese plane and flew to Canton, had supper, slept there, took the train to Hong Kong, and took off for Japan the next morning. We had the press talk to us when we got to Canton, and [they] talked to us again when we got to Tokyo. We stayed overnight in Tokyo and then flew all the way to New York, stopping at Anchorage and I guess at Philadelphia because of the weather. I was very tired. . . .

[No U.S. government official encouraged me to go to Hanoi.] Neither did they try to stop me. Shortly after I got back, I called an old military friend of mine and said that I had been over there and I would be glad to talk to them at the Pentagon, especially since we had seen a great deal of several American prisoners. I thought they would want to know what we knew about where they were and how they were treated and so forth. I was also quite willing to discuss what I had seen in the way of the bombing with the air people, which I did. I also stood before a congressional committee and told them what I had seen and what I thought the burden of it was. And there were other times that I got invited to talk publicly, and I wrote a lot of things for the *New York Times*. . . .

[To say that U.S. political and military leaders should have been tried for war crimes because of the carpet bombing and the use of napalm and antipersonnel fragmentation bombs] gets us into an area which is difficult to be precise about. As to those bombs that spread the needles, I agree with the proposition that any bomb that is unnecessarily painful should be regarded as a violation of the laws of war. But it depends a great deal on what you are bombing on [and] what you are trying to do.

If you are bombing an antiaircraft base, the use of personnel bombs seems to me to be perfectly legitimate. There your enemy is not only the weapons but also the people who are running them. Certainly, if you were sitting in the woods with a rifle, you would say that you would hit those people. I am very strong on the idea that these weapons must be useful in a military way, and the little things that get into you, that give you great pain and make it difficult for the surgeon, are abominable and should be regarded as war crimes, but the mere fact of personnel bombardment is not. It depends upon where and when and how.

I brought this up and thought about it when I was in Vietnam, and I went to their exhibit, a sort of museum of exhibits. The trouble was they hadn't done a good job. They put things in there, but they wouldn't tell you where they came from. There was no way to tell whether some of these personnel bombs had fallen in a place where it was legitimate or where it wasn't, so that it wasn't possible to come to any final conclusion about it.

[Carpet bombing and napalm] certainly were directed against targets that would be difficult to hit without also hitting civilians. But I think where the bombing was heaviest, in an urban sense, was at Haiphong, where there were a couple of cement factories, the headquarters of the railroad, and the port. These were legitimate objectives, despite the fact that bombing those targets would likely cause deaths as well. But they were military objectives, there is no question about that.

In South Vietnam, on the other hand, my little book was very anti-American on the handling of the air war. Because there they were dealing very closely with the Viet Cong and local people. It was like a civil war down there. Quite a number of the things that were done in South Vietnam, which I wrote about in my book, I put that way because I didn't get there, so I never did get to see that part. I never would have. I was never asked to go to South Vietnam. . . .

In the Korean War, . . . there was one point at which the Americans had gone up all the way to the Yalu River and had all of Korea in their pocket. Of course, two days later, the Chinese came into the war and drove us back down the peninsula. But at that point, we were right up at the Yalu River, and I got several calls from newspapermen saying, "Well, we seem to have licked the Koreans. Do you think we should have any war crimes trials?" I answered that if there would be any war crimes trials, they ought not be done the way that we had done them before where it was a one-way street. It was only the victors trying the vanquished. It ought to be done by some neutral body like the UN, which could make a jural body that was open for trials on the sides of the victors as well as the vanquished.

So I had thought about that when this did arise in the Korean War. But matters never came to the point where I was ever asked if it applied. There was basis, certainly, in the Vietnam War for charges of war crimes against the Americans. Look what happened with My Lai. It didn't work very well. We did have war crimes trials, really. There were some other trials as well as [those for] the My Lai people. It was also true that there were things done by the North Vietnamese in the ground war that also were violations of the laws of the war. . . . There certainly were. But of course, that war came to an end in a way which did not make it feasible to have any international trial.

[I did not belong to any organization opposed to the war] . . . I was in favor of the Vietnam War until about 1966. Rightly or wrongly, during that period, I had been under the impression that South Vietnam had been invaded by the North Vietnamese, and I would go along with the secretary of state that this was an aggressive war on the part of North Vietnam. Later on, when I studied it more carefully and wrote the book, it was very much more difficult a question as to whether there really was anything [the alleged invasion by the North Vietnamese] to criticize. Therefore, my criticism of the air force in South Vietnam was mostly a matter of the bombing at low level of the villages and areas where the Viet Cong were thought to be. It was done on a wide scale.

Without pretending to be an international lawyer, in that sense, or having any inside information on it, I cannot see any reason why we shouldn't [resume diplomatic relations with the Vietnamese]. . . .

[The American public] most certainly does not [fully understand the origin, development, and our involvement in the Vietnam War]. But give me a war that both sides do thoroughly understand. It is very difficult to find one. When you compare the Korean War with this war, both were wars that took a lot of our best boys out and caused a great deal of sorrow and death, yet the Korean War disappeared from the minds as something to worry about very rapidly, except for those who were personally hurt. The Korean War ended, of course, in a much different way. We went back to the way things were before the war began: North Korea and South Korea. It didn't leave anything like the wounds not only of people who lost sons but also people who were just ashamed at the amount of carnage that the war caused.

The Vietnam War was a much crueler war, and it went on and on and on. It appeared to me more and more to be a useless war, that it was not going to accomplish anything at all close to the damage that was being done. So at about 1966, I began to think of things the other way, and it had never occurred to me that I was going to go to Vietnam. I didn't write anything about it until the My Lai massacre.

The My Lai massacre made me very ashamed. I was actually in England at the time. I took a period at Churchill College in Cambridge, England, when this happened. I talked mostly to the British about what had happened. The reason that I wrote *Nuremberg and Vietnam* was that it appeared to me that it was time that somebody tried to put together what our policy aims had been at Nuremberg and compared them with what was happening in Vietnam. And that's what the book is all about. I don't think I ever would have thought of doing this after Korea, and I am sure that many other people were much more deeply wounded mentally and upset by the whole thing. . . . Opposition to the war grew and grew and grew to the point where the government could no longer swallow it.

Turning against the war didn't automatically mean that I was turning toward it with a plus for North Vietnam. It meant that as an episode going on there, it seemed to me that the chances of its doing any good were remote, and it seemed to be doing a great deal of human harm. I came to North Vietnam with almost no feelings one way or another about whether I was going to find these people pleasant, get to like them, or how I would feel about the country as a whole. On that score, as I've said, it was quite plain that they were completely prepared to lie, and I am sure that if things had gone badly enough, they would be very harsh on you.

[Although some alleged that Americans who traveled to Hanoi prolonged the war], I very much doubt if there was a very perceptible effect of that kind from the few people that went. . . . Jane Fonda is a most attractive woman and a wonderful actress, and I admire her for those factors, but I think that she — I wouldn't say this about others — but I think that she *was* trying to "hop" things up to portray a support for the North Vietnamese, and to some extent, my colleagues that I went with were that way. But I regarded myself as a newspaperman. I did not go to say yes or no about those things. I wanted to see what I could see and understand and portray, and I was in no sense trying to increase the idea of support for all this.

Joan Baez, you have to know her. She's quite different from Jane Fonda. She's very unpolitical, but she is also very humanitarian and very, very antiwar.. . . The war was going on as a result of American activities [the bombing of North Vietnam] there. So while she was there, she was sympathetic and supportive of the North Vietnamese but not in a political sense. It was in a humanitarian way. As a matter of fact, after the Vietnam War was over and the whole of Vietnam came together, emerged, she turned right around and became anti–Vietnamese government because there was so much indication of vicious things by the Vietnamese, both in South and North Vietnam. As a matter of fact, . . . I had occasion once to call [Cora Weiss] when I wanted to get Joan's address, and she said, "Well, we're kind of out on that. Our friends do not think she went the right way." So that was Joan Baez. It was not a political thing. It was a very antiwar feeling.

I would like to think that I stand as a patriot but as a humanitarian patriot and a law-and-order patriot. I certainly am not a pacifist. How could I be? I spent seven years in uniform, and three of those were during the war. Nor am I in all circumstances against capital punishment. How could I be? I was the chief prosecutor at at least two large trials where the results of my efforts were the execution of the German prisoners. I don't regret having done that. I am in no sense ashamed of it, and I don't believe, therefore, that I can honestly say that — and nothing has occurred since that has turned me to an absolutely anti–capital punishment person.

I've pretty much said that I haven't changed much in [my feelings about the war]. . . . I have been disappointed in the whole of Vietnam. I don't think they started out in a very cool way. They don't seem to me to be very clever economically, either. Things are improving a bit, but I haven't had any impetus to want to go back to Vietnam, at least up to the present time.

I would be inclined to think more or less [that a contributing factor to Vietnam's economic difficulties is the U.S.-imposed trade embargo and not entirely their faulty economic planning]. I am not an economist, and I have not tried to remain fully informed on the situation at all. There may be things that I don't know about, and I could well understand when the war first came to an end, there would still be an awful lot of bitterness that would be very difficult to overcome. But at this date, I would be against maintaining that embargo. . . .

In the tail end of [my book, in] the last chapter, I probably got away from Nuremberg and law and talked about my thoughts about the war. By then, it would have been around 1970, and they were pretty sharp, pretty sharp in the sense that I had really become quite strongly antiwar. It's one of those things that I had occasion to write a good deal about, and once you've written quite a lot about them, you don't have too much more to say. Not only did I write *Nuremberg and Vietnam* but I was on the middle page of the *New York Times* for quite a little spell. I wrote an article for the *Atlantic Monthly* and I did quite a lot of lecturing. I really think I talked myself out. . . .

[With respect to my role in the Nuremberg Trials], I'll have to be accurate about that. There were thirteen Nuremberg trials. In the trial regarded as the big Nuremberg trial, with [Hermann] Göring and the others, I was not the chief prosecutor. I was one of four associate prosecutors to Justice [Robert H.] Jackson, who was the chief prosecutor for the Americans. Of course, there were three other chief prosecutors: the British, the

Russian, and French. About halfway through the first trial, when it became apparent that there would be more trials, Jackson would not stay and do that because he had to get back to the Supreme Court, from which he was on leave. And I was asked to succeed him and become the chief prosecutor for the twelve remaining trials. And I was the chief prosecutor for those.

[After the trials, I returned to] civilian life. I had never been in private practice between my graduation from law school and the time I entered the army. I remained in the army throughout Nuremberg, the reason being that I had a position which was not only legal but also administrative. I had to get stenographers, I had to get really all kind of things, and I knew very well that I would fare much better in the military milieu, in which the whole thing was conducted in the late 1940s, if I stayed in uniform.

I was a colonel at the end of the war, and I also insisted that I be made brigadier general if I was going to do this. I liked that, too, but my real reason for insisting on it was that I would have to ask for people and try to get people and things, and it would be much better. . . . As a brigadier general, I was paid exactly six thousand dollars a year, and my senior underlings [officers of higher rank] were paid ten thousand dollars a year. But in other ways, I profited a great deal. I was given a fine house, an airplane, tennis courts, things like that.

. . . I was chief lawyer for the Federal Communications Commission [before World War II], where I stayed on until about six months after Pearl Harbor and then joined the army in the summer of 1942. I was in the Pentagon on intelligence work for about five months and then was sent to England for intelligence work. . . . I haven't had any cases involving murder or anything of that kind. They were usually cases that involved either matters of money or matters of misrepresentation, things of that kind.

Appendix
U.S. Citizens Who Traveled to North Vietnam: 1965–1972

Name	Affiliation	Year of Visit
Adams, Herbert	NA	1965
Allen, Rev. Michael	accompanied Telford Taylor, Joan Baez; associate dean, Yale Divinity School	1972
Aptheker, Herbert	historian; member, U.S. Communist Party; accompanied Tom Hayden and Staughton Lynd	1965
Arnett, Peter	accompanied Cora Weiss; war reporter, author (with Michael Maclear), *The Ten Thousand Day War: Vietnam 1945–1975* (New York: St. Martin's Press, 1981)	1972
Ashmore, Harry S.	journalist; author (with W. C. Baggs), *Mission to Hanoi: A Chronicle of Double Dealing in High Places* (New York: Putnam, 1968)	1967 1968
Austin, Jan	editorial board, *Ramparts*; editor, *War Bulletin*; accompanied both Eldridge Cleaver and Tom Hayden	1970 1972
Baez, Joan	accompanied Telford Taylor; singer; Amnesty International	1972
Baggs, William C.	editor, *Miami News*; accompanied Harry Ashmore	1967 1968
Barnet, Richard J.	co-director, Institute for Policy Studies; author (with Ralph Stavins and Marcus G. Raskin), *Washington Plans an Aggressive War* (New York: Random House, 1971)	1969
Barrow, Willie	accompanied Irma Zigas; minister	1971
Bennett, Anne	accompanied Ronald Young and Trudi Schutz Young	1970
Benson, Sally	NA	NA
Berrigan, Rev. Daniel	priest; POW escort; author, *Night Flight to Hanoi: War Diary With 11 Poems* (New York: Macmillan, 1968)	1968
Bevel, Diane	Student Nonviolent Coordinating Committee; accompanied Grace Newman	1966

Blumenfeld, Regina	accompanied Eldridge Cleaver	1970
Boardman, Betty	Quaker activist (delivered medical supplies in ketch to Haiphong)	1967
Branfman, Fred	accompanied Susan Miller-Coulter, Tom Hayden, and Howard Zinn; director, "Project Air War"	1972
Brown, Elaine	vice minister of information, Black Panther Party	1970
Brown, Rev. John	Episcopal priest; accompanied Tom Hayden and Rennie Davis	1967
Brown, Robert	accompanied Tom Hayden and Rennie Davis	1967
Burrows, Vinnie	actress; poet	—
Bury, Rev. Harry	priest; International Assembly of Christians in Solidarity With the Vietnamese	1972
Butterfield, Fox	reporter, *New York Times*; accompanied Cyrus Eaton, his grandfather	1969
Caldwell, Clifton	vice president, Meat Cutters Union	1972
Camp, Katherine	Coordinating Committee, People's Coalition for Peace and Justice; national chairwoman, Women's International League for Peace and Freedom; Steering Committee, New Mobilization ("Mobe")	1971
Carmichael, Stokely	chairman, Student Nonviolent Coordinating Committee; member, International War Crimes Tribunal, 1967	1967
Champney, Horace	crewmember of ketch *Phoenix*	1967
Charles, Olga	wife of POW Lt. Norris Charles; accompanied husband back to States	1972
Chomsky, Noam	professor, MIT; accompanied Douglas Dowd and Richard Fernandez; principal organizer, Resist	1970
Clark, Ramsey	former U.S. attorney general; Amnesty International, U.S.	1972
Clarke, Mary	Women Strike for Peace; Coordinating Committee, People's Coalition for Peace and Justice	1965 1967
Cleaver, Eldridge	minister of information, Black Panther Party	1970
Clement, Marilyn	accompanied woman associated with Operation PUSH, Chicago	NA
Cobb, Charles	accompanied Julius Lester; member, Student Nonviolent Coordinating Committee; member, Commission of Inquiry to North Vietnam, International War Crimes Tribunal	1967

Coffin, Rev. William Sloane	chaplain, Yale University; POW escort; Committee for a Sane Nuclear Policy	1972
Collingwood, Charles	CBS News reporter	1967
Collins, Judy	folksinger	NA
Cook, Terrie	Coordinating Committee, People's Coalition for Peace and Justice	1971
Craven, Joseph (Jay)	Coordinating Committee, People's Coalition for Peace and Justice	1971
Davis, Rennie	project director, National Mobilization Committee; leader, SDS; Coordinating Committee, People's Coalition for Peace and Justice; May Day Collective; Steering Committee, National Antiwar Conference; POW escort	1967 1969
Dellinger, David	chairman, National Mobilization Committee to End the War in Vietnam; editor, *Liberation;* Coordinating Committee, People's Coalition for Peace and Justice; POW escort; member, War Crimes Tribunal, Stockholm and Copenhagen, 1967; Committee of Liaison; Fifth Avenue Vietnam Peace Parade Committee; Steering Committee, 1969, National Antiwar Conference; author	1966 1967 1972
Deming, Barbara	editorial board, *Liberation* magazine	1966
Douglas, John	SDS; accompanied Rennie Davis and POWs; filmmaker, *Newsreel*	1969
Dowd, Douglas	professor, Cornell University; New Mobilization Committee to End the War in Vietnam ("Mobe"); New Universities' Conference participant; Resist; Steering Committee, National Antiwar Conference; Coordinating Committee, People's Coalition for Peace and Justice	1970
Drath, Phillip	crewmember of ketch *Phoenix*	1967
Duckles, Madeline	accompanied Cora Weiss and Ethel Taylor; Women Strike for Peace; member, Women's International League for Peace and Freedom	1969
Eaton, Anne	accompanied husband, Cyrus	1969
Eaton, Cyrus	86-year-old Cleveland industrialist	1969
Eaton, Robert	crewmember of ketch *Phoenix*	1967
Egleson, Nicholas	president, SDS; accompanied David Dellinger	1967
Elder, Joseph	American Friends Service Committee	1968
Evans, Linda	member, SDS	1969
Falk, Richard	professor, Princeton University; POW escort; Amnesty International, U.S.;	1968 1972

	author, *The Vietnam War and International Law* (Princeton NJ: Princeton University Press; vol. 1, 1967; vol. 2, 1969; vol. 3, 1972; and vol. 4, 1976)	
Faun, Richard	accompanied Betty Boardman; employed by Canadian Broadcasting System	1967
Feinberg, Abraham	rabbi; accompanied David Dellinger	1967
Fernandez, Richard	minister; Clergy and Laity Concerned About Vietnam; Coordinating Committee, People's Coalition for Peace and Justice; Steering Committee, National Antiwar Conference; National Coalition Against War, Racism, and Repression	1970
FitzGerald, Frances	author, *Fire in the Lake: The Vietnamese and the Americans in Vietnam* (Boston: Little, Brown, 1972)	NA
Floyd, Randy	American Deserters Committee, Sweden	1972
Fonda, Jane	actress; People's Coalition for Peace and Justice	1972
Forest, James	secretary, World Peace Committee	1970
Fruchter, Norman	SDS; POW escort; founding member of *Newsreel*; co-organizer with Tom Hayden of Newark (New Jersey) Community Union Project (NCUP)	1967 1969
Froines, Ann	wife of John Froines, Chicago Seven	1970
Fulmer, Mark	student; accompanied David Kirby	1968
Gartley, Minnie Lee	mother of POW Navy Lt. Mark Gartley	1972
Gerassi, John	author, *North Vietnam: A Documentary* (Indianapolis, IN: Bobbs-Merrill, 1968); member, first investigating team, International War Crimes Tribunal	1967
Gibbons, Harold	vice president, Teamsters Union	1972
Gordon, Lorraine	accompanied Mary Clarke; Women Strike for Peace	1965
Greenblatt, Robert	professor, Cornell University; Steering Committee, New Mobilization; New Universities' Conference; accompanied Andrew Kopkind, Susan Sontag, and Franz Schurmann	1968
Griffith, Patricia	wife of Cornell University chemistry professor; administrative secretary, Nov. 5–8 "Mobe" Committee	1966
Grizzard, Vernon	accompanied Anne Weills, Stewart Meacham, and POWs; SDS; member, National "Mobe"	1968
Gumbo, Judith Clavir	accompanied Nancy Rubin and Genie Plamondon	1970
Hall, Gus	general secretary, U.S. Communist Party	1972

Hamilton, Mary Anne	International Assembly of Christians in Solidarity With the Vietnamese; accompanied Rev. Harry Bury	1972
Hart, Jane	wife of Sen. Philip A. Hart, Democrat, of Michigan	1972
Hart, John	reporter, CBS News	1971
Hayden, Tom	founder, SDS; project director, "Mobe"; author, *The Love of Possession Is a Disease With Them* (Chicago: Holt, Rinehart and Winston, 1972)	1965 1967 1972
Heick, William	accompanied Betty Boardman; employed by Canadian Broadcasting Corporation	1967
Herring, Frances	accompanied Mary Clarke; professor, University of California, Berkeley	1965
Hersh, Seymour	investigative reporter, *New York Times*; author, *My Lai 4: A Report on the Massacre and Its Aftermath* (New York: Random House, 1970)	1972
Hunter, Rev. David	deputy general secretary, National Council of Churches	1972
Ifshin, David	president, National Student Association; Coordinating Committee, People's Coalition for Peace and Justice	1970
Johnson, James A.	chairman, Black Antiwar Antidraft Union; Young Workers' Liberation League; one of Fort Hood Three; accompanied Rennie Davis and POWs; SDS	1969
Kahin, Audrey	accompanied husband, George McT Kahin	1971
Kahin, George McT.	professor of government, Cornell University	1971 1972
King, Alexis	women's liberation movement; accompanied Eldridge Cleaver	1970
Kirby, David	student	1968
Kirkpatrick, Kenneth	American Friends Service Committee	1970
Koch, Jon Christopher	accompanied Harold Supriano, Michael Myerson, and Richard Ward; former radio producer	1965
Koen, Rev. Charles	minister; national chairman, Black United Front	1971
Kolko, Gabriel	historian	NA
Kolko, Joyce	economist	NA
Kopkind, Andrew	SDS; accompanied Robert Greenblatt and Susan Sontag; editor, *New Republic*	1968
Kraft, Joseph	news correspondent	1972
Kramer, Robert	SDS; accompanied Rennie Davis and POWs; founding member, *Newsreel*	1969
Kransberg, Janet	NA	NA

Krause, Ruth	accompanied Mary Clarke; Women Strike for Peace	1967
Lawson, Phillip	Methodist minister; Executive Committee, New "Mobe"	1970
Lecky, Robert	accompanied Paul Mayer; editor, Clergy and Laity Concerned About Vietnam; minister	1971
Lens, Shirley	accompanied Mary Clarke	1965
Lerner, Judith	Women Strike for Peace	NA
Lester, Julius	member, fourth investigating team, International War Crimes Tribunal	1967
Levertov, Denise	poet; accompanied Jane Hart	1972
Lewis, Anthony	reporter, *New York Times*	1972
Livingston, David	president, District 65, Distributive Workers of America	1972
Lockwood, Lee	news photographer	1967
Lynd, Staughton	professor, Yale University; author, accompanied Tom Hayden; editor, *Liberation*	1965
Lynn, Conrad J.	accompanied Hugh Manes; associated with International War Crimes Tribunal; lawyer	1967
Manes, Hugh R.	lawyer; member, Third Commission of Inquiry, International War Crimes Tribunal	1967
Massar, Ivan	crewmember of ketch *Phoenix*	1967
Mayer, Rev. Paul	New York Theological Seminary; People's Coalition for Peace and Justice	1972
McCarthy, Mary	accompanied Franz Schurmann; author, *Vietnam* (New York: Harcourt, Brace, and World, 1968)	1968
McEldowney, Carol	SDS; accompanied Rev. John Brown, Tom Hayden, and Rennie Davis	1967
McReynolds, David	director, War Resisters League; accompanied by a Vietnam veteran	1971
Meacham, Stewart	accompanied Anne Weills and Vernon Grizzard; POW escort; education secretary, American Friends Service Committee; co-chairman, "Mobe"; National Coalition Against War, Racism, and Repression; Coordinating Committee, People's Coalition for Peace and Justice; Steering Committee, 1969, National Antiwar Conference	1968
Meyers, William	member, Lawyer's Committee on American Policy Towards Vietnam; accompanied Richard Barnet	1969

Miller-Coulter, Susan	director, Episcopal Peace Fellowship; New "Mobe"; organizer, March Against Death, September 1969	1972
Mugar, Carolyn	accompanied Tom Hayden and Howard Zinn; Indochina Peace Campaign	1972
Muste, A. J.	82-year-old pacifist; Fellowship of Reconciliation; chairman, Fifth Avenue Vietnam Peace Parade Committee	1967
Myerson, Michael G.	international secretary, W.E.B. Du Bois Clubs; accompanied Jon Christopher Koch, Harold Supriano, and Richard Ward	1965
Near, Holly	actress; accompanied Jane Fonda	1972
Neilands, J. B.	professor, University of California; member, Third Commission of Inquiry, International War Crimes Tribunal	1967
Newman, Grace	sister of Dennis Mora (one of Fort Hood Three); Fort Hood Three Defense Committee	1966
Paley, Grace	National Resist; Greenwich Village Peace Center; poet and author; accompanied Rennie Davis	1969
Parker, A. (Zeus)	college student body president	1970
Peck, Sidney	professor, Case-Western Reserve University; co-chairman, New Mobilization Committee; Coordinating Committee, People's Coalition for Peace and Justice; coordinator, "Mobe"; Steering Committee, National Antiwar Conference; National Coalition Against War, Racism, and Repression; Wisconsin State Committee, U.S. Communist Party (while a student)	1970
Pfeiffer, Egbert W.	professor of zoology, University of Montana; accompanied Mark Ptashne	1970
Plamondon, Genie	accompanied Judith Gumbo and Nancy Rubin	1970
Ptashne, Mark S.	professor of biochemistry, Harvard University	1970
Rappaport, Randy	NA	1970
Reed, Charles	secretary, American Friends Service Committee	1971
Reynolds, Earle L.	captain of ketch *Phoenix*	1967
Romo, Barry	accompanied Telford Taylor and Joan Baez; former U.S. Army lieutenant; Vietnam Veterans Against the War	1972
Rothstein, Vivian	accompanied Rev. John Brown, Rennie Davis, and Tom Hayden; SDS	1967
Rubin, Nancy Kurshan	accompanied Judith Gumbo and Genie Plamondon	1970

Rukeyser, Muriel	poet; Greenwich Village Peace Center	1972
Russell, Margaret	accompanied Mary Clarke	1965
Salisbury, Harrison	editor, *New York Times*; author, *Behind the Lines: Hanoi, December 23, 1966– January 7, 1967* (New York: Harper and Row, 1967)	1966
Scheer, Robert	editor, *Ramparts*; author, *How the United States Got Involved in Vietnam* (Santa Barbara, CA: Center for the Study of Democratic Institutions, 1965)	1970
Schmidt, Phyllis	accompanied Mary Clarke	1965
Schneider, Mr.	member, A Quaker Action Group	1970
Schoenbrun, David	reporter, CBS News; author	1967
Schoenman, Ralph	secretary to Bertrand Russell; author, *A Glimpse of American Crimes in Vietnam* (London: Bertrand Russell Peace Foundation, 1967)	1966
Schurmann, Franz	professor, University of California; author (with Peter Dale Scott and Reginald Zelnik), *The Politics of Escalation in Vietnam* (Greenwich, CT: Fawcett Publications, 1968)	1968
Seeger, Pete	folksinger	1972
Seeger, Toshi	accompanied husband, Pete Seeger	1972
Sontag, Susan	author, *Trip to Hanoi* (New York: Farrar, Straus, and Giroux, 1969)	1968
Stavis, Morton	accompanied Peter Weiss; Lawyer's Committee on American Policy Towards Vietnam; Center for Constitutional Rights	1970
Stetler, Russ	NA	1966
Storey, Rasheed	chairman, Communist Party, New York	1972
Sumi, Hideko (Pat)	leader, Movement for a Democratic Military	1970
Supriano, Harold E.	accompanied Jon Koch, Michael Myerson, and Richard Ward	1965
Swerdlow, Amy	accompanied Irma Zigas; Women Strike for Peace; professor, Sarah Lawrence College; author, *Women Strike for Peace* (Chicago: University of Chicago Press, 1993)	1971
Tabankin, Margerie	accompanied Rev. Paul Mayer; president, National Student Association	1971
Taylor, Ethel	accompanied Cora Weiss and Madeline Duckles	1969
Taylor, Telford	U.S. Army prosecutor, Nuremberg Trials; professor of law, Columbia University; author	1972

Tyner, Jarvis	vice presidential candidate, U.S. Communist Party; national chairman, Young Workers Liberation League	1972
Wald, George	Nobel laureate; professor, Harvard University	1972
Ward, Richard E.	accompanied Harold Supriano and Michael Myerson; freelance writer	1965
Wefers, Mark	student	1970
Weills, Anne	POW escort; member, National "Mobe"	1968
Weiss, Cora	Committee of Liaison; POW escort; Women Strike for Peace; co-chairperson, National Mobilization Committee; Steering Committee, National Antiwar Conference; Coordinating Committee, People's Coalition for Peace and Justice; Jeannette Rankin Brigade	1969 1972
Weiss, Peter	Lawyer's Committee on American Policy Towards Vietnam	1970
Werner, Jayne	NA	1972
Westover, Martha	NA	1970
Williams, Robert	NA	1966
Williams, Mrs. R.	accompanied husband, Robert	1966
Wilson, Dagmar	accompanied Mary Clarke; president, Women Strike for Peace; vice chairperson, Spring Mobilization Committee	1967
Woodward, John	professor	1971
Young, Ronald	member, Fellowship of Reconciliation; coordinator, People's Coalition for Peace and Justice; Washington Action Committee; Steering Committee, New "Mobe"; National Coalition Against War, Racism, and Repression; accompanied Anne Bennett and Trudi Schutz Young	1970
Young, Trudi Schutz	accompanied Ronald Young; national coordinator, Women Strike for Peace; Coordinating Committee, People's Coalition for Peace and Justice; "Mobe"; organizer, 1969 March Against Death	1970
Zietlow, Carl	crewmember of ketch *Phoenix*	1967
Zigas, Irma	Women Strike for Peace	1971
Zimmerman, William	accompanied Rev. Paul Mayer; Medical Aid to Indochina	1971
Zinn, Howard	professor, Boston University; POW escort; accompanied Tom Hayden and others; author, *Vietnam: The Logic of Withdrawal* (Boston: Beacon Press, 1967)	1968 1972

Index

A first initial is used in names of individuals who were interviewed. Names of individuals who were not interviewed are spelled out.

Abolish Peonage Committee, 22
Adams, Herbert, 287
Afghanistan resistance, 198–199
Against the Crime of Silence, 67
Agent: Blue, 71–72; Orange, 9, 71–72, 145, 161, 195; White, 71–72
A Glimpse of American Crimes in Vietnam, 294
Agronsky, Martin, 228
Air America, 78, 113
Air Force, U.S., alleged strategic bombing concept, 70
Allen, Michael, xix, 173, 269–270, 273–274, 276, 280, 287
All Things Considered, 8
Alvarez, Everett (POW), 4
American Bar Association, 256
American Broadcasting Company (ABC) Radio and Television, 252, 256
American Civil Liberties Union (ACLU), 217–218
American Committee on Africa, 205
American Deserters Committee, Sweden, 290
American Friends Service Committee (AFSC), 89, 136, 144, 217–218; antiwar movement effectiveness, 234; membership, 289, 291–293;
American Institute for Marxist Studies, 13
American Legion, 58
American Peace Conference, 7. *See also* World Peace Congress
American Negro Slave Revolts, 23
American Power and the New Mandarins, 183
American Revolution, compared to Vietnam War, xxi, 191–192
American University in Beirut, 111
Americus County Jail, 51
Amnesty International, 287–289
Anderson, Jack, 163
And Justice for All, xvii–xviii
Andrews Air Force Base, 121
Antiwar activists, trips to North Vietnam impact upon selves, xxiv–xxv; A. Weills, 123; E. Boardman, 102; E. Taylor, 148, 156; I. Zigas, 210; M. Duckles, 144; M. Myerson, 9
influence on war, xii, xxii–xxiv; A. Weills, 123; C. Weiss, 180; E. Boardman, 94–95, 102; E. Taylor, 148; G. Wald, 247; I. Zigas, 210, 216; J. Lester, 86; M. Duckles, 144; M. Myerson, 9; N. Chomsky, 193; R. Clark, 263; S. Miller-Coulter, 270–271; T. Taylor, 284
perceptions similar, xxi–xxii, 100
purpose of: A. Weills, 124; C. Weiss, 165–167, 169–170; D. Dellinger, 47, 52; E. Boardman, 89; E. Taylor, 148, 156–157; G. Kahin, 220–221, 228–229; G. Wald, 237; H. Aptheker, 13; H. Manes, 63; I. Zigas, 207, 210; J. B. Neilands, 70; J. Brown, 111–112; J. Lester, 77–78, 84–85; M. Clarke, 1; M. Duckles, 136; M. Myerson, 8; N. Chomsky, 184; P. Weiss, 202; R. Clark, 252–253, 255; S. Miller-Coulter, 269; T. Taylor, 274–275; W. Heick, 103
reaction to trips, ix; A. Weills, 124–125; E. Boardman, 94–96; E. Taylor, 155–156; G. Kahin, 232; H. Aptheker, 18–19; H. Manes, 66–67; H. Supriano, 11; I. Zigas, 211; J. B. Neilands, 73–74; J. Lester, 85; M. Clarke, 5; M. Duckles, 143; R. Clark, 256–257; W. Heick, 108–109
Antiwar demonstrations and protests, xxiv; arrest of E. Taylor, 157; civil disobedience by Susan Miller-Coulter, 272; Lincoln Memorial rally, 34–37; march on Pentagon, 34–37
Antiwar movement
leadership, 75, 234; D. Dellinger, 132, 217, 271; Martin Luther King, 75, 115, 145, 217; R. Clark, 145; Ron Kovic, 67; Students for a Democratic Society, 101, 133; T. Hayden, 205; Women Strike for Peace, 146, 235

military involvement in, 75–76
women lacked recognition within, 120
Aptheker, Herbert, 47; and breaking the
ban on radical speakers, 13; interview,
12–24; McCarran Act and *Aptheker vs.
Rusk,* 13; not prosecuted for North Viet-
nam visit, 19; Pham Van Dong inter-
view, 18
A Quaker Action Group (AQAG), 89–90,
92, 294
Army Air Corps, 113
Arnett, Peter, 52, 168, 178, 287
Ashmore, Harry S., 287
Association of Social Workers, 11
Association of Southeast Asian Nations
(ASEAN), 126
Association of the Bar of the City of Hanoi,
201–202
Association of the Bar of the City of New
York, 202
Atlantic Monthly, 285
At War With Asia, 183
Austin, Jan, 268, 287
Azikiwe, Nnamdi, 24

Ba, Vuong Xuan, 224(illus.)
Baez, Joan, 120, 180; with Bary Romo to
North Vietnam, 293; compared to Jane
Fonda, 284; dissilusion with Vietnam-
ese government, 270; with T. Taylor to
North Vietnam, 273, 275, 287 travel to
North Vietnam, 173; unavailable for
interview, xix
Baggs, William C., 287
Bak Mai, 254
Barnet, Richard J., 166, 202, 287, 292
Barrow, Willie, 206, 287
Bechtel, Steve, 108
Bechtel Corporation, 108–109
Beeler, Carrol (POW), 230
Beheiren conference, anti–Vietnam War, 47
Behind the Lines, 294
Benghazi, bombing of, 261
Ben Hai River, 168
Bennett, Anne, 287, 295
Bennett, James V., 27
Benson, Sally, 287
Berrigan, Daniel J., xix, 52 184; POW escort,
287
Bevel, Diane Nash, 51, 287
Bingham, Jonathan, 202
Binh, Mme Nguyen Thi, 124, 150, 202
Black Antiwar Antidraft Union, 291
Black Panther Party, 40, 47, 134, 287
Black United Front, 291
Blumenfeld, Regina, 288

Boardman, Elizabeth, 103, 287, 290–291;
feelings towards U.S. airmen, 98; interview, 88–102
Boardman, Eugene, 89, 94
Boat people, 87, 162, 179, 259; compared to
refugees from American Revolution,
191–192
Bollenbeck (Captain), 97
Bomar, Jack (POW), 73
Bombing: carpet, xxii, 169, 203, 252, 269,
281–282; civilian targets of, M. Clarke,
3; compared to World War II, 254, 273,
277–278; D. Dellinger, 51; effectiveness,
226–228; G. Kahin, 227, 230; G. Wald,
241; H. Manes, 64; I. Zigas, 207; J. B.
Neilands, 70; J. Lester, 79, 83 ; R. Clark,
254; T. Taylor, 277– 278, 280, 283; W.
Heick, 106; war crimes allegations
related to, 281–282
Bombs: antipersonnel, 51, 64, 281; cluster,
51, 68; "daisy-cutter," xxii; "guava," 64,
66; smart, 226
Bond, Julian, 213
Borge, Victor, 124
Bork, Irving, 41
Born on the Fourth of July, 21
Boston Five trial, 40–41
Boston Globe, 245–246
Branfman, Fred, 268, 288
Bratislava conference, 52, 111–112
Brezhnev, Leonid, 131
Brown, Elaine, xix, 288
Brown, Emily, 111
Brown, John Pairman, 288, 292–293; inter-
view, 111–117
Brown, Paul, 139(illus.), 172(illus.)
Brown, Robert, 112, 288
Browne, Malcolm W., 275
Buddhists, overthrown, 234–235
Buddhist university, 242–243
Bundy, McGeorge, 202, 221
Bundy, William, 61
Bunker, Ellsworth, 243
Burchett, Wilfred, 3, 26
Burns, Glen (POW), 230
Burrows, Vinnie, 288
Bury, Harold, 172, 288, 291
Bush, George, 56, 58, 159
Butterfield, Fox, 288
Buu, Ta Quang, 49

Cable News Network (CNN), 260
Caldwell, Clifton, 288
California, University of, at Santa Barbara
(UCSB), 125, 135
Calley, William, 154, 170

Cambodia: bombing of, 189; Chinese invasion of, 131; protests against invasion of, 37–38, 134; secret war in, 160
Camp, Katherine, 288
Canadian Broadcasting Corporation (CBC), 92, 103–104, 107, 289, 291
Canadian embassy, assistance to crew of *Phoenix*, 107
Canton, China, 281
Capitol Times, 90
Carmichael, Stokely, 288
Carpenter, Joseph (POW), 121
Carpet bombing. *See* Bombing: carpet
Carter, James E., 196, 212–213, 257
Casey, William J., 258
Catholic Church in Vietnam, 245
Censorship, by Pentagon, 208
Center for Constitutional Rights, 201, 294
Center for the Study of Democratic Institutions, 119, 294
Central Committee for Conscientious Objectors, 218
Central Intelligence Agency (CIA), xvii, xxviii, 130–131; Afghanistan conflict, role in, 199; Air America, 78, 113; D. Dellinger distrusted, 30; Indonesia massacre, role in, 248–249; informants, 163; Libya disinformation campaign, 258; POW James Low skeptical of, 122; R. Clark Senate campaign, role in, 256; Vientiane presence, 210
Central Park rally, 39
Chamberlin, Owen, 146
Champney, Horace, 91, 104, 288
Charles, Norris (POW), 52, 168, 172, 173(illus.), 288
Charles, Olga, 168, 172, 174(illus.), 288
Chiang Mai, 125
Chicago Eight trial, 170
Chicago Seven, 290; trial of, 25, 39–47, 118
Chomsky, Noam, 55, 100, 288; interview, 183–200
Christian Century, 114
Christmas bombing of Hanoi, 15, 173, 230, 273, 277–80
Churchill College (Cambridge, England), 283
Church World Service, 168
Civil rights movement, 50–51
Clark, Ramsey, xxiii, 40, 146, 288; Andrei Sakharov critical of, 239; Chicago Seven trial, testimony refused at, 41; Fritz Efaw, request to nominate, 213; interview, 251–264; interview, why agreed to, xxi; requested T. Taylor travel to North Vietnam, 274; said to be

deceived by North Vietnamese, xxvi; Senatorial candidate, 256
Clarke, Mary, xxiii, 288, 290–292, 294–295; interview, 1–6
Cleaver, Eldridge, 40, 287–288, 291
Clement, Marilyn, 288
Clergy and Laity Concerned About Vietnam, 112, 116, 265, 290, 292
Clifford, Clark, 221
Cobb, Charles, 77–78, 81(illus.) 82–83, 288
Coffin, William Sloane, xix, 40, 52, 171, 274; POW escort, xi, 168, 172, 174(illus.), 289
Cohelan, Jeffrey, 74–75, 120
COINTEL (Counterintelligence), FBI program, 32
Cold War, 56, 132, 204, 246; end of, 261
Collingwood, Charles, xix, 289
Collins, Judy, 180, 289
Colorado State University, 101
Columbia Broadcasting System (CBS), 227–228, 265; News, 289, 291, 294
Commission of Inquiry to North Vietnam, International War Crimes Tribunal, 288
Committee of Concern, 269
Committee of Returned Volunteers, 54
Committee for a Sane Nuclear Policy, 5, 289
Committee of Liaison With Families of Servicemen Detained in Vietnam (Committee of Liaison) (COLIAFAM), xx, 25, 52, 289, 295; founders, 165–166; POW families urged to avoid, 155; purpose, 148, 166–167
Committee of Responsibility, 136, 143, 181
Communist Party, xv
 accused of conspiracy, 20
 Indonesia, massacre of members of, 233
 members of: Danbury prison inmates, 28; Gus Hall, 290; H. Aptheker, 20, 287; Jarvis Tyner, 294; Sidney Peck, 293
 Myerson, Michael, former member of, 8
 rationale for existence, 22
Community for New Politics, 74
Congress, ending U.S. involvement, 111, 116
Congress of Racial Equality (CORE), 10
Conn, Lauren, 251
Cook, Terrie, 289
Counterintelligence program (COINTEL), 32
Craven, Joseph (Jay), 289
Crisis, 24
Cuba, travel restrictions to, 14
Cullen, Countee, 24

Culture of Terrorism, 183

Daily News, 39
Daley, Richard, 47, 214
"Daley Dozers," 44
Danbury prison, 27–28. *See also* Dellinger, David
Danny the Red, 133
Davis, Rennie, xix, 289, 291–292; Chicago Seven indictment, 40; Chicago Seven trial, 44–45; Committee of Liaison, 52; with Grace Paley to North Vietnam, 293; with J. Brown to North Vietnam, 111–112, 288; POW escort, 289; with Vivian Rothstein to North Vietnam, 293
Deceptions of the Vietnam War, identified by: A. Weills, 131; C. Weiss, 178–179; E. Boardman, 102; G. Kahin, 234; G. Wald, 247; I. Zigas, 215; N. Chomsky, 187. *See also* Vietnam War
Defoliants, chemical, 72, 154
De L'Estang, François Bujon, 160
Dellinger, David, xx, 87, 289; with Abraham Feinberg to North Vietnam, 290; antiwar movement leadership, 132, 217; Bratislava conference organizer, 112; Chicago Eight trial, 170; Chicago Seven, 25; Committee of Liaison founder, with C. Weiss, 52, 165–166; Communist Party leadership, distrustful of, 28; Danbury prison sentence, as conscientious objector, 27–28; Democratic National Convention of 1968, involvement in, 25; G. Kahin in Hanoi at same time, 230; Ho Chi Minh interview, 25, 48–49; interview, 25–61; in Lewisburg Penitentiary, 28–29; North Vietnam, arranged trips to, 124; POW escort, xi, 168, 172, 173(illus.), 174(illus.); reunification celebration, attended, 54–55, 245; Stockholm War Crimes Tribunal, member, 25
Dellinger, Natasha, 42
Dellums, Ronald, 52, 142
Demilitarized zone (DMZ), 121–122
Deming, Barbara, 289
Democratic lawyers' group, 65
Democratic National Committee, 213
Democratic National Convention of 1968, 25, 40–41, 120; of 1980, 206, 212–214
Desert Storm, 87, 219
Detention camps, 204. *See also* Re-education camps
Dick Cavett Show, 124
Diem, Ngo Dinh, 154, 159, 161, 234
Dien Bien Phu, 55, 62, 119

Dikes, bombing of, 3, 252–253
Djakarta, meeting of Women Strike for Peace in, 1–2, 162, 164
Doenitz, Karl, 197–198
Dong, Pham Van, 231; meeting with A. Weills, 118, 122–123; meeting with D. Dellinger, 48; meeting with G. Kahin, 222(illus.), 223, 228; meeting with M. Duckles, 136, 141–142; meeting with N. Chomsky, 186; meeting with R. Clark, 254
Dooley, Tom, 119
Dotry, Robert (POW), 11
Douglas, John, POW escort, 289
Dow Chemical Company, 181
Dowd, Douglas, 184, 288
Draft: counseling, 5–6, 66, 206, 211, 218–219; reconciliation, resulting from, 212–213
Drath, Marjorie, 88
Drath, Phillip, 88, 91, 107, 289
Du Bois, Tom, 24
Du Bois, W.E.B., 12, 23; clubs, 8, 10, 23, 293
Duckles, Madeline, 289, 294; and bamboo flute gift, 140–141; with C. Weiss to North Vietnam, 136, 148–149, 166, 289; with E. Taylor to North Vietnam, 136, 148–149, 151, 152(illus.), 153(illus.), 289; interview, 136–147; Nam Dinh, visit to, 142; POWs, meeting with, 172(illus.); Vietnam, return to, 144–145
Duckles, Vincent, 143
Dulles, John Foster, 56, 159, 161
Dung, Van Tien, 123

Eaton, Anne, 289
Eaton, Cyrus, xix, 288–289
Eaton, Robert, 91, 289
Ecocide in Indochina, 183
Efaw, Fritz, 206, 212–214
Egleson, Nick, 52, 289
Eisenhower, Dwight D., xxi, 23, 55, 161, 199
Elder, Joseph, 89, 289
Elias, Edward (POW), 52, 172, 173(illus.)
Ellsberg, Daniel, 36
Embargo, against Vietnam, 74, 176, 178
Episcopal Peace Fellowship (EPF), 111, 268, 270, 293
Episcopal Seminary at Yale, 269–270
European Community (EC), 126
Evans, Linda, 289
Explorers' Club of New York, 109

Faculty Peace Committee, 74
Falk, Richard, xiii, 52, 166, 289; POW escort, 168, 172, 173(illus.), 174(illus.), 289

Fall, Bernard, 48
Fall Mobilization Committee, 33
Fanfani, Amintore, 201
Far Eastern Economic Review, 189
Faun, Richard, 92, 103–104, 107–108, 289
Federal Broadcast Information Service (FBIS), 186
Federal Bureau of Investigation (FBI), 264; COINTEL program, 32; E. Taylor, kept dossier on, 155–156; H. Supriano, alleged harassment, 10–11; Jane Fonda, reports on, xvii; W. Heick, interview of, 108
Federal Communications Commission, 228, 286
Feinberg, Abraham, 290
Fellowship of Reconciliation, 218, 268, 293, 295
Fernandez, Richard, 184, 288, 290
Fifth Avenue Vietnam Peace Parade Committee, 7, 30, 289, 293
Finch, Roy, 43
Fire in the Lake, 60, 175, 290
FitzGerald, Frances, 60–61, 175, 290
Five o'clock follies, 170, 178, 179, 188
Floyd, Randy, 290
Fonda, Jane, xvii, xxiii, 290; admired Tom Hayden, 60–61; antiwar activity evaluated, xxvi–xxvii; compared to Joan Baez by T. Taylor, 284; criticisms of POWs, xxvii, 60, 238–239; with Holly Near to North Vietnam, 293; J. Lester's perception of, 85; photographed atop North Vietnamese tank, xv; POWs refused to meet with, 275; Radio Hanoi broadcasts criticized, xxvi, 182; with Tom Hayden to Vietnam, 171; unpopular with supporters of war, xvi
Foran, Tom, 42, 45
Ford, Gerald, 163
Forest, James, xix, 290
Fort Dietrich protest, 101
Fort Hood Three, 291, 293; Defense Committee, 293
Fourth investigating team, International War Crimes Tribunal, 292
Franc, Hans Goren, 251–252
Freedom of Information Act, xvii, 234; FBI surveillance learned through, 155, 163
French Communist Party, 233
Froines, Ann, 290
Froines, John, 40, 43, 45, 290
From Yale to Jail, 25, 60
Fruchter, Norman, 112, 290
Fulbright, J. William, 202, 234; Kahin, G. McT., discussions, 220, 224, 228–229

Fulmer, Mark, 290
Fulton, Richard (POW), 230

Gandhi, Mahatma, 59, 115
Gandhi Society for Human Rights, 175
Gartley, Markham (POW), 52, 139(fig.), 168, 171, 172(illus.), 173 (illus.), 290
Gartley, Minnie Lee, 172, 173(illus.), 174(illus.), 290
Genet, Jean, 44
Geneva Accords, 49, 199, 232, 234
Geneva Convention, 62–63, 148
Gerassi, John, 290
Germany, lack of repentance by, 266–267
Gibbons, Harold, 290
Gilpin, Richard, 47
Ginsberg, Allen, 44
Globe Communication, 163
Goldberg, Arthur, 202
Golden Gate Park, demonstration at, 133, 146
Goodell, Charles E., 234
Goodman, Paul, 30, 43
Gorbachev, Mikhail, 246
Gordon, Lorraine, 1, 290
Göring, Hermann, 285
Grant Park rally, 42, 44
Great Chicago Conspiracy Trial, The, 44
Great Neck Women Strike for Peace, 211
Green, Felix, 81
Greenblatt, Robert, 290–291
Greenwich Village Peace Center, 293–294
Greene, Graham, 65, 107
Grenada, invasion of, 258, 261
Griffith, Patricia, 52, 290
Grizzard, Vernon, 120–121, 123, 290, 292
Gruening, Ernest, 164
Guardian, The, 8
Gulf: crisis in, 260, 262; rallies against, 57–58; war in, 86, 205. *See also* Desert Storm
Gumbo, Judith Clavir, 290, 293

Hainan Island, xxx(map); *Phoenix* sailed around, 104–105
Haiphong: bombing of, 51; considered legitimate military target, 278; I. Zigas visited nearby, 208; P. Mayer visited, 266; *Phoenix* crew arrived at, 88, 90, 92
Hall, Gus, 290
Ha Long Bay, 121, 126, 138
Halsted, Fred, 38
Hamilton, Mary Anne, xix, 172, 291
Ham Rong bridge, 185
Hanoi
    bombing of, 65, 277–280
    Chinese aircraft took T. Taylor, others, out of, 280–281

flight connections taken to, by: C.
Weiss, 169; E. Taylor, 150–151; G.
Kahin, 229; H. Manes, 63–64; H.
Supriano, 10–11; I. Zigas, 206; J. B.
Neilands, 70; J. Brown, 113; M.
Clarke, 2; M. Duckles, 137; M.
Myerson, 8; P. Weiss, 202; R. Clark,
256; S. Miller-Coulter, 269; T. Tay-
lor, 275
Hanoi Bar Association, 202
Hanoi Daily, 123
"Hanoi Hannah," xvi, 155. *See also* Fonda,
Jane
Hanoi Hilton, 4, 171, 278
Hanson, Gregg (POW), 230
Harkins, Paul D., 221
Harriman, Averell, 120–121
Harrisburg Defense Committee, 266
Hart, Jane, 291–292
Hart, John, xix, 225, 227, 291
Hart, Philip A., 291
Hatfield, Mark O., 234
Hayden, Thomas, xvii, xix, 59–61, 184, 291–
292
antiwar movement, leadership in, 205
armed rebellion, trained for, 41
Bratislava conference, selected attend-
ees for, 52
with Carolyn Mugar to North Vietnam,
293; with H. Aptheker to North
Vietnam, 287; with Howard Zinn
to North Vietnam, 295; with J.
Brown to North Vietnam, 111–112;
with Jan Austin to North Vietnam,
287; with Jane Fonda to North Viet-
nam, 171; with S. Miller-Coulter to
North Vietnam, 268; with Vivian
Rothstein to North Vietnam, 293
Chicago Eight, trial of, 170
Chicago Seven, indictment of, 40; trial,
41, 43–45, 118
Newark Community Union Project
organizer, 290
North Vietnam, trips to, 14, 17, 18, 47
Peoples' Park, participation in protest
at, 130
Radio Hanoi, broadcasts over, xvii
Weills, Anne, companion to, 118, 129
Harlem Renaissance, 24
Hegdahl, Douglas (POW), 4, 52
Heick, William, 91, 291; interview, 103–110
Herald Tribune, 15
Herring, Frances, 2, 291
Hersh, Seymour, xix, 170, 291
Hinckle, Warren, 119
Historical and Social Sciences Institute, 229

Hitler, Adolph, 267
Hitler-Stalin pact, 28
Hmong people, 65
Hoa Binh Province, xxx(map), 138
Ho Chi Minh, xxi; antiwar protesters, meeting with, xx; C. Weiss visited hiding
place of, 168; D. Dellinger meeting
with, 25, 48–49; declared independence
after World War II, 54; G. Wald visited
tomb of, 244; leadership of, x; northern
provinces, initial base in, 231; pitied
POWs, 48–49; presented declaration of
independence to Vietnamese people,
159; supported by Vietnamese, 63; sup-
ported U.S. during World War II, 161,
215
Ho Chi Minh Trail, 64, 115
Hoffman, Abbie, 37–38, 43, 45–46, 132; Chi-
cago Eight trial, 170
Hoffman, Julius, 45–46
Hojer, Axel, 63, 69
Holmgren, Arne, 69
Holocaust, the, 193, 204
Hoover, J. Edgar, 19, 131
Horton, Miles, 43
House Un-American Activities Committee
(HUAC), 109, 131
*How the United States Got Involved in Viet-
nam*, 294
Hubbell, John, xvii
Huey helicopters, 71; monitored *Phoenix*,
104
Huggins, Ericka, 134
Hughes, Harold E., 234
Hughes, Langston, 24
Human rights violations, 204
Humphrey, Hubert, 74
Hunter, David, 268, 291
Hunter, John, 90, 97
Hussein, Saddam, 54, 56, 195

Ifshin, David, 291
Ilyushin aircraft, 169
Indochina Digest, 126
Indochina Peace Campaign, 293
Indochina Reconciliation Project, 53
Indochina Resource Center, 234
Indonesia, massacre in, 233, 249
In Retrospect, xxvii
Institute for Policy Studies, 287
Intentioned community, 29
International Assembly of Christians in
Solidarity With the Vietnamese, 288,
291
International Committee for the Red Cross,
258

International Confederation of Disarmament and Peace, 184
International Control Commission, 3, 124, 169; flights sponsored by, 137, 150
International Monetary Fund (IMF), 127
International War Crimes Tribunal, 288, 290, 292, 293. *See also* Russell, Bertrand: War Crimes Trials; Russell, Bertrand: War Crimes Tribunal; Stockholm War Crimes Tribunal
Intervention, 220, 234
Iran, under the Shah, 259
Iraq, Iran's war with, 259

Jackson, Jesse, 206
Jackson, Karl, 192
Jackson, Robert H., 285–286
Japanese American citizens interned during World War II, xvii–xviii
Johnson, James A., 291
Johnson, Lyndon B. (LBJ), xxi, 72–74, 120, 149–150, 234; presidential campaign, withdrawal from, 205; Women Strike for Peace, monitored, 163

Kahin, Audrey, 221, 222(illus.), 223, 291
Kahin, George McT., 291; interview, 220–235
Kalb, Bernard, 4
Katzenbach, Nicholas, 9
Kennedy, John F., xxi, 119, 164, 199; administration, 234; International Airport (JFK), 202
Kennedy, Robert, 42, 202, 234
Kent State University shootings, 37–38
Kenyatta, Jomo, 24
Kerry, John, 248
Khmer Rouge, 127, 131, 176, 189, 199
Killing Fields, The, 190
King, Alexis, 291
King, Martin Luther, 42–43, 115, 145–146; antiwar movement, leadership in, 75, 115, 145, 217; C. Weiss served as treasurer for, 174–175; death influenced S. Miller-Coulter, 270
Kirby, David, 290–291
Kirkpatrick, Kenneth, 291
Kissinger, Henry, 73, 127, 129, 229, 277; China, traveled secretly to, 210; Christmas bombing ignored release of POWs, 173; directed secret war in Cambodia, 160; Nobel Peace Prize undeserved, 160; pacifists attempted to kidnap, 266; Women Strike for Peace, sued by, 163
Knoll, Erwin, 273

Koch, (Jon) Christopher, 8, 11, 291, 293–294
Koen, Charles, 291
Kolko, Gabriel, 291
Kolko, Joyce, 291
Kopkind, Andrew, xix, 290–291
Korean War, 282–283
Kovic, Ron, 60, 67, 213–214
Kraft, Joseph, xix, 224, 291
Kramer, Robert, 291
Kransberg, Janet, 291
Krause, Ruth, 2, 292
Kuwait, 179, 247
Ky, Nguyen Cao, 159, 221, 234

Laird, Melvin, 167
Laos: alleged invasion false, 187–188; civilian targets bombed, 187; refugees interviewed, 186
La Pira, Georgio, 201
Lau, Ha Van, 202, 222(illus.), 223
Lawson, Phillip, 292
Lawyer's Committee on American Policy Towards Vietnam, 203, 292, 294–295
Lecky, Robert, 265, 292
Left, the, 13, 22, 31; New, 31, 97; Old, 31
Lemay, Curtis, 158
Le Monde, 119
Lens, Shirley, 2, 292
Leonardo, New Jersey: civil disobedience at, 272
Lerner, Judith, 292
Lester, Julius, 93, 288, 292; interview, 77–87; interviewed Pham Van Dong, 80
Levertov, Denise, xix, 292
Lewis, Anthony, xix, 292
Lewis, John W., 220
Lewisburg Penitentiary, 28–29
Liberation, 30, 43, 289, 292
Libya, bombing of, 258, 261
Lien, Vo Thi, 154
Life, 78
Lincoln Memorial, demonstration at, 34–36
Livingston, David, 292
Lockwood, Lee, 78, 292
Logan, Donald (POW), 230
Logan Act, ix, 256
Long Island Draft Information and Counseling Services, 218–219
Lon Son tiger cages, 154
Los Angeles Times, 66, 118, 167
Love of Possession is a Disease With Them, The, 291
Low, James (POW), 121–122
Lowell, Robert, 44
Lowenstein, Allard K., 205
Luce, Donald, 168, 252–253

Lynd, Helen (mother), 14, 19
Lynd, Robert (father), 13, 19
Lynd, Staughton, xix, 47, 184, 287, 292
    Bertrand Russell War Crimes Tribunal,
        asked to serve on, 53
    North Vietnam, activities in: 14–19;
        asked to make trip to, 13–14;
        debated M. Clarke about first to
        visit, 1
Lynn, Conrad J., 292

McAuliff, John, 53–54
McBride, John, 251
McBride, Shawn, 251
McCarran Act, 13
McCarthy, Mary, 292
McCarthy, Eugene, 234
McCarthy, Joseph, 29, 233
McCarthyism, 131; HUAC alleged to be
    example of, 109
McEldowney, Carol, 112, 292
McFadden, Judith Nies, 273
McGovern, George, 180, 234; discussions
    with G. Kahin, 220, 228–229
Maclear, Michael, 287
McNamara, Robert, 36, 181, 221; recent
    reassessment of U.S. involvement,
    xxvii
McReynolds, David, 292
Mailer, Norman, 34
Mandela, Nelson, 23, 249
Manes, Hugh R., 69, 73, 292; draft-age
    young men, counseled, 66; interview,
    62–68; Ho Chi Minh, interviewed, 64–
    65; POWs, chose not to meet, 65
Manhattan-Bronx Council of the New York
    State Commission Against Discrimina-
    tion, 205
March Against Death, 293, 295
Marshall Plan, 259
Massacre of the Innocents, U.S. bombing
    compared to, 136
Massar, Ivan, 91, 292
Matsui, Melvin (POW), 230
May Day Collective, 289
May Day in Washington, 38
Mayer, Paul, 292, 294, 295; interview, 265–
    267
Mayhew, William (POW), 139(illus.), 171,
    172(illus.), 173(illus.)
Meacham, Stewart, 120, 122–123, 290, 292
Media reporting believed inaccurate, 5,
    100, 178, 186, 188
Medical Aid to Indochina, 265, 295
Mennonites, deported, 129; leadership in
    antiwar movement, 234

Mescall, James, xvi
Meyers, William, 292
Miami News, 287
Mideast crisis, 217
Miller, Edison (POW), 266
Miller-Coulter, Susan, 288, 293; interview,
    268–272
Mills, C. Wright, 55
Milos, island of, 262
Minh, Duong Van, 221–223
Missing in action (MIA): concern for both,
    159–160; families contacted by E. Tay-
    lor, 160; issue of, 145, 177; packages
    mailed to, 167; U.S. and Vietnamese,
    Vietnamese losses, evaluated against,
    195
Mission to Hanoi, 14, 287
Mitchell, John, 40
"Mobe," 25, 37–38, 51, 291, 292, 293; North
    Vietnam, arranged trips to, 124. *See also*
    National "Mobe"
Mobilization Against the War in Vietnam,
    174. *See also* National "Mobe"
Mondale, Fritz, 214
Montgomery bus boycott, 42–43
Mora, Dennis, 293
Morse, Linda, 41
Morse, Wayne, 62, 164
Moscow conference, attended by Women
    Strike for Peace, 5
Moses, Robert, 14
Movement for a Democratic Military, 294
Mugar, Carolyn, 268, 293
Mumford, Lewis, 66
Murphy, Frank, 188
Muste, A. J., xix, 30, 43, 47, 293; inspired D.
    Dellinger, 59
Myerson, Michael G., 11, 291, 293–295;
    interview, 7–9
My Lai, massacre at, 53, 116, 154, 170, 204;
    T. Taylor ashamed by, 283; war crime,
    evaluated as, 282
*My Lai 4: A Report on the Massacre and Its
    Aftermath*, 291

Nam Dinh, antiwar activists visited,
    xxx(map), 15–16, 142(fig.)
Napalm, use of, 51, 281–282
National Antiwar Conference, 289–290,
    292–293, 295
National Assembly, Vietnam, 128
National Association for the Advancement
    of Colored People (NAACP), 23
National Broadcasting Company (NBC),
    275

National Coalition Against War, Racism, and Repression, 290, 292–293, 295
National Coalition for Peace and Justice (NCPJ), 7
National Council for Unconditional Amnesty, 212
National Council of Churches, 53, 268, 291
National Lawyers' Guild, 52, 67–68
National Liberation Front (NLF), 112; American Peace Conference, attended by, 7; E. Taylor met representative of, 154; M. Clarke met with, 1; postwar leadership role, 232; seven-point negotiating program, 222; Women Strike for Peace, met with, 163. *See also* Provisional Revolutionary Government
National "Mobe," 7, 25, 38, 133, 290, 295. *See also* National Mobilization Committee to End the War in Vietnam
National Mobilization Committee to End the War in Vietnam, 32–33, 124, 289, 295
National Resist, 293
National Security Agency (NSA), 130
National Student Association, 265, 291, 294
Nazi(s), 193, 197–198, 233; Germany, 197–198, 233, 266; occupation by, 252
Near, Holly, 293
Nebraska Alliance, 101
Negro in the Civil War, The, 23
Nehru, Jawaharlal, 23
Neilands, Joseph B., 63, 293; Ho Chi Minh interview, 69, 71–72; interview, 69–76; Pham Van Dong interview, 71–72; Radio Hanoi broadcast, 69, 72
Newark Community Union Project (NCUP), 290
Newman, Grace, 287, 293
New "Mobe," 288, 290, 292–293, 295
New National Mobilization Committee, xx, 32, 293
Newsday, 266
Newsweek, 18
Newsreel, 289–291
New Yorker, 245
New York Theological Seminary, 265, 292
New York Times, quoted, 7, 196, 230; mentioned, 77, 112, 202, 241, 266, 275, 281
New Universities' Conference, 289–290
Nha Trang, xv
Nhu, Mme Tran Le Xuan, 7
Night Flight to Hanoi, 287
Nimitz, Chester W., 197–198
Nixon Richard M., xxi, 20, 60, 150, 220, 227, 245; administration, 40, 221; Cambodia, oversaw secret war in, 160; peace settlement delayed by, 235; southern U.S. strategy employed by, 225
Nongovernment organization, 165–166
North Vietnam. *See* Antiwar activist, trips to North Vietnam
North Vietnam: A Documentary, 290
Noumoff, Samuel, 168
North Vietnam Women's Union, 148, 207
November 5–8 "Mobe," 290
Nuclear testing, protest against, 5, 104, 162, 180
Nung, 229
Nuremberg and Vietnam: An American Tragedy, 274, 283–286
Nuremberg (War Crimes) Trials, 179, 191, 197–198, 200; T. Taylor, U.S. prosecutor at, 273, 284–286, 294

Oakland Army Terminal, 119
Oanh, Do Xuan, 48
Ochs, Phil, 180
O'Neill, Michael, 61
Operation Push (People United to Serve Humanity), 206, 288
Orangeburg, black antiwar demonstrators at, 37
Other Side, The, 14

Paley, Grace, xix, 293
Pan-African movement, 23–24
Panama, invasion of, 258, 261
Paris agreement, 176
Parker, A.(Zeus), 293
Pathet Lao, 189
Patriotism, definition of: C. Weiss, 180; E. Boardman, 94–95; E. Taylor, 157; G. Kahin, 135; H. Manes, 67; I. Zigas, 216–217; J. Lester, 87; J. B. Neilands, 75; M. Myerson, 9; N. Chomsky, 193; P. Mayer, 267; S. Miller-Coulter, 270–271; T. Taylor, 285; W. Heick, 109–110
Pauling, Linus, 151
Peace Corps, 54, 242
Peace Information Center, 23
Pearl Harbor, 286
Peck, Sidney, xix, 293
Pentagon, ix; censorship by, 208; march on, 34–37 (*see also* Antiwar demonstrations and protests); POWs, interest in, 281
Pentagon Papers, 36, 40
People's Coalition for Peace and Justice (PCPJ), 33, 38, 268, 288–291, 293, 295
Peoples' Park, 130
People's Permanent Tribunal, 249
Persian Gulf, 261–262

Persian Gulf War, 86, 130, 158, 170, 176–177, 205. *See also* Desert Storm
Pfeiffer, Egbert W., 241, 293
Phat Xiem, 171
Philbrick, Herbert, 20
Phinney, Richard, 109
Phoenix, voyage of, 88, 90–91, 102; crew-members of, 288–289, 292–293; nuclear testing in Pacific, used to protest, 104
Phoenix Program, 258
Phoenix Trip, The, 88
Phu Ly, bombing of, 106
Phuong, Mme Khanh, 154
Phu Xa, bombing of, 50
Piazza Strozzi, antiwar demonstration at, 146
Pilger, John, 187
Playboy, 119
Plamondon, Genie, 290, 293
Political Affairs, 13, 22
Politics of Escalation in Vietnam, The, 294
Polytechnic University (of Hanoi), 185
Pot, Pol, 54, 127, 176, 192
Power Elite, The, 55
Pran, Dith, 190
Pravda, 199
Prevent the Crime of Silence, 25–26, 183
Prisoners-of-war (POWs)
alive, alleged to be, 58
antiwar activists, escorted by, xi, xx, 287–292; A. Weills, 118, 125–126, 295; C. Weiss 165, 295; D. Dellinger, 52, 289
antiwar movement sentiment, believed unaware of, 149
Clark, R., observations by, about, 251, 257; concerns about, 253
families contacted by E. Taylor, 160
Fonda, Jane, critical of, xxvi–xxvii, 60, 238–239
Harriman, Averell, concerns for, 120
identification of, 167
mail: C. Weiss, role of, in delivering, 165; complaints about, 52; contraband in, x, 167; I. Zigas, carried by, 207, 216; U.S., returned to, by antiwar activists, xxvii, 142, 156, 171, 275
media ignored, 18
meetings with: C. Weiss, 139(illus.), 151; G. Wald, 236, 238, 241; H. Aptheker, 18; J. Brown 114; M. Duckles, 136, 138, 139(illus.), 151; M. Clarke, 4–5; M. Myerson, 9; P. Mayer, 266; R. Falk, x–xi; S. Miller-Coulter, 269; T. Taylor, 278–280, 281

North Vietnamese, preparations by, for meeting antiwar activists, 239
Phoenix crew, observed by, 107
State Department negotiations, 121, 124
torture, accusations of, xi, 51, 161, 198; disputed by George Wald, 238–240
Vietnam, Republic of, discussions with, concerning, xxviii
Vietnam War, prolonged to obtain release of, 178
war criminals, accused as, 148
Project Air War, 288
Project Independence, 56
Protests, forms of, xxiv
Provisional Revolutionary Government, 221–223
Ptashne, Mark S., 293
Pyle, Ernie, 261

Quakers: antiwar movement, leadership in, 101; burned churches, rebuilt, 103; and humanitarian aid, 144; meetings held by, 98; voyage of the *Phoenix*, sponsored by, 104
Quang Ngai Province, 196
Quang Tri, 168

Radio Hanoi broadcasts, xx; by H. Aptheker, 19; disputed by, G. Wald, 242; by Jane Fonda, xvii, xxvi–xxvii; M. Myerson, 9; N. Chomsky, 186; by Tom Hayden, xvii
Ramparts, 35–36, 118–119, 133, 287
Rand Corporation reports, 188
Rankin, Jeanette, 146; Brigade, 146, 295
Ransom, Louise, 206, 212–214
Rappaport, Randy, 293
Raskin, Marcus G., 287
Reagan, Ronald, 126, 130, 132, 159, 247–248; tolerated apartheid, 259; viewed as militaristic, 262
Rector, James, 130
Red River, 203
Reed, Charles, 293
Re-education camps, severity of, 145, 162, 179–180, 232
Religious Task Force, 265
Remington, William, 29
Report to the President by the Commission on CIA Activities, 163
Resist, 184, 288–289
Reunification Hotel, 65, 106
Reunion, 59
Revolutionary Nonviolence, 25
Reynolds, Akie, 91–92

Reynolds, Earle L., 91–92, 104, 107; captain of *Phoenix*, 104–105, 293
Rice, Charles O., 34–35
Rockefeller, Nelson, 163
Romo, Barry, 173–174, 273, 293
Rose, George (POW), 230
Rosenthal, Benjamin, 180
Rostow, Walter, 61
Rothstein, Vivian, 112, 293
Roxy, "Five o'clock follies" presented at, 170, 178–179
Rubin, Jerry, 37–38, 41, 43–46, 132
Rubin, Nancy Kurshan, 290, 293
Rukeyser, Muriel, 294
Rusk, Dean, 13, 107
Russell, Bertrand, 53, 73, 75, 294; Crimes Commission, 66; D. Dellinger endorsed by, for trip to North Vietnam, 47; Peace Foundation, 62, 70; War Crimes Trials, 52; War Crimes Tribunal, 53, 69, 77, 84
Russell, Margaret, 2, 294
Russians, rockets believed operated by, 275
Rustin, Bayard, 42–43

Sabin, Albert, 162
Saigon University, 242
Sakharov, Andrei, 239
Salisbury, Harrison, 77, 278, 294
Salk, Jonas, 162
SANE/FREEZE, 53
Sartre, Jean-Paul, 53, 73
Saudi Arabia, 215
Schanberg, Sidney, 190
Scheer, Robert, xix, 74–75, 118–119, 294; POW mail courier, 167
Schlesinger, James, 163
Schmidt, Phyllis, 2, 294
Schneider (Mr.), 294
Schoenman, 52–53, 62, 70, 294
Schoenbrun, David, xix, 3, 294
Schurmann, Franz, 290, 292, 294
Schutz, Trudi, 171. *See also* Young, Trudi Schutz
Schweiker, Richard S., 159
Scott, Hugh, 160
Scott, Larry, 101
Scott, Peter Dale, 294
Seaborg, Glen, 146
Seale, Bobby, 40, 45–47, 134
Search-and-destroy missions, 204
Seeger, Pete, 294
Seeger, Toshi, 294
Selective Service system: complicated procedures of, 218; influence on U.S. involvement, 111, 116

Seventh Fleet, U.S., 79
Shah of Iran, rule under, 259
Sheehan, Neil, 235
Shoup, David, 196
Sihanouk, Norodom, 4, 64, 119
Silver screen (television), influence of, 111, 116
Sixty Minutes, 239–240, 265
Socialist Workers Party, 37
Sonnenfelt, Helmut, 202
Sontag, Susan, xix, 290–291, 294
Son Tay raid, 203
South China Sea, voyage of *Phoenix* through, 104
South Vietnam: air war in, 282–283; special forces troops of, 68
Soviet Women's Committee, 1
Spock, Benjamin, 34–35, 37, 40
Spring Mobilization Committee, 32–33, 295
Stavis, Morton, 201–202, 294
Stetler, Russ, 70, 294
Stockholm War Crimes Tribunal, xx, 62, 69, 73; investigating team of, 62. *See also* Russell, Bertrand: War Crimes Tribunal
Stone, Oliver, 60
"Stop the Draft Week," 120
Storey, Rasheed, 294
Stratton, Richard (POW), 52
Student Nonviolent Coordinating Committee (SNCC), 10, 77–78, 175, 287–288
Students for a Democratic Society (SDS), xx, 14, 289–291, 293; antiwar movement, influence within, 101, 133–134; Weatherman influence upon, 130
Suharto (President), 220, 249
Sukarno, Achmed, 2, 220
Sullivan, William, 121, 252
Sumi, Hideko (Pat), 294
Supriano, Harold E., 7–8, 291, 293–295; interview, 10–11
Surface-to-air missiles (SAMs), 105–106, 114
Swerdlow, Amy, 206, 294

Tabankin, Margerie, 265, 294
Tagore, Rabindranath, 59
Takman, John, 63, 69
Tan Huoc Province, 82
Tateishi, John, xviii
Taylor, Ethel, xxi, 136, 294; 152(illus.), 153(illus.); with C. Weiss to North Vietnam, 166, 289; interview, 148–164; Jane Fonda antiwar activity evaluated, 164; service clubs, invited to speak at, 155; with M. Duckles to North Vietnam, 289

Taylor, Telford, 294; with Barry Romo to North Vietnam, 293; intelligence work in Pentagon, 286; interview, 273–286; laws of war discussed by, 277–278; lawyer for Federal Communications Commission, 286; with Michael Allen and Joan Baez to North Vietnam, 287; war crimes, discussed by, 276, 281
Teamsters Union, 290
Teheran, hostage crisis in, 257
Ten, Chu Van, 225, 229
"Tendency," towards violent antiwar activity, 31, 129
Ten Thousand Day War, The, 287
Tet offensive, ix
Thailand, University of, 125
Thai Nguyen, xxx(map), 224–225
Thanh, Pham, 143
Thanh Hoa City, 185(map); naval bombardment of, 79; Province, 185
Thanh's War, 143
Thieu, Nguyen Van, 159, 234
Third Commission of Inquiry, International War Crimes Tribunal, 292–293
Thompson, Fred, 121
Thong Nhat hotel, 122
Tiananmen Square, 129
Time, 18
Time-Life, 252
Tirana, Albania, 64
Tonkin, Gulf of, xxx(map); incident in, 100, 102, 215, 234, 260; resolution, 164, 203, 215, 258
Travis Air Force Base, 143
Treaty of Paris, 21
Tripoli, 261
Trip to Hanoi, 294
Trotskyites, 31, 37–38
Truman, Harry S., xxi
Tyner, Jarvis, 295

Union Theological Seminary, 26
United Nations Children's Fund (UNICEF), 169, 249; Development Program (UNDP), 169
United Nations (UN), 282
United States government: control of media, 261; deceptions by, 187, 234, 257–258, 260; embargo, effects upon Vietnam of, 99, 128, 176; lessons not learned by, 261; Vietnam War, why involved in, 55–56, 177–178
United States in Vietnam, The, 220, 226
United States Military Assistance Command in South Vietnam (MACV), 221
United States Peace Council, 7

United States State Department, xxiii, 123, 155; POWs, negotiated return of, 121, 124
United States–Vietnam Friendship Committee, 8

Veterans of Foreign Wars (VFW), 30, 58
Victory celebration, 244. *See also* Dave Dellinger, reunification celebration
Viet Bac, 229
Viet Cong, 132, 282–283
Viet Minh, 132
Vietnam (fig.), xxx
Vietnam, 292
Vietnam, Democratic Republic (DRV), of: disappointed with, 128, 232, 270; human rights violations, accused of, 204; mass executions, allegation of, by, 179–180, 192, 204, 231, 234
Vietnam: The Logic of Withdrawal, 295
Vietnam Day, 69; Committee, 7, 118–120
Vietnam Revisited, 25, 54
Vietnam Veterans Against the War, 248, 263, 293
Vietnam veterans, problems of adjustment of, 116–117, 131, 161, 267
Vietnam War
   Agent Orange affected veterans of, 195
   Americans, believed uninformed about, by; C. Weiss, 178; E. Taylor, 158; G. Wald, 246; J. B. Neilands, 74; M. Myerson, 9; N. Chomsky, 191; R. Clark, 260; T. Taylor, 283
   Geneva Convention violated by U.S. in, 62–63
   lessons learned from, 205, 214, 217, 235
   motive for U.S. involvement in, 55–56, 177, 233
   POW issue prolonged, 178; U.S. involvement concealed in, 54
   U.S. population failed to repent role in, 266–267
   violated law, xi
   violated United Nations Charter, 62–63
Vietnam War Memorial, 54, 107, 117
Vietnam Will Win!, 26
Vietnamese Youth Group, 8
Voyage of the Phoenix, The, filming of, 107
Vy, Nguyen Vinh, 49

Wald, George, 295; interview, 236–250; MIT speech given by, 236–237, 245–246; U.S. government, disappointed with, 247–248; victory celebration attended by, 244–245
Wallace, George, 214

War, laws of, 277–278
War Bulletin, 287
War crimes: Hanoi bombings evaluated as,
  281; T. Taylor discussed with Hanoi
  lawyers, 276; U.S., accused of, 160, 200
War Crimes and the American Conscience,
  236, 273
War Crimes Commission, 202
War crimes trials, Tokyo, 198
War Crimes Tribunal, Stockholm and
  Copenhagen, 289. *See also* Stockholm
  War Crimes Tribunal
Ward, Richard E., 8, 11, 291, 293–295
Warfare: aerial, laws of, 277–278; chemical,
  190, 196 (*see also* Defoliants, chemical)
War Powers Act, 203
Warren, Earl, xviii
War Resisters League, 51, 184, 217–218, 292
Washington, George, 192
Washington, Jerome, 54
Washington Action Committee, 295
Washington Monument, rally at, 38. *See also*
  Cambodia: protests against invasion of
Washington Plans an Aggressive War, 287
Washington Star, 228
Wausau, Wisconsin, 95–96
Weathermen, 39, 118, 129–130
Webster, Barbara, 52
Wefers, Mark, 295
Weglyn, Michi, xviii
Weills, Anne, 292, 295; interview, 118–135;
  North Vietnam, return to, 125–129;
  Tom Hayden, companion to, 129
Weiner, Lee, 40, 43, 46
Weisberg, Barry, 184
Weiss, Cora: antiwar movement leadership
  205; Chicago Seven trial, unable to tes-
  tify at, 41; Committee of Liaison
  founder, 25, 52, 295; with E. Taylor to
  North Vietnam, 148–150, 294; G. Kahin
  in Hanoi at same time as, 230; inter-
  view, 165–182; with M. Duckles to
  North Vietnam, 136, 153(illus.), 289;
  Nam Dinh, visit of, 142(fig.); North
  Vietnam trips, arranged by, 184, 207,
  266, 268–269, 274– 275; with P. Weiss to
  North Vietnam, 203; with Peter Arnett
  to North Vietnam, 287; POW escort, xi,
  165; POWs meeting with, 139(fig.),
  172(fig.); T. Taylor, contacts with, 284
Weiss, Dawid, Fross, Zelnick, and Lehr-
  man, 201
Weiss, Peter, 168, 179, 181, 294, 295; interview, 201–205
Western Union, 163
Westover, Martha, 295

Whitehall Recruiting Station, 35
Who's Who in America, 12
Williams, Robert, 295
Williams, Robert (Mrs.), 295
Wilson, Dagmar, 2, 295
Wine, Swan, 128
Wisconsin Alliance, The, 97, 101
Women's International League for Peace
  and Freedom (WILPF), 136–137, 288–
  289
Women Strike for Peace (WSP), xx, 290,
  292; Amy Swerdlow, 206, 294; antiwar
  demonstrations, 157; C. Weiss, 165;
  Canada, met in, 163, 166, 181; China,
  attempted to visit, 209; current activity,
  146; Dagmar Wilson, 295; Djakarta, met
  in, 1–2, 164; E. Taylor, 148; effectiveness
  of, 162, 164, 181; execution of U.S. sol-
  dier, prevented, 4; Great Neck chapter,
  counseled draft-eligible men at, 218; I.
  Zigas, 211, 295; M. Clarke, 288; M.
  Duckles, 136; Moscow, met in, 1, 5;
  National Liberation Front, met with,
  163; nuclear testing, protested against,
  5, 162, 180; rationale for antiwar stand,
  180; Trudi Schutz Young, 295
Women Strike for Peace, 294
Women's liberation movement, 130
Women's Press, 139
Women's Union (Vietnamese), 270. *See also*
  North Vietnamese Women's Union
Woods Hole, 236
Woodward, John, 295
Works (Colonel), 154
World Bank, 54, 127
World Peace Committee, 290
World Peace Congress, 10. *See also* Ameri-
  can Peace Conference
World Peace Council, 13
World Peace Day, 156
World War II, served in: H. Aptheker, 22;
  H. Manes, 67; T. Taylor, 286
Wright, Eddie, 57

Xiaoping, Deng, 127

Yale Divinity School, 287
Yalu River, 282
Yamashita, Tomoyuki, 198
Years of Infamy, xviii
Yippies, 37, 44, 132
Young, Ronald, 171, 287, 295
Young, Trudi Schutz, 287, 295
Yacobsen, Flodie, 252

Zietlow, Carl, 90–91, 100–101, 295

Zigas, Irma, xxvi, 287, 294, 295; interview,
206–219
Zimmerman, William, 265, 295
Zinn, Howard, xix, 184, 288; POW escort,
52; with T. Hayden to North Vietnam,
268, 293, 295
Zoo, the: POW escorts visited, 121; T. Taylor visited, 278–279
Zumwalt, Elmo, 145